Diaries of Ireland

Diaries of Ireland

An Anthology
1590–1987

Edited by
MELOSINA LENOX-CONYNGHAM

THE LILLIPUT PRESS
DUBLIN

First published 1998 by
THE LILLIPUT PRESS LTD
62-63 Sitric Road, Arbour Hill,
Dublin 7, Ireland.

A CIP record for this
title is available from
The British Library.

ISBN 1 874675 88 0 [cased]
    1 874675 78 3 [pbk]

The Lilliput Press receives financial assistance from
An Chomhairle Ealaíon/The Arts Council of Ireland.

Set in 10 on 12.5 Adobe Caslon by Sheila Stephenson
Printed in Ireland by Betaprint of Clonshaugh, Dublin

Contents

INTRODUCTION   VII

Ludolf von Münchhausen [*19 February – 20 March 1590*]   3

Richard Boyle, 1st Earl of Cork [*27 January 1611 – 1 January 1642*]   9

Anon.: Siege of Limerick Castle [*18 May – 23 June 1642*]   16

Elizabeth Freke [*25 August 1677 – 13 July 1696*]   25

John Stevens [*2 May 1689 – 30 June 1691*]   32

Colonel Thomas Bellingham [*31 August 1689 – 19 July 1690*]   41

John Scott [*15 December 1704 – 14 March 1708*]   46

John Wesley [*23 June 1750 – 28 June 1789*]   52

John Scott, 1st Earl of Clonmell [*2 June 1774 – 13 February 1798*]   57

Lucy Goddard [*2 April 1778 – 27 August 1782*]   61

John Tennent [*12 July 1786 – 13 July 1790*]   67

Theobald Wolfe Tone [*20 June 1790 – 29 December 1796*]   81

Mary Leadbeater [*18 February 1791 – 2 May 1797*]   92

John Fitzgerald [*1 January – 31 December 1793*]   99

Marianne Fortescue [*16 – 27 May 1798*]   106

Richard Farrell [*18 – 28 May 1798*]   108

Anne, Dowager Countess of Roden [*23 May – 11 June 1798*]   112

Elisabeth Richards [*26 May – 22 June 1798*]   116

Sir Vere Hunt [*28 March 1798 – 18 March 1816*]   128

Nicolas Marshall Cummins [*5 April 1810 – 6 July 1837*]   141

Humphrey O'Sullivan [*2 April 1827 – 31 July 1835*]   153

Frances & Emily Ponsonby [*19 September – 2 October 1837*]   163

Sir John Benn-Walsh [*11 April 1823 – 25 September 1864*]   172

William Joseph O'Neill Daunt [*2 October 1842 – 2 August 1869*]   182

Asenath Nicholson [*2 July 1844 – May 1845*]   186

Rev. William Sewell [*12 October 1844 – 23 February 1845*]   191

Elizabeth Smith [*26 October 1845 – 21 July 1850*]   199

William Clements, 1st Earl of Leitrim [*18 April 1857 – 2 January 1873*]   210

John Sarsfield Casey [*7 October 1867 – 9 January 1868*]   217

Thomas Johnson Westropp [*7 July 1875 – 20 March 1879*]   221

Hattie Cowper [*4 June – 6 December 1877*]   226

Joseph Holloway [*8 May 1899 – 1 March 1926*]   231

James Stephens [*24 – 30 April 1916*]   239

Joseph Campbell [*6 June – 22 November 1922*]   244

Lady Gregory [*8 September 1918 – 14 February 1926*]   251

Frank McEvoy [*4 March 1958 – 16 February 1960*]   258

Seán Ó Ríordáin [*11 August 1964 – 21 March 1974*]   265

Gemma Hussey [*15 December 1982 – 22 January 1987*]   268

SOURCES   275

Introduction

From my earliest youth I have followed the maxim, 'Keep a diary and one day it will keep you.' Alas, mine lacks those indiscretions and revelations so important in the making of a bestseller, for as Tallulah Bankhead said, 'Only good girls keep diaries. Bad girls don't have time.' Rereading my diary, I see I had hopes of a forgotten Robert whose name, whenever mentioned, is wreathed in hearts. Every morning I used to rise early in order to kiss Robert though he failed to requite my love, and on the 17th of February 1947 he bit me. I think he was the milkman's horse.

So instead of relying on my own journal I have taken extracts from other peoples'. The diaries I have included in this anthology have been chosen principally because I myself have enjoyed reading them. All except one were written in Ireland; some describe an historical event, others recount 'the trivial round, the common task'. I have arranged them in chronological order with the idea of giving a perspective on the state of Ireland through the years, but I cannot claim that this book gives a balanced view.

The journals or diaries that have survived from the seventeenth and the early part of the eighteenth century were written almost exclusively by Protestants, who were either landed gentry, clergymen, soldiers or visitors. There is a strong tradition in Protestant denominations of keeping journals as an exercise of self-examination, particularly among the Quakers. There are many excellent diaries in Quaker archives, including one by William Penn in the seventeenth century when he came to look at his estates in Cork. On 4 December 1669, when crossing the Blackwater at Cappoquin by ferry, the horses became unruly:

… John Penington was struck overboard and by mighty mercy I and the boatman caught and saved him. Philip Ford's horse slued over and swum back, portmanteau and all, to the other side; and whilst I and the ferryman were saving John Penington my horse and his had well nigh flung us both upon him, and they upon us, which the God of mercy for His name's sake prevented. We returned, John Penington lost his hat, got him to an Inn, put him to bed, plied him with hot cloths, strong waters, and what could be got to preserve him; after two hours stay to dry and recruit him we passed the ferry …

In the nineteenth century, with the advent of a strong evangelical movement, there was an increase in the number of spiritual diaries, filled with pages of pious devotional thoughts and hopes that rewards will not always be only in heaven. J.M. Synge's grandfather was rector of Schull in County Cork, though he called himself 'a poor, feeble worm, unable to do aught of myself for Jesus, and unworthy to name his Name'. On 7 July 1832 he wrote:

The cholera at length at hand. Indeed, I wonder not that such judgements have reached up from the iniquity of these wicked priests who are setting the world in an uproar to accomplish their own base and selfish ends. Last week an anti-tithe meeting was held in Skibbereen and on Monday a similar display of ferocity and rebellion to take place here, all for the purpose of inducing the people to withold from me what is legally my due and exalting themselves on my ruin. But I trust in the Lord and make him my refuge and defence. They can neither hurt me personally nor injure my property without the express permission of God – in some instances these mobs have been guilty of great excesses. I have heard of some such intention here, but the Lord has a bit in their jaws and a chain upon their hands and unless he give the command they can do me no harm. But surely we cannot wonder that God should visit for these things. The very Saturday subsequent to O'Connell's profanation of the Sabbath the cholera was found in Cork ...

I must record that during the Great Famine the Rev. Traill worked indefatigably and courageously, until he died of fever, in his efforts to obtain relief for the thousands suffering from hunger and disease in his parish, and there is no taint of souperism to his good works.

Many diaries have only the briefest entries; some are merely farm logs with the rotation of crops, the buying and selling of stock and market prices all noted down, and some are closer to account books, recording financial transactions. Easily the most common subject in Irish diaries is the weather – there are hundreds of journals devoted solely to the vagaries of the climate. The first official weather diary was commissioned by the Duke of Ormonde in 1682 and was kept in a beautiful spidery hand by John Kevan in Kilkenny, but almost all journals make some reference to the weather each day.

Numerous diaries were written in – or perhaps have been preserved from – times of unrest. At the battle of the Boyne the squeak of pens must have drowned out the sound of the cannons. An assortment of diaries, too, has come down to us from the time of the Rebellion of 1798, and from 1916. But I have found surprisingly few that refer to the Great Famine. Among those from that period, only the journal of Elizabeth Smith gives any picture at all of what it was like. Thomas Edwards, a clerk in the coaching office in Carlow who had to support his parents, sisters and brothers on a tiny income, never mentions the failure of the potato crop or that people were starving. This is, I believe, because the peasantry were endemically impoverished, living always on the brink of starvation; and in a diary one only records a sudden impact. However, travellers coming to Ireland nearly always mention with horror the beggars swarming the countryside; Asenath Nicholson, part of whose diary was included in her book *Ireland's Welcome to the Stranger*, actually came here from New York just before the famine to see for herself why so many destitute people had left our shores for America.

By the second half of the eighteenth century, journal-keeping had become much more widespread. A very curious diary was kept in Carrick-on-Suir by a surveyor, James Ryan. It is written under subject headings such as 'Accidents', 'Rain', 'Deaths', 'Green Wax' and 'A list of subscribers to the new chapel in

Carrick with their occupation'. As such it is more a commonplace book of facts giving a picture of a town rather than of the writer, though there are occasional personal glimpses, especially under 'Excursions' when he describes an outing to Belline, where after having seen the 'improvements we scampered away to Piltown for breakfast; thence we adjoined to Bessborough, saw and admired the paintings and park etc. Then back to Piltown where we dined like the sons of Irish Kings ... The only strife – who should most please.'

Reading diaries, one realizes the frailty of life in every class of society. Up to the end of the nineteenth century a very high percentage of babies died before they were a year old, a common cold often turned to pneumonia, and fevers of all sorts could be fatal. In 1729 Colonel Charles Clinton emigrated to Pennsylvania from Longford on a passage that took from May until October. On the day that they had their last sight of Ireland, two of his children fell sick with the measles and they both died, as did ninety-four other men women and children; I presume that the measles was the cause of many of the deaths though he does not say this. For women, there was the additional risk of childbirth, which had a very high mortality rate. Though divorce was almost unknown, men and women frequently changed their marriage partner owing to death.

What is interesting in diaries relates as much to the perspective of the reader as to that of the writer; the further apart the dates, the more fascinating the trivial details of domestic life, while an introspective diary is of much greater significance to a contemporary. What was eaten for dinner two hundred years ago is of more import than who ate it (unless they were distinguished or infamous). The Rev. Nixon, who lived at Castle Hume in Fermanagh, entertained Mr Tottenham, the Surveyor-General of Leinster, making a party of sixteen on Saturday, 29 April 1769, with a brisket of beef and greens, a roast leg of mutton, boiled cows' heels, mutton broth and cod. Fourteen bottles of claret and four bottles of port were drunk. This meal was at half past three or four o'clock and was followed by supper, when they had cold beef and butter and cheese and drank four bottles of claret, two of port and one of whiskey.

Travel is another subject of consequence, and the difficulties and discomforts are described in detail; many of the diaries on this subject were written by people who had come as tourists or with some specific object in mind. Arthur Young, the well-known agronomist, came on a tour of Ireland in the late eighteenth century. His observations are printed in diary form, though alas his private journal was stolen with his trunk by a servant he had just taken into his employment.

Roads were rough; in 1675 Elizabeth Petty (the wife of the remarkable Sir William Petty who did the first survey of Ireland) went to collect rents and inspect their estates in Kerry. She wrote bitterly in the diary she kept for her husband: '16th June, Wednesday I went from Newmarkett to Killarny butt such a way (or rather noe way) as I am afrayed to tell you, however (I thanke God) I came safe, after haveing beene from 9 a clock in the morning to 9 at night in my coach.' The next day she went over 'to Mangerton with the help of Mr Robert Hassett and his gellding, in paine enough; and some danger, butt with a guard of 70 or 80 horrse, to Phill Heases at Roghty Bridge'.

Another mode of transport was the canal boat, though this too was not always reliable. In 1831 Major Oliver Fry with his daughter embarked at Tullamore on the canal boat for Dublin.

At 2 a.m. I was greatly alarmed as the boat was violently drawn to shore by a riotous mob, who forceably took possession of her with dreadful yells and curses; we expected an attack every moment. The tumult continued for quarter of an hour, before we could learn any circumstance, at length on venturing to look out we found that two fellows were on their way to America, and that their friends formed our assailants being determined to accompany the emigrants part of their journey. The boat was overloaded and in danger of turning over, the water up to the windows, but reasoning was useless and thus we were accompanied for three miles when all departed save the two travellers.

Though the coming of the railway made a huge difference to travel, there is very little excitement about it in the diaries of the day. Thomas H. Edwards, a coaching agent from Carlow, wrote in July 1844, when he was visiting Dublin: 'having nothing to do and never having seen a Railway I set out for Kingstown. I was not nearly as much surprised as I expected to have been.'

The man who had the most pleasure from his vehicle was Lord Louth, who bought a motorized tricycle during Dublin horse-show week in 1900. After a lesson on how to ride it in Phoenix Park, he rode it back to Louth Hall near Ardee in three hours – 'it went simply beautifully' – and for the next few weeks was always out and about until he hit a gatepost when trying to avoid a drunken man in a horse and cart. The tricycle had to be sent back to England for repairs and Lord Louth resumed his very dull life.

Very few diaries were written in Irish until the end of the nineteenth century, the earliest I have come across being ascribed to Father O'Mellan of Brantry Friary in County Tyrone, who was a chaplain in the armies of Sir Phelim and Owen Roe; it deals entirely with the confederate wars of 1641 with little personal detail. One of the best diaries was written in Irish by Humphrey O'Sullivan, a schoolmaster from Callan, County Kilkenny, in the early nineteenth century. By the beginning of the twentieth century literacy was universal and nationalism widespread. Douglas Hyde, the first President of Ireland, wrote some of the brief entries in Irish in the diary he started as a boy in Roscommon, where his father was the Church of Ireland rector. Tomás Ó Criomhthain on the Great Blasket Island, encouraged by Brian O'Kelly, kept a diary from 1918 to 1923.

I have read hundreds of diaries – sometimes with the greatest trouble owing to handwriting that too often seems to have nothing to do with an alphabet, but always with pleasure – and have had a difficult time choosing passages for this book. I have quoted in this introduction from some that I have not included in the anthology. I will conclude with a quotation from Ellen Butler who lived in Ballyraggett in the late nineteenth century, growing older and yellower as she confided sadly to her diary. She ended one volume with the words: 'Now goodbye old book you have been a good fellow and taken down my good, bad & muddled thoughts and actions – I feel mighty hungry notwithstanding the bilious tendencies.'

EDITOR'S NOTE

I have tried to present the diaries in a form as close to the original as possible. I have modernized archaic spelling and punctuation where I think it poses a threat to comprehension or will try the patience of the reader, but in some diaries (particularly the earliest) the orthography is so different from our own that piecemeal 'correction' would be useless; these diaries have been left more or less alone. Where archaisms or apparent misspellings have been retained, they have not been marked with *sic*, because to do so in every case would be needlessly distracting. It would be impossible to achieve total consistency when dealing with thirty-eight separate diarists from five centuries, many of whom have been subject to previous editing. Cuts in the entries are marked with ellipses (...). I have standardized the dating throughout the book, except where it is a distinctive part of the character of the diary, as with the Quaker Mary Leadbeater, who eschewed the 'idolatrous' names for days and months. The diaries are presented chronologically by the first entry except in a few cases where, because of the span or emphasis of the diary, it seemed illogical to abide by that rule.

ACKNOWLEDGMENTS

For their help in assembling this volume I would like to thank the following, in no particular order: Andreas von Breitenbuch, the Royal Irish Academy, Julian Walton, Tim Cadogan of Cork County Library, the Cork Historical and Archaeological Society, Major Cecil Barrow, the Rev. Levingstone Cooney, the National Library of Ireland, the Public Record Office of Northern Ireland, Dan McLaughlin, Imogen Hamilton, Bernard Meehan and Felicity O'Mahony of the Manuscript Library at Trinity College Dublin, John Hunt, Dean Nicolas Cummins, Julia Crampton, the *Donegal Annual*, the late Mrs Hubert Butler, White Row Press, Terry Trench, Marcus Clements, Martin Kevin Cusack, Maura Toler-Aylward, George Stacpoole, Simon Campbell, Nicholas Grene, Mary Morrissey of Kilkenny County Library, Frank McEvoy, Bernie McQuillan, Noel Ross, Eleanor Grene, Anthony Malcolmson, Michael Coady, Seán Ó Coileáin, George Fry, the Religious Society of Friends Library in Dublin, Charles Clements, Patrick Dawson, Chris O'Mahony, Lisa Shields, Ronald Lightbown, Peter and Gilly Somerville-Large, Conleth Manning, Gemma Hussey.

Diaries of Ireland

Ludolf von Münchhausen
1570-1640

LUDOLF VON MÜNCHHAUSEN was born in northern Germany, where he inherited a large estate at Oldendorf. As a young man he travelled extensively, visiting the British Isles, Norway, Sweden, Italy and Hungary. He came to Ireland with the intention of going to two of the great European places of medieval pilgrimage, Monaincha and St Patrick's Purgatory, though as a tourist, not as one seeking Grace.

When he returned home he took up an official position in his sovereign's court at Stadthagen and married Anna von Bismarck. Their descendant was Baron Münchhausen (1720–97), whose exaggerated stories of his travels were turned into the eighteenth-century best-seller, Adventures of Baron Munchhausen.

Monaincha (called Lan Nimmeo in the manuscript) was most likely founded by St Canice of Aghaboe in the sixth century and is on what was an island in a bog very close to Roscrea. It was known as the Island of Life, for no man could die there, but if a woman or animal of the female sex should land on it they would succumb immediately. In spite of these powers, the monks of Monaincha had left the island around 1485 because they found the noxious vapours of the surrounding marshes and swamps highly injurious to their constitutions and settled on the mainland at nearby Corbally where Cronan had established his first monastery. No doubt this chapel is where Münchhausen found the old monk.

The diary was written in very old-fashioned German, interwoven with Latin passages. This translation has been made by Andreas von Breitenbuch, a direct descendant of Ludolf von Münchhausen.

* * *

19 February 1590

Saturday; embarkation at Bristol. The officer who visited the ships did not want to let me board for Ireland for many reasons. I satisfied him with a piece of gold. The wind was north-easterly and at about twelve o'clock we drifted down the river, and after about three miles we set sail and drove between Cornwall and Wales … At night, there was a storm and a lot of wind and because we were low on ballast, we had to reef sail. The women and children cried, there were some who prayed, others yelled, nearly all were so ill that some of them were vomiting and suffered from diarrhoea. I was disgusted by the stench and the howling and feared the roughness of the sea and its danger.

21 February 1590

In the morning, we saw Ireland, drove along it at the right-hand side for a while until we came to a white tower. There, we sailed into a river and, having a good tide, arrived at Waterford around mid-day ... The passage cost five shillings. I took quarters with a German woman from Cologne at Waterford. Here, like the rest of the town, there were hung neither shield nor weapon.

22 February 1590

... Waterford is the most distinguished trade town in Ireland, because here live the richest tradesmen ... ships are leaving for France and Spain and other places, most of them carrying fish like Herring which is widely caught here, and cowskins, which are the income and riches of this country. In return they bring iron, wine and other things ... The houses in Waterford and at other places in Ireland are, although mostly built from stones, bad, rustic buildings ... in this town, and in all other Irish towns, there were all sorts of ecclesiastical monasteries, which are nowadays mostly destroyed. The churches now belong to the reformed religion, but the people still cling to the papal religion which makes me wonder ... The people are unclean, coarse and lazy. They have brains enough for roguery, but they know nothing of arts and subtle craftsmanship. Their greatest pleasure is idleness, they are no good for greater jobs; they prefer to rest nakedly in their houses by the fireplace to working and digging in the fields. I saw seven people dragging at one piece of wood and hardly succeeding in carrying it away. I think that I could, with a little effort, have carried it alone.

I saw them standing in the fields digging, wrapped in their Irish blankets as protection against the cold winds ... What a wonderful country this could be if there were the same people living here as there are in other places. They do not rear hay, for their livestock stay in the open in summer and in winter. They are unclean and impure in clothing and food. The butter is full of dirt and hair because they don't strain the milk. The farmers don't wash the cans and dishes, so everything is covered with dirt. A shirt and the other linen wear will be worn for a quarter of a year. The women in Ireland wear much linen cloth around their heads, they could be called pretty if they only kept themselves cleaner and wore nicer clothes. The men in the country do not wear hats, the boys can run the whole day, like a horse. There were two things I liked well in the Irish houses in the country: a pretty maid and normally a pretty wind, sometimes also a pretty horse.

The Irish love each other vehemently, but hate the strangers. They divorce their wives easily ...

2 March 1590

I took an interpreter and a guide in Waterford, and a boy to carry my things. We boarded a ship going upstream to Carrick, twelve Irish miles ...

4 March 1590

We walked to the north, thirteen Irish miles. Stayed over night in the house of an Irish nobleman. Their houses are normally built like towers and surrounded by a wall. They do not live in these, just keep them as a fortress. Next to these, they have another house, badly built, not as good as our farmers' houses, in which they light a fire right in the middle. Here, the master of the house takes his place with his wife at the top, the domestic servants following according to their ranks. When they have eaten, everybody takes a bunch of straw to sleep on. Each nobleman is bound to house and feed his servants, otherwise they set fire to his house and goods.

In Ireland, he who owns enough livestock and land to live on would be called a nobleman. I wondered about their boorishness and coarseness, for the nobleman of this house had taken off his trousers and stockings, stood in front of the fire and lifted his shirt and let everybody see his backside. Afterwards, when it was mealtime, they threw a rough, unclean plank over the table, on which they put some herrings, some bread, and some salt (the salt looked as rough as pounded gravel). During the meal they made my interpreter ask me some strange and foolish questions. After this we drank from the common mug. Then we were given some water to wash our feet in, which is courtesy in this country. When it was sleeping time, they threw a blanket over some straw and the host with his wife lay down, I next to them and then my guide and the others, we covered ourselves with our coats. This is how we were treated by an Irish nobleman.

When they ride a horse, they have neither stirrups, nor boots nor spurs. They wear a coat of mail over their bodies, a shield hanging from their arm and they have a long spike in front of their saddle and a servant running 10 or 20 steps behind them. The servants only wear helmets and carry a broad sword at their sides, the upper part of their bodies being naked.

5 March 1590

Another four miles to the north, to the island which to visit I have undertaken this journey. The Irish call it 'Lan Nimmeo' which means 'Island of Life'. Half an Irish mile before the island, there lives the Prior with several older friars. Here, an old hermit lay in his bed, giving the visitors to the island his absolution. I made my interpreter ask this very old, decrepit man, if all the things being told about this island of life were true (although I have no doubts, for I would not have undertaken this long pilgrimage otherwise). So I desired to know (in order to be able to meet the infidels elsewhere) wherefore one knew the fact that no one could die on this island. The old one let me know that he himself had been living on the island for 10, 20, 30, 40, 50, 60 (and so he counted the years one after another) 70, 80, 90, 100 and more years without having been able to die on it, neither had he seen one of his friars die there. When one of the others had been tired of life, he would not go to the island anymore, like he himself would not go there any more because he now wanted it to become possible that he could die.

I was glad that the Prior of this place happened to be absent and I was not urged to confession and other superstitious things.

I and my companions crossed the water in a small old boat, rowed by two friars. Coming to this island of life, it is the custom that the pilgrim take off his shoes and stockings and walk around the island eight times on bare feet. I could well see that recently only few had made use of this customary pilgrimage walk. It was an evil walk on bare feet around the island. After I had done so once, just for exploration, and on my own decision, I laid myself down under a tree and let the others walk according to their devotion. Afterwards, they crawl on their knees in the little chapel up to the altar and then again in the large church.

After all this has happened, there is a little stone crucifix, and he who is able to embrace this backwards, i.e. with the crucifix behind you (which is easily done) is void of all sins and has fulfilled his pilgrimage. He who is unable to do so has not done enough penance. My companion, being old and crooked, could not get his arms and hands around the crucifix at his back. Therefore, he was supposed to stay there and do more crawling on his knees and so forth. Because I was tired of this nuisance and although he was of papal belief, I asked him to stretch his arms to the sides, took his hands and pulled them around the crucifix and thus this man too was freed from his sins.

After making a donation (although there is not much need of spending money in wild Ireland, they took this donation), and after having received the old hermit's blessings, everybody is free to go their own way.

The natives think a lot of this little island 'Lan Nimmeo' and they think that there is no pilgrimage any more holy than this … The wood from this island is said to be a protection from poisonous animals in such a way that if in a foreign country (there are no poisonous animals in Ireland) you drew a line of circle in the ground with a piece of wood from the island, no poisonous animal could cross this line or enter this circle.

Giraldus Cambrensis writes that no animal of female sex can get to the island. I do not believe in this … I saw a pair of wild pigeons sitting in the church and I saw a lot of birds' excrement on both the church and the chapel. I would have liked to make a test with a female sheep or a bitch, I was even prepared to do the test with a negress out of some negroes which had been robbed from a ship recently and which I had been willing to buy. But my interpreter and my guide would not let me do so, they said the people would not allow it. We would get into danger. As things were, we had enough to do to get along with these superstitious people.

… I made the Irish pilgrims who came to this island believe that only devotion had driven me here. They paid honour to me, kissed my hands and body and accompanied me for one or three miles and showed me the way, perhaps with the intent of robbery in their minds. I let them know that the journey back home would take me more than a year's time. They had only heard of France and Spain,

England and Flanders and could not know how far it was to Germany. Some of them wondered what an enormous sin I must have committed to undertake such a long pilgrimage, others thought I was a holy man. One of them, whom I had told that my sin was incest with my sister, let me know that my sins were forgiven, even if I had slept with the Holy Virgin.

After I had made my prayer to God in the church and thanked Him for His kindness and made my excuses to Him about taking part in all the jugglery, we made our way back through the swampy, bad path, six Irish miles. Stayed with another nobleman over night.

When I first came to Ireland, I had in mind to visit St Patrick's Purgatory too, but now, knowing the vanity of the Island of Lan Nimmeo and because it would have been a long way to travel, I changed my mind.

In the winter of 1995 I went to Monaincha (Lan Nimmeo). The bog had been drained and was planted with rows of fir trees. My female dog and I walked across along the grass causeway in some trepidation to the island. The weather-worn High Cross was on a cement plinth, huge gnarled beech trees clung to the rocky bank of the island; we passed through the beautifully decorated doorway into the roofless church. It must have looked very much like this when Münchhausen was here 400 years before, with the walls of flat reddish stone and carved sandstone decorations round the windows and chancel arch.

6 March 1590
Go to the south for thirteen miles, stayed overnight in a poor farmhouse.

7 March 1590
Kilkenny three miles. Rested here this day and the 8th March.

Just when I was in Kilkenny, a convict had been condemned to death. Because of this, the women ran through all the lanes crying and weeping, clapping their hands and making a lot of noise, so that the whole town was filled with their lamentations. I wondered what all this was about, because they could not have done worse if the whole country had been exposed to treason. I then heard them crying, but without tears, like they are said to do in all cases of death. It sounded like: 'Dil, dil, dil, dil, Ho, ho, ho!' They are just holding the ordinary court in Kilkenny like they do in all counties four times a year. Justice is very strict in Ireland because the people are of a natural savageness and malignity.

9 March 1590
Through Leinster from Kilkenny, ten Irish miles and hereafter another fourteen Irish miles on horseback.

10 March 1590
Another twenty-four miles to Dublin. For a horse, I had to pay sixteen Pfennigs

each day, had to feed the horse and the servant who ran with it and brought the horse back the next day.

In Dublin I took quarters with Peter von Heren, a shoemaker born in Bruges, for he spoke German ... The people of this place are not as uncivilized and boorish, for this area was given to the English by the Queen of England, so they speak little Irish around here, yes even many of the natives do not speak Irish at all. The houses in Dublin are a lot more dainty than in other places ...

20 March 1590
A Saturday – boarded a ship in Dublin. Because I had no English passport with me, I had to steal myself away from Ireland. After I had ordered a cabin in the large ship, I let the people who normally visit the outgoing ships pass, and after the large ship had raised anchor, I crossed over in a small ship to the large one, and so I left Ireland.

Richard Boyle, 1st Earl of Cork
1566-1643

'GOD GUIDED ME FIRST HITHER *the 28th June being midsummer even, 1588; bringing with me a taffeta doublet and a pair of velvet breeches, a new suit of laced fustion cut upon taffeta, a bracelet of gold worth £10, a diamond ring and £29.8s in money in my purse.' So wrote Richard Boyle, a young English adventurer who arrived in Ireland with few social pretensions and no fortune.*

But though God may have guided him, Boyle was extremely able in looking after his own affairs and ended up as one of the richest men in the kingdom. With unscrupulous determination he pursued wealth and power, acquiring a vast land holding and creating an industrial empire of iron smelting and the export of wooden staves, besides becoming the Lord Treasurer of Ireland. It was not an entirely smooth path to success, for he was imprisoned for fraud, both in England and Ireland, and became an implacable enemy of the Lord Deputy, Thomas Wentworth, Earl of Strafford, who made him return Church property and fined him £15,000 and, what was perhaps more insulting, forced him to move to a less prominent position the elaborate black and gold tomb he had erected behind the high altar in St Patrick's Cathedral in Dublin. The tomb contained the bones of the Great Earl's first wife, her grandfather and parents. From then onwards, he did everything he could to undermine the authority of the Lord Deputy and his testimony in Parliament was the damning evidence that caused the impeachment and execution of Strafford.

In spite of appropriating Church lands and revenues, the Earl was a strong adherent and generous benefactor of the Protestant faith. This may have had more to do with political correctness than bigotry, though when he built the town of Bandon he had inscribed over the gates the words 'Jew, Turk or Atheist may enter here, but No Romanist or other unconfirmed Novellist shall be allowed entry.' Nevertheless, one of his daughters-in-law became a Roman Catholic and the diarist Evelyn said she nearly made a martyr of a little maid-of-honour trying to convert her.

The Great Earl lived in the castle of Lismore, which he had bought from Walter Raleigh and rebuilt. It withstood a siege by the Confederates in 1642 and in the diary is the note: 'Had sent as my gift to Capt. Broadrip £5 in money and also a cloak of mine of black Waterford frieze lined through with blue Tustaffatia, with a riding coat, doublet and breeches, sutable, for defending so well my castle of Lismoor when it was besieged 8 days by the rebels'.

He also spent much time in Youghal (which he spelt as Yoghall), and at Stalbridge, his house in England.

One of his more extraordinary achievements was in 1601, when he brought the news of the victory at Kinsale to London within forty-eight hours. 'I left my Lord President at Shandon Castle near Cork on Monday morning about 2 o'clock and the next day delivered my packet and supped with Sir Robert Cecil, being then the Principal Secretary, at his house in the Strand, who after supper held me in discourse until 2 o'clock and by 7 that morning called upon me to attend him to the Court, where he presented me to her Majesty in her bedchamber, who remembered me, calling me by name and gave me her hand to kiss.' (On a previous occasion Elizabeth had been much taken with his looks.)

He had fifteen children, ten of whom survived him, and they kneel about his magnificent tomb in the Protestant church in Youghal. They are the children of his second wife, Elizabeth Fenton, the daughter of the scholarly Sir William Fenton, the Surveyor General. It was said that the Earl had an appointment with the Surveyor General and while he was waiting, played with Fenton's baby girl and then explained 'he been courting the young lady'. Sure enough, he married her sixteen years later.

Much of his diary, which was kept from 1611 until 1642, records Boyle's financial transactions; there is also a careful chronicle of the presents given and received – gifts at that time being an acceptable way of oiling the wheels for both social and business purposes; but besides this there are many domestic details of the life of a seventeenth century nobleman.

The diary year ends on 25 March, which was the civil or legal year in the British Isles until 1752.

* * *

27 January 1611
Delivered Mr Ross to be made into a jewell for my wife 30 small diamonds and 28 small rubies, which were sett in a feather of gould. And at that time delivered him 32 orient pearles to be holed and 6 Irish pearls, which she wears in a nycklease.

5 February 1611
Given to my Lady Fenton [his mother-in-law] an angell in gold, for which she is to paye me £3, if She live till any two trees at Kilbree now planted do bear fruit; which I hope in God she shall see and pay for.

25 July 1613
Paid Alexander Newtown for the tarcell of a goshawk, 4 ster; which I delivered Sir Thomas Brown to be kept for me; who suffered the hoge to eat my hawk.

'Ster', short for Sterling, was silver money.

10 October 1615
The tenth Oct at night it pleased Almighty God to call my eldest son Roger Boyle from Deptford into Heaven.

30 June 1617

Mr Perckins my taylor certefied me that Mr Thomas Ball paide him £18 ster for my newe nightgown.

1 July 1617

Sir Walter Raleighe came to my howse to whom I lent one hundreth pounds ster; which I borrowed of my cozen Lawrence Parsons: who departed home 3rd July ...

In 1602 Boyle had bought 42,000 acres for £1500 from Sir Walter Raleigh.

25 July 1617

Sent Sir Walter Raleighe as a gift six barres of Spanish iron and a hogshead of salmon, for which I am to paye Roger Carew £3 ster.

23 December 1617

Paid for a murrey satten petticoat that is embrodered and for an apron to give my wife for her New Years Gifte £14.

29 October 1618

Sir Walter Raleigh beheaded at Westminster.

23 September 1619

Given Mrs Walley a pair of sea water green silck stockings, garters and Roses.

6 February 1619

I had from Wm Lyne of Tallaghtbridge a fair young black gelding that the Jury fownd guilty of the death of a man, as due to me for a Deodand, which I bestowed on my servant Roots.

A deodand was a personal possession that, having caused the death of a human being, was given to God, i.e. forfeited to the Crown to be used for pious purposes.

10 July 1620

This night it pleased Almighty God of his great mercy to take out of this mortal life into Heavenly Kingdom my eldest brother, Dr John Boyle, Bicsshop of Cork, Cloyne and Roscarberry for which visittiacon God make me thankfull And uppon the first notice thereof I posted my letters to the Lord Deputy to comend my cozen Richard Boyle, Dean of Waterford to those bicsshopricks.

12 July 1620

My eldest and onely brother, Docteur John Boyle, Lord Bicsshop of Corck and Rosse, was brought dead from Corck and interrred in my vault in my new chapelle in Yoghall; God grant him and me a joyfull resurrection.

13 February 1620

The 13th of this moneth the whale or other great fish was found dead at Ballyallenan neer Ardmoor.

11 March 1620

Mr Charnely sent me cinoman water, Tobacko, marmalade, Sacket & green ginger.

30 December 1621

My Lord Barry (though it wer Sounday), uppon an untimely falling out at dice, wounded Malperos the ussher of my Hall very dangerously with the fire forck. I praye god he may Recover and that the example hereof may teach my Lord better temper and carriage and neither of them bothe hearafter may presume to play upon the Lords Daye.

3 January 1634

Sir Randal Cleyton & his Lady, with my 2 daughters, came to Lismoor, and he brought me a veary Lardge Rounde fair Pearle taken in the River of Bandon, which the poor woman that found it sold in Corke for 2s in money and 4d in beer and Tobackoe; that party sold it againe for 2 cows, who solde it for a 3rd time for 12£ to a Merchant of Corke and then my Cozen Bardsey counseled Sir Randall Cleyton to buy it for me, who paid for it in ready gold 30£ ster; and I bestowed it for a New Years gifte on my daughter Dongarvan: It is worth a 100 marckes, and weighs 18 graines.

29 January 1634

Given to one Mr Humfrey, a young gent that was in wants (who wrott me that he served the Lo Keeper of England) half a peece.

20 January 1635

My daughter Dongarvan having at play lost £40 this Xtmas, and being drained drye of money, I supplied her with 20 peeces, and she to play them and if she loste them, then is she to add other 20 peeces of her own for play and the loss or gain be equally divided in half till more be gotten, or that lost by her at play.

4 March 1638

Mr Daniel O'Swillevant sent me 44 cane apple trees to plant; where of I sent the Earl of Bristol 4, to his Lordship's son in law, Mr John Freke 2, the rest are planted in my orchard at Stalbridge and in my servant William Rideout's garden with seven young stocks grafted there with Harvie apples. The grafts where of the said Mr Frekes sent me who also bestowed upon me twelve younge pear trees of the last years grafting viz Boncritteens and Burgomynes which I leave growing with him and one with Mr Rideout till the next season that they are fitt to be removed into my orchard.

9 November 1639

This daye I received the letters of my two youngest sons, Francis and Robert Boyle, and from their governor, M. Marcombes, that they all three with their two servants arrived safely from Rye at Dieppe the last day of October, 1639. The great God of Heaven bless guide and preserve them in their foreign travels and in his due time return them unto me in health and prosperity. They stayed not at Paris above ten days and came to Geneva the 28th of November 1639.

Robert Boyle became the distinguished philosopher who enunciated Boyle's Law, which states that the volume of gas varies inversely with its pressure.

21 November 1639

My daughter Mary did this day as she had many times before, declare a very high adverseness and contradiction to our counsels and commands touching her marriage with Mr James Hamilton, the only child of Lord Viscount of Clandebieus, although myself and all my sons and daughters, the Lord Barrymore, Arthur Jones and all other her beste friends did most effectually entreat and persuade her thereto and I command too.

Mary had refused to marry James Hamilton in August and the Earl had crossly referred to her as 'My unruly daughter' and cut off her allowance.

26 December 1639

My second son; Sir Lewis Boyle, Knight Baron of Bandonbridge, Lord Viscount Boyle of Kynalmeaky, was married in the King's Chapel in his court of Whitehall to the Lady Elizabeth Feilding, one of the Ladies of the Queen's Majesty's privy chamber, and daughter of the Earl of Denbigh. And the King was pleased to honour their marriage with his own presence, and to give the lady to my son to be his wife at which nuptial there was much revelling, dancing and feasting, and the King and Queen brought the Bride to her bedchamber in Court; where her majesty and all the ladies of honour did help to undress her and put her into her bed and when her husband was bedded with her, the King and Queen kissed and rekissed her, and blessed them bothe, and so did I, And it was, is and shall be my prayer to my God to bless guide and preserve them with health and long life and to make them fruitful in virtuous children and in good works to his glory Amen.

The Queens Majesty presented the bride with a rich necklace of pearle valued at £150, which the Kings majesty put about her neck. But Kynalmeaky was not in good order for a bridegroom.

1 January 1639 [The year ended on 25 March]

The new years giftes given me from my children this day were those: the Earl of Barrymore a beevor hat and band; his lady, six laced falling bands and six pair of cuffes; my son Dongarvan a pair of embrodered gloves; his lady twelve handkerchies and four nightcappes; my daughter Jones, 2 sherts laced, my daughter Bettie 4 shurts laced; my daughter Mary 4 nightcappes. Mrs Faulkerner, a book of Sermons called the 'Souls Conflict' etc, my Lady Stafford a bale of dice; a dozen pair of cards and a very curious French watche, all enameld which I bestowed on my vocall wife, the young Lady Mary Fielding, daughter of the Countess of Denbigh; and my son Broghill presented me with a pair of gloves ritchly embrodered with silver, which for a New Year's gift I bestowed on my Cousin John Naylor Fitzthomas of Grais In [a barrister].

20 January 1639

This day my son Broghill was at my table at dinner with me. He was secretly called away by a message from Charles Rich son of the Earl of Warwick to answer a challenge he brought him from Mr Thomas Howard son to the Earl of Berkshire. Whereupon Broghill secretly avoided the house bought him a sword and found Jack Barry, whom he made choice of to be his second and went both in Broghill's coach with their seconds into the fields, where they fought with their single Rapiers and both returned without any wound onely Broghill took away the fringe of Mr Howard's glove with the passage of his rapier that went through from his hand between his arme and the side of his boddy, without any other harme and thereupon their seconds parted them, and made them friends and so they came home supped together and all this for Mrs Harrison.

Mrs Harrison was being courted by Broghill and she accepted him, but after the wedding day had been fixed and the clothes bought she threw him over and married Howard.

2 June 1640

This day Mrs Taylor of Bandonbridge who was security for Richard Ticknor and had forfeited the lease of his dwelling house and shop in Bandon town to Paul White having made it over to White and he to me to secure me of £20 which in ready money I had lent gratis to Richard Ticknor. Mrs Taylor this day brought and paid me the £20 in gold which twenty pieces when I had received and she bemoaning unto me the poverty of herself and her seven fatherless children, I in commiseraton of her necessity, forgave her for the forfeiture of her lease, her four year's rent and freely gave back unto her the twenty pieces she had then paid me.

3 June 1640

My daughter Mary being by me allowed £100 a year for her maintenance in apparell & all other her necessities etc. (except her diet and lodging) was the 21st May 1639 paid £25 for her quarters allowance beforehand, which payment beforehand was to supply her for and until the 28th of August 1639 since which time for her disobedience in not marrying Mr James Hamilton, son and heir of the Lord Viscount Clandeboys as I seriously advised her. I have from the 21 May, 1639 till this third day of June 1640 deteigned my promised allowance from her and not given her one penny. But this day William Cheattle hath by my order delivered her one payment a £100 which pays her for and until 21th August next and then she is to be paid other £25 and so every quarter hereafter, beforehand and other £25.

That winter, Mary had had to make a piece of the best bedcurtains do for a winter waistcoat. Sometime later, Mary caught the measles, and Mr Rich was so attentive that the family suspected an entanglement and packed her off in Broghill's coach to Hampton, but she nevertheless married Rich, who inherited the title of the Earl of Warwick. She became well known for her piety and charitable works, but it was not a happy marriage. Her diary refers to quarrels – 'Had this afternoon with L. dispute wherein I was confidant I was in ye right but he in ye dispute growing violently passionate I still inconsiderately held on ye dispute which made him in his passion break forth most bitterly.'

24 April 1641
I have formally paid my son Dongarvan £30 did this day pay him other £30, being £60 for the half years diet in London of my daughter Mary and Franks wife, ending at May next, for themselves and their two maids.

1 September 1641
Sent by Travers to my infirm cozen Roger Vaghn a pot of Sir Walter Raleigh's Tobackoe and Thomas Letshums bill whereupon I lent him £30 with my letter of attorney to my cozen Henry Fitzwilliam Boyle of Hereford to receive it as my free gift.

18 December 1642
Sent to Sir Percy Smith's house in Yoghall towards our Xtmas, a hogshead of claret wine had from Josua Boyle for £4, and a great cheddar cheese given me by my Lady Stafforde.

1 January 1642
I presented my cozen, the Lady Smith with 2 sugar loaves for her new years gifte, and with my great cheddar cheese which Lady Stafforde gave me in England, and the Lady Smith sent me sixe cambrick hankerchers laced.

Anon.: Siege of Limerick Castle
1642

IN 1641, A GENERAL ARMED RISING *was planned in which Dublin Castle was to be
seized and the government's northern strongholds captured. The insurrection had an
inauspicious beginning, as a drunken man revealed the plan to the authorities, leading
to the arrest of many of the leaders. In the North, the Irish rose in a mass against the
English settlers, and the bloodshed there became a focal memory for anti-Catholic feeling for centuries to come. Farther south there was a complicated pattern of alliances. The
extreme Roman Catholic section desired national independence, while the moderates,
though wanting their religion to be restored to its former predominance, did not wish
for a break with England. There were the Protestant Royalists led by the Earl of
Ormonde and the Puritans who were hostile to Protestant Episcopacy, Catholicism and
Royalty. In England the government was in turmoil with the Civil War.*

*Early on, the 'Insurgents' or 'Confederates' took possession of Kilkenny and
Waterford and then went west to besiege Cork, but there they were repulsed. They
marched on Limerick under the leadership of General Gerald Barry, who had served for
a time in the Spanish Army. The citizens of Limerick opened the gates to them, the roy-
alist garrison in the Castle alone refusing to capitulate.*

*The commander of the Castle, Captain George Courtenay, son of Sir William
Courtenay, had only sixty regular soldiers under his command, but with auxiliaries and
others could muster two hundred men.*

*The Confederates took vigorous action to cut off all chance of relief for the besieged,
throwing a boom of aspen trees, across the Shannon so that the three vessels that came
up the river could not reach the Castle. They mounted a gun on the Cathedral tower so
that they could shell the defenders and protect themselves while they mined the walls.
For this, excavations were made under the outer wall of the Castle, which were roofed
and propped up with dry timber, and smeared with tar and other combustible matter.
At a given signal the woodwork was set on fire, and being rapidly consumed, the roof of
the cavern fell in, carrying down with it a large part of the wall. This made further
resistance impractical and the fortress was surrendered on honourable terms.*

*The Lord President is supposed to have died of grief when he heard that the Castle
at Limerick had been lost, but as he had been ill for some time, his death from whatever cause was not unexpected. The Confederates treated the defeated Royalists with great
generosity, allowing them to leave unmolested with their baggage.*

*The author of the diary is anonymous, but must have been a civilian of some
authority and mentions being a friend of Oliver Stephenson, one of the most gallant of*

the Confederate leaders. The diarist calls Stephenson 'a kinde acquaintance of mine' who arranged for the remnants of the garrison to go to Kinsale by boat rather than the much more hazardous route overland.

* * *

18 May 1642

After long & tedious watching in severall houses upon Wednesday May 18 1642 we came into the castle of Limerick about one of the clocke where within 3 hours after the towne began to lay at us with ther muskets that none of the castle durst issue out after that. None of the castle hurt that day or night but one poore old woman killd without the castle halfe an howre after our coming in.

19 May 1642

The enemie layd at us more fiercly and from the adjoyning castle killd John Skegge, a little girle & boy & hurt some 3 women & children, a bullet shot from the enemy rebounding from the wall was catcht in a boy's mouth without hurt the boy laughing.

22 May 1642

Ther came up into the river a pinnace of his Majesty's with two other ships even within shot of the towne about 8 of the clocke in the morning but the winde being full against them & the tide not great that they could not come neare, they bestowed some shott into the towne & fell downe with the tide, they returnd againe in the afternoone but could not come neere enough to the towne for want of winde & water, and after the bestowing some 60 shott at the church steeple where the rebells had set up a flag of defiance against them and at a new erected bulwarke on Thomond's side from whence the enemy offered to gall the pinnace & boates, they fell downe againe with the tide and that night perceiving the winde full against them and that the waters would be too lowe to doe service they fell downe towards Bunratty wher they might safely Anchor till better winde & tide as we thought, but returned not as we hoped, this day 6 or 7 great pieces were shot off from the castle which did some damage to the towne we had noe hurt of man woman or child with us.

25 May 1642

They shot not soe much as before till the afternoone and then fiercely, yet none killd that day or hurt, on the same night was heard some digging hammering and sawing in one of the row of houses on thee east side of thee castle betweene 12 and 1 of the clocke.

26 May 1642

In the morning we attempted the firing of the house but to noe purpose for by the unskilfullnesse of the gunner the fire tooke soe slightly that it tooke noe effect but was easily put out, a great gun was alsoe shot of and a Sacre at the bridg castle, but both (as he used to doe) missed, great shooting all that day on both sides but none killd or hurt of ours, thos workemen in the houses, went on still as we could heare them but could not hinder them. From the time we came in to this day were burid amongst us of sicke weake & poore that dyed ther 21 besides the 5 that were killd.

The great gun on the platform next the town was described as being so large that it required thirty-five yoke of oxen to draw it.

27 May 1642

We could heare the workemen still at worke in the houses but we could not hinder them. Towards night they shot more nimbly and from the steeple slew one woman, that night 2 boys were put out at the port holes of the gate they fired some houses on the north end of the castle which burnt downe to the ground, 4 other boys & men were let downe to fire the houses on the east side, but missed the full purpose, for the fire tooke not effectually and that which was fairest burning was put out doe what we could, it being at the end farthest from the winde all boys & men came in safe againe.

29 May 1642

They shot but litle at us all day long but still we could heare them going on with their worke yet could not guesse whether they labourd to undermine us or goe on with a trench which we could not discover by reason of thos houses which we could not fire, at night a boy belonging to one Mr Clare a minister was let out at the port-hole of the gate for discovry.

31 May 1642

Before or about 6 of the clocke in the morning Beeche the gunner of the castle got up some and calld for more them that were supposed to have most skile in gunnery, & removing a gun upon the water platforme to charge it with case shot and to turne it for clearing the south end of the castle, violently throwing in the shot into the gun fired it, killd himselfe and 3 others in the place and hurt 6 more whether this was done by ignorance or mischance, or else wilfully desperat I know not but many thought the later, because he had soe shamefully performed his duty before, & indeed was abhorred of all as alsoe that the day before a boy was let into the castle wch was suspected to bring some letters, torments could not make the boy to confesse it, but upon kind usage and promise of reward he avered that he had brought a letter to the sd Beech of a sheete of paper. Besides this great mischance, we had but one man hurt in the arme that day of this Beech much more was said even by all but nothing good.

There was small shooting of either side none hurt of ours, this evening was the moone at the full, but she was not fuller of light then our hearts were of heavinesse feare & sorrow, in that the tides and the windes had beene now 3 dayes full & faire for us and yet noe ships appeared, noe helpe noe comfort noe newes came to us, hunger sicknes and weaknesse increased and our enemies still girt us round about more strictly from Thursday last to this Thursday night were buried 38 besides 4 that were killed with the great gun, one woman by the enemy and a boy that was wounded the weeke before in all 44. Soe that from May 19 to this 2d June were buried 70.

Ther was not much shooting from either side, in the afternoone of the same day one Adam Darling going about to mend some blindings on the street platforme in removing a wool pack ther chanced to light upon certain letters which were tied to a stone which 20 to one they had not fallen backe againe outwards, one from the right Ho.ble the Earle of Corke to Cap. Courtney the other from my brother Oliver unto myselfe which were throwne up by a wellwishing hand, they bore date May 16 & 19, 1642 this was the first title of any newes that we could heare of anything done abroad since we were shutt up and the first hope of comfort that we had although that alsoe were far off, this day was discovered a kinde of skreene which the enemies had made to cover the worke that they were about in St Nicholas' churchyard.

Little or noe stir of either side, the mines went on, both of their sides and ours & could heare one an other worke as we assuredly conceived.

In the morning about 6 of the clocke a shaft of our mine falling soe close upon one of theires that some earth falling downe by an unskilfull boy the alarme was raisd but the bustle was such that we came to discovery of each other, and as we heard our men killd Michael White a friar, who was in the mine, all that day they fought under ground & the night following, but noe man of ours hurt then fell they to pouring in of water upon us, as we had done before upon them, but our men cleered it there and went on in an other drift to crosse them elsewhere.

Ther was still labouring on both sides and some part of the day the enemy shot hard at us but we had none of our men hurt either above or under ground this afternnone was descried a great ship under saile coming up the river wch cast anchor about Bunratty which began to stir in us some little sparke of hope of reliefe.

13 June 1642

Early this morning one Robert Vivian a mason stole out of the castle by the bucket rope that drew water which was much discontent unto us, this forenoone we descried 3 other ships which came up and cast anchor by the first which did somewt encrease our hopes but ther they lay and advanced not towards us, our enemies incroched still upon us by ther mines and took an other station against us in one Smith's house over against our gate on the north end of the castle, and shot at us from thence and from the Bps house. At night some of ours were againe sent out to fire the houses on the east side, but failed (though they had well kindled it) the enemye being soe many and soe ready to quench it notwithstanding our constant shooting.

15 June 1642

This morning about one of the clock Vivian that before had stolne forth came to the watergate, called and was let in, averred that he had beene with the Earle of Thomond and had made relation of our estate and that the earle replied (after some doubt of his fidelity) that the Lo. President with an army would be shortly with us for our aide and that 3 of the ships should meete him ther and that himselfe alsoe with 300 foot and competent horse would come to the assistance of them, but whatever was the truth the man was much doubted whether he had been ther or noe. This night we set out our Cresset light upon our highest platforme that they of the fleet might see some token of our distresse and that we were not as yet taken for we had noe meanes to certifie them of our estate, They shot dangerously at us on all sides but hurt none of ours this day.

16 June 1642

In the afternoone we descried one of the ships moving and advancing towards us, she anchored about a mile and halfe from us and sent up a long boate towards the towne who vewed about and returnd to the ship againe, some few shots were made at a fort that the enemye had made not far from the towne on Munsters side, and at some other straglers that waited to trouble them on Thomonde side, that night was let downe a man who undertooke to swime to the ship to make our state knowne unto them of whom we had hope that he reached to them, this night alsoe some 16 of our men went out thinking to spoile some of ther mines which indeed they had done to good purpose had they been backed with some helpe, or stood all to it lustily themselves, but both wanting, not doeing much, but discovering what they could not helpe they came all in againe 2 of our men wounded, one of wch namely Will. Mannering dyed within 3 dayes, if they had

had helpe they might have brought away 2 small iron pieces that they found mounted in the mine a good way from the castle and bent into the water for hindering the long boate or pinnace that we expected to bring us powder, one of thes they shot of the other they cloyed and brake the carriages but could not bring them with them nor throw them into the river for want of helpe the enemy coming in soe fast upon them.

17 June 1642
This morning the ship advanced some what neerer to the towne but made noe shot at it, some shots were spent at some others without the towne that sought to anoy them the other ships kept still below much to our discomfort the winde and tide being now fitt, and more was our discomfort that this morning was perceived a great cracke in the bulwarke of the castle from the top to the bottome which before we doubted to be undermined which forced us to draw backe one of the best pieces we had in the castle which (with a minion) was ther planted as the strongest and most important place of the whole castle not long after the tide being out the rebells foreseeing or then perceiving that the ship had not water enough to ride ther brought out of the towne a couple of small guns and planted them in a place of some advantage on Thomond side and shot some 6 or 8 shots at her, and others with muskets from the bushes and ditches on both sides the river played upon her, about 2 of the clock in the afternoone she floated againe and made them satisfaction and quietly kept her station, about 4 of the clocke we descried two other ships and a pinnace making up towards us which rekindled comfort and hope in us and presently upon ther approach towards the first ship we alsoe descried some land forces on Thomond side in severall companies to the number (as we guessed) of 300 foot & horse wch increased our hopes thinking the Earle of Thomond had conducted them (as we were formerly tould) but joy was quickly turned to a cold blast to our distressed hearts for we could perceive some of the rebells to goe unto them (as very rebells as themselves) and people that began to run away with the catle and goods to returne & stay and divers boates from the towne to fetch divers of them over the Shanon, but out of our reaches yet we ventured many a shot at them (And to increase our woe we discovered an other drift of our enemyes mine which was run within the wall of our castle at least 20 foote this was found by boaring wch for the present was plyed with water as long as we could make it run, but presently after we could heare them working in severall other places, all which we were not able to prevent soe that great was our feare sorrow and care our enemy being soe numerous fully supplied and fed, and we in want of implements and timber for our workes and mines, our men weake sicke and overwatch'd; diseases amongst the poore men women and children, bread and drinke scarse to be had and that not altogether soe much for want of corne and malt as for want of quernes to grinde it and worse for want of fuell to dresse it, the miserable crowd of poore men,

especially women & children helping to spend out wt they had that had provision, was cause that many starved & dyed & even all wanted for when the best in the castle for love or money could not procure phisicke, cordials, comfortable or scarce ordinary good food, how could it be with the poore that wanted almost all these things and had bad lodgings with all, and that which grieved the hearts of many and did them small comfort in the litle they had was the woeful yelling of the many miserable sicke starving and dying for want of which they were not able to supply them with, soe that now to see halfe a score carkeses together stretched out, meanly shrouded, lying on the ground ready to be inter'd was a lesse discomfort (a thing hard and horred to a tender nature) then to see and heare the woefull wailes and wants of a foure fould number round about halfe living and halfe dead (and that neither the full nor wanting may rejoyce an iminnent feare of death every houre hanging over all such was our present state of misery yet the lord in mercy did preserve a remnant for wch for ever blessed be his name).

19 June 1642

The ships lay still, our enemye plyed ther worke, wound about us still under ground, our danger still increased, an other cracke perceived in our bullwarke and for supply or helpe in this case, our materials and hands were skant and weake, this afternoone they of the towne carried over two brasse pieces the best they then had which they planted that evening upon Thomond side to beate upon the shipps where they lay, which the next morning they did, we heard not above 3 shot sent from the shipps that day, they beate upon our castle and into it that day not as formerly, but as God would have it hurt none of us.

20 June 1642

This morning early they began to beate upon the ships with aforesaid 2 pieces, and when they thought they made a good shot great was ther joy and shoutes, but surely they shot soe dangerously at the great ship that she was forc'd to slip ther cable and leave a good anchor behinde them which was to the enemy ye occasion of many a brag.

    This was done before 8 in the morning, which noe sooner ended, but presently an other accident happned of a litle comfort to us for a mine that had beene sunke middle of the east curtaine by one Robert Pope which had not been much accounted of, nor the man cherished or assisted in it, as he deserved, yet he carefully followed it on, and this morning it fell just with a mine of the enemyes, and himselfe being diligent in it, was present and discovered the approach, and after calling for helpe which came but thinly to him at first he himselfe first made in to the enemyes mine, and presently after some others followed, soe that he cleard the myne of thes few that then were in it, pulld downe all ther timber and brought it into the castle, and presently began a new drift to meete with an other mine wch we conceived to run southward towards our bullwarke all this was done without hurt to any of ours, most part of this day the enemye shot sharply at us from the castle at Thomond bridg and which did much over top us, yet hurt neither man woman or childe, but killd 2 cowes that were in the castle yard but ye joy of our good speede in the mine lasted us but a litle while, and was but (as is said) a lightning before death, for presently the houses on the east side of the castle were filled with men, that we could not fire them as we attempted, and at evening were cleaving hewing and breaking of wood and sticks which gave cause of feare yt they intended the firing of some other mines neere or under the bullwarke which was too true as aferwards appeared for.

21 June 1642

About one of the clock in the morning the upper part of the wall of the bullwarke fell down almost as low as the sally port doore, but this was not soe great signe of the fire underneth as that which followed the same day, this breach caused a generall alarme amongst us, but the enemy (as God would have it) bet not on, or then scarce perceived it, but not long after we perceived that ther was fire below under the eastern curtaine, by the smell and smoke that brake out in some cabins that were built within the castle against the wall, as alsoe by some smoke that brake up by the side of the trench without soe that then we saw that we were in imminent danger, the increasing whereof we could not prevent, but must goe on to an impossibility of our subsisting which I suppose was sufficient cause which moved our Capt to write to the Generall of the rebells &c. concerning one point of their letter formerly written to him, which was what honourable tearms they meant upon which they would have him to yield up the castle unto them, they answered his letter presently desiring him to come forth to parley and they would send in hostages for his safety, to that he replied that he might not goe forth of the castle himselfe, but that he would (if they pleased) send forth two other unto them naming Alderman Lellis an Alderman of the city and A.J. wch they refused but wrote to the captaine to propose his demands which not long after was done and set downe in 9 articles which together with a letter from our Capt was sent unto them, but it was somewhat toward evening and noe answer returned that night and we conjectured and probable it was that they stayed to see the event of their fire under our walls which soe continued to the encreasing of our sorrow that we feared the falling of a great part of our eastern curtaine before the next day, and this evening was a brasse falcon to be conveyed into one Smith's house for the battering of our gate.

Euery houre begat us new cause of feares and we doubted to be assaulted before the next morning, which if they had done, such was our case that without speciall providence we had beene undone from Thursday June 9 to this Tuesday ye 21 were buried 113. Soe that since we were shut up the number was 223.

22 June 1642

This day ther was noe shooting from either side as if ther had beene a formall ces-sasion. In the afternoone the Bp of Limerick dyed, and in the evening the enemy sent to our Capt that they would accept of the two aforenam'd to treat with them and accordingly they went out and after much debate got quarter for life and goods we were to have accomodation for houses and necessaries during our aboad in the towne & horses and carriages to covey us to Corke we paying for what we tooke.

23 June 1642

This day we yeilded the castle and carried the Bp to his grave & buried him in St Munchin's Church, and every one of us began to carry out our goods out of the castle too houses assigned us, we had civill usage from the soldiery, and our for-mer acquaintance in the towne gave kindly visits …

Ther dyed of our company the smale time we stayd in the towne 57. We did impute the cause of this mortality to our change of dyet, &c. so that the number of our dead did in this short time amount to 280.

Elizabeth Freke
1641-1714

ELIZABETH FREKE of Rathbarry Castle, County Cork, subtitled her diary 'Some few remembrances of my misfortunes which have attended me in my unhappy life since I were married.'

The eldest daughter of Raufe Freke of Wiltshire, she was a cousin of Nicolas Culpeper, author of the 'London Dispensatory', which may account for her interest in cures and recipes – four hundred appear in her diary. In 1671 she eloped with her cousin Percy Freke on 'a most dreadful raynie day, a presager of all my sorrows & Misfortunes'. After her only son was born, she accompanied her husband to Ireland, leaving the baby behind with a nurse who dropped him, breaking his hip very badly, but no one noticed for three months. Her father then summoned her back to England but would not let her see the child for some time, as it was so likely to die (in the diary, the lives of Elizabeth and her family are frequently despaired of by doctors and surgeons).

She travelled back and forth between Ireland and England, quarrelling with her husband. Her father, to whom she was devoted, gave her large sums of money, which her husband would take to purchase more land in Ireland. In the end her father bought her an estate at Bilney in Norfolk, which she managed to retain for herself. She lived first of all in a thatched house, farming the land until the tenant's lease ran out, then she moved into Bilney Hall. She settled here permanently, after her last visit to Ireland in 1694. Percy Freke came to Bilney when he was ill and his subsequent death caused her much histrionic grief and expense. She says she 'never knew sorrow until this misfortune', then tots up what the funeral had cost her.

She was paranoid about people cheating her, though she says with satisfaction that God often brought retribution to her enemies. But it must be said, when a George Morlly was arrested for stealing her coach mare, she attended the court, but at the last moment she would not prosecute him as he would be hanged. This infuriated the Justices and the Bench and it cost her 'near £10 and many troublesome journeys', but she says endearingly: 'This Miserable criminal stood in iron fetters before me, bowing which pierced my heart.'

She did suffer the most dreadful accidents – once falling down stairs, she knocked out her teeth. Another time she set herself on fire when she was having a quiet read of her will and on a further occasion she was beaten up by ruffians, but she survived it all. She continued complaining that her son never wrote to her, her family neglected her and that her employees were dishonest until she died in London in 1714 and was buried in Westminster Abbey.

*Her diary, which was kept with greater regularity in the latter years of her life –
the first part being more of a memoir – was written in a large folio volume bound in
white vellum that had been given to her as a present by her husband.*

*She came to Ireland first in 1676, landing at Youghal, and was met by Percy
Freke's mother, but as there was 'no place fit to lay her unfortunate head', she stayed at
Rostellan Castle, which belonged to the Earls of Inchiquin. Here, she says, her mother-
in-law mistreated her so much that she had a miscarriage. She spent about eight months
in Ireland, until summoned back to England by her father. In 1677, at the time of the
first entry below, she is returning to Ireland with her husband.*

* * *

25 August 1677

But K. Charls & K. James had commanded an imbargoe on all ships & passengers, nott to cross the seas withoutt their permitt, which was denied us, soe wee
wentt privattly off att pill [Crokerne Pill, upon the Avon] in a Boatt to A shipp
… my second time of goeing for Ireland.

26 August 1677

Wee were all like to be lost by most tempestuous winds and raine, butt, by Gods
Mercy, we putt in att Illford Combe, where I stayed Sunday, Monday & Tuesday,
& a Wensday by two of the clock in the morning, the 28 of August, the wind
changed, & I wentt wth Mr Freke to sea againe, & came thatt night within a
watch of reaching Watterford; butt on a suden, aboutt sunsett thatt nightt, the
wind changed, with the most hidious tempest of wind & raine, wch brought us
backe againe next day att nightt to Lundy, wher we lay wth 4 ships more, dis-
pairing of life, and our mast all downe, our cabin shutt upp, & our anchors lost.
We lay roleing till nextt night, when, being In a despratt condition, we attempted to shoot the Bay of Barstable, wher all that saw us on the hill gave us over for
Lost. Butt by Gods greatt Mercy wee safe landed att Barstable, aboutt sun-set-
ting, wher wth Captaine Jeffryes, we staid a weeke.

5 September 1677

When we wentt to sea againe, & by Gods Mercy to me, wee all landed safe in
Cork Harbour, tho' persued by several Algeriens …

*Pirates from the North African coast were a very real danger in the seventeenth centu-
ry. The Rev. Devereux Spratt had embarked in a boat from Youghal in 1641 with about
six passengers but before they were out of sight of land they were all taken by an
Algerian pirate who put the men in chains and stocks. When they reached Algiers, Spratt
was sold into slavery but was given more liberty than normal, which allowed him to
preach the gospel, and even after his ransom was paid, he stayed on for a further two*

years in order to minister to the other Christians. He eventually returned to Ireland and became the clergyman in Mitchelstown where he did keep a diary, though alas he had not kept one during the time he was in captivity. In failing to abduct Mrs Freke, the Algerian pirates had a lucky escape.

The Frekes spent only a short time in Ireland and were again in England in 1679 when Mr Freke's mother died and they returned to Cork.

16 September 1680

I came with my husband & son to Rath Barry, wher my husbands sister Barnard had cleered my house of every thing goode in itt, even to seven years letters wch past between us befor I were marryed, & my cirtificate of my privatt marriage the first time; This I thought very hard to me; besides, She was pleased to take away all my plate, to the value of neer two hundred pounds, though I had itt before I marryed, and it was engraven with my own coat of arms in a lossenge. Of two dozen of silver spoons of my own, I had not one left, or one scrip of my best lin-nen − all was conveyed a way by my husband's sister Barnard pretending Itt was her mothers, & though Mr Freke was her executor, neither hee nor my selfe had the vallue of five shillings (as I know of); only she sentt my husband a bill of eighty pound for burying his mother. But with much adoes & high words I gott a Little of my plate a gaine.

This was the good usage I had in the familly, she laying the death of my hus-band's mother to my doore (for carrying away her son) att neer fouwre score years of age.

30 April 1682

I left Rathbary and went to King-saile [Kinsale] with my son to a tend for a shipp for England, wher affter a fortnight weighting I had the oppertunity of A man of Warr in which I putt my self & son, I haveing noe friend to take any care of me.

In a later entry she says that her husband's 'last parting wish att Kingsaile, was thatt he might never see my face more etc. This stuck deep in my stomack, tho' to this day I never Lett my Father, or any friend I had, know of the Least difference between us, or any unkind usage from the Family I have Received In thatt Home or elce where.'

10 May 1682

We wentt outt to sea, as to my best remembrance, a Sunday morne … where by Gods infinite Mercy (affter striking three times on the sands) wee landed safly att the Pill att Bristol with my son and fowre servants.

In spite of his expressed desire never to see her again, Percy Freke followed her to England to get what money he could from his in-laws and then to bring her back with him.

26 July 1683
I took shiping att Pill, incognito, and by Gods greatt goodness & Mercy to me though such turbellent times by reason of plots in England, we both came safe to Corke the Satterday following, being 29 of Jully.

29 July 1683
We were both garded like prisoners before the Maire of Cork for English plotters stole over, who, being one Mr Covett, well known to my familly, was over and above civell to us & treated us both like a gentleman, saying hee would & dared be security for us and our name, and affter 3 or 4 bottles of wyne drunk in his house, hee released us, giveing order for the presentt landing of our clothes, & our other goods on ship due to our quality, to the amasement of all Beholders.

Thus God provided for us When we had none to help us, and itt was the whole reportt of Cork thatt my husband was by the order of King James hanged up on ship board att Minhead for making his escap for Ireland withoutt his permitt (which we could nott gett).

1 January 1683 [The year ended on 25 March]
My Deer Father sentt mee over to Ireland a hundred pounds for a New years gift being my unhappy birthday, & ordered mee, thatt iff Mr Frek Medled with itt, itt should be lost, or he to answer itt with the Irish intrest to my son. Butt Mr Frek took itt from me.

26 March 1684
Mr Frek ... contractted with John Hull for the rentting of Rath-barry, for a lease of one & forty years comencing the May day following, at the yearly rentt of two hundred & fiffty pounds a yeare, and a thousand pound for our living stock of horses, aboutt thirty working horses besids coach horses and sadle horses; cow-beasts and plough oxen about three hundred; and sheep two thousand five hundred; and lambs seven hundred.

24 April 1684
Butt oh, the saddest of the fattes thatt ever a tended poor mortall was mine, for on the 24 of April, my God took to himselfe by death my deer deerest Father ...

1 May 1684
John Hull, Mr Frek's tenant, by six a clock in the morning came to Rathbary when our house was full of company, & with Sr Emanuell Moor, his unkle, demanded the possession of the house, tho' by his faithfull promise we had three weeks time to remove all our goods. Nothing could prevaile butt wee must bee imediatly thrown outt of doors wch we wer thatt day & I with them; butt the country learning of this inhumanity, sentt us in carts & horses to remove our

goods as fast as we could to Donowen, aboutt a mile distant from Rath Barry, Wher by the way we lost neer halfe of them, the whole country coming to see this cruellty to us – However, late att night, I gott up behind Mr Freke and wentt that night to Cloghein neer Clanikilly [Clonakilty] to my cosin Hester Gookins ...

Butt my greatt God avenged my cause on this bruit Hull, for in 3 or 4 year-es, King Jams 2d Came for Ireland, & seised by the Irish all thatt ever he had in the world, & gave away our estate to Owen Macarty, the loss of which, with all his goods & his own estate, brok his hartt, he haveing nothing left for his wife and familly to subsist on; he lyes buried with one of his children in the open part of the church of Rathbarry a mongst the common Irish, to his etternal infamy.

Mrs Freke spent the next eight years in England, where she frequently says she had no place to lay her unhappy carcase or for those of her son and her three servants. She spent most of this time on her estate in Norfolk, where she lived in a thatched cottage by her-self 'with ease and comfort, tho every day threatened by neighbours' and took up the business of husbandry on the farm.

In 1692 she acceded to her husband's wish that she should return to Ireland, and landed in Cork.

12 November 1692

I came with my servants a horseback to Rathbarry, from whence I had bin absentt eight yeares, where, when I came, I found my house quit burntt downe, only two little rooms, & neither a bed, table or chair or stool fitt for a christian to sett on,-dish or plat to eatte outt out of, – or meat or drink fitt to suffise nature; and on the Land ... only two sheep and two lambs & three or 4 garron horses, worth about ten shillings a piece. And this was the fifth time I came to bare walls & a naked house since I was married.

In this most deplorable condition I staid till neer Christmas when the Irish parliament adjorned and Mr Frek came home ...

However in this miserable place I stayd, allmost frightened outt of my witts, for fowre yeares and a halfe, and sicke all the time with the colick & vapours, soe thatt I hardly wentt downe stairs (butt as I were carryed to the garden) all the time I were in Ireland ... and though I have undergone more than mortoll tongue can speak, I never knew whatt vapours were till this prospect given mee in Ireland, the misfortune of which I expect to cary with mee to my grave.

17 May 1693

Mr Frek left mee att Rathbarry and landed in England and went with my son to Billney wher they stayd aboutt a fortnight, & they fetched all my plate, linnen, my best beds, and other goods I had bin eight yeares a getting together, and all I had worth carriage or removeing they brought away all unknown to mee for Ireland, to furnish Rathbarry, in hopes by itt to make mee reside in Ireland, and, which was most my concerne, my downe feather bed I allwaise lay inn; soe thatt of my eight years industry att Billney, I had nothing good now left mee. This is the hard fate of Eliz Freke.

16 August 1693
However, Agust the 16, the greatt & good God, brought both my husband and son safe home to mee at Rathbarry when I did nott the least look for either of them; for which Mercy the Lord make me for ever most humbly thankfull. Eliz Freke.

26 November 1693
A greatt Dutch ship was cast away & lost with all the passengers in her on Rathbarry strand by overshouting his course for the Old Head of Kingsaile, and was dashed all to pieces amongst our rocks, and every creature in itt drowned with all the goods in itt, butt fowre men Mr Frek took upp amongst the rocks and buried them in Rathbarry church ...

3 November 1694
Mr Frek was made shriff of the County of Cork, doe all I could to the contrary. He kept his first Asises in the City of Cork, wher I were with him, and did putt against the Asises two and twenty handsome proper men, all in new liveryes to attend him, beside those that run by his horses side; Ld Chiefe Justice Pyne and Sr Richard Cox being the two Judges wher thatt Asises, were condemned eight and twenty persons to be hanged & burned, – And one young English man, an only son, whose life I begged, itt nott being for murder (I concidered my own condition thatt have butt one child) – And his father an estated gentleman in Devonshire. E. Freke.

2 June 1696
My son, Mr Ralfe Freke, was of age of one & twenty yeares when I gave him for a new yeares gifft two hundred pounds (200£) which my deer Father sentt me for my birthday presentt two months before he died, & five pounds for a purse to putt itt in.

I left Rathbarry in order to goe for England, affter I had stayd ther 4 yeares and a halfe, a miserable Life, most of the time very sicke of the distempers then reigning affter K. Jams wars ... I rested my selfe a week or more att Castle Mahon. From thence I wentt to Cork to try for shipping by my selfe.

25 June 1696
In my impatience of being gone, I ventured my selfe on board a very cracy shipp of Captaine Townesend, with a maid & another woman, a man & a boy and my husbands nephew, Thom Crosby, who was vexation enough to Elizabeth Freke, for whom I wer to get a place in a shipp to serve the king as a volenteere.

1 July 1696
I landed att Plymouth affter a weeks saile ...

6 July 1696
We wentt againe to sea, where we lay beatting up & downe the sea till Thursday, in a tempest and mists, nott knowing where we were, which forced us to an anker for two days more in a tirrible storme, our shipp & boatt both very crazy, itt durst nott stirr againe any more to sea, & our boatt nott worth a crowne. Thus were I sentt outt of Ireland by long sea, or round the whole Lands End, and in this storme we att last ankered on the Goodwin Sands ...

12 July 1696
I sent for the Queens pillatte boate and put my selfe and my family in itt at a ginny a person & though with greatt Hazard, by Gods greatt Mercy to mee we landed safe on the beach att Deale, wher the boatt-men & all belonging to mee jumpt on the shore. Butt I nott being able to stirr with my sickness and jorney were by a great wave carried away againe to sea, that everybody thought mee lost when on a suden a nother greatt wave forced my boatt to the beech againe and I in itt, where aboundance of the people looking att mee, by their strength & iron graples pulled itt soe far on the shore as to take me outt, butt I was In sencible now, till they demanded five guineys for bringing five of us from the Good-win sands ...

13 July 1696
We Landed att Deall, Wher I hired the Canterbury coach for London, & a horse for my cosin Crosby & two horses for my servantts. & att Maudlin in Kentt I were besett by five high way-men, one of which told mee I would never reach Cittingbourne & bid my boy behind my coach drinke hartily for itt was the last he would ever drink. From these blades they rid & wee drove for itt, & I most humbly thank my God, just gott to the Townds End before them to Citting-bourne. I came from Cittingboure to Rochester and soe to Gravs End.

On the 17, Latte att night I Landed att Billingsgate, when coming outt of the boatt, a roghy watter man stole every ragg of my clothes, and a mantue & pet-ticoat I would not have taken thirty pounds For, being sure thatt I shall never be Mrs of the like againe. In this pickle I got a coach and came aboutt midnight to my deer sisters, the Lady Norton, att her house ...

She never returned to Ireland.

John Stevens
16??-1726

John Stevens first came to Ireland around 1685 as part of the entourage of the Lord Lieutenant, the Earl of Clarendon. When Clarendon fell from favour, he recommended Stevens to Lord Rochester, describing him as 'an honest, sober young fellow and a pretty scholar whose father is a page of the backstairs to the Queen Dowager. He is a Roman Catholic.' In spite of this commendation, Stevens was not employed at court and he became a Collector of Excise in Wales. A fervent Jacobite, when he heard that the Prince of Orange had landed at Torbay and that James II had fled, he determined to follow his lawful sovereign to France and offer his services in assisting his return.

In January 1689 he embarked at Billingsgate on a hooker with forty or fifty other passengers, but the only seamen were the Master, who was almost blind, and a little boy. Not surprisingly, they got lost, ran aground, and almost foundered several times before reaching Calais. After a short uncomfortable stay in Paris he made his way to Brest, where Louis XIV had provided twenty-five men-of-war to take the 1500 men of James's army to Ireland.

* * *

Thursday 2 May 1689
We landed at Bantry, which is a miserable poor place, not worthy the name of a town, having not above seven or eight little houses, the rest very mean cottages … Two nights that we continued here I walked two miles out of town to lie upon a little dirty straw in a cot or cabin, no better than a hog-sty among near twenty others. The houses and cabins in town were so filled that people lay all over the floors. Some gentlemen I knew took up their lodging in an old rotten boat that lay near the shore, and there wanted not some who quartered in a sawpit. Meat, the country brought in enough, but some had not money to buy, and those who had for want of change had much difficulty to get what they wanted, the people being so extreme poor that they could not give change out of half a crown or a crown, and guineas were carried about the whole day and returned the whole. Drink there was none, but just at our landing a very little wort (infusion of malt before it is fermented into beer) hot from the fire, which nevertheless was soon drunk; and good water was so scarce that I have gone half a mile to drink at a spring …

Saturday 4 May 1689

Much of the morning was spent in looking for horses; at last with much difficulty Mr Lazenby bought a little nag, on which we laid his, Major Price's and my clothes in two portmanteaus, and having loaded our horse marched afoot driving him before us twelve miles to Dunmanway ...

Thursday 9 May 1689

We set out [from Cork] having hired a man and horse to carry our clothes, and marched with much difficulty, the way being hilly and my feet very sore, to Rathcormack a little town, which was very full, yet afforded us good quarters.

Stevens went via Kilkenny to Dublin. He was seriously embarrassed for money and in Dublin had to sell his rings, which had belonged to his father, and even the silver hilt of his sword – he says wryly that 'it might be truly said I live by my sword'.

Eventually he was given a lieutenancy in the regiment of the Lord Grand Prior and in the early autumn of 1689 skirmished round Dundalk. In October the army returned to Dublin and his regiment wintered in Trinity College. Stevens is censorious that this opportunity was not taken to train and discipline the troops, most of whom had come straight from the mountains and bogs and had never fired a musket.

In May 1690 they returned to County Louth and skirmished again around Dundalk, but by the end of June they had withdrawn to the south bank of the river Boyne.

Monday 30 June 1690

Early in the morning the enemy appeared on the tops of the hills beyond the river, some of the poor country people flying before them. They marched down and spread themselves along the sides of the hills where they encamped, but so as we could not discover them all, a great part being covered by the higher grounds. Part of our cannon was carried down and planted on the pass, or ford, which from thence played upon some regiments of theirs, and did some but not considerable execution. After noon they began to play upon us with their cannon and some mortars, but no considerable damage was received on either side.

A trooper from the Williamite side, Gedéon Bonnivert, also kept a journal for a short time over the battle of the Boyne, which records the narrow escape of King William:

'Monday the last of June we march'd towards Drogheda where the Ennemy were, and we came within sight of the town at 9 in ye morning. There we drew up our horse in three lines and came in order of Battle upon the brou of a long Hill. There we saw the Ennemy and weare so neare them that we could heare one another speak, there being nothing but the River between us. As we were drawn up we had the order to dismount and every man stand by his horse's head. We had not been there long but some of the king's Regiment of Dragoons were detach'd and sent to line the river side: so they begun to shutt at the Ennemy and those of king James's army at 'em. They had not been long

at this sport, when the king passing by the first Troop of his Guards, the Ennemy fir'd two small gunns at him one of the bullets greas'd the king's coat: then they play'd on till three of the clock upon us and shot a few men and horses ...'

I have endeavoured to extract from Stevens' description of the battle only the part that he actually witnessed.

Tuesday 1 July 1690

Very early the tents were thrown down, the baggage sent away, but the soldiers ordered to carry their tents, some of which were afterwards together with their snapsacks laid in heaps in the fields with some few sentinels, the rest thrown about as they marched, but in conclusion, as the fortune of the day was all lost ... [The enemy] gained the ford having done much execution on some of our foot that at first opposed them and quite broke such of our horse as came to rescue the foot, in which action the horse guards and Colonel Parker's regiment of horse behaved themselves with unspeakable bravery, but not being seconded and over-powered by the enemy after having done what men could do they were forced to save their remains by flight, which proved fatal to the foot. For the horse in general, taking their flight towards the left, broke the whole line of the foot, riding over all our battalions. The Lord Grand Prior's wherein I served was then in Duleek Lane, enclosed with high banks, marching ten in rank. The horse came on so unexpected and with such speed, some firing their pistols, that we had no time to receive, or shun them, but all supposing them to be the enemy (as indeed they were no better to us) took to their heels, no officer being able to stop the men even after they were broke, and the horse past, though at the same time no enemy were near us, or them that fled in such haste to our destruction ... What few men I could see I called to, no commands being of force, begging them to stand together and repair to their colours, the danger being in dispersing; but all in vain, some throwing away their arms, others even their coats and shoes to run the lighter ... I thought the calamity had not been so general till viewing the hills about us I perceived them covered with soldiers of several regiments, all scattered like sheep flying before the wolf, but so thick they seemed to cover the sides and tops of the hills. The shame of our regiment's dishonour only afflicted me before; but now all the horror of a routed army, just before so vigorous and desirous of battle and broke without scarce a stroke from the enemy, so perplexed my soul that I envied the few dead ...

The Lord Grand Prior's regiment but a little before consisting of 1000 men including all officers, now gathered to about 400, and the most part of those in such posture as promised rather the repeating their late shame, than the reveng-ing of it on their enemies. Many officers were not exempt from having their part of the disgrace with the soldiers, above half being missing when we endeavoured to rally, some were not heard of till we met in Limerick, and some stayed in Dublin ... Of those who appeared several had thrown away their leading staves, others their pistols they were before observed to carry in their girdles, and even some for lightness had left their swords behind them ... Brigadier Wauchope ... commanded our brigade to march up the hill ... What with the ill example of the officers and what with the terror that had seized the army, when we reached the top of the hill despite all commands or persuasions the men instantly slunk away, so that within half an hour or little more we had scarce eighty left together ... we marched or rather fled till it was quite dark, when the Duke of Berwick ordered to halt in a field about five miles from Dublin, there being now left together the colours of only five or six regiments and at first halting not above 100 men in all, though before morning we were much increased, sentinels being placed on the road to turn all soldiers in to the field. In this place we took some rest on the grass till break of day.

Wednesday 2 July 1690
At break of day those few drums there were beat as formally as if we had been a considerable body, but it was only mere form and we scarce shadows of regiments, the bodies being dispersed and gone. What was left in dismal manner marched as far as Dublin, where when each commanding officer came to view his strength, shame of marching in such case through the city we not long before had filled with expectation of our actions and hopes of gathering part of the scattered herd caused us to halt in the fields without the town. The colours of each regiment being fixed on eminencies that all stragglers might know whither to repair, in the space of near three hours each regiment had gathered a small number, the Grand Prior's as one of the most considerable being then 100 strong. Thus we marched through the skirts of the city, passing over the river at the Bloody Bridge, which is the farthest off in the suburbs, being either quite dispersed or gone other ways, we halted again in a field at Kilmainham, a hamlet adjoining to the city. The general opinion was that we were to encamp in the park till such time as our men came up ... But about noon we were all undeceived, the other three regiments having orders to march ... our lieutenant-colonel marched us away, which did not hold above a quarter of an hour when we were reduced to only twenty men with the colours. On the road we overtook the Lord Kilmallock's Regiment, which was untouched, being quartered in Dublin when the defeat at the Boyne. The whole day was a continual series of false alarms, the greatest reached us within two miles of the Naas, where Kilmallock's officers attempting to draw up their men to line the hedges, the confusion and terror of the soldiers who had never seen the enemy was such they were forced in all haste to march away.

It was ridiculous to see the brother of the traitor [O'Donnell] ... pretend to take authority upon him here, and order us to line the hedges, when at that time our whole strength was but six musketeers, eight pikes, four ensigns, and one lieutenant besides myself, to this was that by the day before hopeful regiment reduced, and yet not one of the number killed, unless they perished who were left drunk when we fled which were four or five. For our comfort no enemy was within twenty miles of us, but fear never thinks itself out of danger. We followed Kilmallock's men with such speed it had been hard for an enemy to overtake us, and that regiment though till then untouched was in such a consternation that when they came to the Naas they were not 100 strong. Here being quite spent with marching two days without rest or food I used my utmost endeavours to persuade O'Donnell ... to take up quarters for the few men that were left, to refresh them that night, and be the better able to march next morning, but all in vain. The general infection had seized him and he fancied each minute he stayed was to him time lost and an opportunity given to the enemy to gain ground upon us. Therefore following the dictates of his fear he hasted away commanding all to follow him, but necessity pressing more than his usurped authority, I stayed a while in the town with an ensign who had a lame horse, and having refreshed ourselves with bread and drink which was all the town afforded, we followed both on the same lame creature five miles to Kilcullen Bridge, where we could hear no news of our men, though they lay there that night. So inconsiderable was a regiment grown that it could not be heard of in a town where there are not above twenty or thirty houses and but three good ones. Here we took up the remaining part of the night in a waste house, and rested the best we could till break of day.

Thursday 3 July 1690

We were roused out of a dead sleep, proceeding from excessive weariness not from the easiness of the beds which were no other than the planks, at break of day by a great number of dragoons and others riding through the town as fast as their horses could carry them, and crying the enemy was within a mile of them. Being awaked and our lodging nothing pleasant we set out on our lame horse and having travelled five or six miles were overtaken by the Duke of Tyrconnell and his family, some whereof challenged the horse, and indeed he had the king's mark, they being too strong for us to cope with, for then might was the greatest right. They carried him away leaving us afoot weary, and without friends, or money. In this condition being desperate we attacked a village with design to force away a horse under the colour of pressing, but in reality was not much better than robbing. But the women of the village, setting up the cry soon gave the alarm to all men that were abroad, who flocking in with their roperies or half pikes had put us to the rout again, but that I had my leading staff which being longer than their weapons terrified and made them give way where I came, but whatever gained I was forced to lose to protect my companion, who having no weapon but his sword was too hard set, and doubtless had he been furnished with a half-pike we had got the better of the whole village and forced away two horses. As the case stood we were obliged to quit our pretensions and march off without horses, but not without some peals of curses for our good intentions and the good bangs I had given some of the men in the skirmish. Thus disappointed we struggled with weariness in hopes to reach Athy; when a great shower of rain falling increased our misfortune, making the ground so slippery we could scarce draw our tired limbs along. Now again in extremity it pleased God to relieve us, for a friend of mine, one Mr Dowdall, over taking us well mounted took me up behind him and a cornet of Luttrell's Regiment my companion, I having long refused to ride unless he were mounted, thus they carried us four miles to Athy. Hoping the rain would cease we stayed till almost evening refreshing ourselves, and it being then too late to travel took up our quarters at Shanganagh, a small village a mile from Athy and found the best entertainment we had met with since the unhappy rout ...

Friday 4 July 1690

Meeting a servant to one of our lieutenants I borrowed a horse he had, and pressed or forced away another about a mile from our quarters, but without saddle or bridle, which was very uneasy, but anything more tolerable than going afoot, and thus mounted we got about noon to Kilkenny, which is sixteen miles. To do justice I restored the horse to his owner before entering the town, contrary to the advice of all present, but as it was unjust to detain the horse without any other pretension but force so it was inhuman to do it after the poor man had followed sixteen miles afoot upon my promise of restitution. Nor was the manner of taking the horse unpleasant, for at least twenty of the poor people flocking to his defence with several weapons. I frightened away and kept them all off by presenting a matchlock I had taken from the lieutenant's man, though without powder, ball, or so much as a match. All the shops and public-houses in the town were shut, and neither meat nor drink to be had though many were fainting through want and weariness ... hearing that the stores at the castle were broken up and much bread and drink given out, I resolved to try fortune there and found drink carried out in pails, and many of the rabble drunk with what they got ... Our colours and some officers were now in town but no soldiers, so the ensigns were ordered to strip their colours, and thus we set out on our way to Limerick, my ensign having met me and furnished me with a mare he had taken up upon the road ...

The Jacobite army spent the rest of the month in and around Limerick regrouping and making occasional sorties. On 9 August the Williamite troops surrounded the town and the siege lasted until Saturday the 30th, when the Williamite side withdrew, very much to Stevens's surprise.

The army settled down to winter in Limerick in very poor conditions. The garrison lay in empty houses, which had neither beds nor straw to lie on; their clothes were worn to rags and most of them were barefoot 'for their wretched shoes and stockings could scarce be made to hang on their feet and legs'. They were issued with half a pound of salt beef a day and half a pint of barley, oats or wheat in grain with which to make their own bread. The brass money with which the army was paid was virtually worthless.

Stevens expresses great admiration for the men 'who never mutinied nor were guilty of any disorders more than happen in armies that are best paid'.

In the spring of 1691 the natural son of the Duke of Tyrconnell, Brigadier Talbot, was made colonel of the Grand Prior's Regiment, which was, Stevens says proudly, 'one of the eldest and best in the army'. In June they marched out of Limerick northwards to Athlone which was again being besieged.

Monday 22 June 1691
Very early Brigadier Talbot's and the Lord Iveagh's Regiments of Foot relieved the trenches on the north side of the town upon the fords of the river, where they lay all that day and night without anything worthy of note happening, but spent the night pleasantly in raillery with the enemy on the other side.

Tuesday 23 June 1691
We continued in the same post all the day, much of which was spent in a sort of voluntary cessation on the banks of the river, where the guards on both sides discoursed familiarly till some general of the enemy's coming down broke off the communication, and we fell to firing at one another for a short space, and then ceased without any harm done on either part.

Thursday 25 June 1691
There was a general muster in the morning; soon after we had orders to be all ready in half an hour, and presently again to decamp; which was done, and we marched down about a mile nearer to the town, where we encamped on a ground much like the last, but far from the water. The enemy had now mounted more cannon and played most violently without intermission on the castle …

Friday 26 June 1691
The enemy's fire at the castle continued very hot all day, but nothing else of note happened.

Saturday 27 June 1691
… At night we marched in and relieved the trenches on the left of the bridge, which was defended by several companies of Grenadiers.

Sunday 28 June 1691
… About one in the morning the enemy, creeping over their barricades of faggots on the bridge, made up the broken arch with planks, both sides plying their small shot and hand grenades without intermission; yet they did their work and retired. No sooner was it done than five or six of our men, getting over our work of faggots on the bridge, notwithstanding the enemy's continual fire, took up the planks, and throwing them into the river, returned in safety. This great and small shot never ceased firing, and some time before noon the enemies with their

grenades fired our faggots on the bridge, which, being very dry and not covered with earth, burnt most furiously. I was commanded with a detachment of forty men of our regiment, and other officers of the other regiments in the town with proportionable numbers of their men, to put a stop to the fire, which notwithstanding all our endeavours raged so violently that it took hold of the houses adjoining to the bridge. The enemy in the meanwhile bent thirty pieces of cannon and all their mortars in that way, so that what with the fire and what with the balls and bombs flying so thick that spot was a mere hell upon earth, for the places was very narrow which made the fire scorch, and so many cannon and mortars playing on it there seemed to be no likelihood of any man coming off alive. However we threw down one house, and the men, being hasty to run off with the timber for their own security, they gave a stop to the progress of the fire, which then began to decline till it quite ceased. We had very many men killed here of the detachments that came to work, and the rest being gone off, a French major we had in our regiment, besides the Irish, commanded me back to my post. And this I think was the hottest place that ever I saw in my time of service. The fire being quite put out, a new traverse of faggots was raised where it stopped. Many who had served long in France said they had never seen such furious firing for so long a time, and, besides the bombs, the enemy threw out of their mortars a vast quantity of stones; besides that place being so close the cannon balls which struck against the castle walls beat off abundance of stones from them, which did as much mischief as the others. The whole action continued about four hours, most of the men who once got away returning no more, which made the work the longer for those who were forced to continue at it. By this means only seven of my detachment were killed and nineteen wounded out of forty, and I received no hurt myself. Yet returning to my post in the trenches I was knocked down with a stone that flew from the castle wall, which only stunned me, a good beaver I had on saving my head. Another stone from the wall gave me a small hurt on the shin, which was not considerable. At night most of the officers standing about a barrel of powder to be distributed among the men, a bomb fell in the midst of us, but we all lying down, it pleased God it took not the powder, and we all escaped unhurt. About midnight we were relieved by Colonel Nugent's Regiment, and lay the remainder of the night on the bivouac in the ditch of the castle.

Monday 29 June 1691
With the dawning of the day we marched to the camp. This morning some of the enemy's Grenadiers advancing were so well received that we heard they lost above a hundred. Two officers and five soldiers of ours, venturing up to the enemy's faggots on the bridge, set them on fire and the wind favouring us destroyed them all. After this the enemy fired only some odd shot all the day, and continued as quiet in the night.

Tuesday 30 June 1691

Most of the day passed in silence. In the afternoon on a sudden the whole camp was alarmed, and we marched down to the bridge within a mile of Athlone where we understood the town was taken, the enemy having entered both at the bridge and ford without the least opposition made on our side. The Regiments of O'Gara, Cormuck O'Neill and others that were in the works, quitting them at the first onset without firing a shot, so that there was no time for any relief to enter the place. Some of the enemy who ventured without the castle were driven back without any loss, whereupon they retired and secured themselves within, whilst our men who had quitted the town ran in great confusion over the bog. All our army stood at arms near the place but could do nothing, the castle being strong on the land side. In this posture we continued till towards night with manifest tokens of fear in most men's faces, as if utter ruin had been hanging over us upon the loss of the place, though the army was untouched, and except the defence of the Shannon, no loss sustained. At night we returned to the camp, threw down our tents and made all ready to march.

The journal breaks off on Sunday 12th July, just at the start of the battle of Aughrim, where in spite of a much braver stand, the Jacobite army was disastrously defeated. The second siege of Limerick resulted in an early Jacobite surrender and the signing of the Treaty of Limerick.

Stevens probably sailed with the Wild Geese for the Continent. By 1695 he was back in London where he published translations of books from the Portuguese and Spanish.

Colonel Thomas Bellingham
1646-1721

HENRY BELLINGHAM was granted lands at Gernonstown in County Louth, which is about ten miles south of Dundalk on the main Dublin road, by Oliver Cromwell. (The name Gernonstown was changed to Castlebellingham at the end of the seventeenth century.) His son, Thomas Bellingham, kept this diary from August 1688 until September 1690.

At the opening of the diary, Thomas Bellingham was living in lodgings at Preston in Lancashire with his wife, Abigail. His sympathies were with the Protestant cause though he took no active part in the political events in England. The exchange of kings is unemotionally noted in the diary. He placed a bet on when the Prince of Orange would land. 'I gave Mr Hebson half a crown to receive 4 for it if the Dutch invaded us before twelfth day next.' He won as the Prince landed on the 5th.

James II's departure is even more unemotionally recorded: 'On the 28th December, 1688: A hard frost. We had an account of ye King's being gone towards France.'

At the end of August 1689 Bellingham crossed to Ireland to join the Williamite forces under the command of Schomberg. He visited Gernonstown, which was more or less in the front line. His house there was burnt down by the Jacobite army retiring to their winter quarters in the autumn of 1689, though Bellingham did not seem greatly concerned. After the war, he built a new house for himself about fifty yards from the old castle.

In 1690, after passing the winter in Preston, he returned to Ireland and was an aide-de-camp and guide to King William during the Battle of the Boyne.

* * *

31 August 1689

We landed all our horse and encamp'd att White house. I met Capt. Francis Purefoy, who carryed me with him to Carrigfergus and treated me very obleigingly. Sir Henry Ingoldsby's Regiment quarter'd here. Some of them behaved ill att the seige. Lews, Capt of the Grenadeeres, was dismissed for Cowardice.

They marched southwards, the Jacobite army retreating from Newry.

6 September 1689

I gott Protection from the Duke for my tenants. There went a detachment of above 50 horses with Count Schomberg. We marched about 5 in the the evening.

Came within 2 miles of Dundalke, about 10 att night, where we stayed all night, and sate on horse backe in the raine. They likewise marched upp ye Earl of Meath with some foot.

7 September 1689

We came early this morning to Dundalke. Ye army came in entirely before 12, and encamped on the north side of the bridge. This town scap'd the fury of the enemy. We found here some stores of corne and a good cellar of sacke. I gott a quarter at Wm Gunnell's.

10 September 1689

A party of foot and horse came with me to Gernonstowne. The enemy were there that morning and tooke Mr Smith and Courtney. They returned Smith after using him very ill. A deserter came in from Maxwells dragoons.

12 September 1689

Scravenmore came to Gernonstowne and drank with me. Mr Buttler our Curate came to us from Mr Townlys.

14 September 1689

Capt Ed Griffith came here with a party. We saw some of the enemy upon the mount of Dromcath (Greenmount). I had severall messages that K James came with his whole army to Ardee. We putt our small garrison in good order and kept guard all night.

15 September 1689

The alarum continues. The drums are heard as from Maperstowne bridge. I sent an express to the Generall, who brought orders for our speedy marching away, which we did, and reached Dundalke before one. I dined with the Duke [Schomberg] and was civilly treated.

The armies continued skirmishing between Dundalk and Drogheda. The Williamite army suffered dreadful losses because of dysentery.

3 November 1689

Cold weather. Severall of ye sick are sent in carts to Carlingford, and dye by the way. Strict orders are given out for all soldiers to lye in their camp. I was on board the yatcht in order to procure a cabin, and came home in Sir John Topham's calash.

4 November 1689

Very wett weather. A messenger came in with an account of the enemyes being decamped and leaving a garrison in Ardee, which they have strongly entrenched.

In the afternoon Joan McGuire brought me the newes of my house being burnt yesterday morning, and in the evening deserting it. Att night Franck Young came in, whom I introduced to the Duke. He sayes the enemy in very ill condition – they have sent most of their forces into winter quarters – and that K James was to goe from Ardee tomorrow … Toby Purcell assured me that he saw the Doggs in the Irish army plucke upp their dead bodies and eat them, insomuch that att his coming here he was much afraied they would fall upon him. Here are some discontents amongst the great ones about the mismanagement of this campaigne. Severall of our men died in the way to Carlingford, being left in the highwaye.

5 November 1689

Most dismall weather of wind and raine. I was a considerable time this morning with Colonel Stewart, who spoke freely with me of great matters. He seemes much dissatisfyed att the cold reception here of the Derry and Eniskillen men, and sayes that Douglas [a Lieutenant General] was charged with mutining, because he spoake freely about the soldiers being abused for want of pay and other necessaryes.

Michael, my miller, came and confirmed the newes of my house being burnt, and the tenants and neighbours were under dismall apprehensions of being all destroyed by the Irish.

6 November 1689

Still miserable weather. Severall officers came into our quarters, being driven by the extremity of the weather. I sould my horse and furniture to Capt Wescomb for 18 guineas. I was late with Kirkes officers, and was most friendly treated by them, and carried several tokens from them for their wives and others.

Major General Kirke was a senior officer during the campaign.

7 November 1689

This morning I delivered my horse at the Generalls. Some horses were taken away from wthout the lines, as was said by the enemy, but beleiv'd by some of the army to the North. I sould my beavour to Rollston. I gott a certificate from ye General of my good service during this campaigne.

8 November 1689

Bitter weather – wind, raine, and haile. I came on board the yatcht Peggy Stanly, and the miller came to me from home. I received Kirkes adieu and had a noble bonefire att parting.

He spent the winter with his wife and family in Preston, where he was ill for almost two months.

He came back to Ireland on 30 May 1690. His arrival is recorded by another diarist, the Rev. Rowland Davies, who was a chaplain in the Williamite army. '30th May, 1690 – I walked to Belfast, and dined with the Colonel, Major and several others at Mr Rourke's. After dinner, Captain Bellingham came to us being newly arrived from Liverpool, and gave us an account that the Parliament was adjourned on Tuesday last, and the horse-guards marched from London; that his Majesty was speedily to move thence towards us, and will bring with him four thousand men and that all the army in England are paid off to the 1st Inst …'

King William arrived on 14th June at Carrickfergus, and a couple of days later Thomas Bellingham was received by him and kissed his hand.

20 June 1690

Very great showers. I went to Hillborough. Saw ye K [King] and drank of his wine … 2 dragoons were brought in prisoners. I was with my Lord Meath and Mr Neway att their tents, and brought Hunter ye Quaker's wife behind me home.

The Williamite army marched south – there was a skirmish at Moyragh Pass.

27 June 1690

Very hott. About 2 this morning I moved towards Dundalk, and entered it about 6 with Lieut General Solmes and Major General Kirke. The towne is wholy deserted, but strongly fortified. No inhabitants left but Capt Bolton and his wife, who are both stript. Our army encamped about a mile south from Dundalke, being now entire, Douglas party having joyned ours. J. White and I went as farr as Lurgan race, and sate there some time eating bread and cheese.

Lurgan race is the mill stream at Lurgan Green, three miles south of Dundalk.

30 June 1690

Very hott. I called at Mr Townley's in our march towards Boyn. I was some time with ye King on the hill of Tullaheskar, from wher he viewed Drogheda, and then went towards Old bridge. On the side of Boyn lay the enemyes camp which, the King going to view, he was hitt by a cannon shot on his shoulder, wch putt us into the greatest consternation imaginable; but, blessed God, it proved but a slight hurte. He went round his own camp, and was received with ye greatest joy and acclamations imaginable. The cannon fired att each all the afternoone.

Amongst the Bellingham heirlooms are the knife, fork and spoon used by the King on this day.

1 July 1690

A joyful day. Excessive hott. About 6 this morning ye King gott on horseback and gave the necesary orders. Kirke ordered me to bring him some account from the enemy. I brought him a youth, one Fyans, who came that morning from

Drogheda. I carried him to the King, who was then standing att the Battery, seeing his cannon play att the house of Old bridge. He had sent early a strong detachment of about 15,000 men, with Douglas, towards Slane, who passed the river without any opposition, and putt the enemy to rout who were on that wing. He sent another detachment of horse to the left, to goe over att the mill foord; but, the tide coming in and ye foord bad, the passage was very difficult, most of them being forced to swim, insomuch that they could not come upp time enough to assist our foot, who went over ye foord att Old bridge about 11 of ye clock. The enemy had laid an ambush behind the ditches and houses on the other side of the water, who fir'd incessantly att our men as they were passing the river, who as soon as arrived on land immediately putt those musqueteers to the rout and advanced farther into the field in battalion. Here the brave old Duke Schomberg was killed and Dr. Walker (The Governor of Londonderry during the siege) ... The enemy advanced towards us and made brisk effort upon us; but we soone repelled them with considerable loss on theyr side. They made 2 other attempts upon us; but were still bravely beaten back; and when our horse of the left came upp ye enemy quite quitted that feild, having left severall dead bodyes behind them ... the enemyes horse of Tirconnell's Regiment behaved themselves well, but our Dutch like angells. The King charged in person att the head of the Eniskilliners, and exposed himselfe with undaunted bravery. He pursued allmost as farr as the Naul, and left them not till near 10 a clock att night. I was his guide back to Duleeke ... I returned to the camp att Oldbridge, having left the King in his coach att Duleeke, where he stayed that night. I was almost fainte for want of drink and meate.

2 July 1690
Very hott ... By one come from Dublin this morning we hear the enemy have quitted Dublin, and left only some few of the militia. We stayed all this day att Duleeke, where I saw Mr French and conferred with him about correspondence and intelligence. I wrote to England.

4 July 1690
Very hott. I waited on the King with an account of the stores and provisions that were in Dublin and 20 miles around. I presented him with a baskett of cherryes, the first he eat since he came to the kingdom. He tooke them with his own hand very kindly ...

Ten days later, Thomas Bellingham was made sheriff of Louth and returned to Gernonstown where he 'mowed his grass and reaped his corn'.

19 July 1690
Hott weather. We had a markett. I sent the cattle away. In the afternoon I went to Lurgan (Green) to shoot rabbetts.

John Scott
c. 1685-1709

IN HIS REMARKABLE BOOK Two Centuries of Life in Down, *John Stevenson quotes extensively from the diary of John Scott, a divinity student who lived at Donaghadee.*

John Scott, the son of Captain Matthew Scott, a mariner, was partly educated in Glasgow and there is an entry in his diary describing his journey home. It took nine days but gave him plenty of opportunities to go and listen to sermons preached in Irish and in English. He was licensed to preach in 1707, after he had undergone many examinations by the ministers of the Down Presbytery of the General Synod of Ulster. Alas there is no record of him after 1708 and I presume that he died young.

* * *

Friday 15 December 1704

I was att home and in company wth my father who was same day under Physick, when Hugh Campbell wth Wm. Pinkstane came to my father wth his Bill of Cost: presented it, & after some time, he was provoked, tho' no cause was given, to give my father a blow, whereupon I gott up, gott him in my arms & desired him to be sober, and att length gott him pulled from my father and then interposing betwixt them quit him, he made towards my father the second time, I again interveans & desires him to give me the blow & not meddle with father, & so I gives him a blow with my fist on the face he was afterwards pretty sober, only told me he would give me a blow another time, and promising the same elsewhere namely Pinkstan's in the audience of Capt. Montgomery, Jon MCormick of Newry & Arch Milling he was indeed as good as his word, for same night Fraiday 15th he came in Street door & chamber door being open; & as he entered the room door he drew his oak cudgel with this expression, 'were you not a base villan to beat me so in the morning' & so let drive att me, but ever blessed be my God, who at all times safeguards his own, destined one of the beams of the house to receive it from me, & when it was over, namely, the blow, I clapt in to him & gott hold on him and att length gott him under me, and so beat him with my fists untill I was allmost weary, and at last I gott him putt out of the house, & while att the door & chamber window he threatened to put me from preaching & to burn the house upon us.

Wednesday 14 March 1705
I was att no sermon. The Sabbath before Mr Hamilton had given intimation that there would be no weak days sermon because of the sowing.

John Scott fell in love with the daughter of the Rev. Henry Hamilton of Donaghadee, Jean Hamilton – whom he often referred to in the diary as 'Doâ'. When he wrote about their meetings he did so in Latin, though as he was not very proficient at the language, the text is scattered with English words. For greater ease of reading, John Stevenson made a 'sense' translation which I have followed.

Friday 16 March 1705
I was att work all day only in the evening went down to Mr Hamilton's where I spent some space of time with the mistris.

Tuesday 17 April 1705
I went to Belfast and bought a hatt price 5s: 10d and two yards & 3 quarters of broad-cloath at 5 as I judge it may be, because it was not paid then p yeard. I returned same night.

Wednesday 15 August 1705
I heard Mr Hamilton on Jon 4:2 & was domi p diem. Memorandum that same day I went to Tho. Wrights who was going to my father to Dublin & gave him the key of my father's chest & at my return I overheard Janet Barkley cursing Jon Blair whom I reproved … I was a little out of humour through her & she was pleased to declare throughout the town that I abused her when God knows it was the glory of God & the good of her poor soul that I designed by the reproof by me reached her, but I fear poor woman she is given up of God.

Scott had ridden to Antrim the day before the following entry.

Saturday 8 June 1706
I slept till near 4 in the afternoon, about 5 it was noised through the town that the Meeting house was on fire, as soon as I got my shooses on my feet & my coat on my back, I ran as fast thither as possibly I could and found true what was noised, but blessed be God it was soon quenched, so that it did not much harm, the occasion of it was Jamie Allen the collrs son his firing a musquet at a bird that was upon the house, and the weather being dry & the forrage of the gun carring to thatch set it on fire by him not designed I am persuaded.

Monday 20 September 1706
I was in Donoghadee it being a fair day. I was sometime with Mr Ja. Hamilton in Ja. Kennedy's & Ja. Hay's, God pardon the sin of mispending time, precious time. Memorandum Mr James Hamilton sent with Mitchel to Edr. {Edinburgh] for a perriwig about five & twenty or thirty shillings in price. Mitchel was to return within 6 weeks.

In 1707 he courted Jean more assiduously.

Saturday 1 November 1707

I was in Donaghadee about eleven o'clock. I went to Mr Hamilton's and met in the entrance Mrs Jean, to whom I had spoken and she promised to meet me about 6 o'clock near the church. At that time I disclosed to her what was in my mind, and to console me she said that she would think over the matter about which I had spoken. I was with her about two hours and we separated near the church.

Monday 3 November 1707

I was in Donaghadee and in the evening went down to Mr Hamilton's. I had only a word with Doâ. I went with Mr Henry Hamilton, Mr Hamilton, Mrs Jean and some others home with Mr James Hamilton and lady to their lodgings in William McMechans's and again accompanied Mr Hamilton and wife with, especially, Mrs Jean, home and supped with them.

Tuesday 4 November 1707

I was in Donaghadee during the day only in the evening went to Mr James Hamilton's lodging where I meet with Doâ. I went home with her to her pater's and from thence came straight home.

Friday 7 November 1707

I was in Donaghadee and in the afternoon went out with Mrs Jean Hamilton, Mr James Hamilton & his wife to Killachyes we returned home same night; and I at my return went down to Mr Hamilton's went in and meet Doâ in the small room, where about the space of an hour I was with her and had indeed a desirable time tho' still very nice.

Monday 10 November 1707

I was in Donaghadee during the day and in the evening went down to Mr Hamilton's and met Doâ in the small room, where I was with her for six or seven hours – father and mother in Belfast.

Wednesday 12 November 1707

I was in Donaghadee and did preach on Rom: 8:1:1 dined in Mr Hamilton's. I was in the evening in Mr Hamilton's, and took occasion to signify to Mrs Hamilton quam maxumum amorem I had for Doâ Jean her daughter she told me she would not be my foe but rather my friend, for which I returned her many thanks. I was for some time at the Turf stack same night cum Doâ.

Thursday 13 November 1707

I was domi p diem and in the evening went down to Mr Hamilton's & meet Doâ in the small room where I was with her about two hours. I supped in Mr Hamiltons. I gave Marrion Hamilton a handkerchief and gloves.

Friday 14 November 1707
I was in Donaghadee all day and in the evening went down and meet with Doâ in ostio we were in the guest chamber from 6 to ¹/₂ 9 Mrs Hamilton came and called Mrs Jean and so we were necessitate to part. I came straight home.

Saturday 15 November 1707
… In the evening went down towards Mr Hamiltons but did not see Doâ and again I went and did not see her; I came home and about 9 of the clock I went down and meet with Doâ. I was with her about half an hour and gave her gloves.

Wednesday 19 November 1707
I was at sermon & heard Mr Hamilton on Isai: 55:2. In the evening I was about 2 hours with Doâ from whome I had the following encouragement … which was that if she did not alter she would accept of and in due time reward my service; but if she altered then she was to be free.

Friday 21 November 1707
I was working all day only in the evening went down to Mr Hamilton's there supped with Mr Bigger after supper I met with Doâ at the haystack and stood about a quarter of an hour with her, and at the same time presented her with a broadd piece of gold, of which with much pressing she did accept.

Wednesday 26 November 1707
I was in Donaghadee and going to sermon went to Mr Hamilton and was told by Marion Hamilton that Doâ was gone to Mr Moor's of the Roddins, whereupon I returned home and went not to sermon, but took horse and went straight to Mr Moor's, but found her not there, which was to me most disquieting. I came from there straight to Mr Wallace's where I found her & had only two words with her and returned home to Donaghadee so burdened with concernedness for her absenting her father's house that I thought I shold never have got to Donaghadee, when I came to Donaghadee I went down to Mrs Hamilton and entreated that she would tomorrow send for Mrs Jean she told me seeing me so much concerned that she would.

Tuesday 2 December 1707
I was resolved to have gone to the presbytery but it proved a bad day I stayed at home; I went down before daylight to Mr Hamilton's and was cum Doâ in the guest chamber from half eleven till ¹/₂ three in the afternoon: in the evening I just saw her she being bussied making a furbelow'd skerf in order to go to Dorothy

Hamilton's burial. I gave, memorandum, to Isabel a hankerchief and pair of gloves.

Friday 5 December 1707
I was in Donaghadee and in the evening went down to Mr Hamilton's, and was with Doâ in her closet from 6 to 10 of the clock. I did same night present her with a little bottle; she was pleased by her carriage towards me to evidence and more concernedness for me and love to me than ever formerly.

Monday 8 December 1707
I was in Donaghadee & working all day only in the evening I went down to Mr Hamilton's and was told that Mrs Hamilton and Mrs Jean were gone to Crebuy. I sate for some time with the children & came home much disconsolate that I was not favoured with a sight of Doâ.

Thursday 18 December 1707
I was working all day only in the evening went down to Mr Hamilton's and was with Doâ in the guest chamber from 6 to 8 of the clock, she told me that her father same day after breakfast was speaking to her and telling her that he would not further her to keep me any longer company; because my father had never taken occasion to make known to him what was betwixt her and me, which same night occasioned much indisposition to me, for about the space of an hour I was very bad and thought I should have fallen by; Mrs Hamilton came in and told me that Mr Hamilton was not in the least dissatisfied with me, but he thought my father might have spoken to him.

Monday 22 December 1707
I was working all day, only in the evening I went down to Mr Hamilton's and was with Doâ in the guest chamber from six of the clock to nine, my father did same night to Mr Hamilton make known the respect I had for his daughter Mrs Jean; and his reply to him was that he would give me his daughter to wife, rather yea and sooner than to many with 400 p annum wherewith my father was mightily taken; and indeed no wonder for it was much more than he was expecting or looking for from him.

Sunday 14 March 1708
I was in Donaghadee and in the morning was taken with a pain in my head which did oblige me to keep my room, about ten I went to bed, resolving to sweat for it, the which I did vehemently till 8 at night. Memorandum that same day about 1 in the afternoon my father was seized with the gravel and continued most violent to 6 of the clock. Munday's night about 7 of the clock at night Mr McCracken, Mr Hamilton, Mrs Hamilton & my dear Mrs Jean came to see my

father who then was much tormented. Doâ came to the back of the bed to me where I had occasion to see and speak with her and had from her 3 oscula [kisses] which were at that time to me very refreshing.

His courtship continued until Tuesday 20 July 1708, when the diary comes to an abrupt end and nothing more is heard of John Scott. He did not marry Jean Hamilton, who five years later became the wife of the Rev. Robert Gordon of Rathfriland, a widower. When she died, the Rev. Gordon wrote in his diary: 'On the Thursday following being the 8th of September 1726 my heart my life my brightest and best of wives departed this life at 12 at night. She was a godly woman, most exemplary to me and her children for true piety. She died, much lamented & the 10th of September was buried in the Reverend Mr Alexr Gordon's grave in the churchyard of Ballyroney. This great loss I fear will never be made up for now I must say I never knew her fellow in all respects. We were marryd I bless God thirteen years except twenty days and O that I may have grace to follow her footsteps and may her children imitate her in her pious ways.'

The Rev. Gordon married yet again to Esther Scott, who was John's sister. Altogether he had twenty-five children, though thirteen of them died young.

John Wesley
1703-1791

THE FOUNDER OF METHODISM, *John Wesley was the fifteenth child of a Lincolnshire clergyman, a distant relation of the Wellesleys who lived at Dangan outside Trim, County Meath, from whom the Duke of Wellington is descended. John Wesley was first of all educated by his mother, a strict disciplinarian who before her children were a year old had taught them to 'fear the rod and to cry softly ... that most odious noise of crying of children was rarely heard in the house'! She expected him to learn his alphabet in one day and on the next day he began reading the first chapter of Genesis. John went to Oxford and was ordained. In 1735 he went to Georgia in the USA as a missionary and it was on his return that he became an ardent evangelical.*

For fifty years he rode about the British Isles on horseback, preaching often several times a day in the open air. He is said to have travelled 250,000 miles altogether, sometimes riding as much as 90 miles in a single day, and to have given 40,000 sermons. In 1751 he married a cantankerous widow who for the first four years accompanied him on his journeyings, but became jealous of his relationship with his female helpers and in one quarrel is said to have dragged him about by his hair. After this they lived apart.

Wesley came to Ireland over twenty times, going about the country, preaching two or three sermons a day. Though he describes the thousands that came to hear him preach, which often included soldiers from the barracks, the actual members of his societies who were drawn from the Church of Ireland and non-conformists sects were quite few in number. In 1760 he wrote that the societies in Connaught contained little more than two hundred members, those in Ulster about two hundred and fifty, and those in Leinster a thousand.

It was not until after the death of Wesley that Methodists became a distinct body and no longer part of the Church of England.

John Wesley is described as a man of short stature with very bright and piercing eyes. He would get up at four and often preached his first sermon at five. As he rode along he would read a book, and though he did not write as many hymns as his brother Charles, they published together a collection of psalms and hymns. Samuel Johnson said: 'John Wesley's conversation is good, but he is never at leisure. He is always obliged to go at a certain hour. This is very disagreeable to a man who loves to fold his legs and have out his talk.'

The journal of John Wesley is a most remarkable work, covering twenty-six volumes in its complete form. Wesley himself abridged it to a four-volume edition for publication. While he was travelling he recorded the events of the day briefly in shorthand with careful reference to the texts that he had preached on.

John Wesley

His first visit to Ireland was in 1747 and he was again here in 1748. In June 1750 he had been threatened by a mob in Waterford and spent the night in a village on the Carrick road.

* * *

Friday 15 June 1750
We set out at four, and reached Kilkenny, about twenty-five old Irish miles, about noon. This is by far the most pleasant, as well as most fruitful country, which I have seen in all Ireland. Our way after dinner lay by Dunmore, the seat of the late Duke of Ormonde. We rode through the park for about two miles, by the side of which the river runs. I never saw either in England, Holland or Germany, so delightful a place. The walks, each consisted of four rows of ashes, the tufts of trees sprinkled up and down, interspersed with the smoothest and greenest lawns, are beautiful beyond description. And what has the owner thereof, the Earl of Arran? Not even the beholding it with his eyes.

The 2nd Duke of Ormonde had fought for William III at the battle of the Boyne, but after the succession of George I he had joined the Jacobites and gone into exile, and an attainder was passed on his English title and estates. On his death his brother, the Earl of Arran, became de jure *3rd Duke of Ormonde.*

My horse tired in the afternoon; so I left him behind, and borrowed that of my companion. I came to Aymo [Emo] about eleven, and would very willingly have passed the rest of the night there; but the good woman of the inn was not minded that I should. For some time she would not answer: at the last she opened the door just wide enough to let out four dogs upon me. So I rode on to Ballybrittas, expecting a rough salute here too from a large dog which used to be in the yard. But he never stirred, till the hostler waked and came out. About twelve I laid me down. I think this was the longest day's journey I ever rode; being fifty old Irish miles, that is about ninety English miles.

Saturday 23 June 1750
I heard, face to face, two that were deeply prejudiced against each other, Mrs E— and Mrs M—. But the longer they talked, the warmer they grew; till, in about three hours, they were almost distracted. One who came in as a witness was as hot as either. I perceived there was no remedy but prayer. So a few of us wrestled with God for above two hours. When we rose, Mrs M— ran and fell on the other's neck. Anger and revenge were vanished away, and melted down into love.

Calling at Kenagh in the way, I unexpectedly found a large congregation waiting for me; to whom I declared Jesus Christ our 'wisdom, righteousness, sanctification, and redemption'.

On his visit to Ireland in 1756, he visited the North.

Monday 19 July 1756

No sooner did we enter Ulster, than we observed the difference. The ground was cultivated just as in England, and the cottages not only neat, but with doors, chimneys, and windows. Newry, the first town we came to, (allowing for the size) is built much after the manner of Liverpool. I preached soon after seven to a large congregation, and to a great part of them at five in the morning: afterwards I spoke to the Members of the Society, consisting of Churchmen, Dissenters, and Papists (that were); but there is no striving among them, unless to 'enter at the straight gate'.

At the end of his visit in 1758, when he was leaving from Waterford, he wrote:

Tuesday 1 August 1758

The captain with whom we were to sail was in great haste to have our things on board; but I would not send them while the wind was against us. On *Wednesday* he sent message after message: so in the evening we went down to the ship, near Passage; but there was nothing ready, or near ready for sailing. Hence I learned two or three rules, very needful for those who sail between England and Ireland. 1. Never pay till you set sail: 2. Go on board till the captain goes on board: 3. Send not your baggage on board till you go yourself.

In 1762 he was again in Kilkenny.

Saturday 10 July 1762

We rode to Kilkenny, one of the pleasantest and the most ancient cities in the kingdom; and not inferior to any at all in wickedness, or in hatred to this way. I was therefore glad of a permission to preach in the town-hall, where a small, serious company attended in the evening.

Sunday 11 July 1762

I went to the cathedral, one of the best-built which I have seen in Ireland. The pillars are all of black marble; but the late bishop ordered them to be whitewashed. Indeed, marble is so plentiful near this town that the very streets are paved with it.

At six in the evening I began preaching in the old bowling-green, near the castle. Abundance of people, Protestants and Papists, gathered from all parts. They were very still during the former part of the sermon, then the Papists ran together, set up a shout, and would have gone further, but they were restrained, they knew not how. I turned to them and said, 'Be silent; or begone!' Their noise ceased and we heard them no more; so I resumed and went on with my discourse, and concluded without interruption.

When I came out of the green, they gathered again, and gnashed upon me with their teeth. One cried out, 'Oh, what is Kilkenny come to?' But they could go no farther. Only two or three large stones were thrown; but none was hurt, save he that threw them: for as he was going to throw again, one seized him by the neck, and gave him a kick and a cuff, which spoiled his diversion.

Thursday 13 May 1773
We went on through a most dreary country to Galway, where at the late survey, there were twenty thousand Papists and five hundred Protestants: but which of them are Christians, have the mind that was in Christ, and walk as he walked? And without this, how little does it avail whether they are called Protestants or Papists? At six I preached in the Court-house to a large congregation, who all behaved well.

Friday 14 May 1773
In the evening I preached at Ballinrobe, and on Saturday went to Castlebar. Entering the town, I was struck with the sight of the Charter-School: No gate to the court-yard! A large chasm in the wall! Heaps of rubbish before the house-door! Broken windows in abundance! The whole a picture of slothfulness, nasti-ness, and desolation! I did not dream there were any inhabitants, till the next day I saw about forty boys and girls walking from church. As I was just behind them, I could not but observe, 1. That there was neither master nor mistress, though it seems they were both well; 2. That both boys and girls were completely dirty; 3. That none of them seemed to have any garters on, their stockings hanging about their heels; 4. That in the heels, even of many of the girls' stockings, were holes larger than a crown piece. I gave plain account of these things to the trustees of the Charter-School in Dublin; whether they are altered or no, I cannot tell.

Sunday 16 May 1773
I preached in the grand-jury room, morning and evening, to a lovely congrega-tion, whose hearts seemed to be as melting wax.

By 1778, he usually travelled by chaise.

Monday 18 May 1778
There were two roads to Sligo, one of which was several miles shorter, but had some sloughs in it. However, having a good guide, we chose this. Two sloughs we got over well. On our approaching the third, seven or eight countrymen present-ly ran to help us. One of them carried me over on his shoulders; others got the horses through; and some carried the chaise. We then thought the difficulty was past; but in half an hour we came to another slough: being helped over it, I walked on leaving Mr Delap, John Carr, Joseph Bradford, and Jesse Bugden, with

the chaise, which was stuck fast in the slough. As none of them thought of unharnessing the horses, the traces were soon broke: at length they fastened ropes to the chaise, and to the strongest horse; and the horse pulling, and the men thrusting at once, they thrust it through the slough to the firm land. In an hour or two after we all met at Ballinacurrah.

While I was walking, a poor man overtook me, who appeared to be in deep distress: he said he owed his landlord twenty shillings rent, for which he had turned him and his family out of the doors; and that he had been down with his relations to beg their help, but they would do nothing. Upon my giving him a guinea, he would needs kneel down in the road to pray for me; and then cried out, 'Oh, I shall have a house! I shall have a house over my head!' So perhaps God answered that poor man's prayer, by the sticking fast of the chaise in the slough!

In 1789 Wesley paid his last visit to Ireland and went on his usual gruelling itinerary, visiting all four provinces.

Sunday 28 June 1789
In the conclusion of the morning service, we had a remarkable blessing; and the same in the evening, moving the whole congregation as the heart of one man.

This day I enter on my eighty-sixth year. I now find I grow old. 1. My sight is decayed, so that I cannot read a small print, unless in a strong light; 2. My strength is decayed, so that I walk much slower than I did some years since; 3. My memory of names, whether of persons or places, is decayed, till I stop a little to recollect them. What I should be afraid of is, if I took thought for the morrow, that my body should weigh down my mind, and create either stubbornness, by the decrease of my understanding, or peevishness, by the increase of bodily infirmities: but thou shall answer for me, O Lord my God.

John Scott, 1st Earl of Clonmell
1739-1798

'IT IS HARD TO BELIEVE *that the office of Lord Chief Justice could be attained by a man most superficially read in law, and whose antecedents, as false trustee and otherwise, had been wholly at variance with truth and justice' – so wrote a contemporary of John Scott. Copperfaced Jack, as he was known, was born in Tipperary, went to Trinity and was called to the bar. With a 'happy talent to turn everything to his advantage', as Henry Flood said sourly, he was made Solicitor General, Attorney General and Lord Chief Justice in quick succession.*

The basis for his fortune was derived from having held lands in trust for Catholics – an arrangement made possible by the Penal Laws – and then dishonouring the agreements. His political pliancy and willingness to be bought assured him of the patronage of the government. But even in high office he did not abandon his disreputable cronies – chief of whom were the flamboyant Buck Whaley and the notorious Francis Higgins, nicknamed the Sham Squire – and he was to be often seen with them on the Beaux Walk in St Stephen's Green. The papers of the day record him attending the many sumptuous entertainments of the 'Shamado', 'where he loved by undignified buffoonery to set the table in a roar'. The Sham Squire, owner of The Freeman's Journal, *was an extremely unpleasant character who is believed to have betrayed Lord Edward Fitzgerald in 1798. He and Lord Clonmell conducted an unscrupulous campaign against John Magee, a popular journalist and printer who owned the patriotic* Dublin Evening Post. *Clonmell, the Lord Chief Justice, issued a warrant for his arrest with the order to find an enormous sum for bail or else remain in prison until trial, which was held over for more than a year. After his release Magee put in the paper that he was going to spend £4000 of an inheritance on Lord Clonmell and advertised a Grand Olympic Pig Hunt that took place in the fields he had rented next to Clonmell's country house near Blackrock. Eight thousand people attended who were provided with free whiskey; then, greased athletic pigs were released and they and the drunken mob overran and destroyed the gardens of Neptune House on which Lord Clonmell had spent much time and money.*

Lord Clonmell died on the very eve of the outbreak of the rising on 23 May 1798. Before his death he had been very careful to destroy his papers but his diary survived and his family published it – as a memorial, I can only think, to his industry and to his intentions.

* * *

2 June 1774

This day the first session of Lord Harcourt's administration closed and the Parliament was prorogued.

I am, I believe, thirty-five years old this month, just nine years at the bar, near five years in Parliament, almost four years King's Counsel. Tomorrow, Trinity Terms sits. I therefore resolve to enter into my profession, as upon a five years' campaign, at war with every difficulty, and determined to conquer them. I have given up wine. I will strive to contract my sleep to four, or at the most, six hours in twenty-four; give up every pursuit but parliamentary and legal ones. If I continue a bachelor until I am forty years old, and can realize £2000 per annum, I will give up business as a lawyer, or confine it merely to the duty of any office which I may fill. I will exert my industry to the utmost in law and constitutional learning for these five years, so far as temperance, diligence, perseverance and watchfulness can operate; and then hey for a holiday.

29 February 1780

AIR – Sharp sea air opens the bowels. I never went to Temple Hill, and I have heard many costive persons say the same, that it did not send me to the water-closet ... N.B. Examine this subject of air and the effects of different kinds of it.

5 July 1780

The Exchequer rises. I take final and absolute leave of tea, snuff and of wine at dinner or any liquor, but water; soup too makes me thirsty and fat. Sleep one nap only, at one time, from this day.

13 May 1781

From a heartfelt sense that by intemperate guzzling, stuffing and sleeping, I have impaired my health, slackened my vigour, activity and exertion, lessened my reputation; not added to my business; grown ignorant of my profession, cheap to others and hateful to myself. I am firmly persuaded the severest discipline is more healthful than indolence or sensual indulgences and that I must sink speedily, if I do not rouse – I do here solemnly and alone vow to the Great and Almighty Power to whom I am indebted for my existence and for blessings innumerable which I have abused and not advanced myself when seeing the fairest prospect of riches and honour before me. Feeling that I may be chancellor of Ireland, unless I am insufficiently accountable to God himself and my friends for my future conduct and the disposing of my time. That I will from this day, whilst at the Bar, devote twelve hours a day to Parliamentary and professional pursuits with my whole heart and every word and action, thought and power of my mind and body pointed like ordnance to the taking that fortress and being able to keep it.

23 June 1784

Five years married this day – forty-five years old. Five years reading, at twelve hours a day, would establish my reputation on the Bench, and make the rest of my life easy. Cromwell would have done it, and did a thousand times more.

20 January 1785
… A perpetual state of rivalry with all the judges, especially with those of my own court, must be my constant object.

Downes is crowing over me; he is cunning and vain, and bears me ill. *Dilgence* is *necessary*. Hewitt is dying. Boyd is drunken, idle, and mad. Diligence will give me health, fame, and consequence.

Downes succeeded Clonmell to the Chief Justiceship of the King's Bench and though hardly ever known to laugh, he was comparatively honest. Hewitt died ten years later and Judge Boyd is described by Jonah Barrington as having a face 'like a scarlet pin-cushion well studded'.

25 April 1787
Three years this term Chief Justice; twenty-two years this term called to the bar. Lord Chief Justice Patterson my sincere friend dead; his intended successor Carleton a worthless wretch, though I am his maker; Lord Chancellor Lifford, a declining, insincere trickster; Lord Pery and the Provost, old watchful, adverse jobbers; no confidence to be placed in Lords Hillsborough, Shannon, or Tyrone, nor indeed in any other public character; Bennet likely to ascend the King's Bench; adverse to me; Henn, his kinsman, and at best a fool; Bradstreet, able, double, and dying. Thus I stand a public character *alone*, but at the head of the law courts, Assistant Speaker of the Lords, and in receipt of £15,000 per annum!

Lord Lifford held the office of Lord Chancellor for twenty-two years and his obituary recorded, 'Slow he was, in the highest degree, increasing tenfold the usual dilatoriness of the Court of Chancery.'

17-20 September 1789
SIZE I see no reason why men should not change their weight and bulk as soon as horses or other animals in a few months, if they are determined to do so.

Lord Clonmell was grossly overweight.

20 September 1789
A view, as Lord Bacon advises, frequently of one's actual and comparative situation, mine is as follows, shortly:

Fitzgibbon made chancellor, and Carleton a peer, these, with the Archbishop of Cashel, are likely to unite to less me in the King's Bench and House of Lords. *Quere* – How to prevent them? Magee, the printer's case, will be brought into Parliament by an opposition to worry the Marquess of Buckingham through my sides. *Quere* – How best to turn this incident to advantage, in and out of Parliament? From what I have seen of circuit, I wish never to go again. Nothing can keep me up but temperance, exercise, and diligence to law.

19 October 1789

I concluded sitting to Stewart. In the last month I have become a viscount; and from want of circumspection in trying a case against a printer I have been grossly abused for several months. I have endeavoured to make that abuse useful towards my earldom.

He achieved his earldom four years later.

14 September 1790

I have had a picture painted by Stewart, and lost a fourth front tooth – it is time I should learn to keep my mouth shut, and learn gravity and discretion of speech, which I hitherto never yet practised; temperance and eyes ever watchful, would be of use.

4 November 1790

King William's birthday. Saturday is the first sitting of the term. This day Lord Fitzgibbon exhibited the most superb carriage that ever appeared in Ireland; he seems to have got the summit of his vanity, chancellor, minister, and mummer.

13 February 1798

The arrival of Lord Moira in this country to throw it into confusion, as apprehended, by encouraging the malcontent Papists and Presbyterians. N.B. *I think my best game is to play the invalid, and be silent;* the Government hate me, and are driving things to extremities; the country is disaffected and savage; the Parliament corrupt and despised. Be discreet and silent.

His diary ended a few weeks before he died:

This book is now concluded, avail yourself daily and hourly of its manners, observations, and advice; and endeavour to make the residue of life exemplary to others and honourable to yourself; securing respect and esteem in old age, if you cannot have the love and affection of youth.

Lucy Goddard
17??-1802

MRS LUCY GODDARD was a childless widow who, though based in Dublin, paid lengthy visits to her friends and relation. She must have been attractive or perhaps it was her fortune that captivated her suitors as she received a number of proposals, none of which she accepted. On her travels she was accompanied by a maid and usually a little dog.

Her great crony was Lady Elizabeth Fownes, who lived at Woodstock, near Inistioge in Kilkenny. She was also the friend and confidante of Sarah Ponsonby, the ward of the Fownes', whose elopement with Eleanor Butler is recorded in her diary.

It is hard now to understand the shock to society caused by two unmarried women leaving home without their families' approval. It was a revolt, if only a tiny one, against the rigid mores of the time. The background of the case was as follows:

Eleanor Butler was the daughter of the de jure 16th Earl of Ormonde, a Roman Catholic, who had inherited the estates from his cousin and lived in Kilkenny Castle. Eleanor was born in 1739 and educated at a convent in France, where she was described as having 'an uncommon strength and fidelity of memory; and that she expresses all that she feels with ingenuous ardour, at which cold-spirited beings stare'. When she was thirty, she met Sarah Ponsonby, then a child of fourteen at school in Kilkenny. Eleanor, bored and lonely, found an eager pupil to be guided in her reading and education. They continued to correspond after Sarah had grown up and had had a season in Bath and several in Dublin. Sarah was an orphan who lived with her cousins the Fownes'. Lady Elizabeth Fownes, the châtelaine of Woodstock, was devoted to her, while her husband Sir William was so much attracted to his ward that he attempted some form of seduction. Sarah repulsed these advances vigorously, 'taking no pains, when Lady Betty does not perceive it, to show my disgust and detestation of him. But I would rather die than wound Lady Betty's heart.' In Kilkenny Castle, Eleanor Butler too was unhappy and frustrated; her family had suggestd that she should retire to a convent in France as she had shown no desire to marry.

On 30 March 1778 they took their future into their own hands: 'Miss Butler left the Castle just as the family went in to supper and was not missed for two hours. 'Tis supposed she changed her clothes in the porch and got on a horse (which she had never done before) to ride several miles of a dark night.' Sarah climbed out of a window carrying a pistol and her little dog Frisk. With the help of a labourer, the women met up in a barn and walked over the hills to Waterford, where their indignant relations caught up with them and brought them back – Sarah to Woodstock and Eleanor to stay at Borris House, where her sister was married to Mr Kavanagh.

Lucy Goddard was in Dublin at the time of the notorious elopement in 1778.

Thursday 2 April 1778
Got a letter from L.B.F. [Lady Betty Fownes] and Mrs Medows telling me that Miss Butler and Miss Pons. [Sarah Ponsonby] had run away the Monday before. Wrote to both with a fretting heart.

Friday 3 April 1778
Having no account of their being found, staid at home to think of them.

Saturday 4 April 1778
Got a letter from Mrs Tighe, another from Sir William to tell me that they were catched and in safety ... Went with Mrs Rochfort to the Italian opera, where we were well frightened with the riot between the army and mob and did not come home till one.

Mrs Tighe was the daughter of the Fownes' and her family inherited Woodstock.

Monday 6 April 1778
Got letters from Lord S., Izod., and L.B.F. telling me Miss Pons. was very ill. Went with Beck and Mrs Rochfort to 'School for Scandal'.

Wednesday 8 April 1778
At Dean Ledwick's, after that play'd a rubber of whist with Mrs Kinsbury, who had been brought to bed the Saturday before. Went through two mobs, one pulling down a house of ill fame, the other attacking a Press-gang from Bloody Bridge.

Wednesday 22 April 1778
Got a letter from L.B.F. to tell me Miss Butler had again absconded from Borris on Sunday night, wrote to L.B.F.

Thursday 23 April 1778
Got another letter to tell me Miss Butler was, and had been, at Woodstock concealed by Miss Ponsonby from Sunday till Monday night without their privity.

Lady Eleanor and Sarah announced their unalterable intention of leaving together and Lucy Goddard hurried to Kilkenny to offer advice.

Friday 24 April 1778
Set out with Jane, dined at Mrs Eustace's Naas, upon excellent mutton chops.

Saturday 25 April 1778
Dined at the Royal Oak and got to Woodstock at nine. A most terrible long jaunt it was. Found them all in distraction. Saw my poor Miss Pons. but Miss Butler did not appear.

Sunday 26 April 1778
Saw Miss Pons. again who came down to dinner, but Miss Butler not till evening when she came in to tea but did not speak to me.

Monday 27 April 1778
Spoke to them both. Gave them my best advice which they seemed to take well, and I hop'd from their manner would have been followed. They both dined with us.

Tuesday 28 April 1778
L.B.F. made me go with her to talk to them. They seemed to have grown hardened in their resolution of going together. Mr Park came with Mr Butler's permission that they should go together and talk'd in vain to dissuade them from it. They would not show themselves below to-day.

Mr Park was the agent to the Butlers.

Wednesday 29 April 1778
Sir William wrote to Sir W. Barker and Col Lyons to acquaint them of their resolution, and to Mr Butler entreating he would come for his daughter.

Thursday 30 April 1778
The ladies did not come down to dinner for fear Mr Park should be questioned about Miss P.

Friday 1 May 1778
L.B. and I set out with Mr Park who was going to Kilkenny at eight in the morning. We parted from him on the road and then breakfasted with Mr. Izod to whom by Miss Pons. desire I told the secret transaction between her and Sir William. Returned to dinner when the ladies joined us and Miss P. play'd cards in the evening.

Saturday 2 May 1778
I talked again to Miss Pons. not to dissuade her from her purpose but to discharge my conscience of the duty I owed her as a friend by letting her know my opinion of Miss Butler and the certainty I had they never would agree living together. I spoke of her with harshness and freedom, and said she had a debauch'd mind, no ingredients for friendship that ought to be founded on Virtue, whereas hers every day more and more show'd me was acting in direct opposition to it, as well as to the interest, happiness and reputation of the one she professed to love. Sir W. joined us, kneel'd, implored, swore twice on the Bible how much he loved her, would never more offend, was sorry for his past folly that was not meant as she understood it, offered to double her allowance of £30 a year, or add what more

she pleased to it even tho' she did go. She thanked him for his past kindness but nothing cd hurt her more, or wd she ever be under other obligation to him. Said if the whole world was kneeling at her feet it should not make her forsake her purpose, she would live and die with Miss Butler, was her own mistress, and if any force was used to detain her she knew her own temper so well it would provoke her to an act that wd give her friends more trouble than anything she had yet done. She, however, haughtily, and as if it were to get rid of him, made Sir W. happy by telling him if ever she was in distress for money he should be the first she would apply to. They dined with us and I never saw anything so confident as their behaviour.

Sunday 3 May 1778
Sir W. read prayers at home, Miss P. one of the congregation. The fact of their carriage being come was known to all but L.B. We ply'd the Game of the Goose … all dull but the girls. At night Miss P. on going to bed gave me an embrace.

Monday 4 May 1778
She call'd at my door. I w'd not open it. At six in the morning they set out as merry as possible.

Friday 15 May 1778
All went to Kilkenny. The family at Woodstock dined at Mr Park's, I at Mrs Hamerton's, where I heard Sir William's gallantry to Miss Pons. was beginning to be whisper'd. I paid a visit to the Castle but not a word was said to me of Miss B.

Thursday 28 May 1778
Set out with Miss William, Lady B and Miss Blount, who did not know where they were going, to Thomastown. Here by my secret appointment we had a tolerable dinner.

Friday 29 May 1778
Went to see the Barn the ladies had taken shelter in for a day and near two nights. Mr Tighe and family arrived.

This was on the women's first escapade, when they were found in Waterford dressed in men's clothes.

Sunday 31 May 1778
At 3 in the morning was waked by Sir William's roars who said – and the whole house thought – he was dying of strangulation or gout in the stomach. He was bled, bathed in warm water. I took an opportunity to tell him the cause was in his mind. Fell asleep at five and wak'd pretty well at eleven.

Saturday 6 June 1778
Sir William told me before Mrs Tighe his illness, as I said, was his own fault that he was punish'd for.

Sunday 14 June 1778
The Blunts and Doctor Young left us as did Mr Park the day before, having first wrote to Miss Ponsonby an account of Sir William's death.

Monday 15 June 1778
Mr Izod's cariage came for me. Jane, Bess and I got to Chapel Izod at one o'clock, where was Mr Hearn, I, his wife and daughter, a prating foolish girl, toss'd up with the notion of having a large fortune.

Mrs Goddard went to stay with a relation living just outside Kilkenny city.

Thursday 9 July 1778
A good deal of company at home. I had heard in the morning of my dear Lady Betty Fownes' death the Tuesday before at eight at night and did not make my appearance among them.

Saturday 11 July 1778
Was asked to the Castle would not go. Went with Mrs Medows to Chapelizod. Mrs Baker, the Harry Bakers, and Bob Wray dined there. We had for our dinner a hog's cheek with beans under it, three chickens roast, a cut of salt salmon two inches wide, Mr Izod's own pudding and a salad. And our leavings of this, which there would not have been any of but that in complaisance to each other or rather charity we stinted our appetite, was all that was for the servants in the kitchen. In short, none of us got enough and the servants were worse. Came home and play'd chess with Fanny till twelve.

Thursday 30 July 1778
Mrs Medows got up at six o'clock and chatted till eight, when Jane, Bess and I set out in a return'd chaise. When we had gone about a mile I heard a noise made me fancy something was wrong in the carriage but it turned out to be some live cockerells the post-boy had put under the seat. They flew out and frightened me.

Friday 31 July 1778
Got to Dublin in time for supper.

Meanwhile Sarah Ponsonby and Lady Eleanor Butler had arrived in Wales, where they bought a cottage in Llangollen and settled down. Strongly influenced by the Romantic Movement, they achieved a reputation for learning and culture. Much of their time was spent laying out and improving their demesne and overseeing their little farm, where the three cows all had names; their garden was neatness itself, with forty-four different kinds of rose and a fashionable shrubbery. They enlarged and gave Gothic features to the house.

The Ladies of Llangollen, as they have become known, captivated their visitors, who described them variously as 'the most celebrated virgins in Europe', 'enchantresses', or less flatteringly as a 'gossip shop between England and Ireland'. They lived together for fifty years in perfect harmony and delight with each other.

Lucy Goddard remained a friend of Sarah Ponsonby's, though Lady Eleanor was often acerbic about her letters in her journal: 'Feb 5th 1788 – Letter from Mrs Goddard. Written on the cover Don't open this till the bearer is gone. Bearer went. Open'd Mrs. G's letter – it contained nothing particular … Feb 25th – Letter from Mrs Goddard, Bath as usual no date. I wish she were not so tiresomely communicative of her odious dreams.'

In 1782 Mrs Goddard stayed with them in Llangollen on her way back to Ireland from Bath.

Friday 27 August 1782

We lay at Salop, and Saturday the 28th we got to Llangollen. At 3 o'clock before we had done dinner Miss Butler and Miss Ponsonby came in search of me, and with them we walk'd to their cottage. Beck etc follow'd in a chaise, left me there, went to her inn and, not choosing to take a second leave, I did not see her again … As for me I staid with my fair friends in their very pleasant habitation till Saturday 13th Oct. in which time Mrs Bond and Mrs Elizabeth Barrett dined with us and another day Lady Dungannon, upon whose civil invitation we went Tuesday the 8th October to dine with her at Brynkinalt and made our way to her by Chirk Caslte the seat of Mr Myddleton, a man of £16,000 a year who about four years ago married the nursery maid that wont now accept a settlement of £1000 a year because she thinks she will get more. I was quite charm'd with the castle which is very well furnishe'd, but this is all I could see while I staid at Llangollen as during that time there was but one fine day.

When Lucy Goddard died in 1802, she left Sarah Ponsonby a legacy of £100 and an annuity of thirty guineas a year for life. This generous bequest became a major part of the Ladies' income, which was always precarious.

Lucy Goddard lived in Dublin, but often made extended visits to Kilkenny. When not at Woodstock, she spent time with the Warrens at Lodge just outside the city or she stayed with Mr Izod in Kells as a paying guest at Chapel Izod. There was an idea that he might marry her. It would not have been an easy relationship, as they quarrelled constantly and she accused him of being particularly mean over food.

Mrs Goddard was converted to Methodism by John Wesley (as was Lady Betty Fownes' daughter, Mrs Tighe). She became obsessional, alternating between doubts and wild religious ecstasies possibly brought about by the excessive fasting that she indulged in and was the cause of her death in 1802.

John Tennent
1772-1813

THE FATHER OF JOHN TENNENT came from Scotland and was the Minister of the Secession Congregation at Roseyards, County Antrim; he also rented a farm at Bally-robin. The family consisted of five boys and three girls, of whom John was the sixth child. His eldest brother, William, who was a partner in a sugar house, became a successful banker.

John resolved on becoming a grocer and was apprenticed in Coleraine at the age of fourteen to Samuel Givin.

* * *

12 July 1786
My father agreed with Samuel Givin that I might serve him four years and ten guineas (fee paid). Samuel Taylor bought the indentures from H. Newton. Cost 6/-, with liability to go to school.

4 January 1787
Ben told me to go down to the cellar for a piece of bacon, and I would not go down, whereupon he put me down by force and hurt me very much.

Ben was the younger brother of Sam Givin and the senior apprentice.

May 1787
Ben tells William Gregg that I would beat him; he says I would not, and we were going to fight. Instead of fighting we contracted a friendship. Went with William Gregg in a boat at 2 o'clock in the night when he was almost drowned.

20 June 1787
I went to school unto Samuel Patterson. Stayed one day perhaps in the week. S. Givin would still find some excuses for to detain me at home part time.

August 1787
Continually fighting with Ben who did all that lay in his power to hurt me in every manner of way.

May 1788
About this time a most dreadful epidemic disorder raging. It is kind of a cold and

affects the persons like a fever. Reading Robinson's History of America with other books which I received from my brother William from Belfast. Nancy was blacking my shoes on Saturday night or Sunday morning – S. G. asks her 'Whose shoes are them?' – she says 'John's'. Says he, I shall have no such attendance and is continually vexing me so that I wish I had never come to him.

7 September 1788
I was digging potatoes in the field the day before I went home when I lost my pocket handkerchief; when I came back on Saturday night, as I was leaning over the counter, when somebody threw it in to me.

Nancy Kelly and Ben Givin was talking about me when N. told Ben that I was as good as him. He took it so ill that he never spoke to her for a fortnight.

17 September 1788
S.G. came to me & asked me if I had put any tea in the tea-pot in which he had seen some. When N. Kelly came in he put the same question to her. When she answered that she had and that she had bought it, not satisfied with this, as soon as we were sat down to breakfast, he began discourse by saying 'I cannot help thinking, John, but you know something of this tea. N.K. could never afford to buy tea and use it every day, which I understand she does frequently, without you giving her some of my property in an unlawful manner. I would be very sorry to suspect you, but I am well aware of the great temptations that apprentices are exposed to if they be so innocent as to be led by servants.'

18 September 1788
Next day, he sent me to Bushmills with an account of J. Miller's (although I had a very sore boil on my thigh); and as soon as I came home set me to carry flour from the back house into the kitchen. About 8 o'clock at night, N. Beaton came down & testified that N.K. had bought tea from her shop, the same day that he found it in the tea-pot – at which he was greatly enraged at N.B. Mind and ask Sam Givin, when I am going to leave him, if he be satisfied about the above affair.

28 September 1788
Rainy weather. Nothing material occurred. The Russians and Germans are at war with the Turks & Sweden.

4 October 1788
This week employed on carrying meal from William Robb. The harvest mostly all in. Rainy weather. Sam Givin more ill-natured than ever.

7 October 1788
I put my name in white paint upon the room. S.G. says 'Take a cloth and wipe that name of your's from off the wall which you are so fond of putting up.' Charles

Synd of this town and Miss Allen of Antrim were married. A method for putting blue letters on knives: take a polished blade and hold it over the fire until it is blue, then oil-colour white such letters you wish should remain. Then after this process, pour some warm vinegar on it, which will take off the blue colour, and some fresh water will take off the oil colour.

17 October 1788
I will endeavour to give a pattern of the way of life which I lived with Sam Givin for a week (in which it varies very little through the whole I have been with him). First, then, on Sunday slept till eight o'clock, then breakfast is ready for us. If not up in time I receives a great scold from S.G. Goes to meeting Mr Simpson's at 11; comes home again; 2 – dines on boiled mutton or beef; takes a walk with Robert Henry or some others until 6; comes in again; reads till 9, or writes this book; goes to bed at 10. Monday rises at 7; puts up the signs, cleans the shop; if not very busy sent to collect debts, let the weather be ever so bad. Continually doing one thing or another for S.G. – but never put to post any books for my learning – nay, I believe he did all in his power to prevent my getting any benefit from him. About 8 or 9 he goes out to drink – shuts the shop. I goes down to Robert McKinney to get my hair dressed, for I never can get it done in his house until the shop is shut. Goes to bed after supper of potatoes and milk. Rise as yesterday, the same manner until Saturday – and so on, a continued round of insipidity and vexation, being obliged to keep company of a man I hate.

25 October 1788
This day I am 16 years of age, and I perceive myself growing more wiser and better than I have been for this long time. This day I went to Killead, being Mr Moore's Communion Sabbath, and my father being there ...

1 November 1788
Holiday was begun with carrying some sugar from a store over the street. Ended thus: S. Simson came and drank punch with Samuel Givin. Interim, I am busy in the shop. Simson goes away – I go to bed without any supper. No uncommon thing for me. As I am going to my bed S.G. says 'You best put out that candle and go to bed' – for fear of burning his candles.

4 November 1788
Being Tuesday: was celebrated for being the anniversary of the Glorious Revolution – being just a century elapsed since that period and likewise it being King William's birthday.

17 November 1788
Nothing material, only the king very bad.

21 December 1788
… I am just afflicted with a grievous cold – notwithstanding I have to be in the shop. I went to Richard Cunning to learn geometry.

25 December 1788
Christmas. Went out shooting. S.G. stayed in the house to be in the shop. After I came I dined on mutton and turnips, which was the same we had for dinner all Christmas I have been at Coleraine. Stormy weather. I am writing this on a box as I am going to bed, 11 o'clock Thursday night.

1 January 1789
S. Givin was at Londonderry and whilst he was away we lived quite happily.

3 January 1789
This evening a girl of Mrs Wilson's brought a sailor into bed to her. Now her mistress's bed was just beside hers; her mistress hearing an unusual disturbance got up to see what was the matter, and having found out the cause of it, alarmed Mr Fulton; so the fellow went off and she kept the girl.

11 January 1789
This day I had a quarrel with N. Kelly, our girl. When I had come out of the meeting, I says 'Nancy's to be turned off,' upon which she threw some water on me, and I took and twisted her a little, and went up stairs, where she threw a turf after me and broke a jug. Frosty weather.

5 February 1789
I bought a fiddle from B. Givin for which I gave him 6/6d on condition he would learn me five tunes, and he bought a new one from Robert Molloy and paid 13/- for it; and report was circulated that N. Gault, a daughter of Charles Gault of this town, gave a little drummer some money (11s 4¹/2d) and had too familiar intercourse with him. It was said she behaved in the same manner with a fifer that was here before. However it may be, she has certainly hurt her character very ill by these transactions. S. Givin, on going to Balleymoney, the horse throwed him in a hedge of thorns and scratched his face.

12 February 1789
Thursday: Nancy Kelly left the service of S. Givin, who she had served two years and a half. She did me many kind offices, which it is my duty never to forget. We had indeed many outfalls, yet never any very serious ones.

15 February 1789
Samuel Givin, on N. Kelly leaving him, hired a woman of the name of Sarah

McLaughlin (an old woman) and so was Nancy Kelly for he never hires any but old women. Sam Givin, when he would see Nancy and me together would watch us, for he could not bear to see us speaking together. Tomorrow Sam Given intends going to Belfast, which if Nancy had been here, nothing could have made her more happy than his absence, as indeed his presence is not very agreeable to me.

25 March 1789

On this night the inhabitants of Coleraine, wishing to celebrate the happy recover of the King, they ordered the town to be illuminated. First the soldiers quartered here marched in full dress to church, and after they came out fired four rounds; then about 7 o'clock the whole town was illuminated. No one had anything remarkable, only Captain Douglas, who had very elegant transparent paintings on four windows: first window, 'Our prayers were not in vain, Hallelujah!' second window, 'The Anointed of the Lord is well, and we are happy'; third window, 'The King is well, Huzzah'; fourth window, 'Long live the King!' The whole concluded with bonfires and some fireworks which were ordered to be played off by Captain Douglas, but as he was showing some deceptions for the entertainment of the populace, they crowded so about him that one of the sentinels who was guarding the door had to push them off, and pushing a man rather severe, the man struck at him, at which Captain Douglas was so offended that he ordered all to be given over, to the no small mortification of the people, who vented their curses against the man who had been the occasion of their losing their diversion.

14 April 1789

This evening I went to the bowling green (a place where persons of every description goes in the time of Easter to divert themselves), and stayed till eight, then come home and shut the shop and went out and drank some porter, and so went to bed.

16 April 1789

S.G., being summoned to the assizes, went this day ... Some people said I was too great to Nancy Gault. Indeed, I sent a letter, William Gregg having wrote it (for this reason: if it was found out, I might say I did not write it). I was a long time importunately waiting an answer, when one Saturday night N.G. comes into the shop. Our girl, who had given her my letter ... went to the door. N.G. in a great rage began a scolding the girl, saying she had given her a letter without any name at it and said it was enough to use a common whore so, and commanded her to tell who gave the letter. Accordingly our girl told it was me, upon which she went away, and said no more about it from that day to this.

1 May 1789

Mr S. Givin went out to his father's, I suppose to consult about his marriage with a Miss Garraway. When he came home we had to tell him that a vessel from Dublin which had arrived in Portrush had got a plank started, in consequence of which some goods he had on board would be damaged, which, together with an order from his father not to marry Miss Garraway without a fortune (which she had not got), put him in a very bad humour.

2 May 1789
I got a pair of shoes from W. McFarel near Bushmills. Fine weather. An affair has happened in this town which has convinced me of the reality of people being really in love! Miss Kennedy of this town some time ago took a great liking to Isaiah Briens, and she at last owned to him that she was deeply in love with him and offered if he would marry her to give four thousand pounds and as much more at her mother's death, which he refused, because he thought she was not young nor handsome enough, which indeed she is not, and he is a little smirking chap.

3 May 1789
This day I was appointed an assistant at the Sunday school, there being four young men appointed every month to help the four masters that is paid for attending there constantly. They go in at 9 o'clock and comes out at 11; in the afternoon goes in at 3, comes out between 4 and 5 and concludes with singing a hymn by the children and a prayer by John McKeirney to the Father of Mercies for His blessing on this institution. The people does not attend near so much now as when it was first set on foot, and I suppose that it will soon grow that no one will attend.

9 May 1789
William Gregg, having slept out of his master's house different times, he at last found it out, upon which they parted, which I think is the greatest misfortune that can befall a young man and to have to leave his apprenticeship before his time is out – let him or his master be in the fault, for the world will too readily blame the boy, which should make every apprentice extremely cautious and circumspect in his behaviour.

17 May 1789
Hazy, wet and uncertain weather – what different effects good and bad weather has on me! Good makes me light and cheerful, but bad heavy and dull. I am too much inclined to melancholy.

27 May 1789
Miss Garraway, a young woman whom S.G. was courting, died – and I believe it was happier for her than if she had lived and married him.

2 June 1789

Ben went to his father's. We have not been anyway intimate, but very cold to each other this long time, and are likely to continue so, as neither of us (I am sure) cares how long it may continue. It originated in a small dispute where we had some words and blows.

6 June 1789

This night B. McKinney came and dressed Ben's hair. When he had done I brought him up to my rooms to dress mine, when S.G. came in, and in a great rage called if he would go away he would shut the doors on him (and cried to Ben where the powder was, for fear I had taken it), although he did not shut them for an hour after.

Mr Wesley, the founder of that sect called Methodists, preached in Mr Kyle's meeting house three times.

There was some sort of a fracas, the description of which is torn from the diary.

29 July 1789

… He wanted Garner to get out a warrant for us and Garner said he would. Accordingly a report spread that there was one. S.G. first told me of it, Mr McCausland having told him. When I heard it I was grieved to find I had done such a thing that the people would be talking of, and as I would be counted no better than Allison, who was a great blackguard, to prevent it from spreading I went up to Mr McC. and he said that I must give Garner some money and settle it, and so I intend the first time I see him. Young men ought as much as possible to keep out of bad company, or they will soon be counted as bad as them …

1 August 1789

Lighted candles the first time: the Summer quarter is out, and I do never mind such an unpleasant and wet season, there being not two days dry in it all. Sent the box to Belfast for books.

8 August 1789

I having not been at my father's since May, I thought S.G. would not hinder me from going. Accordingly I asked him. Says he, 'How long will you stay?' I said till Friday. 'I can't possibly let you stay that long, but you may stay till Monday.' I told him I would not stay so short a time. The excuse he made was that he was going out to the country himself although he has no intention of going any place.

9 August 1789

Notwithstanding his refusing to let me go, this morning he said I might go, so I set off, and arrived there at 2 o'clock … The next day being the ordination of Mr E. at Skilraghts we concerted a scheme to get there…

The next morning we got all things ready and set off. When we had gone the length of Clough we met the two Miss Rowans.

We just got to the Kilraghts in time to see him ordained. We were then invited to the ordination dinner in Archibald Wallace's. Accordingly P.E., sister Peggy and I set off (my mother and the Miss Rowans going to Ballyrobin). I went along and dined with the ministers, the ladies dining in another room. After dinner we drank tea, and then came off having spent a very agreeable evening.

10 August 1789

We went away to the Giant's Causeway; at Carcoulogh we got Miss P. Rowan. Being Dervock fair, we had some difficulty in getting through it. We got to the Causeway in the evening; they said it was not worth going to see, only for the sake of the ride etc. But I really think it an admirable piece of God's work. When we came home we went off to the fair; we there met G. McCleland and some ladies, who returned home with us and drank tea. After tea at 9 o'clock we set away for Dunbought, my aunt having to go to the assizes next day (when we went there it was almost day-break).

On Thursday morning after breakfast I went off for Ballyrobin. When I came home I was dull, restless and uneasy, owing to my want of sleep on the preceding night.

Next day being wet, I did not go to Coleraine, but on Saturday I went off at 6 o'clock. When I came to Coleraine I was very much surprised to hear there was a warrant out for me about that affair in Portrush which is spoken of before.

16 August 1789

This night eight nights ago, a parcel of boys broke into a garden of R. Giveen's; one of them attempted to take the gun from a soldier, who was placed there to watch, upon which the soldier shot him. In consequence of the wound the man has died. This morning a party of men again went in and broke down all the trees in the garden, and brought them to Mr Giveen's door and tied them to the rapper.

23 August 1789

John Allison and I went down to Portrush to settle that affair with Garner; but before we went down, wishing to have a pair of pistols we went to Mr Armstrong's for a pair, but he was not in the house. However, the room door being open, we took the liberty of taking the pistols, and then went off to Portrush. Nigh Portrush we charged the pistols, John almost quite filled his. At Portrush we got Garner and filled him full of drink and gave him some money, after which he signed a paper never to trouble us any more. By this time John was quite drunk; when we got to the middle of Portrush, I fired off my pistol in the air, and likewise John his, which immediately burst to pieces; we then came off home. As soon as we were home I went up to Armstrong who was in bed (I being very uneasy about the pistols) with my pistol. He seemed very angry that anyone should take his pistols without leave.

22 September 1789
... Last night, on S.G.'s coming home from the funeral of William Gray's wife, he enquired if a £20 bill that he had left in the window had been sent off. On finding it had not, he was in a great passion, and more so when it could not be found. Next day it was brought to Ben, he had dropped it out of his pocket. However he tore it up as S.G. had wrote off to stop payment.

R. Henry, apprentice to James Hazlett, has got a child by a whore ...

6 November 1789
This morning two men came to buy some copper. I went out to the back house to show it them; they enquired the price of me; I told them it was 14d per lb. After they had brought it in to be weighed, I asked S.G. the price of it; he said 14^{1}/2d; I told them that was the price. However, after they had got it cut and weighed, and was going to pay for it, they would only pay at the rate of 14d, from my telling them at first. Upon which S.G. was angry at me, and bid me to go to Mr McNaughton and swear I had not told them. I went down with them, but not to swear; however the men payed at 14^{1}/2d, as Mr McNaughton was not up. Now he had sold copper at 14d, which made me tell them that price, but as they were strangers he wished to have more.

12 November 1789
Went to Dunluce fair to buy a fat cow. Having never been there before I was the more willing to go as it really is worth going to see.

? December 1789
... Went about eight miles through bog ... wind and rain, all in obedience to my honourable and generous master. I hate the word; he is fit to be a master hardly for a savage ... A pale and meagre visage, with his forehead full of wrinkles and almost continuous gloom, is the countenance you see when S.G. approaches: his pale face makes them say he is afraid to take his food. I am sure he appears when taking it as if he grudges anyone to enjoy it more than himself, as we often dine together without saying a word, but sits as if we were all of different languages, and like as many mutes.

25 December 1789
Christmas: celebrated as usual: one party keeps it by going to Church, the shop-boys by going a fowling and then gets drunk in the evening by way of thanksgiving. I for my part in the morning went through the fields with a gun, and then came home and eat part of a fowl. Afterwards I concluded the evening by taking

a hearty jug with some young lads – the thing I did not do this six weeks as I found it was very injudicial to my health.

29 December 1789

Came to town this day Mr O'Neill and Mr Rowley and the Earl of Cork to be present at Mr Jackson's election into this borough in the room of his father deceased. In the evening they went off for Ballymoney where Mr O'Neill and Mr Rowley are to give the freeholders of the County of Antrim a dinner in order to solicit their votes in opposition to Lord Chichester and Mr Leslie, who are likewise candidates for the representation of the county. Likewise came this day the Earl of Massereene on a visit to it, the first since he left the Bastille, France where he was a prisoner twenty years for debt. My father went through this town on his way to Newton. A very wet and stormy day.

1 January 1790

Welcome comes this day, the first day of the last year of my apprenticeship. On account of non-attendance at the Quarter-Sessions held at Derry S.G. was fined (by the sheriff, who came to town on purpose to collect the fines) forty shillings. I was in the back house, doing something about emptying casks, when I was called to the shop by S.G. to weigh a pound of molasses. I was a little angry at him for calling me in to do such a trifle, as I thought he did it merely to show his authority, so I did it very angrily. He took notice of it and asked me why I did his business in so careless a manner. I told him I thought I did it very properly, and did not see how he could find fault with me, if he did not do it merely out of ill nature, and further told him I did his business better than he deserved, as all the knowledge ever he gave me I could have acquired in the half of the time I had been with him. (I thought I had no reason to be afraid of telling him my mind, though I was bound to him, provided I did not exceed the rule of good manners.) He made some excuse about my writing such a bad hand and the like (just like the excuses and wiles villains make when they want to cheat you), and he said I had been spoiled by my friends in offering me a place in Belfast, and said I perhaps was as well where I was, as where I was going. I was somewhat nettled at him, and was going to give an answer that would have vexed him, but people coming into the shop prevented any further altercation, and he has not thought proper to resume it again.

5 January 1790

A little boy, about 13 or 14 years of age, of the name of Keaton, went into James Black's shop, and the drawer of money being open, took it, and what money happened to be in it, away. However, fortunately an apprentice of J. Caldwell's saw him coming out with it, he immediately seizes him, till more help came and secured him, and sent him off to Derry.

16 January 1790

A Methodist preacher belonging to the band of music of the 16th Regiment came to town this evening. On account of the novelty of a preaching soldier, and his having the name of a great orator, great numbers of people went to hear him.

17 January 1790

Went to hear the above soldier (Mr Smith) in the Market House. The house began to fill at 4, and against 5, when he came in was quite full. He had done singing the hymns, and was holding forth with great emphasis when suddenly a form broke. Immediately the cry rose: the house was falling. The hurry, confusion and noise this occasioned put a stop to his preaching, and the house being so full, and everyone striving who would get out first, really made the house all shake. Many was thrown down and was crushed greatly, some lost their cloaks, hats, and some their wigs, and from the whole there was such a confusion that I think will prevent some of them from going to such a crowded place again. The noise of children acrushing and of women calling for their children, together with the tumbling and crushing of forms made a scene of terror and dismay as is not easy to be conceived. But at last they got quit without any material damage – only the ladies got their caps and hats somewhat roughly handled.

25 January 1790

Went this evening to a raffle for a dulcimer and put in 1s. 1d. to the number of 40. I lost – it is a scandalous place to go to. However, it was the first ever I was at in this town.

A Miss Alan of this town was married to Tom Lyons of Derry some few days ago.

9 February 1790

Was sent to Dervock for money by S.G. Being 10 o'clock before I went away, it was three when I got there, however, back I must come this night ... On the road I was very tired and somewhat hungry; I went into a house to rest myself. The dinner was ready, the good woman of the house very courteously asked me to partake, which offer I did not think proper to refuse (though naturally shy of taking favours of that kind). After taking a potato or two, I came away, and being well rested, came home here cheerfully ...

12 February 1790

A girl in this town, finding herself with child, went over to Inishown to be delivered. She brought it back the length of Maggilegan Rocks, and there inhumanly murdered it, and put it in a hole of one of the rocks, where it was found by some fishermen. When she heard that it was found, she this day absconded (her name is Murphy)!!! The above is a dreadful instance of the depravity of human nature, yet alas it is too common a practice for women to kill their children to avoid the shame attending on their having them.

16 February 1790
John McSuly brought me a hat from Dublin, which S.G. had wrote for at my request.

13 March 1790
Just now I hear S.G. scolding the girl for washing down the stairs – 'You are eternally scrubbing and cleaning, I am sure I can't see the use in it,' says S.G. She makes answer, 'I never was with anyone before who would scold me for cleaning their house. It costs you nothing, for you won't buy me freestone, but I have to get it where I can. So I don't see what you can scold me for.'

Much more did they say to one another, of much the same purport. They very frequently take a turn at scolding, after S.G. comes in from his cans, and us all gone to bed only the girl and himself where they can take a turn at it in comfort by the fireside without anyone to disturb them. However, the next day they will be as well pleased at one another as if nothing had happened.

25 March 1790
A dog belonging to S.G. was said to be bit by a mad dog some time ago. This evening he bit a son of Rector Heyland's. Dr Thomson ordered the dog to be kept up to see if he was really mad, but S.G. killed the dog. Now they can't tell whether the dog was mad or not.

On my first coming to this place I thought they drank tea every evening, but in a night or two's time I found they did not. However, when S.G. went out to his cans, about 8 or 9 o'clock, Ben generally ordered the kettle to be boiled and made tea unknown to him. From that time to this, he continued to do it, and S.G. never found it out, till unfortunately this night he came in so unexpectedly that he saw us all at it, but I happened to be above stairs, so he did not see me.

26 March 1790
This has been a very busy week, having three vessels to discharge at the quay at once.

8 April 1790
This day a case was tried at Londonderry which ought to be a lesson to magisterial pride. A man having some business with the mayor of Derry (Mr Bateson), seeing him in the street, went up to him, and took off his hat and put it on again. The mayor, being offended at his speaking to him with his hat on, ordered him to take it off, and on the man's refusing, ordered the sergeants to put him in Jail, which they did. A while after, the mayor being sensible he had acted wrong, sent

to the jail to liberate the man, but he would not come out, but stayed in four days. He then brought an action against the mayor which was tried in Dublin, and sent down from thence on a *nisi prius* to be tried in Derry. So this day it was there tried, and to the honour of the jury, they fined the mayor £350, which together with costs would be no less than £500 – which it cost him for wanting the man to take his hat off to him! It was observed as a droll circumstance that the man happened to be a hatter.

Dry weather, but extremely cold and frost, which has made the ground so hard that it is with great difficulty they can get it harrowed.

20 April 1790

This day it has come on to rain, which was very much wanted. S.G. said to me this morning (because I happened not to rise soon enough), 'I wished you would rise earlier and open the shop, for I don't believe you have opened it six times since you came here.' Now if I was to rise ever so early I would not get the key of the shop until either Ben or him would get up, and as soon as ever he comes down he flies and opens it, and without I would rise at 5 or 6 and sit moping in the kitchen for an hour or two till some of them would come down, I could not get opening the shop, and for all the bother he makes about opening it, he only lifts one leaf and all the rest I have to open, and the shop to clean out. Other apprentices when they rise can get the key when they please and never opens till 7. Now if he would not open it before that, I would be up in time to open it.

11 June 1790

This evening there was bonfires in this town in consequence of Messrs. Rowley and O'Neil having got the representation of the County Antrim in opposition to E.A. McNaughten and Mr Leslie. One Reynolds, a tobacconist, one of Leslie's partisans, drove down one of the tar barrels that was burning, which so provoked the mob that was standing round it that they followed him over and made a bonfire before his door, which, when he came out to put it out, the mob then catched him and gave him a complete beating, and then paraded through the town with a blazing tar barrel accompanied with loud shouts of 'Rowley and O'Neil!'

4 July 1790

… I began seriously to reflect on the many difficulties and hardships I had undergone in my four long tedious years of bondage. I immediately returned my most fervent acknowledgements to that great, wise and merciful God, who had preserved me therein and brought me through my time with joy …

I thought then of that day I came here. Just a little before I left home my father called me into the room and says 'John, have you seriously considered what you are going to do? Are you determined, and do you think you can serve a strange man four years – mind it is a long time, and I'd have you to think well about it before you get yourself bound, as after that it will be too late for you to draw back.' I said I did not fear to be able to serve it well enough. He said no more, but recommended me to the care of Heaven. So I departed; his words, however, made so strong an impression upon me that they never left my memory, and they frequently occurred to me during my apprenticeship.

13 July 1790
Yesterday I left Coleraine. Before I came away S.G. got another prentice of the name of Hamilton from Dungiven. He got four years of him, and £20 of a fee – washing etc. as I had. On Monday I intend going up to Belfast, as I cannot get away rightly before that time.

After he had finished his apprenticeship, John Tennent went to Belfast, where his brother William had found a place for him. The brothers both joined the United Irishmen. In 1797 John was in the Netherlands with Alexander Lowry, a member of the executive committee from County Down. They visited Wolfe Tone, who was on board the Vryheid *in expectation that the French would be sending an invasion fleet to Ireland. In his diary, Tone wrote: '... set off for Texel to see Lowry and Tennent. After dinner we walked out to a pretty little farm, about half a mile from the town and sat down on a hillock, where we had a view of the fleet riding at anchor below. I then told them that I looked upon our expedition, on the present scale as given up ... I saw they were a good deal dejected by the change of plan and consequent diminution of our means and did my best to encourage them ... We agree that we would stop at no means necessary to ensure our success rather than turn back one inch from our purpose. After this discussion, we returned to the inn, where we supped, and, after divers loyal and constitutional toasts, retired to bed at a very late hour.'*

Rather than return to Ireland and almost certain arrest, John Tennent instead joined Napoleon's army and was made an officer in the newly established Irish Battalion. He represented his unit at Napoleon's coronation in 1804 and fought in the Napoleonic campaigns in Spain, Holland and Germany. He took command of the 1st battalion of the Irish Regiment at Landau in 1810 when Napoleon named him a Knight of the Legion of Honour. He died on the retreat from Moscow in 1813.

Theobald Wolfe Tone
1763-1798

'THIS EXTRAORDINARY MAN went to Paris with a hundred guineas in his pocket, unknown and unrecommended, and came near to altering the destiny of Europe,' the Duke of Wellington said of Theobald Wolfe Tone.

The son of a Protestant coachmaker in Dublin, Wolfe Tone became a barrister but was more interested in politics. This was the time of 'Grattan's Parliament', when legislative independence had been achieved, but the administration was still under the control of the British government appointee, the Lord Lieutenant. There was mounting pressure for parliamentary reform and Catholic Emancipation, to which Tone contributed by writing pamphlets. One, called 'An argument of behalf of the Catholics of Ireland', contended that parliamentary reform and Catholic Emancipation had one common interest and one common enemy. In Ulster, the reform movement was supported by many Presbyterian businessmen who had formed secret committees. In 1791 they invited Tone to Belfast and it was here the Society of United Irishmen was born; in November of that year the Dublin Society of the United Irishmen came into existence. Tone's ambition was 'to break the connection with England, the never-failing source of our political evils, and to assert the independence of my country ... to substitute the common name of Irishmen in place of the denomination of Protestant, Catholic and Dissenter'. At this time, the Catholic Committee under the leadership of John Keogh employed Tone as their agent and some of their members went to Belfast in July 1792 to celebrate the anniversary of the taking of the Bastille with a review of the Volunteers and an address to the people of Ireland in favour of the Catholic claims.

In 1793 Catholics were given the right to vote but not to sit in Parliament. Tone continued to work for complete separation from England, but facing the likelihood of arrest for treason, he and his family left for America. Early in 1796 he arrived in France, where he persuaded the members of the Directoire to send an expedition to invade Ireland, but owing to the weather and inadequate seamanship, the force did not even land.

In 1798, when the rebellion in Ireland was almost over, the French sent two invasion forces – one that landed at Killala but was soon compelled to surrender, and a smaller expedition with Tone on board the flagship farther north. This was defeated off Lough Swilly and Tone was captured and sentenced to death. Before the execution could be carried out, he cut his throat with a pen knife; this did not kill him, but when he heard the surgeon say that he would die instantly if he moved or spoke he said immediately, 'This is most welcome news you give me. What should I wish to live for?'

Wolfe Tone wrote his diary for his wife during the times she was not with him. He gave his associates nicknames, and he calls himself Mr Hutton.

His great friend and supporter, Thomas Russell: Clerk of the Parish or P.P.

William Sinclair, a Belfast linen manufacturer: The Draper.

Thomas Braughall, a member of the Catholic Committee: T.B.

Richard McCormick, a member of the Catholic Committee: Magog.

There are other associates who had nicknames, but they do not appear in these extracts from the diary.

* * *

20 June 1790

My idea of political sentiment in Ireland is that in the middling ranks, and, indeed, in the spirit of the people, there is a great fund of it, but stifled and suppressed, as much as possible, by the expensive depravity and corruption of those who, from rank and circumstances, constitute the legislature. Whatever has been done has been by the people, strictly speaking, who have not often been wanting to themselves, when informed of their interests by such men as Swift, Flood, Grattan, &c.

14 July 1791

I sent down to Belfast, resolutions suited to this day, and reduced to three heads.

1st, That English influence in Ireland was the great grievance of the country.

2nd, That the most effectual way to oppose it was by a reform in Parliament.

3rd, That no reform could be just or efficacious which did not include the Catholics, which last opinion, however, in concession to prejudices, was rather *insinuated* than asserted.

17 July 1791

I am this day ... informed that the last question was lost. If so my present impression is to become a red hot Catholic; seeing that in the party, apparently, and perhaps really, most anxious for reform, it is rather a monopoly than an extension of liberty which is their object, contrary to all justice and expediency.

11 October 1791

Arrived at Belfast late, and was introduced to Digges, but no material conversation. Bonfires, illuminations, firing twenty-one guns, volunteers, etc.

Thomas Digges was an American from Maryland. He has been suspected of being an informer.

12 October 1791

Introduced to McTier and Sinclair. A meeting between Russell, McTier,

McCabe, and me. Mode of doing business by a Secret Committee, who are not known or suspected of co-operating, but who, in fact, direct the movements of Belfast. Much conversation about the Catholics, and their Committee, &c., of which they know wonderfully little at *Blefescu* [Belfast] ... Went to Sinclair, and dined. A great deal of general politics *and wine*. Paine's book [*The Rights of Man*], the Koran of Blefescu. History of the Down and Antrim elections ... P.P. very drunk. Home; bed.

13 October 1791
Much good jesting in bed, at the expense of P.P. Laughed myself into good humour. Rose. Breakfast ... Much conversation regarding Digges. Went to meet Neilson; read over the resolutions with him, which he approved ...

14 October 1791
... Four o'clock; went to dinner to meet the Secret Committee ... P.P. made a long speech, stating the present state and politics of the Catholic Committee, of which the people of Blefescu know almost nothing. They appeared much surprised and pleased at the information ... The Committee agree that the North is not yet ripe to follow them, but that no party could be raised directly to oppose them. Time and discussion the only things wanting to forward what is advancing rapidly. Agreed to the resolutions unanimously. Resolved to transmit a copy to Tandy [Napper Tandy, a Dublin politician], and request his and his fellow citizens' co-operation, from which great benefit is expected to result to the cause, by reflecting back credit on the United Irishmen of Blefescu ... Home at 10. P.P in the blue devils – thinks he is losing his faculties; glad he had any to lose ...

15 October 1791
Digges came in to supper, I had been lecturing P.P. on the state of the nerves, and the necessity of early hours; to which he agreed, and, as the first fruits of my advice and his reformation, sat up with Digges until 3 o'clock in the morning, being four hours after I had gone to bed.

23 October 1791
... Dinner at A. Stewart's, with a parcel of squires of County Down. Fox hunting, hare hunting, buck hunting, and farming. No bugs in the northern potatoes; not even known by name, &c. A farm at a smart rent always better cultivated than one at a low rent; *probable enough*. Went at nine to the Washington Club. Argument between Bunting [the musicologist] and Boyd of Ballycastle ... Persuaded myself and P.P. that we were hungry. Went to the Donegall Arms and supped on lobsters. Drunk. Very ill natured to P.P.; P.P. patient. *Mem.* To do so no more. Went to bed ...

24 October 1791

Wakened very sick. Rose at nine. Breakfast at Wm. Sinclair's, per engagement; could not eat. Mrs Sinclair nursed me with French drams, &c. Rode out with P.P. and Sinclair to see his bleach green. A noble concern; extensive machinery. Sinclair's improvements laughed at by his neighbours, who said he was mad. The first man who introduced American potash; followed only by three or four, but creeping on. The rest use barilla. Almost all the work now done by machinery; done thirty years ago by hand, and all improvement regularly resisted by the people ... Great command of water, which is omnipotent in the linen. Three falls, of twenty-one feet each, in ten acres, and ten more in the glen if necessary. A most romantic and beautiful country. Saw from the top of one mountain Loch Neagh, Strangford Loch, and the Loch of Belfast, with the Cave Hill, Mourne, &c. &c. Sinclair a man of very superior understanding. Anecdotes of the linen trade ... Ireland able to beat any foreign linens for quality and cheapness ... German linens preferred, out of spite, by some families in England, particularly by the royal family. All the king's and queen's linen German, and, of course, all their retainers. Sinclair, for experiment, made up linens after the German mode, and sent it to the house in London which served the King, &c.; worn for two years and much admired; ten per cent cheaper, and 20 per cent better than German linen. Great orders for Irish German linen, which he refused to execute. All but the royal family content to take it as mere Irish. *God save great George, our King!* ...

25 October 1791

Joy's! [Henry Joy McCracken, Secretary of the Whig Club] paid my fees to the Northern Whig Club, and signed the declaration ... Dinner at McTiers ... A furious battle, lasted two hours, on the Catholic question ... Bruce an intolerant high priest, argued sometimes strongly, sometimes unfairly ... We brought him, at last, to state his definite objection to the immediate emancipation of the Roman Catholics. His ideas are, 1st, Danger to true religion, inasmuch as the Roman Catholics would, if emancipated, establish an *inquisition*. 2nd, Danger to property by reviving the Court of Claims, and admitting any evidence to substantiate Catholic titles. 3rd, Danger, generally, of throwing power into their hands, which would make this a Catholic government, incapable of enjoying or extending liberty ...

The next year, Napper Tandy with members of Catholic Committee visited Belfast on the anniversary of the fall of the Bastille. Tone was already there.

13 July 1792

Rise again with a headache. Go to the Donegall Arms. No Catholics by the mail; very odd ... Will they come or not? ... Weather bad. Afraid for tomorrow every way; generally in low spirits ... Hear that several Catholics have been seen ... find

Magog, Weldon, and others, to a large amount. The hair of Dr Halliday's [Secretary of the Northern Whig Club] wig miraculously grows grey with fear of the Catholics. Several comets appear in the market place. Walk the Catholics about to show them the lions. See a figure of commerce at the insurance office; the Catholics mistake it for an image and kneel down, take out their beads and say their prayers before it ...

14 July 1792

Knocked up early by Neilson; get on my regimentals, and go breakfast with the Catholics ... Drums beating, colours flying, and all the honours of war. Brigade formed, and march off by ten; 700 men, and make tolerable appearance. First and second Belfast companies far the best in all particulars ... Ride the Draper's mare. The review tolerably well ... A council of war held in a potato field, adjacent to the review ground ... take the word 'Catholic' out, and put in the word 'Irishman' of every religious denomination. Procession. Meeting at the Linen Hall, astonishing full ... Carry the question with about five dissenting voices among whom are Joy and Waddel Cunningham ...The business now fairly settled in Belfast and the neighbourhood. Huzza! Huzza! Dinner at the Donegall Arms. Everybody as happy as a king but Waddel, who looks like the Devil himself! Huzza! God bless everybody! Stanislas Augustus, George Washington: *Beau-jour.* Who would have thought it this morning? Huzza! Generally drunk – Broke my glass thumping the table. Home, God knows how or when. Huzza! God bless everybody again, generally. – Bed, with three times three. Sleep at last.

11 August 1792

... Hear just now that if we go to Rathfriland we shall be houghed ... Arrive at length at that flourishing seat of liberality and public virtue. '*I fear thee*, O Rathfriland, *lest that thy girls with spits, and boys with stones, in puny battle slay me.*' Stop at Murphy's Inn ... Get paper and begin to write to Dr Tighe, Mr Barber, and Mr A. Lowry ... Stopped short by the intelligence that the landlord will give us no accommodation! Hey! hey! The fellow absolutely refuses. He has cold beef and lamb chops, and will give us neither, but turns off on his heel ... A striking proof of the state of politics in this country, when a landlord will not give accommodation for money to Catholics ... Some of us determined to make the boors of Rathfriland smoke for it, if they attack us, particularly McNally, who has ridden from Newry armed, merely to assist us in case of necessity ... The gentlemen of the town have learned, as we presume, that we are prepared, and therefore make no attempt to duck us, as they had lamented they did not do on our last visit. Leave Rathfriland in great force, the cavalry in the front. See about 150 Peep-of-day-boys exercising within a quarter of a mile of the town. Suppose if we had attempted to lie in the town, we should have had a battle ...

19 August 1792

Go to mass; foolish enough; too much trumpery. *The king of France dethroned!!* Very glad of it, for now the people have fair play. What will the army do! God send they may stand by the nation. Everything depends upon the line they take. *Our* success depends on things which some of us are such fools as not to see. Ride to Rosstrevor; more and more in love with it; dinner; thirty people, many of them Protestants, invited on the occasion. Dr Moody, the Dissenting minister, says grace; bravo! all very good; toasts excellent. United Irishmen mentioned again, and the idea meets universal approbation ... wonderful to see how rapidly the Catholic mind is rising, even in this Tory town, which is one of the worst spots in Ireland; sit till nine; set off for Dundalk, and arrive about twelve.

27 August 1792

Tinnehinch. Read the manifesto to Grattan and Hardy; Grattan thinks it too controversial and recommends moderation in language, and firmness in action. The manifesto taken to pieces, and at least three-fourths struck out; many passages supplied by Grattan himself, Mr Hutton taking them down from his dictation: no man bears criticism half so well as Mr Hutton ...

Tinnehinch was the house at Enniskerry presented to Grattan by the nation in gratitude for the part he played in the achievement of parliamentary independence. The house was originally the best inn in Wicklow, much frequented by Grattan himself.

5 October 1792

Left Dublin at eight in the evening in a post-chaise with Mr Braughall, commonly called in this journal T.B. ... An adventure!! Stopped by three foot-pads near the park gate, who threaten to exterminate the postboy if he attempts to move; T.B. valiant, also Mr Hutton. Mr Hutton uses menacing language to the said foot-pads, and orders the postboy, in an imperious tone of voice, to drive on. The *Voleurs*, after about three minutes' consideration, give up the point, and the carriage proceeds. If they had persisted, we should have shot some of them, being well armed. Mr Hutton in a fuss; his first emotion was to jump out and combat on foot; very odd! but his fear always comes on *after the danger*; much more embarrassed in a quarter of an hour after than during the dialogue; generally stout, and would have fought, but had rather let it alone; glad we did not kill any of the villains, who seemed to be soldiers. Drive on to Kinnegad – another adventure! The chaise breaks down at three in the morning; obliged to get out in mud, and hold up the chaise with my body whilst the boy puts on the wheel; all grease and puddle; melancholy! Arrive at Kinnegad at past four; bad hours!

6 October 1792

Set off at eight; sick for want of sleep; meet Dr French, Catholic bishop of

Elphin, at Athlone; seems a spirited fellow, and much the gentleman ... arrive late at Ballinasloe, and get beds with great difficulty. Meet Mr Larking, the parish priest, a sad vulgar booby, but very civil to the best of his knowledge. Mr Hutton falls asleep in company; victuals bad; wine poisonous; bed execrable; generally badly off; fall asleep in spite of ten thousand noises; wish the gentleman over my head would leave off the bagpipes, and the gentlemen who are drinking in the next room would leave off singing, and the two gentlemen who are in bed together in the closet would leave off snoring; sad, sad; all quiet at last, and be hanged!

In 1795 Tone knew that he was likely to be arrested for treason, so he and his family sailed for America. On the first day of 1796 he sailed for France and it was at Brest that the invasion force prepared to sail for Ireland.

12 December 1796

The Etat Major came aboard last night; we are seven in the great cabin, including a lady in boy's clothes, the wife of a commissaire, one Ragoneau. By what I see we have a little army of commissaires, who are going to Ireland to make their fortunes. If we arrive safe, I think I will keep my eye a little upon these gentlemen ...

13 & 14 December 1796

Today the signal is made to heave short and be ready to put to sea ... (*Evening*.) Having nothing better to employ me, I amuse myself scribbling these foolish memorandums. In the first place, I must remark the infinite power of female society over our minds, which I see every moment exemplified in the effect which the presence of Madame Ragoneau has on our manners; not that she has any claim to respect other than as she is a woman, for she is not very handsome, she has no talents and (between friends) she was originally a *fille de joie* at Paris. Yet we are all attentive and studious to please her ... General Watrin paid us a visit this evening, with the band of his regiment, and I went down into the great cabin, where all the officers mess, and where the music was playing. I was delighted with the effect it seemed to have on them. The cabin was ceiled with the firelocks intended for the expedition; the candlesticks were bayonets stuck in the table; the officers were in their jackets and *bonnets de police*; some playing cards, others singing to the music, others conversing, and all in the highest spirits ...

15 December 1796

... We are all in high spirits, and the troops are as gay as if they were going to a ball. With our 15,000 or more correctly 13,975 men, I would not have the least doubt of our beating 30,000 of such as will be opposed to us ... The signal is now flying to get under way, so one way or other the affair will be at last brought to a decision, and God knows how sincerely I rejoice at it.

16 December 1796

At 12 today the *Fougueux*, a 74, ran foul of us, but we parted without any damage on either side ... At half after 2, made sail, the wind still favourable, but slack. Settled our *rôle de combat* ... We are all in full regimentals, with our laced hats, &c., which is to encourage the troops ...

17 December 1796

Last night passed through the Raz, a most dangerous and difficult pass, wherein we were within an inch of running on a sunken rock ... This morning, to my infinite mortification and anxiety, we are but 18 sail in company, instead of forty-three, which is our number. We conjecture, however, that the remaining 25 have made their way through the Yroise, and that we shall see them tomorrow morning ...

18 December 1796

At 9 this morning a fog so thick that we cannot see a ship's length before us. *'Hazy weather, master Noah';* damn it! we may be, for aught I know, within quarter of a mile of our missing ships, without knowing it ... The Captain has opened a packet containing instructions for his conduct in case of separation, which order him to cruise for five days off Mizen Head, and, at the end of that time, proceed to the mouth of the Shannon, where he is to remain three more, at the end of which time, if he does not see the fleet or receive further orders by frigate ... he is to make the best of his way back to Brest. But we must see in that case whether Bouvet and Grouchy may not take on themselves to land the troops ...

19 December 1796

This morning, at eight, signal of a fleet in the offing ... rose directly and made my toilet, so now I am ready ... I see about a dozen sail, but whether they are friends or enemies God knows. It is a stark calm, so that we do not move an inch even with our studding sails; but here we lie rolling like so many logs on the water. It is most inconceivably provoking; two frigates that were ordered to reconnoitre have not advanced one hundred yards in an hour, with all their canvas out ... At half past ten we floated near enough to recognise the signals, and, to my infinite satisfaction, the strange fleet proves to be our comrades, so now we are quit for the fright, as the French say; counted sixteen sail, including the Admiral's frigate, so the General is safe ... I was mistaken above in saying that the *Fraternité* was with the squadron which joined us ... Adm. Morard de Galles, General Hoche, General Debelle, and Colonel Shee are aboard the *Fraternité*, and God knows what is become of them. The wind, too, continues against us, and altogether I am in terrible low spirits ...

20 December 1796

Last night, in moderate weather, we contrived to separate again, and this morning at eight o'clock we are but fifteen sail in company, with a foul wind, and hazy.

At *ten*, several sail in sight to windward; I suppose they are our stray sheep. It is scandalous to part company twice in four days in such moderate weather as we have had, but sea affairs I see are not our *fort*. Captain Bedout is a seaman, which I fancy is more than can be said for nine-tenths of his confreres.

21 December 1796

... this morning, at daybreak, we are under Cape Clear, distant about four leagues, so I have at all events once more seen my country; but the pleasure I should otherwise feel at this is totally destroyed by the absence of the General, who has not joined us, and of whom we know nothing ... At the moment I write this we are under easy sail, within three leagues, at most, of the coast, so that I can discover here and there patches of snow on the mountains. What if the General should not join us? If we cruise here five days, according to our instructions, the English will be upon us, and then all is over ...

22 December 1796

This morning, at eight, we have neared Bantry Bay considerably, but the fleet is terribly scattered; no news of the *Fraternité* ... All rests now upon Grouchy ... he has a glorious game in his hands, if he has spirits and talents to play it ... At half past six cast anchor off Beer Island, being still four leagues from our landing place; at work with General Chérin writing and translating proclamations, &c., all our printed papers, including my two pamphlets, being on board the *Fraternité* ...

23 December 1796

Last night it blew a heavy gale from the eastward with snow, so that the mountains are covered this morning, which will render our bivouacs extremely amusing. We are here, sixteen sail, great and small, scattered up and down in a noble bay, and so dispersed that there are not two together in any spot, save one, and there they are now so close, that if it blows tonight as it did last night, they will inevitably run foul of each other unless one of them prefers driving on shore. We lie in this disorder, expecting a visit from the English every hour, without taking a single step in our defence, even to the common one of having a frigate in the harbour's mouth, to give us notice of their approach ... we are now three days in Bantry Bay; if we do not land immediately, the enemy will collect a superior force ... In an enterprise like ours, everything depends upon the promptitude and audacity of our first movement, and we are here, I am sorry to say it, most *pitifully languid*. It is mortifying, but that is too poor a word; I could tear my flesh with rage and vexation, but that advances nothing, and so I hold my tongue in general, and devour my melancholy as I can ...

24 December 1796

... we made signal to speak to the Admiral, and in about an hour we were aboard. I must do Grouchy the justice to say that the moment we gave our opinion in favour of proceeding, he took his part decidedly, and like a man of spirit; he instantly set about preparing the *ordre de bataille*, and we finished it without delay. We are not more than 6,500 strong, but they are tried soldiers who have seen fire, and I have the strongest hopes that, after all, we shall bring our enterprise to a glorious conclusion ... It is altogether an enterprise truly *unique;* we have not one guinea, we have not a tent; we have not a horse to draw our four pieces of artillery; the General-in-Chief marches on foot, we leave all our baggage behind us; we have nothing but the arms in our hands, the clothes on our backs, and a good courage, but that is sufficient ... we are all as gay as larks ...

It is inconceivable how well that most inconceivable of writers, Shakespeare, has hit off the French character in his play of Henry V. I have been struck with it fifty times this evening; yet it is highly probable he never saw a French officer in his life ...

25 December 1796

... Last night I had the strongest expectations that today we should debark, but at two this morning I was awakened by the wind. I rose immediately and, wrapping myself in my great coat, walked for an hour in the gallery, devoured by the most gloomy reflections ... if we are taken, my fate will not be a mild one; the best I can expect is to be shot as an *émigré rentré*, unless I have the good fortune to be killed in the action ... Perhaps I may be reserved for a trial, for the sake of striking terror into others, in which case I shall be hanged as a traitor, and embowelled, &c. As to the embowelling, *'je m'en fiche';* if ever they hang me, they are welcome to embowel me if they please. These are pleasant prospects! ... This day, at 12, the wind blows a gale, still from the east, and our situation is now as critical as possible ...

26 December 1796

Last night, at half after six o'clock, in a heavy gale of wind still from the east, we were surprised by the Admiral's frigate running under our quarter, and hailing the *Indomptable* with orders to cut our cable and put to sea instantly; the frigate then pursued her course, leaving us in the utmost astonishment. Our first idea was that it might be an English frigate lurking in the bottom of the bay which took advantage of the storm and darkness and wished to separate our squadron by this stratagem ... Captain Bedout resolved to wait, at all events, till tomorrow morning ... The morning is now come, the gale continues, and the fog is so thick that we cannot see a ship's length ahead ... we have been now six days in Bantry Bay, within five hundred yards of the shore, without being able to effectuate a landing; we have been dispersed four times in four days and, at this moment, of forty-three

sail of which the expedition consisted, we can muster of all sizes but fourteen ...
I confess, myself, I now look on the expedition as impractible ... This infernal
wind continues without intermission, and now that all is lost I am as eager to get
back to France as I was to come to Ireland.

27 December 1796
... At half after four, there being every appearance of a stormy night, three vessels cut their cables and put to sea. The *Indomptable* having with great difficulty
weighed one anchor, we were forced at length to cut the cable of the other and
make the best of our way out of the bay, being followed by the whole of our little squadron, now reduced to ten sail, of which seven are of the line, one frigate,
and two corvettes or luggers.

28 December 1796
Last night it blew a perfect huricane. At one this morning a dreadful sea took the
ship in the quarter, stove in the quarter galley and one of the deadlights in the
great cabin, which was instantly filled with water to the depth of three feet. The
cots of the officers were almost all torn down, and themselves and their trunks
floated about the cabin ... I concluded instantly that the ship had struck and was
filling with water, and that she would sink directly ... As I knew all notion of saving my life was in vain in such a stormy sea, I took my part instantly, and lay down
in my hammock, expecting every instant to go to the bottom; but I was soon
relieved by the appearance of one of the officers, Baudin, who explained to us the
accident. I can safely say that I had perfect command of myself during the few
terrible minutes which I passed in this situation, and I was not, I believe, more
afraid than any of those about me.

29 December 1796
At four this morning the Commodore made the signal to steer for France ... I
spent all day yesterday in my hammock, partly through sea-sickness, and much
more through vexation. At ten we made prize of an unfortunate brig, bound from
Lisbon to Cork laden with salt, which we sunk.

Mary Leadbeater
1758-1826

MARY LEADBEATER was the granddaughter of Abraham Shackleton. He was a Quaker who had come from England to Ballitore in County Kildare in the early years of the eighteenth century and founded a boarding school that numbered Edmund Burke and Napper Tandy among many distinguished pupils. The school was carried on by Mary's father, and when she was a young woman she went to London with him where they were entertained by Burke and met Sir Joshua Reynolds and the poet George Crabbe, whose verse they much admired. Mary herself published The Cottage Dialogues and Cottage Biographies, collections of short pieces on the lives of Irish peasants. Later, her diaries and memoirs were edited as the Annals of Ballitore (1862). They give a vivid picture of the village and its people. In those days Ballitore was shaded by avenues of large trees; the houses were very simple, with earthen floors, casement windows and hall doors that opened with an iron latch (though these were soon replaced by locks), wooden floorboards and sash windows.

In 1791 Mary married William Leadbeater, also a Quaker, who farmed a substantial property in the neighbourhood. They had a son, Richard, and five daughters, Elizabeth, Jane, Deborah, Sarah and Lydia.

In the decade of the diary from which I have selected the entries, one can feel the mounting political tension: robberies become frequent; there are unexplained disappearances; soldiers are often billeted on the family and horses are 'pressed' or seized by the army. As the situation deteriorated, the Quakers resolved to destroy their firearms and thereafter to hold no weapons, which probably saved many of their lives in the years to come.

On the 24 May 1798 the mail-coach was stopped in Naas. This was the signal for the start of the insurrection. At first the United Irishmen were successful. In celebration in Ballitore, they asked Mary Leadbeater to give them anything of a green colour, but she told them she could not join any party. 'What not the strongest?' they asked in surprise and they left the green cloths that covered her parlour tables.

Soon the tide was turned against the rebels, and though her husband, her brother and John Bewley tried to arrange terms for the surrender of arms, the village was 'delivered up for two hours of unbridled license of a furious soldiery'. The insurgents had fled and it was the innocent, and even many of the loyalists, who were plundered and murdered indiscriminately, and had their houses burned. The Leadbeaters' house was searched and a soldier pointed a musket at Mary, which terrified her almost out of her wits; they called her names that she had never heard before, and outside the door they shot her great friend the doctor who, she said, had never lifted his hand to injure anyone. *Though none of Mary Leadbeater's own family were killed in the rebellion, tragedy struck during this time, when her youngest daughter died after setting herself alight with a burning taper that she was carrying upstairs.*

   I have preserved Mary Leadbeater's style of dating her entries. Quakers do not call days and months by their 'idolatrous' names, but refer to them numerically.

* * *

18th day, 2nd Month, 1791
Busy above stairs where I had the company of a sweet little Redbreast who sought shelter this cold snowy day and now and then repaid our entertainment with a song; yet escaped to its natural element before the day closed.

2nd 3rd Month, 1791
I went to the mill with sister and the children, there were many things to be admired but nothing I admired so much as my blooming husband.

25th 5th Month, 1791
Mother's arm began to be whipt with nettles for a numbness.

22nd 6th Month, 1791
Rose early and was delighted with our little sheep shearing of about 5 sheep; I sat in the hay yard knitting while old Ned Burne was at work; his conversation was an entertainment. I often admire with what forcible description the simple language of those people abounds. Speaking of my lamented Sally Haughton he says, 'What a brave swinging girl she was and as white as a curd!'

   My father looked on a bit but when he retired, 'Long may you live, many a man got a share of your money, and that with satisfaction, for you never grumbled at paying any man.'

2nd 8th Month, 1791
Sister kindly proposed to lend us the washing machine to try it.

3rd 8th Month, 1791
The washing machine performs 'wonderfully'. Washed with 2$^{3}/_{4}$ pounds of soap. 26 sheets, 8 bolster cases, 13 pillow cases, 14 shirts, 25 shifts, 12 towels, 12 aprons, 6 tablecloths, 5 napkins, 4 pr stockings, 1 petticoat, 1 flannel ditto, beside kitchen cloths and rubbers.

5th 8th Month, 1791
In the forenoon mother and I paid a visit at Prospect. We saw the churning machine at work and were much pleased with the industry and simplicity which

reigns here. Isaac Waring found a swarm of bees when a youth, he tells us, and from that time was never without bees till he came to this country and left them behind. Now the other day another swarm was found near his present dwelling. May it be a lucky omen.

24th 8th Month, 1791

Father, mother and I breakfasted at Lord Aldborough's. We were kindly received and entertained; after breakfast walked in the gardens and were taken to ride in an open carriage called a caravan. When we returned partook of a cold repast and returned home to dinner. The Earl and his amiable lady were kinder than ever I think.

This is at Belan near Ballitore where now a rotunda temple and two obelisks stand incongruously in fields, the only remnants of the desmesne.

26th 2nd Month, 1792

I dreamed I ate something which I did not know whether it was sweetened with honey or sugar but when I had swallowed it, I said 'I believe that I have eat what I should not eat'. Next day at dinner at Brother's we had a plum-pudding, which was made of minced meat, which Sister had made before she read the pamphlet, and thought it a pity to throw away. Now tho' I remembered my dream I ate of it, foolishly, and yet I think my palate is no great object of gratification to me. I repented when I had done and my stomach was sick in the evening. But I got another reproof, I was with the children looking at the picture of the slave ship, and explaining it to Jane Chandlee, who looked with great attention and I think with tears in her eyes, and when I asked her would not she rather eat no sugar than have poor people brought over in this manner to make it, she readily answered, 'Yes,' but added 'thee eat sugar today.'

7th day 8th Month, 1792

Sitting round the tea table we were much surprized by a cow which was walking gently into the parlour and had advanced a good way in the door. Fortunately we had our old knight errant Mansergh (William not being there) who soon dismissed the stranger.

26th 1st Month, 1793

Wm Leadbeater employed a person to cut furze, a stranger but one expert at the business, who earned 2/2 per day. He earned a crown, and then not choosing to finish, got his money to go home to Rathcool. Soon after Wm being by the road side saw him setting out on his journey, completely equipped as a decrepid old beggar.

25th 3rd Month, 1793

A press of horses, my mother's filly and my Nell taken. The soldiers came down to the market, the people concealed their horses and attempted to resist. It was well there was not foul play. Chas. Coote interposed. They let the filly back, but took Nell to Carlow, from whence Tom Manders who followed brought her after ten at night.

The Leadbeaters returned to live with her mother at The Retreat.

3rd 5th Month, 1793
Wm and I once more became inmates of the Retreat. Elizabeth we found asleep in her little bed beside our own. When she awoke and missed her nurse we had a toilsome time with her especially her father who took the trouble on himself, however she pretty soon settled and he watched.

21st 8th Month, 1793
Wm had his great coat stolen, which he forgot on a potato ridge. Is it possible it could be made a prize by any of those to whom he sells potatoes at so low a price as has greatly relieved them and has been a check on those who were willing to get exorbitant prices from the poor for the necessaries of life?

24th 8th Month, 1793
I made ointment for the worms and strained my hand with pounding the herbs, also Tansy Whiskey.

13th 9th Month, 1793
Elizabeth having frightened me today by climbing upon the mangle I was thinking while settling her bed in the evening, how unsafe it was to lose sight of her, when Nancy came to look for her, and not finding her with me seemed alarmed, we went into the garden and found her standing on the top of the high step ladder, pulling ivy from the wall; it was the side next the wall, it was unsteady and just below were the auricula pots. I looked upon her escape as a great favour.

10th 12th Month, 1793
In the afternoon 6 soldiers were brought here by their captain who said he had authority to do it, spoke civilly, but determined and they staid. About 100 they say were in and about the village, they are on their way to France, from whence they seem not to expect to return. Their Captain, Arabine of the 58th they say walked most of the way from Naas, giving his horse to a tired soldier and carried his firelock. They were very civil, helped to churn. Elizabeth admired them, I believe, and went among them.

11th 1st Month, 1794
M. Webster to tea. She brought an alabaster baby which she had dressed for

Elizabeth whose astonishment or delight it is hard to tell which prevailed. In her eagerness of love she soon bit off its nose.

7th 2nd Month, 1794
My heart ached to see poor tired looking soldiers in great numbers march by, preceded by a band, and followed by a number of luggage cars, on almost every one of which was a woman or two, and every woman almost accompanied by one, two or three children.

19th 5th Month, 1794
A fine morning, Molly Hudson, Eliz and I preparing to go to Athy on the spoke wheel car – a report comes that the Militia, who were pressing for horses there on 7th day, were still at that work, yet being unwilling on an uncertainty to give up our visit, Wm mounted his filly and came with us. We had a pleasant ride and found several horses and cars waiting without the town till the officers should be quite cleared out. Wm ventured us inside the turnpike, and then sent Jos back to wait without the town with the horses and car. We went to Josa Webster's from whence having sat a while with Molly in her school, we walked towards Brother's. We perceived Jos. was venturing into town and soon after learned that the press was going on. I turned back to tell Jos. who soon understood the matter, and was making his way back but the soldiers who were about seizing another horse, seeing ours left that prey and with their officer on horseback pursued hotly and were near overtaking, when another coming their way, engaged them. Jos. slipped the car off the horse and galloped out of the town. Josa Webster securing the car, and all escaped though narrowly. The town was in confusion, people hiding their horses, the country business stopped and no civil power exerted to protect the inhabitants from these military wrongs. However they soon after departed and horses were seen in the streets again.

11th 6th Month, 1794
Our silly bashful young mastiff Watch leaped through a pane in the parlour window in which Jane Chandlee was sitting.

29th 6th Month, 1794
The funeral of Toole's child which died of the quinsey passed by, attended by boys carrying garlands, flowers and white rods.

17th 7th Month, 1794
About 7 o'clock this morning I suppose near a hundred men came into this village, in order to tender oaths to people that they would neither join the militia or the army, but be true to their cause. Though I saw them I did not understand their business, till I saw Jos. Manders hide in the hole under the kitchen stairs,

where I locked him in. They got at the workmen and made them swear and attacked old Richard Manders for the same purpose, but he withstood them and with Wm's assistance got from them. They did not ask Wm, but some of them attended to his remonstrance of what danger they ran of the law and I suppose went home. The main body after moving about the village some time, assembled in R. Hudson's field near the high road, forming a ring, some kneeling, others lying.

On the 10th of the 8th month, her second daughter, Jane, was born.

11th 8th Month, 1794

I got up after dinner and staid up some hours, till Richd Manders sent me to go to bed. About 4 this afternoon, my dear little Jane left me being escorted to her new abode by M. Hudson, Jane Chandlee and Elizabeth. Knowing that I could not bring either a nurse or an assistant in nursing into this family, and being perhaps too easily put off attempting the entire care of the infant if I could nurse, which was doubtful, I had engaged before to send the babe out. How we are reconciled to difficulties! I who so hardly resigned Elizabeth to a nurse in the house, could now determine to send out her sister, though not less dear; though it caused me a pinch.

16th 6th Month, 1795

Wm deeply engaged repairing the house once Abby Widdows, now our intended habitation. Eliz. being bold I inadvertently called her 'Honey'. She reproved me saying I should not call her 'Honey' when she was bold; a while after, 'Now I am almost good, thee may call me Honey.'

21st 7th Month, 1795

Last night a letter came from Thos. St Lawrence to Wm whose tithe not having been taken last year, because the Proctor did not come the day of drawing the hay, and Wm would not open his gates for him after. Our priestly neighbour wrote in a high strain and threatened with the Bishop's Court. Wm wrote a reply dictated by the spirit of meekness to which a milder answer came. We remain in doubt whether these ecclesiastical menaces will not be put in force, and I hope honestly desire to suffer patiently.

The Leadbeaters attended a Meeting of the Friends in Dublin and returned by canal boat.

30th 10th Month, 1795

John and Mungo Bewley, Wm and I went in the early boat. It was much crowded. I sat just within the door of the state cabin and for some time amused myself with the scene of a little (perhaps inoffensive) coquetry in a very pretty woman, who I believe concealed from those who sat opposite, the length of her chin by the riband of her hat, and a pretty gentleman vis à vis who took some pains to display the ring which adorned his white hand. But no real satisfaction was to be found in thus entertaining myself; and when I exchanged this warm carpeted cabin for the damp, dirty floor of the other, I was much more comfortable and in that I was with my own company and also several other friends and some plebians. Wm and I deferred breakfast till we got to Sallins about 10 oclock. From thence we rode home and I enjoyed my seat on Nell and the sidesaddle once more though the day was rough. On top of the jail at Naas is fixed the head of Connor, the schoolmaster who was hanged by being a Defender and who showed on his trial a spirit worthy of a better cause. The wretched spectacle was shocking to humanity. Going to Dublin we saw a magpie quite white near the first turnpike.

19th 12th Month, 1796
Rose about 5, and called the girls to set about churning and went up to finish dressing. On my return to the kitchen found the fire made, and things ready as I thought to begin, when being desired to see was the milk in order, I found it churned and the butter ready to take up, for my two girls who in age are little more than children, had rose in the night, made a fire, finished the churning, raked the fire and went to bed.

The little girls were only five and two years old.

2nd 5th Month, 1797 – Dublin
During the Yearly Meeting of Friends the tenor of the testimonies was much to warn of approaching troubles, and to exhort us whither to fly for refuge, encouraging with the hope of safety. Samuel Emlen mentioned the robbers which were in the land and spiritualized thereon. This calamity seems at present chiefly in the King's County. Josiah Manliff was attacked three or four times, John White desperately and repeatedly fired at, till at length in his own defence he shot a man it is supposed; his house was sadly abused, and he has left it. One Knipe a clergyman and Bagly and his wife, farmers, were murdered, and even dear worthy Joseph Inman was put in danger of his life, for after he had thrown out what money he had, they fired into his room.

John Fitzgerald
17??-1795

JOHN FITZGERALD was a schoolmaster or usher, as assistant teachers were called, who taught for many years at St Stephen's, the Blue Coat school in Cork.

In 1783 he published The Cork Remembrancer, *which contained 'A Chronological Account of all the remarkable Battles, Sieges, etc., and other memorable occurrences that have happened since the Creation and more especially for the city of Cork'. There was particular emphasis on executions, 'by rope and faggot', of criminals. Thomas Crofton Croker wrote of John Fitzgerald: 'The Author made a point of being present at the death of every criminal whose execution he has recorded; and that he generally marched in procession from the gaol to the gallows. On one occasion it is reported of Fitzgerald, when being confined to his bed by a severe illness, he actually petitioned the Judge to postpone an execution until he was sufficiently recovered to become a spectator.'*

At the time of the diary, which covers the year 1793, he is tutoring boys and occasionally girls and also making a good income from writing letters and petitions.

He lived in Drawbridge Street, Cork, with his son Johnny, to whom he was devoted, and frequently records giving him presents. He was fearful that the boy might be 'drawn' into the militia but they hoped to avoid this with a medical certificate.

For the month of October he failed to make any entries in his diary, probably because he was suffering from an ailment connected with his convivial habits. The doctor told him not to take any more spirits, but his abstinence lasted a very short time for there is only one sad entry about drinking a pot of green tea. Soon he and Biddy were back to quaffing pots of Cork porter.

The diary is kept on a daily basis with meticulous reference to the weather. In the first half there are descriptions of the recruiting campaigns both for the regular army and for the Cork Militia. There are allusions to seeing a comet which the astronomers have not been able to identify; Arthur Ponsonby suggests it is the effects of Cork porter.

Fitzgerald was originally a Roman Catholic but later conformed to the 'Reformed Religion'; this would appear to be mainly for political and career reasons.

It is a very unselfconscious diary and though the extracts are short, they convey the atmosphere of a prosperous eighteenth-century town, which Cork was at this time.

***

1 January 1793
A desperate and very cold day, with repeated heavy showers of hail and rain. Coal 8s 8d per barrel; at yards, 5s 5d.

3 January 1793

Very heavy rains most part of the day and night. King's proclamation put up this day. £5 for able seamen; £2.10s for ordinary seamen, and £1.10s for landsmen, to continue till 1st of February. A great many convicts on board a lighter, and on a loft near Bridewell, from different parts of Ireland, and destined for Botany Bay. This was the most dreadful day of rain that ever happened.

5 January 1793

A smart, cold day without rain, but freezed very smart after nightfall. Four companies of the 58th marched out of town this morning for ——. The remainder of the 69th marched here from Kinsale. Beastly. Johnnie and I drank three pots of Irish porter in my parlour, which I paid for. This was the first liquor I drank since St Stephen's day.

6 January 1793

A dismal, gloomy, dark day, with some slight rain after nightfall. Betty Mackey, Johnnie and I drank six pots of Cork porter between us. I fell out with her about her desiring me never to mention anything about Maurice begging my pardon, and told her never to come inside my house again. She was very hearty.

12 January 1793

Very cold, with rain and sleet. Dr Orpen called to know how I was whilst I was abroad. Remained drinking porter and punch at Bat Murphy's till after midnight; it cost me 1s.1d.

26 January 1793

A very fine soft day. Played cards; we all lost a jug of punch each. I had a tod and pot of porter myself, and made 1s.7¹/₂d.

30 January 1793

Dark, dismal weather. Convicts from all our prisons went down the river for Cove [Cobh]. Breakfasted with Sheriff Allen.

31 January 1793

A cloudy, black sky with rain. Put on my new soled shoes for the first time. Stayed at home all night.

11 February 1793

Wind, and cold rain. I saw the comet very visible in the S.W. quarter. Got Mayberry's guinea, who began Euclid with me the 5th inst. Paid the doctor Dunscombe's money, £5.2s.4¹/₂d. The Lord Lieutenant's proclamation (of 8th inst.) was posted on the South Gaol for detaining all French ships in the Kingdom.

12 February 1793 – Shrove.
A fine mild day. Ate a pancake at Mr Mann's. A young child left at James Gogan's door. Began to teach Stewart by himself, after finishing Dunscombe, finding it out of my power to teach him along with Mayberry and Busteed, who are both learning Euclid.

17 February 1793
A smart cold day, dark and gloomy, with frost; heavy rain after nightfall. Sir William Clarke and his Volunteers were up the Dyke. A new ribbon for my hair. Mr Grannd, the Usher, came first to Mr. Sandiford. A very cold morning, the day turned out fair and agreeable. The Pressgang, four lieutenants and two midshipmen, the band, drums and colours, went through the town to enlist seamen. Press warrants, it seems, will be issued immediately.

In the early 1790s the government, alarmed by the French Revolution and fearing rebellion and invasion, set up a militia. The force was made up of Irish peasants and artisans with many English non-commissioned officers. Officers were, in most cases, Protestants. Units were quartered away from their county of origin. In 1794 County Cork had raised twenty-four companies, but quartered seventy-four.

23 February 1793
A dark gloomy day, with an almost invisible mist of rain from morning to night. Nothing but recruiting parties about the town; light horse, artillery, and foot parties beating about for men. Sir Wm Clarke's rendezvous all in uproar with music and drumming. Paid 5s.5d to Charles Keeffe for a new pair of shoes for Johnny. Sir Wm Clarke lost his purse and 20 guineas, beating up with flambeaux at 10 o'clock at night for volunteers.

26 February 1793
A cold rainy day, a high wind and rain at night. M. Connell and the Weavers' recruiting party, and Sergeant Cummins offered 5 guineas for [men] 5ft 4 ins and upwards. They had two tierces of porter, a fiddler placed in a truckle, and the whole band of music, fifes and drums, beating up for Volunteers in independent companies. 10 guineas for 5ft 7in, and 20 guineas for men 5ft 9in and upwards. A great scarcity of coals; 8d a peck at the hucksters, and 14s a barrel at the quays. Fresh butter 12d a pound; potatoes 5d a weight; 4lb 4oz in the 6d household loaf; brown sugar 12d a lb. The wife of John Connell the barber gave 5d this evening for half a peck of coals and 4½d in the morning. John Cotter gave a guinea for two barrels this day to old Sullivan in Morgan's Lane, and Jas Cogan gave a guinea last night for two barrels to a man in Cove Lane. The town all in an uproar with recruiting, and vast numbers enlisting.

28 March 1793

A severe cold dry day, wind N.E., some snow; a smart white frost at night. Norry Wool bestowed on me a nice bit of pickled pork, a pretty bit of corned beef, three pigs' tails, and a fine rasher of bacon for my Easter Sunday's dinner. Wrote a petition for Joshua Andrews in Bridewell, and got 2s 8¹/₂d for my trouble at Bat Murphy's, where I was all night.

Good Friday, 29 March 1793

Assizes began. Lord Chief Baron Yelverton, Baron Hamilton, and Serjeant Chatterton read their commissions. Bernard Blake and his son put into South Gaol this day for the murder of Richard Moore, Esq., in Bandon, about 10 p.m. last night. Two houses in the S—— Square-lane were blown up with powder, and a man and woman severely bruised, but no life lost. I heard Father Calnan preach a sermon at Broad Lane Friary. This was a very beautiful dry day, with sunshine.

3 April 1793

Jeremiah Geany, Dan. Shea, and M. Rourke were executed on a wooden gallows near Blackpool bridge for the murder and robbery of Edward Russell, 12th May last. Sheriff Clarke only attended the execution; Sheriff Foster was not present. They all walked to the gallows, Rourke first, Shea second, and Geany was hanged last. They arrived at the gallows at 5.10 p.m., and were cut down at 6.30. It was a charming evening, dry, and the sun shining, though there were several showers in the morning. Johnny and I went to Shinnicks and saw the execution.

7 April 1793

Rain most part of the day. One of the band of the 28th Regt. abused Thos Woodward at Bat Murphy's about Paine's principles. Paid Daniel Skelly 6 ¹/₂d for newspapers.

Paine is presumably Thomas Paine, author of The Rights of Man, *published in 1791 in answer to Burke's* Reflections on the Revolution in France.

30 April 1793

Rain at different intervals during the day. Rev. Mr Blackwood, rector of Rathcormac, got up in his sleep and threw himself out of an attick window.

4 May 1793

Very heavy rain all the forenoon and torrents the whole evening. Catherine Murphy, for personating Mary Donovan, and getting 46lb of wool from Denis Buckley; and Mary Ahern, for stealing wearing apparel from Michael Rumnick, were pilloried at Broad Lane. Catherine Murphy to be confined six months, besides her being once pilloried, and Mary Ahern to be confined nine months and pilloried a second time.

13 May 1793

Bitterly cold weather, and windy all day. Sir Thomas Roberts' Bank stopped payment. An officer walked from Kinsale Fort to South Goal Bridge in an hour and forty minutes, and won a wager of £100.

26 May 1793

A remarkably warm day. John Connor, Paddy Ahern, and I, took share of 14 pots of porter at Cotter's. I paid six, Connell three, and Ahern five pots, went home like a Bachanalian Prince.

3 June 1793

A fine agreeeable day; continued rain all night. Began to teach young Sam Hobbs. A spirited resolution in this evening's papers by the True Blues and Union Volunteers on account of being prevented firing on the Parade to-morrow, the King's birthday.

4 June 1793

Heavy rain during the day; evening mild and agreeable. The 40th and 58th Regts. fired three vollies each on the Grand Parade. Two six-pounders, one officer of the train and some artillery went to Lapp's Island and fired 21 rounds each in honour of the King's birthday. General Moucher was on the Parade and hindered the Volunteers from firing. Not one of the citizens joined in the huzza. Army under arms all night to quell the Volunteers.

8 June 1793

Dark moist weather; new moon between 2 and 3 p.m. Young John Allen called to see me at my house. Mr Sandiford was brought from Sunday's Well to his own house this day, preparatory to his final exit. Bat Murphy's wife invited me to go boating with her tomorrow, which I declined. John Terry was whipped from gate to gate for violently assaulting Humphrey Moore in the North Gaol.

19 June 1793

As usual a gloomy morning. In the afternoon the sunshine was charming. Johnny, Jack Devitt, and Macoy, the shoemaker, were out till past one in the morning playing the German flute through the town, and outside my window.

12 August 1793

Heavy rain most part of the forenoon. Sent a letter to R. Hickson Esq., Surveyor of Dingle. Dr Harris paid me a visit, and ordered me to boil the bark of elm to a decoction, about one-third, and take a teacup full twice a day. We had a heavy fall of rain the whole night. Miss Carney poisoned herself.

9 September 1793
A fine, agreeable dry day. Began to attend Wetham this a.m. Dreamed that two teeth in my upper left jaw fell out; thought that John Lyne, the butter-buyer, showed me one of his teeth that fell out first.

29 September 1793
A dark sky, but the day was fair. The fleet put into Cove that sailed last Tuesday. Great mortality among the horses, and two of the transports missing; 27 horses died on board Lieut. Dunscombe's Transport. They were throwing out dead horses all the day at Cove, and boatmen picking them up for the sake of their skins. A troop of the 5th and 12th missing in two transports. They met a storm.

1 November 1793
A severe cold raw day and night. I was fine and easy most part of the day, but at night a renewal of my torments began again. Gave Dr Bagnell this day half a guinea, being his second visit. Candles burning all night.

3 November 1793
Lieuts Todd, Ford, and Ensign Upton and Mr Moore, late of the 43rd Regiment, drowned at Cove. Dark, cloudy weather; a new moon but no rain. I had no kind of meat for food, and took tea. Dr Bagnell told me Johnny had a fever, and it was not safe for me to lie with him, but love made me disobey his directions.

5 November 1793
A cold raw morning, and a little frost. I was roaring like a bull all day until 6 p.m when Dr B gave me some drops, which gave me instant ease. Betty Mackey staid up all night with me, I was so bad.

7 November 1793
A very heavy fall of rain most of the day and night. I continued roaring without intermission from 11 a.m. till 3.30 p.m. but, being able to screech no longer, was obliged to stop with hoarseness, sore throat and violent headache. The Mayor and two deputy governors were at St Nicholas' Church to receive Mulligan and Purcell's lists.

21 November 1793
Gloomy weather all day, and obscure horizon. Ned Daly eloped [played truant] most of the day, and I discharged him, as his mother would not allow me to whip him. No paper from Megul.

22 November 1793
A dismal day, almost resembling night. Dr Bagnell gave me a strict charge never

John Fitzgerald

to be intoxicated; not to drink spiritous liquors, and but very moderately of any kind of liquor. William White, tobacco twister, abused Johnny about his dog, who was going to bite him. Philip Clements killed his wife this day, and afterwards cut his own throat.

24 November 1793
Gloomy weather, without rain. The last five companies of Col Bagnell's Militia arrived in town, and so did the entire Regt. of the Limerick Militia. Johnny, Mr Devitt, and I took share of a 2nd pot of green tea and two quarts of three penny beer; wrote a letter for D. Leahy to F. Belliam, Esq.

10 December 1793
A dark sky, an obscure horizon, inclined to moisture. Wore my new great coat for the first time. The little woman, descendant of an Indian prince, 2½ feet high and 47 years old, was buried this evening. The little man was looking at her.

11 December 1793
Very dark, guttry day, hazy weather. Bought a decanter …, a tumbler …, two white plates …, a three-pint mug …, and a pair of copper buckles for Johnny, for an English shilling. Part of the 22nd Regt. arrived here from Kinsale yesterday. Dr Orpen told me that if my son Johnny was drawn to serve in the militia, he would certify his ill state of health, and get him off.

25 December 1793
A great fog all day, the weather was mild and fair, without rain. Johnny and I dined at home and took three pint jugs of punch royal between us. A party of the Tipperary Militia went to St Nicholas Church, played on their instruments, and sang all the Psalms. Alderman Lawton paid me a visit in my own house, but sent me neither wine, stout or porter for a Christmas gift. The remainder of the Tipperary Militia marched with fife and drum to the North Chapel.

31 December 1793
This being the last day of the year, was consequently the last rainy day, and in reality a more incessant day of heavy rain did not happen in the year before. Breakfasted at Mr Main's house. Simon McCarthy (next door) affronted Johnny, and desired him never again to go for any more water into his house.

Marianne Fortescue
1767-1849

THE AUTHOR OF THIS DIARY *was the daughter of John (Bumper Jack) McClintock of Drumcar, Dunleer, County Louth, who was MP for Enniskillen and Belturbet. Her nephew became the 1st baron Rathdonnell. She married Matthew Fortescue of Stephenstown, County Louth. He was one of the numerous descendants of Faithfull Fortescue, who had acquired the ecclesiastical lands at Dromiskin when he came adventuring to Ireland in 1615.*

The Fortescues had a house in Merrion Street, Dublin, where they were staying when the rebellion of 1798 broke out (Marianne was recovering from the birth of a stillborn child). Shortly afterwards they returned to Stephenstown, where, except for Mr Fortescue spending a great deal of time with his Militia Corps, nothing much happened.

* * *

16 May 1798
Fortescue, Jack and I went yesterday to Malahide – we had a very pleasant drive and passed some very nice places – we went on our return to Burnet's gardens at Richmond – there was not a great deal to be seen there, but it was neat – we came home to dinner – the children and all are well – the weather is coldish.

22 May 1798
We have been driving about and have had company since I last wrote – this morning I went with Jane to Peter's church & heard the Bishop of Ossory preach a very good sermon an hour and twenty minutes long ...

Lord E'd Fitzgerald was taken up on Saturday evening last – this town is in a great fuss, the streets quite full of military & taking up quantity of arms – Fortescue the children & I all thank God well.

24 May 1798
We went yesterday to Rathfarnham & saw a number of beautifull birds – the golden pheasant exceeds any bird I could have formed an idea of. The place is beautifull, the house has some fine rooms & fine paintings. We returned to town before three – I drove about the streets – we had company at dinner – there have been a number of men taken prisoners & some brought in Dead. The United destroy'd three mail coaches last night, burned one & cut others to pieces – the

whole town is in confusion – God send it may all end well & soon as 'tis quite shocking to hear every moment the things that are happening – Jack left us at ten o'clock and went in the Cork mail – we believe it has escaped.

Jack Fortescue was her brother-in-law and was in Holy Orders.

25 May 1798
Still sad work going on with the United – Martial Law was yesterday proclaim'd in this town – all yeomen out every night – Jack Fortescue return'd to town & had only got as far as Naas – the Mail was attacked – the horses very providentially took fright at the firing and ran off – the coach was upset & by that means they all escaped (I mean the passengers) with their lives – there was a shocking battle at Naas. Jack saw thirty-nine lying dead and six hung – we suppose a vast number more must have been kill'd – the army got five h'd pikes from the defenders who dropp'd them in running off – The Mail Jack got safe with into the Post Office at Naas – where we hope it remain'd safe – Fortescue is pretty well – the children very well – I feel unpleasant from the idea of the dreadful situation we all are in – God send us speedy deliverance.

27 May 1798
We are still going on in the same way – the Rebels are defeated in all the battles hitherto fought – there were three men hung yesterday on Queen's Bridge – God send there may be soon an end to it – the weather is uncommonly fine – I long most amazingly to get down to Stephenstown – The North we still hear is quiet – on the door of every house in this town there is a list of the inhabitants posted up & we are liable to have our houses searched at any time for fear of conceal'd arms – Fortescue & the children are this day very well.

Marianne Fortescue returned to Stephenstown on 2 July 1798.

Richard Farrell
1776-1850

THE DAY OF THE RISING of the United Irishmen was fixed for 23 May 1798. It was to be proclaimed by the burning of the mail coaches and the extinguishing of the street lights, but as the organization was infiltrated with informers, many of the leaders were arrested before this date and their military commander, Lord Edward Fitzgerald, was mortally wounded when he was betrayed and captured. The rebellion went ahead, but in the provinces, not in Dublin, and without proper leadership.

Richard Farrell was called to the Irish bar in 1801, was a King's Counsel in 1831, and ended as Commissioner of the Insolvent Debtors' Court. As Assistant Barrister of the County of Kilkenny from 1824, he was the first Irish Catholic to administer justice under English rule since the days of James II, and this even before the Catholic Emancipation Act of 1829.

* * *

18 May 1798

The City of Dublin was proclaimed to be in a state of disturbance according to the provisions of that ever to be remembered act called 'The Insurrection Act'. This appeared to every man unacquainted with party secrets a most unnecessary exertion ... Now it is remarkable that the City of Dublin never presented such a face of tranquillity in the ordinary times of peace – not a house or street robbery to be heard of – an instance of drunkenness, *that once almost inveterate cause of riot* and disorder which long disgraced that city, was rarely met with ... The night of this day I was at the Promenade and afterwards went to a very pleasant ball – the number of entertainments through the town this evening was so great as to exceed anything that was usual – in the party where I was all was mirth and gaiety ...

19 May 1798

I did not go out into the streets until evening. When I approached the Castle I found its avenues guarded and nobody permitted to pass: the guards told me there was a prisoner there under examination. I passed on without much anxiety, and in the course of the evening I heard a report of the capture of Lord Edward Fitzgerald, to which I gave little credit or attention.

20 May 1798

I soon learnt the fate of Lord Edward and that he was at the Castle the evening before when I passed it. The public mind seemed much agitated – the countenances of some expressed great grief, a few open joy, but most were serious. The yeomanry reviewed in different quarters of the town, and paraded the streets in great numbers. There was but one subject of conversation and that was the unfortunate Lord Edward. From the commencement of the war he appeared the declared opponent of the Government, and the champion of the independence of this country – some say he took a lesson in politics from his lady Pamela, said to be the daughter of that unnatural and detested monster *Égalite* – Lord Edward, whom I have often seen, was in the middle size and of hard make, like Flint – his engaging countenance was good natured as well as enterprising – he was remarkable for dressing like an English groom or, as we are told, like a French Jacobin ... I supped at Murray's in Great George's Street where, as I was accustomed, I expected to meet a pleasant party – but nothing could raise the dejected spirits of this party – the females were in tears all day – and in entertainment it is not the province of men to take the lead.

22 May 1798

I was at the Courts. It was the last day of the Easter term ... Returning from the Courts in company with Thomas Moore, who was a Crop [he had short hair], a soldier perceiving this endeavoured to twist a stick from a man going by in order to knock Moore down, fortunately for Moore the man kept his stick – such outrages as this had been commonly committed in the course of the last winter by both parties ... Nothing could surprise me more than to hear Byrne the bookseller in Grafton Street was taken into custody this morning – this man always appeared to me a man of the greatest discretion and caution ... In the evening I heard reports of the operations of the military in that quarter of the town called the Liberty, a place that contained as much misery and as much wretchedness as any street in Europe. The military had been flogging some unfortunate wretches in order to extort confession, they likewise burned any house in which they found concealed weapons ...

23 May 1798

All the streets of the City were blockaded by yeomen, who pursuant to orders from Government commenced a general disarming of the citizens of Dublin – I strolled about the town for three hours in company with my friend James L. McLeader whom I had long wished to converse with – he said this day presented a scene to us which history could not parallel – a soldiery composed of citizens seizing on a capital ... How men of their order in society whose feelings had not been blunted by long professional custom which alone I thought could reconcile a man to those inhuman and barbarous modes of punishment could all at once bring themselves to assist at the infliction of those tortures on their fellow citizens ...

24 May 1798

The yeomanry were employed in the same service of searching for arms and improving themselves in the science of flogging – this morning the Northern Mail was burned on the road, about three miles from Dublin … the apprehensions of Government from this and advice that there was to be an attack on the City made them proclaim Martial Law this evening. I was in the Castle Yard listening to the reading of the Proclamation when I saw Mr Braughall coming out of the Secretary's office and going in custody to Kilmainham – during the few minutes he waited in the yard before the guard was ready to accompany him I noticed the ferocious conduct of some of the yeomen to a man of Mr Broughall's respectability of character, his rank, the age of the man whose grey hairs should secure him from insult … A common soldier permitted in the hearing of the poor gentleman to say, 'What a pity it is to be cramming gaol with these rebels when we could despatch them here,' pointing to the gate, and at the same time remarking what a fine place to hang a weight …

Braughall was liberated on giving bail 'himself of £1000 and two sureties of £500 each'.

25 May 1798

I accompanied Pat Smyth to Lord Gormanstown to consult with him on the measures to be taken by his troop; here we met a Mr Ennis, a member of the same corps – nothing could equal the distracted state of mind those men displayed, undetermined what side to take, wavering between inclination and prudence – the heart was fixed on one side and safety did not appear certain on the other side … I gained admittance with great interest into a Court Martial which was sitting in one of the rooms of the House of Commons upon trial of two yeomen belonging to the Rathfarnham corps who fought on the side of the rebels the evening before – there was not a person beside myself in plain coloured clothing – it was to me a cruel sight to see the lives of my fellow citizens disposed of in this summary manner …

26 May 1798

My sisters had been so frightened during this week that we are anxious to send them to England if we could have met a proper person to accompany them – my father proposed to me my accompanying them – to this I assented without any great reluctance … I could not be a yeoman, and no man could appear in the street if in plain clothes without being liable to insult … Last evening I was in Dublin, passing through Kevin Street in company with my friend Morris I saw one of the cavalry with a scissors in his hand cropping the hair and ears of a decent man because he discovered him with a false tail … The fellow, enraged at our looking without approbation on his conduct, came up; asked me if I was a Crop – and then made me pull off my hat – when fortunately he discovered *my poor little tail* – it was so brutal and cowardly in the fellow, with a case of pistols in his hand and his sabre by his side, to offer such an insult to any man of the appearance of a gentleman who had not the power to resist.

27 May 1798

There were great movements of the military through town, they seized every coach, public or private, every jaunting car, in short, every vehicle that could expedite their conveyance to the country – in the evening my sisters and myself went down to the waterside, but here we found to our grief our passports would not answer ... I met Mrs Dunn, the wife of Councillor John Dunn – when she understood I was going to the Castle to get my passport rectified she gave me hers, and desired me to mention her name to Lord Castlereagh and also to Captain Bruce, one of the aides-de-camp – I took her carriage and drove for the Castle; no Castlereagh to be found here – I then drove to his house, a considerable distance, but he had just left home – back again to the Castle went I – and here I saw Bruce. He was very civil but could do nothing for me ... It was now eleven o'clock and I was afraid to walk through the streets, therefore I took the carriage up to Morris's where I slept ...

28 May 1798

Alderman James, by authority of Lord Castlereagh, gave us the proper passports ... This night we set sail without a sigh of regret after the land we quitted except at the recollection of scenes of suffering which we had so laterly witnessed ... the packet was full of passengers, more than could be well accommodated ... When we landed at the Head we found the principal inn crowded with emigrant Irish ... We were fortunate to get off from this place immediately after our arrival. We joined Mrs Dunn and her two sons in a post coach and four, and thus we posted for two days until we got to Oswestry where we parted – we found in this lady a very agreeable and genteel companion, but though a woman of good understanding it was most strangely blinded by religious prejudices – she credited all the vulgar tales of Popish plots, Popish proscriptions, etc. etc.

Richard Farrell and his sisters went to Birmingham. They spent two months there, where they 'met with the greatest civility – I do not know that there can be more true civility found in any man than in an Englishman, when one has a proper introduction'.

On his return to Dublin later in 1798, and on his twenty-second birthday which he celebrated with much reflection and moralizing on his character and future, he writes of his choice of profession: 'If I trust in my natural abilities alone, I must be content to range the very lowest walks of the profession, but if I make the best use of all the opportunities so happily afforded me, though I may not be the first, yet I feel that I shall be far far from the last of my profession.' He does not mention that his religion would in any way be a handicap to his career.

Anne, Dowager Countess of Roden
1730-1802

ANNE, COUNTESS OF RODEN, widow of Robert Jocelyn, 1st Earl of Roden, was the sister of the last Earl of Clanbrassil, who left her Tollymore Park in County Down and part of his estates at Dundalk. She spent much of her time at Tollymore, which is picturesquely situated on the edge of the Mournes overlooking the sea. The house has since been demolished but the demesne with its numerous follies is now a forest park.

Her eldest son, Robert, raised and commanded a fencible corps of cavalry during 1798. They were nicknamed 'The Foxhunters' because the sergeants promised recruits a day's fox-hunting every week. It was Lord Roden's Foxhunters who pursued and slaughtered over two hundred insurgents who had gathered on the Curragh in order to deliver up their arms, and it was to him that the French General Humbert surrendered at Ballinamuck.

Her third son, Percy, became Bishop of Clogher but was caught in flagrante delicto *with a guardsman in the White Hart public house in Westminster. He absconded while waiting trial and was said to have fled to Scotland where he became a butler.*

Lady Roden began writing the diary shortly after the death of her husband in June 1794. At the beginning it is an introspective diary – 'This day I have indeed much to lament for the faults of my own temper...' – but soon only the most trivial events, if any, are recorded: 'The same as usual' ... 'I can't recollect' ... 'I think I was at prayers'. It is during the rising in 1798 that the diary becomes interesting.

Lady Roden was sixty-eight at the time. She and her daughter Louisa and their friends the Miss (Hely) Hutchinsons, sisters of Lord Donoughmore, had just returned from Dublin to Tollymore Park.

* * *

23 May 1798

Louisa, the Hutchinsons, and I came to Tollymore Park. This day begun those dreadful scenes in and about Dublin which, as we came farther north, we were ignorant of for two days: dreadful indeed they are, but mercy has attended us, and Oh, surely it has attended me and supported me under the dreadful apprehensions from reports yesterday that this shocking rebellion had broke out at Belfast and Drogheda, so that all I loved on all sides was in danger, except the single one who was with me; and even we appeared from that report to be between two fires, which would soon destroy us. God Almighty supported me for some hours that I endured this misery, and at last He granted me the mercy to know this report was false. His protection of my beloved son in his brave undertaking against these unfortunate rebels is a mercy for which my heart is too narrow to conceive or to return praise ... These threatenings continued; but the Province of Ulster was supposed to be quiet, nor was there any danger apprehended. In this persuasion we remained for some days, and we were enjoying ourselves as comfortably as I could.

7 June 1798
Mr Moore and Mr William Moore came to see me, and gave me some instances that seemed to be convincing that the Province of Ulster was likely to continue quiet. In the evening, Gray asked me if I should not like to have some of the troops, that were at Bryansford, guard this house. I was rather startled at the question, as I apprehended he might have heard some alarming account; and he slightly said No, and I refused the guard. In less than an hour after, I received an express from Harriot, to inform me that there was a rising at Larne, which they hoped would soon be under, but urging me most eagerly to set out for Belfast, for which purpose she had sent her horses to meet me at Saintfield, and also an order from General Nugent that the six dragoons that were stationed in Bryansford should escort me. This account was most alarming. We waited for break of day, and set out in our chaise and Miss Hutchinson's chaise. Louisa recollected that Captain Wolseley was in the neighbourhood, and wrote to ask him to accompany us, which he most kindly complied with; and we found him upon our road at Clough. We got with perfect safety to Belfast, and saw nothing alarming. The two Miss Hutchinsons, Louisa, my three little children and our two maids, Davis and Miss H's footman, were all that went with us. Hammy Gray also accompanied us as far as Belfast. When we arrived within two miles of it, during which time we had met nothing alarming, Captain Wolseley took his leave of me, as there were troops from thence to the town. In his return he narrowly escaped being taken on that road which so few hours before we had travelled in safety. The next day Saintfield, where we had changed horses, was in the hands of the rebels.

Harriot is her eldest daughter who was married to Chichester Skeffington; he is called Chitty in the diary and he later became the 4th Earl of Massareene.

The 'three little children' to whom Lady Roden refers are her orphan grandchildren, whom she was bringing up.

8 June 1798
We got to Belfast about ten o'clock, and found Harriot in a worse situation than I expected. She had not seen Chitty for two days and nights, during which time he had been in the Battle of Antrim. It was a desperate one, where, by the brave but rash intrepidity of Colonel Lumley, part of the 22nd were cut off, and the yeoman cavalry were probably saved by the means of Chitty's coolness and recollection. Poor Lord O'Neill was murdered this day as he was going to a meeting of magistrates, not at all in the act of fighting. We were told Chitty was safe, but I

could hardly believe it, not seeing them return; but after some hours the troop returned, and he safe with them. Lord O'Neill lingered some days at Lord Massareene's, where he died. Before we got to Belfast the only friends in whom Harriot could have comfort were fled to Scotland, so that when I got to Belfast she was well-nigh overcome: the only gleam of earthly comfort she had was seeing us. The troop had been delayed in their returning by conveying of prisoners. They entered the town with the greatest acclamation through the streets. The emotion was strong upon this sight; but the doubt of the sincerity of these testimonies of joy damped the luxuriant feel one might have had. When Chitty came to us he bore every mark of the most terrible feelings, joined to the most manly firmness and tenderness to us. The question was this day what we were to do. Chitty did not seem at this moment to advise us to leave Ireland, but we heard that General Nugent had thought it necessary to send Mrs Nugent away. Every hour brought accounts of increased disturbances. This day was passed, indeed, in a most agitated state.

The United Irishmen in the North had risen and, under Henry Joy McCracken, they attacked Antrim town, but were defeated. A force of 4000 men led by Henry Munro, a Lisburn draper, for a time was more successful round Saintfield, but were beaten at Ballinahinch. McCracken and Munro were executed along with other leaders of the rebellion.

9 June 1798

Chitty seemed strongly of the opinion we ought to sail. He told me if an exceeding large force came upon the town, they might seize the boats, and leave us no means of escaping, and that there was now a very good little coal boat in which we might go. This day was also past in suffering, seeing him only for short minutes, when he rather wished to avoid than to see us. His eagerness to put us on board was very great, and at nightfall we (those I have named above) went down to the quay and embarked on board this little vessel (The Liberty, Captain Cargo). Poor Chitty put us on board, and then was obliged to leave us. Soon after, Harriot had the misery of hearing the trumpet sound to arms. The river of Belfast is such a difficult passage, except with every favourable circumstance, that, as we had not these, we were soon a-ground, by the fault, as the Captain said, of the Pilot. All confidence being entirely lost in our countrymen there was no security in our minds that this was not intended. As we lost a tide by it, and remained little more than a stone's throw from the land, if God had permitted us to see it, they might have made us a prey: but it was not permitted. There was an engagement near Saintfield, in which our troops were driven back.

10 June 1798

The ladies upon the deck had the misery of seeing the York Fencibles flying over the bridge of Belfast, to which, as we lay a-ground, we were very near, indeed. We made very little way any part of this day, and got aground again. People were constantly coming to us from the town, by which we had the comfort of hearing that the Yeomanry Troop had not been out the night before, when that dreadful trumpet sounded. They had been so harassed at Antrim, it was almost necessary to spare them this night if it was possible. This evening we had some prospect of sailing, but the Pilot (without whom the Captain dare not sail) did not come on board till barely time for the tide, and then half the crew had left us. All this appeared to me extremely suspicious, but as there was no mending the situation, it was needless to express my fears; there was terror enough spread amongst our fugitives by cruel and false reports which were continually brought from the town. While we were in this situation, Mr Salmon (Mr Skeffington's clerk) brought down the King's boat, out of which he replaced our crew, and worked jointly with them and a servant of Mr Skeffington's (Denis) till twelve o'clock to get us off, which they effected.

11 June 1798

We began to sail and landed at Portpatrick, I think, between three and four in the evening. We brought with us a maid servant and her child, who had lived many years in the family.

The ship was wonderfully crowded – we lay in the hold fifty-three, women and children – and tedious and woeful as the time we were confined there was, I never heard a complaint from any person, except the cries of the poor little innocent children. Harriot had brought some mattresses which were very useful; one of them, spread over some dressing boxes belonging to the passengers, was my bed for the most part of forty-five hours, and I fear, I fared a great deal better than most of my companions. In one thing I fared well indeed, by the strength and spirit it pleased God to give me, never to sink at this strange and unexpected situation. I ought to mention every comfort it pleased God to give us, though it cannot probably tell half: our poor Captain, who I believe to be one of the best-hearted creatures in the world, showed us such kindness and feeling as one only could have expected from a much higher style of education. When we landed, the town of Portpatrick was so completely full of military, going to Ireland, and fugitives from thence, that we had no hopes of a bed of any kind: we could only get a dirty bed-chamber in the inn to eat our dinner: but the regulating officer, Captain Carmichael, from whom we received every civility and assistance, found us out some rooms at the Minister's house, Mr McKenzie, who, with his wife, joined in affording us every comfort in their power. Mrs Nugent who had got a lodging at an ale-house gave Harriot and child a bed there.

They stayed in Scotland until 19 September, returning when the rebellion in the North was well over – their stay there prolonged because of the bad fevers that attacked the grandchildren.

Elisabeth Richards
1778-1863

ELISABETH RICHARDS was living at Rathaspeck, just outside Wexford, with her mother and sister at the outbreak of the 1798 rebellion. Her diary begins on 27 May, when the rebels had taken Wexford. The rumours that all Protestants were to be massacred caused panic, though in actual fact Elisabeth and her relations were treated with remarkably little malice.

Elisabeth Richards's diary ends abruptly on the day after the defeat of the rebels at Vinegar Hill.

Some years later, Elisabeth Richards married Count von Stirum, an émigré Dutchman, and her diary resumes from 1805. Van Stirum, who called himself 'an exiled, ruined, banished man', came from a distinguished Dutch family. In Wexford, he had various businesses and a farm, none of which were a financial success. With high hopes he went off to be aide-de-camp to the Prince of Orange, but he returned to Wexford after only a few months. In 1821 the whole family went to live in Holland. Elisabeth had had ten children, all of whom survived during the length of the diary, though they had many illnesses and were a constant worry to their mother.

I have taken these extracts from a transcription made by a granddaughter of Elisabeth Richards in 1917. I have retained the spellings of names of people and places, though in some cases I think the granddaughter read the names of places incorrectly.

* * *

Saturday 26 May 1798 – Rathaspeck
We this day quitted Clonard, after spending a happy week there; we came round through Wexford, where we learned there had been a general rising in the County of Kildare, but the insurgents had been defeated; it was also reported that the neighbourhood of Govey and of Oulard was much disturbed. Our trunks of clothes that went off this morning for Dublin are I think in some danger. I much fear that the people of this country are more inclined to insurrection than is apprehended: sullen melancholy was expressed this day in the countenances of every individual of the lower class, it can have no cause but the banishment of their priest Dixon and of ten men found guilty, by the Magistrates of the County, assembled at Wexford, of disloyalty – these rebels were sent off this day to Duncannon fort, escorted by a troop of Yeomanry.

Whitsunday 27 May 1798 – Clonard

At church, to my unspeakable astonishment, I heard that Bagenal Harvey, Edward Fitzgerald and John Colclough of Bally Feague had been taken up on suspicion of disaffection to the Government, and lodged in jail, that the rebels in great force had attacked Carlow, nearly destroyed Gullagh-street, but at length had been repulsed. After Divine Service we walked to Fairfield, the news we had heard was the subject of conversation, it was treated lightly until a servant of Mr Sutton's rode up in haste to the hall-door and told us that his master and mistress had sent him out to let my mother know that the people at the other side of the water were up, that they judged the country to be very unsafe, and begged we would go to town immediately. Horrorstruck we ran home. My mother had the lower windows barred, and in breathless anxiety we awaited the return of our servants whom she had sent to town to take the oaths of allegiance.

An hour had elapsed when I saw my nurse running down the avenue. I asked her what was the news. She said: 'Good news, the people had dispersed and the danger was over.' My mother had the hall-door opened and we ventured to come out. At that moment a strange man came from the shrubbery and we were running back to our fortress. My nurse knew him to be one of Mrs Hatton's workmen. I ran to ask him for his mistress. She was at Clonard he said, and begged we would go to her immediately, she sent to my mother a note she had received from a lady in Wexford; by that we learned that the insurgents were in force and had put to death some men who would not join them. The danger seemed evident to my mother and she determined to wait no longer for the carriage, but to walk across the fields to Clonard with the man who had brought the note. I often turned round to look at Rathaspeck. I fear the sadness with which I gazed at it is prophetic.

In the evening flying reports reached us that a detachment of the North Cork Militia, consisting of 200 men, had been sent against the rebels and was cut to pieces with the exception of Col. Tooke who commanded it, and 5 privates. This was thought to be impossible, too soon we found it to be a dreadful certainty. From the back windows we see several houses in flames. 'Good God, what a scene.'

Monday 28 May 1798

The morning passes in listening to reports and looking through a spy-glass. At about three o'clock George Reade rode out to demand Mr Hatton's fire arms, he confirmed the dreadful intelligence of a second defeat of the King's troops at Enniscorthy, of the burning of part of the town, of the murder of Mrs Burroughs, of d'Arcy Howlin, etc. He represented in the strongest colours the dangers to which we should be exposed by remaining in the country; assured us we should be perfectly safe in town, it would be fortified, he said, in such a manner that the rebels, if they did attack it, would not be able to make the least impression. My mother and Mrs Hatton seemed fearless of danger, yet the latter was not totally disinclined to go to Wexford. I wept and supplicated my mother to make an effort to save our lives and properties. I represented to her that there would be time enough that evening to go to Rathaspeck, take our papers from there and proceed to Wexford; she scolded me for my tears and forced me to silence. What will be our fate? I will not go to bed. The rest of the family can sleep as usual, the smoking ruins of Enniscorthy are in sight. How can they rest?

Tuesday 29 May 1798

The Donegal Militia, commanded by Col. Maxwell, is arrived at Wexford, also Col. Colville, Capt. Young and Soden of the 13th who have volunteered their services for our defence. My mother and sister are gone to Rathaspeck to secure our papers and anything of value that is portable. (Mr Hatton and Miss Jenck to town.) I wished to go with them, but there was no room for me on the car; their absence was spent in questioning every passenger and looking towards Rathaspeck through the spyglass. I was uneasy for my mother and sister. At length we all again were assembled. Towards evening we heard the rebels were collecting on the Mountain of Forth.

Wednesday 30 May 1798

At four o'clock my mother called us – during the night the rebels had collected in great force at the Three Rocks. Through the telescope we plainly saw them in large bodies, marching and countermarching, and tossing their pikes as if in joy; numbers on horseback were also performing a kind of exercise. About six o'clock we saw part of the garrison march towards the rebels, they were met by them (on the high road that leads from Wexford to the mountain of Forth, to Jaghmon), a volley of musketry was fired, we saw an officer fall from his horse, we afterwards learned it was Col. Watson, and in the course of a few minutes the King's troops began a precipitate retreat.

Our distress aggravated by uncertainty of the fate of the army and what our own might be, so near to a conquering mob, at first approached despair. At length a stupid horror pervaded my senses. I feared without being able to think at the extent of our misery – all that was most dreadful.

In the course of this morning a man rode into the court-yard with a White handkerchief tied to his hat, a green bough in the front of it and a drawn sword in his hand; everyone crowded round him, the servants seemed joyful. He demanded, or rather *commanded*, that provisions should be sent to the camp. 'We are starving, Ma'am,' said he to Mrs Hatton, 'send us provisions or' – he struck his sword with violence on the head of a pump, near which he had stopped his horse and without waiting for an answer, rode off. His orders were instantly complied with, though not without objections from Mrs Hatton. 'Government may confiscate my property for assisting rebels.' 'If you do not comply, we shall be murdered,' was the reply by all.

An old man was dispatched to the Three Rocks with a car loaded with bacon, potatoes, etc. etc. for which Mrs Hatton received thanks from the rebel chiefs. Reports now reached us that the Yeomanry had abandoned their posts – got on board vessels with their families, and that the town was nearly deserted. About one o'clock, Mrs Clifford came to Clonard from Wexford, she looked distracted. 'Ladies,' she said, 'I am sorry to be the messenger of bad news, the army has left Wexford, it is in possession of the rebels; every *Protestant* is to be murdered tonight; you cannot escape, all we have to do is to prepare for death.' I looked around me with horror. I felt there was no possibility of concealment or flight, the infernal pikes seemed already to glitter at our breasts. – I shrieked, and for a moment was all mad. Crowds of the Enniscorthy victors now began to fill the house – some of them wearing the uniforms of the murdered Yeomen, flushed with victory and glorying in the blood they had shed. They told that they or some of their friends had met the 13th Regt. on its way to Wexford, and that not a man but the Commander had escaped. Some of Mrs Hatton's servants repaired to their victorious confederates as soon as they knew to a certainty that the army had retreated, the mask was thrown aside. Those men who the Sunday before had solemnly taken the oath of Allegiance, did not hesitate to join the rebels. About six o'clock a vast number of the insurgents on horseback and on foot marched in a tumultuous manner from the Three Rocks to take possession of the town, they passed by the gate of Clonard, and to our inexpressible satisfaction promised protection to Mr Hatton. An evening of listless anxiety was followed by a night of apprehension. We could hear shouts – or rather yells of joy, from the town that struck terror to our hearts. I sat up late – death I imagined would have additional horrors if unthought of, and notwithstanding the assurance of safety that had been given us, to that only did I look forward.

It was one or two companies of the Meath Militia that had been defeated by the rebels. They had two field pieces which were taken by the latter and contributed to the defeat of the Donegal Militia at the Three Rocks.

Thursday 31 May 1798
Mrs Hatton received a threatening letter from a man with whom she had had some money dealings, he required that she should give him up some lands or £700; a rebel guard which had been sent to protect her by Gen. Roche (a tenant of Mrs Hatton's) confined the bearer of the letter in the Garden-house, and sent information of the Threats contained in it to the rebel camp at the Windmill Mills. The guard was reinforced. One servant, and an old Cotter came from Rathaspeck to see us; they wept for us: the marks of attachment they showed us made me cry too. Some people who had flown from Wexford to Clonard told us a massacre of the Protestants was intended and would undoubtedly take place. A servant of Mrs Hatton's of the Protestant religion overheard some Papists say that they would first murder the Orangemen, and the Protestants too, although it should be five years afterwards; William Hatton, who is an original United

Irishman, assured us there would not be a massacre, but that if we were uneasy, he would endeavour to procure a boat to take us to Wales. It is said that Capt. Boyd has been taken out and put to death at the Three Rocks. We spent a melancholy evening, although we know him but little, some of our tears were for his sufferings.

Friday 1 June 1798
On foot, unattended, and bearing in our hands green boughs, the emblem of *Unity*, Mrs Hatton, my mother, my sister and I set out from Clonard, we met several parties of armed men on the road, they suffered us to pass unmolested. The great body of the Insurgents had been drawn off towards Ross. One or two corps were exercising in the Windmill fields. The town presented a melancholy spectacle, houses quitted. The streets strewed with broken glass, pieces of furniture and articles of ladies dress. Confusion, astonishment, ferocity was alternately expressed in the faces of those we met, and some viewed us with exaltation, whilst others invoked 'the Saints and Angels to guard and bless us'. William Hatton met us and accompanied us into town, he desired us to hide our sorrow – every one succeeded, but me. In hopes of seeing Gen. Roche, and by his means forwarding our scheme of departure, we walked long on the quay. He had set off for Govey of Vinegar-hill an hour before we had arrived there. Disappointed and fatigued we reached Mrs Hatton's house in George's Street, there a more distressing scene than any we had yet passed through awaited us. Several Protestants terrified at the report that a massacre of all those who possessed their religion was intended, had abjured their faith and suffered themselves to be Christened by Romish Priests from whom they had obtained written Protection, which ran nearly as follows: 'I beseech you for Jesus Christ's sake, protect A.B., his (or her) children and property, who I certify to be a true friend of the Roman Catholic Cause'; signed Corrin, Parish-Priest of Wexford. A lady who had conformed through fear, was very urgent with us to follow her example. My mother consented, my sister did not object, my heart objected at such hypocrisy; Mrs Hatton condemned it, fortified with her approbation, I resolved to avoid even the appearance of a change of Religion. Mrs Rock in the strongest terms represented the danger to which we should expose ourselves by refusing to submit to the ceremony of being Christened by a Priest. She knelt to Mrs Hatton, she shed tears, she caressed, she coaxed me, my determination she could not shake, although she heightened the struggle between the love of my Religion, the dread of committing sin should I seem to renounce it, and the fear of a violent death ...

Mrs Hatton, ever thoughtful, had sent for Mr Corrin, she would enquire from him if there was any foundation for Mrs Rock's fears. He assured her there was not and gave us *Protection*, omitting the words 'friends to the Roman Catholic Cause'. A little tranquillized, although disappointed in our hopes for getting to Wales, we then returned to Clonard. Exhausted by the fatigues and emotions of the day, I lay down on the bed as soon as I came in. After an hour of unrefreshing sleep, I went to the dining room, dinner was already over. I had not sat five minutes, when Miss Mary Byrne crossed the court-yard, accompanied by a servant of Mrs Hatton's, bearing an enormous Pike. She entered the parlour with an air of exaltation, her countenance was glowing and had much the expression a painter would give to Bacchante. She begged to speak to my mother in private, they left the room together; her escort had followed her in, he was asked by William Hatton to sit down; he drew a chair to the table where my sister and I sat, we whom he had so often waited on, – we rose. At that moment, we were sent for by my mother. Miss Byrne had informed her that the massacre of the Protestants would take place that night, unless we consented to be Christened by a Priest, we must die. The conflict of the morning now renewed, Miss Byrne threw her arms round me, kissed off my tears, professed the utmost sincerity – the tenderest regard for me and entreated that I would only 'consent to become a Christian'. 'Oh,' she exclaimed, 'This is a glorious day for our religion, not a creature put to the sword, you know not what was to have happened: *we* were all to have been *murdered.*'

I was too much exhausted to attempt discussing with her; I told her no force could induce me to change my religion, that it was not from the prejudice of education, but from conviction that I was a Protestant, that I could die, but not become a Roman Catholic. 'Well then, my dear Eliza, I will die with you, I will stay here with you tonight. We shall be murdered, but I too can die.' She then urged the insignificance of the ceremony that would save our lives. 'Merely to suffer the Priest to make a cross on our foreheads.' Mrs Hatton was as unwilling as I was to submit even to that, but at length overcome by entreaty, and seeing Miss Jenck inclined to go to town, we ordered the mule and car to be got ready for her and for me, who were unable to walk. Miss Byrne in raptures – I in despair. 'Never, Mrs Hatton,' said I, 'will I abjure my Religion.' 'Nor I either, my dear girl, we will speak to Mr Corrin in private, we will explain our sentiments, *we* will stand together, let the others do what they please.'

We soon reached the gate of the Chapel-Yard – where we alighted. Several pikemen were in the yard and some unfortunate Protestants, returning as I supposed from abjuring their faith, for sorrow was painted in every countenance. Mrs Sutton was among them, I went to her and entreated she would tell me what ceremonies she had been obliged to go through. Miss Byrne endeavoured to prevent her answering me. I perceived she wanted to hide the truth from me, I turned to her with a haughtiness which I wondered I dared show, and desired she would leave us, as I wished to speak to Mrs Sutton alone. She seemed confused and left us.

Mrs Sutton told me she had been obliged to say she believed in Transubstantiation, Saints, in short the whole creed of the Papists.

Miss Byrne had deceived me. I was in the snare, how Alas should I escape? I was called to go into the convent, we went up the narrow dirty staircase, at the head of it, a door lay open. I looked in and saw a large low room filled with wretched converts. The sight of those unhappy beings, together with the heat and close smell, overcame me, I fell sick and scarcely know how I got downstairs. We were taken into a room on the ground floor, to wait for the Priest who, it was said, was engaged 'preparing souls for heaven, bodies for the grave'.

When the grand massacre took place, those who had been christened by the Priest were to have been sacrificed first lest they should change religions again. If they died in the Catholic faith, they were assured they would go to Heaven.

Mrs Hatton said she would not see any Priest but Mr Corrin and she insisted on his being sent for. Whilst we were waiting it occurred to me that he might not come and I should be christened by force ... It began to grow dark, my agitation increased. I pretended to be near fainting to have an excuse for leaving the room. Mrs Hatton came with me. I said to her 'Oh Mrs Hatton, we may now get away, the guards will not find us, we may escape.' She agreed that we would return together to Clonard.

We had walked on for some time, when she recollected, that she had left her little granddaughter in the Convent. She said, she must go back there for her. This was a dagger to my heart, but I made no opposition to her wishes and we returned to the convent. Mr Corrin had come there during our absence; he assured us no massacre was intended, reproached Miss Byrne for having unnecessarily alarmed us, offered us his protections, his house and behaved with that benevolence which one expects of ministers of the Gospel.

He accompanied us to Mrs Hatton's house in George street, on the way he harangued several groups of men, on the wickedness of giving out such a report. 'If', said he, 'any of you have such an intention and execute it, you will draw down on you the vengeance of God and man.' They unanimously protested they had not, yet there was something in their countenances I did not like. They seemed astonished, but not convinced by his words. We slept, or rather lay in town this night. I scarcely closed my eyes, when I did I was tortured by terrible dreams.

Saturday 2 June 1798
This morning brought us some consolation, Lord Kingsborough (Col. of the North Cork Militia) and two officers of his regiment have been taken prisoners by the crew of the armed boat that had been fitted for sea by order of Mr Keagh [Matthew Keogh], the rebel commander of the town; letters were found with them which say that 10,000 men had marched from Dublin against the Wexford rebels, – Oh what joy for us.

Mr Keagh came into a lady's house, where we had gone to see some friends, he had Lord Kingsborough's sword; my mother addressed him as 'Captain Keagh' – he scarcely noticed what she said, he laid his hand on the hilt of the sword, exclaiming: 'I am now Colonel, this is Lord Kingsborough's sword.' In a pompous conceited manner he then mentioned his intention of sending an express to Govt. offering to spare the lives of the prisoners the people had taken, if those of their party which were in the hands of Govt. were protected. Miss Shunt begged he would enclose a few lines from her to her brother, he said he would – adding 'make haste and do not write fiddle faddle, I shall be obliged to read what your write'. Lord Kingsborough had been conducted to Mr Keagh's house, the mob wanted to see him, and to have him taken. Mr Keagh's authority availed to keep the people quiet, but he could not induce them to disperse. A boy of about 14 of the name of Lett, a relation of Beachamp Bagnal Harvey, rode up the street, the mob collected round him, asking if they should not get a pitch-cap for Lord Kingsborough. (A favourite amusement of Lord K. and his Reg.t was putting pitch-caps on the 'Croppies' as the rebels were then called.) 'No, no, we will have none of those doings,' he replied – and such was his influence, that it was urged no farther.

We returned to Clonard more tranquil than we had left it, although fully convinced that we were prisoners; no application for our removal from Wexford would be listened to by the Committee. 'For some time', said William Hatton, 'You must *content* yourselves here.'

Sunday 3 June 1798
My mother and Miss Jenck went to the Catholic Chapel.

Tuesday 5 June 1798
All Mrs Hatton's men servants had been summoned the day before to the neighbourhood of Ross, to be ready for an attack on the town; judging by what I had already seen, I expected it would fall into the hands of the rebels. About four o'clock a servant of Mrs Hatton returned, he was immediately *asked* (not desired) to come into the parlor to tell the news. 'Is Ross taken?' 'Faith they have it now, if they keep it.' …

Wednesday 6 June 1798
Some women who came to Clonard today said that the Barracks and Market house of Ross were still in Possession of the King's troops. I was in an extasy of joy, I exulted over William Hatton, I reasoned with him, he listened to my loyal arguments with good humour, but without conviction; he provoked me. I left the room and for revenge I pulled the odious green cockade out of my hat, and trampled on it; it was a satisfaction to me to insult the rebel colours.

Friday 8 June 1798
At breakfast Miss Jenck said with a tone of great kindness that she wished it was possible we could remain always together, but it could not be. 'And why not, Molly dear?' 'Oh, because Mrs Richards must go home and see about her own affairs.' This was an unexpected speech. It was followed by a dead silence. Miss Jenck interrupted it and manifested unusual vivacity. My mother had ordered a car to come for her from Rathaspeck this day, intending merely to visit it. Miss

Jenck's conduct determined my sister and me to accompany her and to remain at home. With a breaking heart I bade Mrs Hatton farewell, she was more affected at parting with us than I ever remember to have seen her. The day was enchantingly fine, yet how melancholy did Rathaspeck seem. The hall still retained the marks of the rebels who had drank here. The furniture of the room was displaced, all seemed neglected, forlorn. I reflected on what we had been, what our future prospects were. I threw myself on the first chair, I listened to nothing that passed. I felt as if every moment I could have died of grief ...

Saturday 9 June 1798
... The Miss Jooles came to see us this evening, they are freer from bigoted zeal than I could have supposed Catholics to be; they did not speak of religion and seemed truly Loyal. From the time they left us until we retired to our bedrooms we were gloomily silent. Alas, we could not speak comfort to each other.

Sunday 10 June 1798
My sister feigned illness and did not rise until it was too late for any of us to go to the Chapel, as the servants seemed to suppose we should. About ten o'clock a heavy cannonading was heard towards Duncannon Fort ... Betsey having heard my sister was not well, came to see her, she says *the people* are determined no Protestant shall enjoy a fortune such as ours, they exult at our fall. Betsey says that a low shopkeeper intends to marry me as soon as affairs are a little settled. I will never consent. I am indignant. The King's troops, the Misses Jooles tell us, have retaken Arklow. A Mr Codd, who was intended for the Priesthood, but now commands the *Rathaspeck Corps*, sat two hours with us this evening. He says he thinks the lives of Mr Kellett and Mr Edwards are safe, because their wives are 'Romans'.

Monday 11 June 1798
... Today we drove to Clonard on a common car attended by two of our servants armed with swords. Coming out of the avenue gate, we met three women who sneered at us and looked exultingly at our shabby equipage. I was vexed, but how cheering is the sight of a friend. Mrs Hatton's warm embrace banished every uneasy sensation from my mind. Miss Jenck was all kindness, she seemed to wish we should forget her late behaviour to us ... From Clonard we proceeded to Wexford. Oh, what a dismal scene. The shops all shut, pikemen guarding every avenue to the town. Distrust, fear, anxiety painted on the countenances of everyone we met. We called on Mrs Sutton, Mr Slay (a rebel chief) had given her a newspaper. Its contents inspired us with hopes which we did not dare manifest in her presence ... Mrs Sutton told me she had heard that the burning of the Barn at Scullabogue had been ordered by one of the rebel chiefs. That such an action was permitted will be shame, eternal shame to the Irish name (near 100 Protestant men, women, and children were burned to death in the Barn at Scullabogue.)

Tuesday 12 June 1798
Mr & Mrs Sutton, William Hatton and Count Kersbrat, a French emigrant, dined with us; whilst we were at tea a party came to search the house for Mr Ogle. They had got information from the Camp at Vinegar Hill that he was concealed here, or at one of the Clonards. They were civil to us, but talked of the punishment they would inflict on those who concealed Mr Ogle in a manner that made us shudder. Someone assuring the rebels that Mr Ogle was not in our house, he took up the French Count's stick, saying 'there is one old rascal here at any rate'.

It was said the sailors were committing excess in the town. My mother requested William Hatton to stay this night at Rathaspeck. He consented, but got so drunk after supper, that had the house been attacked by them, he could not have afforded us the slightest assistance.

Wednesday 13 June 1798
I drew the whole morning, the weather is too warm to take exercise, it is the finest I have seen in Ireland. How little are our feelings in unison with this bright sunshine ... Bagnal Harvey has resigned his chief command to a Priest of the name of Roach. This is the age of wonders. The rosary is exchanged for the sword and Ministers of the Prince of Peace for the flames of Civil Disorder.

Thursday 14 June 1798
The insurgents have failed in their attack on Borris ... After tea I walked with my mother. The evening was delicious, seated in the Elm-bower breathing air perfumed with woodbine and syringa. My heart was heavy, all my thoughts gloomy ...

Friday 15 June 1798
I had been drawing with some tranquillity when Betsey came to tell me that Col. Shante had been taken to prison. An orange color'd screen, found at Artramont by Mrs Dixon, was the pretext for arresting him; she says the engravings on it are symbols of the deaths the Orange faction intended to have inflicted on the Roman Catholics. The people say that Col. Shante was the chief of that society and that their meetings were held in a room of his house. On his way to jail some of the mob cut at him, others threw him down. He has not been materially hurt. He is to be tried and if found guilty, to be shot ...

Saturday 16 June 1798
A party of ruffians came to search the house for arms ... My mother assured them she had not any, but they were welcome to search the house ... In a loft they found a blunderbuss covered with dust and without a lock. It served however as a pretext for reproaching my Mother with a breach of faith. One Connick, who had found the blunderbuss, insisted on my sister's opening her writing-desk he thought he said, it might conceal Pocket-Pistols. The Impertinence of this man,

and the tone of authority assumed by the whole party, overcame my mother's spirits, she wept bitterly. I felt indignation, and a wish to be revenged.

Sunday 17 June 1798

We did not go to Chapel. I dare say the people wonder, no one however asked us to go there since Mrs Byrne's ineffectual attempt to make us Catholics … After dinner, my sister and I walked to Fairfield, the Miss Jooles returned with us. There was a strange-looking old man at the Lodge. I entered into conversation with him. He spoke of the rising in the North, the present disturbance, he said had been foretold 25 years ago by a stranger who came to his father's house. He told me he said: 'it would be better for me to put the value of a cow into my land in the year of 97 than that of a hen in 98' and 'That we should have peace until 99' … The reason he assigned for the failure of the rebels before Ross was, 'Their being commanded by B.B. Harvey' (a Protestant gentleman of good fortune), but now, he said, 'they have got one of the right sort at their head (Priest Roach) they'll take it with all pleasure'. Father Murphy, he said, had been cruelly treated by 'the army' at Arklow, 'they wanted to burn his chapel and he in it, Miss, but his head would not burn; no nor all the faggots in the county wouldn't have burned it, so at last they sent in a soldier for him and cut it off'. Had I not been afraid, I would have said to him that the head of that soldier who entered the flaming Chapel must have been made of the same materials as the Priest's.

Wednesday 20 June 1798

The rebels have been driven from their Camp at Lacken. MacDonald with a faltering voice told us so. Such good news, so unexpected, so unhoped for. It has been confirmed by a number of flying, trembling wretches who vainly endeavour to conceal their terrors. With exhilarated spirits we walked to Fairfield, from thence through a telescope we plainly distinguished 11 English ships of War. The entrance of Mr Neyler of Gurtinnanrogue with a sad countenance increased my satisfaction. I guessed he had heard what was good for us, bad news for him. … It was late when we left Fairfield, the evening was cold and blustery – at intervals we heard the roar of the cannons. Some men we met told us there was an engagement at Fowkes' Mills; my mother and I resolved not to go to bed until we knew the event … my sister and I sat down in the back parlor, the wind whistled through broken panes of glass, dark clouds flew across the sky. We were silent … listening to the sound of musketry, which one heard now and then in the intervals of the storm … About 11 o'clock we were so anxious to know what the result of the engagement had been, that my mother begged of the housemaid to go and inquire of the guard that was kept at the cross-roads, if they had received any intelligence from Fowkes's Mill. She soon returned and brought word that some men she had spoken to said that they had left Fowkes's Mill, the King's troops were giving way and by this time they supposed they were beaten. It seemed so odd … that we gave but little credit to this account.

Thursday 21 June 1798

At two o'clock in the morning, one of our servants and one of the guard … returned from Fowkes's Mill. The girl who opened the door for them brought us word that the King's troops had been defeated … Desponding and almost heart-broken I threw myself on a chair in my bedroom. I know not how long I remained there, I was stupefied with grief …

After breakfast we walked to Mrs Jooles's. There we heard that the rebels had been defeated at Fowkes's Mills, this morning at Vinegar Hill and that they were flying in all directions. How happy we were now. About 5 o'clock we walked to the Avenue gate, the green boughs and pikes have nearly disappeared, crowds of women and children and a few men, were flying from Wexford. Many sought refuge at our house; they said the King's troops were encamped at the Windmill Mills, that they plundered every house and shot every man they saw.

We again went to Fairfield. Mr Codd, who had commanded the Rathaspeck Corps and a Mr O'Brien, nephew to Mr Corrin the Priest, were there. They wore their swords, cross-belts and green collars. The deep, the manly regret that Mr O'Brien seemed to feel for the overthrow of his party interested me for him. His countenance expressed despair, his arms were folded, his mind seemed abstract-ed from the surrounding objects; some one observed 'we shall now have the bless-ings of peace restored'. 'Yes,' he replied, with a smile of agony and indignation, 'there will be peace, but we shall all be slaves.'

O'Brien was sentenced to nine years' transportation.

Friday 22 June 1798

More troops have marched into Wexford, a body of rebels that had been encamped at Kilinick, and afterwards at Benville, have retreated, they have not been pursued. Two of Lord Mountmorris's Cavalry shot at a man within a short distant of Rathaspeck. An unfortunate rebel who had sought protection here, I thought would have lost his senses when he heard the report of the gun, he cried, he tore his hair. His pusillanimity made me feel more of contempt than pity for him. All the morning we listened to the shrieks and complainings of female rebels. They almost turned my joy to sorrow. As we were going to dinner, the father and brother of the rebel I before mention rode to the door, they were let in and endeavoured to indicate their conduct to my mother. The father showed a *protection* given by Lord Kingsborough, 'to the county of Wexford at large'. He cannot have a right to give one, I think it will not even protect Mr — when he goes into town.

Dinner was scarcely over, when Capt. Jooles sent us word he was arrived at Fairfield. My sister and I ran there without even …

The diary breaks off here.

Sir Vere Hunt
1761-1818

It is said that in eighteenth-century Ireland the first two questions asked as to a young man's respectability and qualifications, particularly when he came as suitor, were, 'What family is he of? Did he ever blaze?'

Vere Hunt had had his first duel by the time he was eighteen, in which year he had also ridden a race, fallen in love with an actress, left college, taken to gambling and sat on a Grand Jury.

His family, the Hunts, had lived at Curragh Chase near Adare in Limerick since the early seventeenth century and were descended through the female line from the Earls of Oxford. (In the hope of gaining the extinct title, succeeding generations called themselves de Vere.)

All this must have made an acceptable c.v., for in 1782, when he was twenty-two, Vere Hunt writes: 'Captain Hill speaks to me about Miss Pery – I go and see the Bishop [her father], I dine with him. – propose for his daughter – accepted – broke off in consequence of a misunderstanding with my father. Renewed.'

I do not think his marriage was a happy one; in his diary he always refers respectfully to his wife as Lady Hunt, but on the whole they lived separate lives. Their only son, Sir Aubrey de Vere, was a poet, as were his sons; one of whom wrote the 'Snowy Breasted Pearl'.

Vere Hunt was created a baronet after he had been High Sheriff of the county. He was also, for a short time before the Union, a Member of Parliament for Askeaton, a seat that had cost him £5000. It was in a effort to recoup his losses that he voted for the Union even though he opposed the measure. In the diary he comes across as something of a maverick and enthusiast, though many of his schemes failed. He took a theatre company around the south of Ireland – unfortunately he did not keep a diary for this period and there survive only brief notes; he owned a coal mine at Glangoole in Tipperary, for which he laid out and built the village of New Birmingham. In one entry in his diary he writes, 'Too wet to lay out Oxford Street.'

One of his more colourful ventures was the purchase of Lundy Island in the Bristol Channel, though after spending some months there during a winter he was most anxious to leave; negotiations for the sale of the island to the government continued for many years.

Because he was such a heavy gambler he was always in debt and spent much time in London, where the entries record a constant whirl of financial transactions and also his ceaseless pleadings with the government – and Castlereagh in particular – to pay the money they owed him for raising a regiment and for Lundy Island. In the end he was arrested and spent many months in the Fleet, the debtor's gaol, though it does not sound as if it was much hardship – he was often on day release, usually had people to dine with him and played bowls in the prison yard.

* * *

28 March 1798
The County [Limerick] met at one over the Exchange. I proposed that it be recommended to landlords to give a temporary abatement to poor tenants on account of the fall of grain, and to pay tythes for those under £10 a year rent. It was negatived. A memorial was sent to the Lord Lieutenant signed by thirty-six Justices to proclaim the entire county as in a state of insurrection. Dined at Harry Fosbery's and got drunk.

1 April 1798
Left Limerick at twelve, got home to dinner, and found Lady Hunt and Aubrey in good spirits considering the dreadful state of the county which was this day proclaimed in rebellion. Fixed to send them to England, put up the rules of the Insurrection Act for the information of the poor people and had a small guard of my own people ... Determined to put the house in a state of defence and made up different doors and windows with stone and mortar.

9 April 1798
My dear wife & darling Aubrey went to Limerick on their way to Dublin & probably England to avoid the dangers of this unhappy distracted county ... A guard mounted. Then came back to dinner, lonesome! I cd not eat a bit.

11 April 1798
Went with John Waller's Corps, thirty-eight in number, to Askeaton, arrived there at four & found thirty of the Tyrone Militia under arms. Searched different houses in town and got seven firelocks and some swords, etc ...

17 April 1798
Heard that my Uncle Harry's son, Phineas, was the head of the United Irishmen about Cappah, but that he gave himself up to General Sir James Duff and made a full discovery.

19 May 1798 – Dublin
Dined at Tom Quin's. At nine an express came for the Surgeon-General, who dined with us, to go off to dress Lord Edward Fitzgerald's wounds, who had just been taken by Major Sirr and Justices Swan and Ryan.

23 May 1798 – Dublin

The town in great confusion and a rising expected every hour ... Went to the Castle, saw Lord Edward Fitzgerald's uniform ... Lord Rossmore showed me an impression of the Great Seal found on Lord Edward ... People taken up every instant and flogged by military law to get confessions ... Determined to send my family off without delay, called with a hackney coach for Lady Hunt, Aubrey and Jenny Bindon, and set out for the *Prince of Wales* Packet. She could not sail, the wind being foul, and we all slept on board. Heard from Captain Hill of the *Lady Fitzgibbon* that Frank Arthur, Dr Hargrove, Doctor Ross (all from Limerick) and others were apprehended, and from my Uncle William Hunt that his son Billy was taken up.

He went to England, where he was much occupied with recruiting, and in May 1799 he took the regiment to the barracks in Guernsey. In January 1800 he returned to Dublin.

17 January 1800 – Dublin

Got into the harbour at daylight and after landing, proceeded to Dublin on foot and put up at Quin's Hotel in Crow Street. In the evening to the House of Commons and most warmly welcomed by Lord Castlereagh. Called on Lord Glentworth and consulted him on my expectations from Government. Strongly advised by him not to take any bargain, as those who acted steadily and honourably to the Government would be more liberally treated than if they made a contract.

19 January 1800 – Dublin

Lord Glentworth and I had another conversation and he suggested to me to ask for the Government of Limerick when it may be vacant, and promised me whenever the County or City Militia were vacant he would get it for me. I dined with him.

21 January 1800 – Dublin

Conversed again with Lord Glentworth and spoke on the subject of a peerage. He seems averse to my pressing Government but to leave matters to themselves. Found my situation very unpleasant, pledged to Lord Castlereagh through Lord Glentworth to support a measure which my honour was bound to but my soul revolted at.

3 April 1811 – Curragh Chase

This morning at four o'clock departed this life, John Leahy, who lived for seventy or eighty years with my father and me, and who lived as a pensioner with me for the last twenty years. His honesty and fidelity were great, and I sincerely lament the departure of so old, tried and valuable a domestic. Ordered a coffin to be made for him of the old elm-tree, coeval with himself, or rather antecedent to him, which was blown down last winter. Kill a lamb and dine on a forequarter of it, fish etc. Dr Lee the parish priest of Adare with me. After dinner, he and I go up to Leahy's house, where I give directions for his wake, funeral etc. Lee sleeps here.

13 May 1813 – Dublin
Lounge to the Exhibition of Paintings by Irish artists at Dublin Society House, and very much amused at it for above an hour. Dead game, vegetables and fish pieces by Doctor Richardson – very capital. Landscapes by Petrie and Sadleir – very well done. And some pictures by Allpenny – pleasing. A full-length of Mr Foster, the late Speaker, by Sir William Beechy, also hangs there. From thence I went to see the Museum of the Dublin Society, and the library belonging to it. I was highly pleased at both, and determine, when I can spare fifty guineas, to become a member of that useful institution.

... I remarked some things which might, on a future day, be applicable to Currah, viz., the geometrical staircase, specimens of models of various implements connected with husbandry and domestic management ... Lounged from the Museum to an auction in Clare Street, of a Mr Isaac who, after having furnished his house in a most magnificent style, found out his error and miscalculation as to his means to support it; and all, of course, went to the hammer – Going! Going! Just going! Gone!!!

Dined at Lelands. They all went in the evening to a concert at the Rotunda and I went home quietly to bed.

17 May 1813 – Dublin
Look in at Gilbert and Hodges, see some books bespoke by Aubrey, and see for the first time the celebrated Archibald Hamilton Rowan, who walked in attended by two monstrous and beautiful Danish dogs.

27 May 1813 – Dublin
A fine day at last. Go out at eleven o'clock in James Hunt's jaunting car with his son Harry to the Botanic Gardens at Glasnevin, and much disappointed at not meeting Doctor Wade the Botanic Professor there. Spent two hours very pleasantly, viewing the plants and arrangements, attended for the most part by the head-gardener, who seems to have considerable technical knowledge of the profession, but by no means sufficient depth of knowledge, genius, education and comprehension, to entitle him to be the head of so considerable a national institution.

The plants in general have undergone a removal and new arrangement this season, on which account they do not appear in so flourishing a state. I particularly remark here the following shrubs trained to a twelve-feet wall, and most beautifully covering it, viz., Pyracantha, Phillacca, Alatimus and Acacia. Saw three plants of large-leaved Mountain Ash, exactly the same as the Curragh accidental variety of it which, I was informed, came from Lee and Kennedy's Nursery as Surbus Hebrides.

Saw a good collection of Irises, some varieties of Box, a Gold Arbor Vitae, some varieties of Holly, many of Poplars and Willows, a very beautiful Pine, the Aleppo, the leaves like the Scotch but delicate, and the branches weeping, and the lower branches all successfully laid. A Siberian Stone Pine grafted, common-cleft way, on the Scotch, and perfectly thriving. In the flower-garden, I noticed a large globe flower with orange flowers. Went all through the Hot-houses which are capitally stocked, and a most curious and extensive variety. Returning very hungry, having had no breakfast, I gratify myself with cold lamb, a pint of porter, and a tumbler of punch at the Globe Tavern in Essex Street.

In the evening, I stopped and went through the Richmond Institution for the Industrious Blind, and saw some employed weaving coarse canvas, and others basket-making, which they did very clumsily. I also went through the Farming Society's Concerns in Summerhill, which establishment seems very complete. The workshops for carpenters, smiths and the various persons employed in making agricultural implements are extensive, commodious and well laid out. In the yard are many new and curious machines and implements of husbandry; and, adjoining the house in the rear, is a small compartment of ground laid out in beds, and the various grasses and greens for cattle are systematically classed and arranged there.

I should not omit that, on my way to Glasnevin today, I went over a great school, established on the Lancastrian plan, situated close by the Bridge, which seems to be most attentively and well conducted.

Returned at nightfall, jaded to death. Took refuge in an obscure tavern in Anglesea Street, the Shakespeare, where I took a crab, bread and butter, a pint of porter and two tumblers of raspberry punch. Strolled home and got to bed and rest, which I never more wanted, at ten o'clock.

28 May 1813 – Dublin
Walked into town and met Major Sirr near the Castle, who stopped me and told me exultingly, as if I had been, which God forbid, an enemy to Catholic Emancipation, that the question was lost, a majority of four being against it in the Commons. I surprised him not a little, when I replied I was most heartily concerned to hear it … Thence to Nick Mahon's where I dined sumptuously on fish, no meat as per following bill of fare: – Salmon, fresh herring, potato pudding, asparagus, sole, haddock epergue, turnips, asparagus, salt fish, turbot, removes, rice pudding, pies, cheese, etc. The company, three ladies, Doctor O'Shaughnessy, Catholic Bishop of Killaloe, Doctor Reynolds, Counsellor

O'Gorman and his brother, the two Mr Everards and two or three others. Home at eleven, smoked a pipe and then to bed.

4 June 1813 – Dublin

Very fine day, and being the King's birthday, the town was in bustle and hurry from morning till night. In the early part of the day a Review in the Phoenix Park, where all ranks and classes were crowded together to see poor soldiers sweating and stinking, and great Militia officers, from the mighty Colonel to the puny Ensigns, exhibiting their bravery and military acquirements. City Buckeens on hired horses and with borrowed boots and spurs; young misses slipping away from their mammas to meet their lovers; old maids taking snuff, and talking and thinking of old times; pickpockets waiting for a lob, and old bawds and whores for a cull; handkerchiefs in constant employ, wiping dust, sweat and dander from the face and head; coaches, landaus, gigs, curricles and jaunting cars in constant jostle and confusion in the backstreet to avoid paying money and the shops open to try to get some; mail coaches making a grand procession through the principal streets.

A Levée at the Castle, attended as usual by pimps, parasites, hangers-on, aidecamps, state-officers, expectant clergymen, hungry lawyers, spies, informers, and the various descriptions of characters that constitute the herd of which the motley petty degraded and pretended Court of this poor fallen country is made up. Alas, poor Ireland.

I spent the day lounging about, seeing what was to be seen, and, in proud feelings of superior independence, looked down with utter contempt of the weakness of an administration, imbecile, evasive, and mouldering into contempt; and every loss of public opinion and respect ever must attend the paltry pretended administration of this despicable and degraded country.

After dinner take a rambling circuit over Westmoreland Street and up Anglesea Street. Lounge into booksellers' shops, then to Crow Street to see, according to ancient custom, all the blackguard boys collected to insult and pelt with small stones, gravel, periwinkles, etc. the ladies who go to the Play on this night. Boxes being free for the ladies, consequently it may be supposed what degree of respect is due to that class of the tender sex who avail themselves of enjoying a theatrical treat.

5 June 1813 – Dublin

Dined at the Griffin Tavern, a private and obscure, but comfortable place, No 3 Dame Court. Very good veal cutlets, cold lamb, bread, cheese etc., ale, and a tumbler of excellent punch for 3s 1d. Walked in the evening with Jerry Barrett who I met, and treated him at the Griffin to ale and punch. A piper, according to the evening custom of the house, played in the Box-room, for the entertainment of young attorneys, buck-shopmen, bankers' and merchants' clerks, and those

under-rate would-be sprigs of dash and fashion, who roll into this and such houses to pass their evenings over a plate of cockles and a pint of beer. I, however,
remarked some who possibly pilfer the till now and then to enable them to gratify in this sort of luxury, extend themselves in their expenditure and boldly call
out 'Waiter, a kidney, and be sure let it be nice.' Another, with a gentler voice,
'Waiter, a naggin of raspberry and *meteerials*.' Another, 'A tumbler, half and half,
mix it yourself waiter, and make it stiff, with a slice of lemon on the top.' They
all seemed delighted with the piper, but it was a great annoyance to me who
would have been much more highly gratified by the eccentric anecdotes of Jerry
Barrett than the musical strains of the Orpheus of No 3 Dame Street Lane. Heavy
and affected in my chest the entire of this day, and very glad to get home to my
bed at ten o'clock.

11 June 1813 – New Birmingham
Awake at three o'clock and remain so, coughing incessantly till six. Then, by the
help of tongs, pulled a wire that runs across the ceiling of my barnish-looking
room and procured the appearance of a chamber maid who seemed much disappointed in my not inviting her to my bed, my thoughts being on much better sub-
jects. I did not pity her chagrin but ordered her to send Thomas to me and to
have the carriage brought to the door. I get up at half past six and set out in an
excellent carriage to Maryborough where arriving at half past eight, I have the
misfortune to be transferred to a deal box not more than double the size of a
sedan, which Mr Phelan, the inn-keeper, insisted was a most capital posting
chaise and I was the first gentleman that faulted. I was obliged to be satisfied and
on proceeding drove to fortune, as the handy boy scientifically announced it, until
I got to Abbeyleix where I made him stop on the account of my wanting breakfast, and seeing there some capital carriages at an inn lately set up under the
patronage of Lord de Vesci, I discharged the lad and sent him back with his shay
discomforted at his disgrace. Proceeded after breakfast to Johnstown where
arrived at half past one and leaving it at two arrived at four at New Birmingham.
This day was as wet as ever a day came. I stopped at Dr Meighams, the parish
priest at Pasterville and gave him a dozen Dublin herrings having bought some
this morning in Monasterevan. And I dined myself on another dozen and some
Glangoole eels. Joe Hunt and Mrs Hunt with me. Dr Connor came in the
evening. He considered me much worse than I think myself as I increased coughing and oppression. This evening as well as repetitive pulse I have travelled in a
very weak state forty miles to dinner. It would quicken the pulses of a strong man
in perfect health. He ordered me a blister to my chest and a bottle of pectoral
stuff. Slept at Joe Hunt's in a room most comfortably appointed. Rested tolerably well but had several courses of coughing. Found on my arrival in New
Birmingham, that poor Paddy the weaver died this morning and had not a coffin. Gave a pound.

29 June 1813 – Curragh Chase

An Holiday. St Peter and Paul's day. Compelled the men to work much against their inclination. Father Halpenny the priest, coming to christen Edmond Ryan's child, made a great rout about it, and although I was convinced on enquiry that the holiday was one usually kept, and would otherwise on so finding it out have dismissed the men from work, yet the tyrannical and overbearing manner of Sacerdos in his interference between my tenants and me, obliged me rather than yield to him to continue a compulsion which I felt unpleasant in doing.

1 October 1813 – Curragh Chase

… Reynard the Palatine, and lessee to the impropriate tithes of Adare, besieges me with an horrible bill for tithes, claiming about £26. Having this day paid Mr Croker his tithes or balance of them, I had hoped I would have some temporary respite from sacerdotal harpies and legal depredations, but alas! I am doomed for ever to be a martyr to the imposition and dunment of this class of taxation so truly irritating and obnoxious to my feelings, as well as to the general feeling of this kingdom.

13 October 1813 – Lanespark (having spent the night at Pallace Inn)

Up at eight, after nine hours confinement with my knees to my chin in a camp-bed, schoolboy-sized, scantily curtained and obliged to make up a sufficiency of covering with the auxiliary box-coat of an unknown rascal who was put into a second bed in the room before I was well asleep. I thought on his first entry he might be a robber, as I had no idea of a male companion being billetted on me, but when, by the glimmering of a solitary coal in a pigmy grate, I perceived the fellow stripping, for he brought no candle, my apprehensions on that subject subsided.

The first lodgment of his habiliments, the aforesaid cloak, was made on the only chair in the room, which was at my bed-foot as a support to the end of the mattress, three feet longer than the bedstead, and which was turned up against the chair. The fellow plunged into bed with a crash that shook the room, and the quivering of the bed-posts and creaking of the sacking bottom, for at least a minute after he made good his lodgment, bespoke the ponderous qualities of its possessor.

After spending an hour in grunting, groaning, hiccuping and belching, to my great annoyance, a temporary cessation of his noisome and noxious easements was succeeded by a nasal overture, indicative of his being at length in the chains of repose. I then made that gentle seizure of his coat which I had long meditated and, dragging it through the foot curtains, I made myself the more comfortable for the night.

The morning came and displayed a wyatt window with three panes broke, and the sugar-paper substitute for them blown by the storm of the night on the floor. I looked for my companion and found he had gone. I looked for the coat, which was also gone. I looked for my own clothes, and found all was safe. The rascal therefore was more honest than I expected, or otherwise was afraid of the gallows, which latter construction is, I think, the fairest to be put on him.

I got up, shaved with cold water and a deceitful-looking glass with so many curls and shades in it, one part of it making my face as round as a buttock of beef, and the other part making it as lank and as sharp as a hatchet, that I wondered how my throat escaped in the operation.

After abusing the house and everything in it, except the interesting waitress, I stepped in to a tolerable carriage, to which were hampered a pair of poor unfortunate woe-worn remnants of post-horses. My stage being but three miles, it was judged they had so much work in them, and the last penny was to be taken out of them ...

Arrive at New Birmingham at 10 and find everything wrong. Joe Hunt's cows on my lawn, the entire of it ploughed with un-rung swine, geese dragging the remnants of grass & ducks repasting on worms. The town filthy, dung-heaps at every quarter and turf ricks made in the streets!!!

30 October 1813 – Dublin

Dine at the Ormond Tavern on mock-turtle, a beefstake and raspberry punch. An antiquated gentleman with few ideas but a great appetite, sat in the box with me and greedily devoured a bloody beefstake as thick as a deal board. The only information I could extract from him was that Taverns are dearer now than they were forty years ago, and that the Ormond Tavern then went by the name of the Bird-House, in consequence of there being an aviary in it. His countenance was horrible, his eyes goggled, blear and raw, and his breath was pestiferous. Adjourned to the Hotel, read Hunter's *History of Botany Bay* till ten, and then to bed.

3 November 1813 – Dublin

Omitted in my journal yesterday that I saw the new Lord Lieutenant, Lord Whitworth, for the first time, it being his weekly day of giving audience, and of keeping up the mockery of state in this fallen and degraded sham-court.

He drove in from the park with his wife, the Duchess of Dorset, and one aide de camp, in a plain coach and four postillons in buff cloth, plain jackets, and two out-riders. The castle seemed deserted, few, I believe, seeking audience; and except the mere hangers-on, secretaries and clerks, two or three Generals and Judges, I presume, from appearance, His Excellency was not much annoyed by visitors.

6 November 1813 – Dublin

Dined at Hemy's Commercial Tavern, notwithstanding the glorious news, on a plain and humble dish of tripes, a pot of porter and two tumblers of punch; and after paying the extravagant sum of 3.9½d for my collation, I lounge to James

Hunt's who, I find in overflowing loyalty, drinking the alternate health of the gallant leaders among the allies. I join in his conviviality, drink tea with the ladies, leave it at ten, drop into a book-auction, buy two volumes of the *Anthologia Hibernica* for 5.10d, and read them in bed till one. MEMO: – John Kemble made his first appearance this night in *Macbeth*.

8 November 1813

This being the first day of the Grand Illuminations for the victory of the allies, I amused myself looking at the Show in Sackville Street till ten, and then perambulated the streets in view of this ebullition of loyalty, reading insincerity and disappointment in the countenances of nine-tenths of the blaze-gazers, and considering everyone but myself an idle fool, who strolled about in view of this wax and tallow exhibition.

These celebrations were for the defeat of Napoleon at Leipzig.

13 November 1813

Dine at Nick Mahon's, a party of twenty-four. Dinner magnificent. Having sat at the head of the table, was consequently obliged to devote my time more to the slavery of carving, and ceremonious attentions, than to the luxury of masticating the delicious viands before me, and the sensuality of gormandizing soups, fish, flesh and fowl, assorted and cooked in the most inviting manner, and accompanied with appropriate sauces sufficient to create keen and exurient propensities in the most debilitated and picktooth appetite. Turbot with never-to-be-forgotten lobster sauce succeeding soup, and mock-turtle stewed in Madeira succeeding turbot, produced claimants succeeding claimants on my patience, and in unremitting pressure evinced their determination that no respite should be granted to me.

Each dish was in its turn disposed of, and tantalus-like, I had the mortification to help the last portion of each, and see its china repository flit from my view in the clumsy and hasty grasp of a coarse, unhandy and unfeeling knight of the shoulder-knot, who kept me in constant agitation and dread of having my ear cut or my clothes besauced in his pro and con placing and replacing dishes, and thrusting for replenishment the plates of the rapacious and unsatisfied cormorants, to whose gratifications I was this day doomed to take an active part.

The second course at length arrived, and before me were placed, three plump and substantial sweetbreads. Fortunately for me, the ladies preferred wild fowl. Under the circumstances, I felt more for myself than for the gentlemen, and I neither recommended the dish to them, or offered to send any round. What then did I do? Why, I eat them all, and much good may they do me, and before the removal of the cloth, I successfully accomplished the making good the time I had lost by a further devoural of one plate of apple-pie, another of blancmange, and another of jelly, two custards, two lemonades and a brandy-peach. Thank God, the ladies did not stay long after the removal of the cloth, and I made a

most comfortable exchange from the chilling situation of being a master-of-cer-
emonies to a parcel of women I cared nothing about, to a warm position near the
fire between two bishops, viz., Father Toohey of Limerick and Father
O'Shaughnessy of Killaloe. The rest of the company were, Counsellors,
O'Connell, O'Gorman, Scully and Finn, all celebrated orators of the Catholic
Board, Mr MacNevin, Mr Richard O'Gorman, Mrs O'Connell, Mrs
O'Gorman, beautiful; Mrs Finn, Miss Mary Hussey, Mrs Kelly and several of
minor note whose names I did not know.

I spent a most pleasant evening, the wine excellent and the conversation var-
ied, enlivening, amusing and instructing. We adjourned at ten to the drawing
room, where there was an addition of about twenty people, four cardtables, and a
grand pianoforte at which the Miss Sharkys, the Miss Meades, and Miss Mahon
played and sang delightfully and alternately, and the rest of the company amused
themselves as usual, in hearing, seeing, admiring, lounging, whispering, taking
snuff and drinking tea. I left at half-past eleven, came home, took a pint of porter,
read the *Evening Post* and went to bed.

16 November 1813 – Dublin

Dined at a tavern in Dame Court on whiting, veal cutlets, and oysters in shells.
In the opposite box to me sat a most communicative man who appears to have
been in business in the Liberties, and to be new-retired from it and living in the
country. His name Burgess, he amused me with a detail equal to a gazette account
of the Rising in 1803 under Emmet, in which he, according to his own account,
was the most valiant hero that fought the Battle of Thomas Street on that memorable night. He was then a Liberty Ranger, but, preferring the Line to the
Yeomanry, he joined the Twenty-first Regiment and, if he is to be believed, he
acted more as their Commanding Officer than as a Volunteer. To his judgment,
skill, local knowledge of lanes, alleys and posts, as well as to his gallantry in heading and encouraging the troops, and the extermination of rebels by his own
hands, was, as he assured me, this Insurrection put down. I believed him, polite-
ly of course, and asked him what reward he had got, wondered he did not get a
Red Ribbon, a Baronetage or some such mark of royal gratitude, to which he
proudly answered that he sought no such distinctions, that the honourable recollection of his having been a saviour of his country, as every weaver in the Liberty
well knew, was a sufficient reward to him …

14 November 1813 – Dublin

Strolling about, I see hungry expectants, legal, clerical and military, some old
beaux, some vain country gentlemen, and some remnants of the Irish nobility,
rolling in hackney coaches in costume to Lord Whitworth's humbug levee. Poor
things, how grand they think themselves going in state to the Pseudo court. In
perfect contempt of the mockery, I sojourned to McDermott's Tavern, where I

dined with Chadwick and his friends; the one a faded relic, the other a plump, maukish, gawkish, unlettered, coarse, ordinary lump of flesh. They both ate beef-stakes and veal cutlets as voraciously as if a meat repast was a treat to them; and as to Raspberry Punch, when that made its appearance, they seemed perfectly intimate with it and received it most affectionately. I was sick of the bitches, and leaving them to the care of their friend, I went home to sup and bed.

18 October 1814 – Bruff
Arrived in Bruff at half past one. Fair day there and meet many friends in Bennett's Inn, all in desponding strains, lamenting the decreased value of fat cattle, the best fat cows bringing this day but twelve guineas each. Milch cows high from £18 to £20, pigs tolerably high, sheep low. Set out at two o'clock for Tipperary and meet near Kilballyowen a very fine threshing machine for Decourcy O'Grady. Soon after I had the misfortune to find myself in a crashing machine, for, crash went the front spring of the crazy depository in which I was journeying, and, having extricated myself by a judicious leap-out from the ill-fated vehicle, I perambulated ankle-deep to the aforesaid Bruff, when, then and there arriving, I found the parlour of the Inn occupied by Cork butchers and discontented farmers to whose society I would have unfortunately been consigned for the day but for the hospitality of John Bennett who invited me to his house, where I fared capitally both in board and bed. I was highly pleased at seeing there in a very small square pond opposite his hall door, duck, mallard, cooter and various other wild fowl in great abundance and perfect tameness, and I was particularly amused by the eccentricities of Standy Bennett who, in his way, is both clever and entertaining … he is about to publish a book of poems, which of course I will be among the first to have. In bed at eleven and sleep like a top.

19 October 1814 – Curragh Chase
Eat a most hearty breakfast, voraciously commixing cold roast beef, eggs, toast, bread and butter and tea. John Bennett sat with me and gave me an account of the proceedings of the county: – the fall of rates, the elopement of tenants, break-up of half-gentlemen, stilling of putteen, disobliging conduct of bankers, security of money and increase of taxes. Sated with an abundant breakfast and over-loaded with his commonplace communications, after putting on a clean shirt, purchasing a pair of spectacles and a pair of sleeve-buttons, I set out at one and arrived at Currah at half past four.

4 May 1815 – New Birmingham
Annoyed very much this evening by an itinerant sow-gelder who announces his arrival in town by the uncouth blasts of an abominable horn, to the terror of swine doomed to emasculation, and the disturbance of quiet citizens, retiring to rest at close of day.

18 March 1816 – Curragh Chase

Remove everything from the old to the new cellar, and a most disgraceful stock it was for a baronet's cellar, once well furnished, and into which in former days, two pipes of port were often put in together, two hogsheads of claret brought together, and varieties of white wines' etc. Thanks to the French Revolution and the Warlike ministers who have now taxed wines to nearly a prohibition, and taught the aristocracy of the country to drink putteen. To commemorate them I shall record my stock:- 10 bottles of claret, 1 of Methylin, 4 of Hock, 2 of Madeira, 20 of Barsac and Hermitage, 3 dozen of vinegar and 4 dozen of cyder. Send to Rathkeale for a quarter of mutton, no sheep being now *here* but six cull ewes in lamb and a Kerry horned gale. Such is the remnant of a fine flock, lost by the mange and the neglect and indolence of my servants ...

After dinner sleep four hours, overcome by eating and vexation.

Nicholas Marshall Cummins
1783-1838

AT THE TURN OF THE eighteenth century Cork prospered, largely because it was from there that the British army was victualled during the Napoleonic wars. The Cummins family were merchants who, besides a large British trade, imported and exported to the West Indies. They were a close family who married into a small circle of friends and relations. Many of them had the same names, making it very complicated for a genealogist.

Nicholas Marshall Cummins had married Martha Swete in 1807, when she was eighteen. At the beginning of the diary they lived in Cork, but in 1814 they moved to Dunkettle House in Glanmire; today the house is called Woodville.

The Cummins were haunted by ill health, and most of their children died as infants; Nicholas graphically describes the symptoms of various diseases suffered by himself and his family. He was a devoted family man and he agonized over his eldest son's education, his laziness and use of 'low corrupt words'. (It was this son's letter to the London Times *from Skibbereen during the Famine that made the outside world realize the catastrophe that was happening in Ireland.)*

With the beginning of the nineteenth century a strong evangelical movement swept through the Church of Ireland with which the Cumminses were very much involved. Nicholas wrote up his diary every few days and the entries include lengthy descriptions of sermons he has heard and the theological discussions in which he has participated. He must have been somewhat verbose, for he often writes happily that it fell to him 'to take on the burden of conversation'.

After reading the diaries, one is not surprised that many of the later Cummins chose to make their careers in medicine or the Church.

At the beginning of the diary the Cummins have two children, Marshall and Martha.

* * *

5 April 1810
I rode to Kinsale and took a small house at Scilly for the bathing season at £4 per month, then returned the same evening.

9 April 1810
My dear Martha accompanied me to Kinsale in her father's gig and after examining the lodgings I had taken she found they would not answer, so we forfeited

the 20/- earnest and took a very commodious house from Miss Bishopp by the single month at £8 completely furnished except with linen. We dined at the Inn and supped with Mr Robert Warren, a gentlemanly sensible man.

19 April 1810
On Monday I rode to Kinsale early to prepare for the family. I laid in coal etc. then went in to bathe … Miss E. Shaw and Miss Willis came with Martha – the two following days turned out wet – so that we could not keep the children as much in the air as we intended.

There is an amendment in little Marshall's health already. His sister is pained and hurt in her bowels from the effect of teething.

I returned to Cork this morning and got in by eight. My father has not been quite well for some days back – he loses his rest with pain occasioned by flatulence in the stomach and bowels ...

Oh how thankful ought we to be for the great blessing of health, how dareful to use that and every mercy received at the hand of Providence to the glory of God and the good of our Souls and those of others.

12 May 1810
My sweet little daughter died last night at ten o'clock, without any very violent struggle. She bore her tedious painful illness of a month's continuance with the utmost patience, and was mercifully favored with that calm composure in her expiring moments, which had been remakable in her temper since she drew her first breath.

28 July 1810
We have had a good deal to do this week with Sugars. D.J. Murphy is come home – Trade and manufactures are low but likely, I trust, to mend – we have had abundance of rain.

6 August 1810
Joseph Cummins set out for Dublin on his way towards England. His ostensible motives are to procure orders for Butter; to make some efforts for recovering the 'Friendly Emma's' contested insurance and to apply for our claim on the Underwriters, Samuel Barnett. I think Martha suspects he has a hope of meeting Dorothea Wilmot – if so, I think he is pursuing and indulging an attachment that will end in bitter disappointment whichever way it turns out – for in the first place I doubt whether she would marry *him* were she uncontroul'd by parents and friends, and secondly I am persuaded her father would not consent, and thirdly, I think that if every obstacle were removed and the cordial approbation of all parties obtained, Joe would feel himself uncomfortable in the midst of so highly polished and fashionable a circle as the Wilmots and Chetwoods, and in the last

place there does not appear *undoubted* evidence of D.W.'s being a decided Christian. She is indeed a sweet engaging creature, well informed, soberly inclined and in Martha's company might advance in divine knowledge and be employed in the active duties of a gracious woman – yet there is a hazard.

Joseph was a younger brother of N.M. Cummins; Dorothea Wilmot was the sister of Martha Wilmot, who had visited the Princess Dashkoff in Russia, and also of Catherine Wilmot, who had gone on a European tour with Lord and Lady Mountcashel.

21 September 1811

Nearly the whole of this day has been spent in consulting with Joshua Carroll and Owen Madden respecting a very ambiguous letter received from J.K.C. [his brother, Joseph Cummins] in which the latter has deviated from his instructions apparently, and involved himself and me in an unprofitable, if not losing speculation in Beef and Pork, to the amount of sixty thousand pounds … commit it to Him who ordereth all things well, and purpose thro' his guidance and help to do what is right.

23 September 1811

I am sorry Joe Cummins has undertaken so extensive a part of the Beef and Pork Contract. I wrote to him today, and I fear I have expressed my difference in opinion with him too freely to persons not much concerned in knowing it.

8 November 1811

At twelve last night my beloved wife began to feel the pangs of child birth. I hastily put on my clothes and ran off (on foot) for Doctor Gibbings – he seemed uneasy at finding no conveyance ready for him – but did not refuse to accompany me – the night was wet and dark. I sat in the parlour reading first the testament and afterwards Dr Claudius Buchanan's 'Christian Researches in Asia' until at 3 quarters past two the happy intelligence of my dear wife's delivery of a son was announced by her mother. After having returned thanks to our Gracious God … I solemnly dedicated my infant to His service and imploring blessings on the babe – I resumed my studies till perhaps near four and was then favored with refreshing sleep till near eight. Praise ye the Lord! HALLELU-JAH!

25 November 1811

The Lord has for some days been visiting me with a little gentle chastisement. My left arm pit is sore. May he accompany his visitation with a Blessing, for Christ's sake, Amen.

12 December 1811

This morning I perceive my poor father's eyes inflamed from sitting with Dunsterville, Urquhart and McCarthy to a late hour last night, listening to most improper discourse, and witnessing perhaps needless indulgence if not intemperance in Wine ... I fear we have all been deficient in our duty to those with who we are compelled to associate when we see them grievously sinning and yet hold our peace – it is hard to know how to act ...

23 December 1811

Accounts have been received of the capture of a vessel called the 'City of Cork' on which we shipped 725 tierces India Beef worth about £8200; 30 barrels Beef worth about £160 and 40 Tierces Pork worth upwards of £300. She was carried into Calais. If the contractors have neglected insuring, it will be a heavy loss, and I fear must be a serious disappointment in any case.

23 January 1812

Yesterday evening a fire broke out in J.G. Newsom's store let to D. Callaghan, and destroyed it. Ben Swete and I stood on Patrick's Bridge at about twelve at night and saw the principals of the roof falling in. The tide was in, the night was moonlight and clear. It was an awfully magnificent spectacle. We were thankful that none of our friends were likely to suffer.

Martha says she had a faintishness during the night.

8 February 1812

Since the commencement of my dear Martha's illness I have occasionally had a fullness in my head, and a nervousness – the most disagreeable time to me has been the night, when I have sometimes apprehended an attack in a degree similar to hers. Last night I slept in her room for the first time since her illness. She is tolerably well this morning, thank God, and I have but little remains of the uneasiness in my head.

11 June 1813

On Monday last Martha went on a boating party with Mr Boland and the Parkers of Passage. She had requested leave to go out to sea some day in Mr B's pleasure boat, hoping it may be beneficial to her poor head and stomach if she were to get thoroughly sea sick. Mr B. accordingly made this party.

Dr Bigger and his two daughters, Mr Quarry, Ann, Ellen and Miss H. Pearde accompanied Martha. The day was fine and all things made agreeable, but I suffered much alarm when it approached eleven at night before they returned. I was not without apprehension that an American privateer might have captured them. It proved to have been occasioned by the delay in casting anchor at Roche's tower during dinner.

On the following day my dear wife's head as bad as usual.

13 January 1814

Martha gains ground rather slowly. She dined below stairs for the first time on

Tuesday 11th inst. My little Patty also delicate, coughs much and has an eruption on her skin. Marshall and John continue at Sundays Well. Marshall went to Mr McNeil's school on Tuesday.

17 January 1814

On the second day after Marshall went to school Mr McNeil found it necessary (as he thought) to give him a smart whipping; the marks of which having been perceived by his Aunt Charlotte she made a complaint of it to Mr McNeil whereupon he wrote Martha the following letter:

Madam … 'The correction I assure you was very slight; the reason of its infliction was not, by any means, the child's not having his lesson, but his having persisted in a course of falsehood. He affected not to know his letters, and in words of one syllable … after having been whipped, it so much improved his memory and ability, that he was able to get by heart two columns of words of one syllable, and seven or eight words of two syllables in a very short time. I think him a very smart boy, but in candour I must say that he appears to have been greatly indulged, and that it will require time and perseverance to conquer him … With respect to the degree of severity with which the child was corrected, I can only assure you that it was very slight. The instrument was a rod consisting of two twigs of birch and he only got three very moderate strokes. Indeed I could scarcely have supposed it possible that this explanation should have been necessary.'

22 April 1814

On 20th I dined at Dunketttle with my father and family. The purpose to remove thither in about a fortnight.

Today my father spoke of some hints thrown out … that Martha had invited Lucy Swete to our house in order that Joe may be attracted by her. He said he did not believe that Martha had done so, but if she had, he could see nothing wrong. He mentioned his high respect for Mr Swete's family, but thinks rather unfavorably of any match for Joe except that with Miss Mary Harrison. If Joe should have entirely ceased to think of that young lady, my father's opinion seems to be that he should rather form a connexion with some family with which we are yet unacquainted, in order that his sisters may thereby be brought into notice. Perhaps too my father thinks Joe entitled to an advantageous match in a pecuniary point of view, but on this subject he is silent.

23 May 1814

Sally Whelply who had lived in our employment about two years and four months has been dismissed in consequence of her having married Richard Swords without the approbation of her mistress. I never knew any servant who conducted herself better than she. She is about to take the place of Housemaid at Lord Forbes'. I fear she will find it a dangerous situation.

28 May 1814

Yesterday our entire family dined at Dunkettle, I mean the inmates of my house. Before dinner my father, Mrs C. [Nicolas Cummins' stepmother] and I walked towards Factory Hill, when we arrived at the foot of the wood, Joe overtook us on horseback. He alighted and apparently in high spirits addressed himself aloud to me before my father etc. He spoke of his attachment to Miss Flemyng, of the excellence of her father and mother, and of a conversation he had just had with her father respecting her. He told us that he was very kindly received, that no questions were asked him respecting his own property, and that he had not named the subject when Mr Flemyng acquainted him that his daughter's was 4000 pounds, not in cash, but I think, as Joe expressed it, in some East India or other stock perhaps. Mr Flemyng, he said, proposed to lay all particulars before my father and me this day at eleven o'clock. I replied that we would attend at the place and time appointed, that I believed Mr Flemyng to be a good man, but that I was unacquainted with his family. Joe then rode on towards Annmount where this young woman has been and is on a visit, and we pursued our walk.

When my father and I were alone, he asked my opinion of the projected match; I only added to my former observation an expression of disapprobation in the gentlest degree, on account of the suddenness and precipitation with which so close an intimacy had been contracted.

There were other opportunities of communication between my father and me alone in the course of the evening, but he did not avail himself of them to speak of the business which one would think should seem highly important at present. Susan is deeply distressed at Joe's desertion of Lucy and attachment to one who has not drawn her regard or esteem. Mary thinks with Susan, but is less affected. James pities and I am sure prays for his brother. Charlotte is in Bandon, having left Joe under the persuasion of his steady affection to Lucy.

One o'clock. My father and I have been at Mr Flemyng's. He laid before us several accounts current of the Trustees to his wife's fortune … After slightly glancing over the papers I told Mr F. that his verbal statement would be sufficient to me without any written documents, but that when it should be needful, those might be submitted to professional friends; that I regarded the matter of the connexion itself as so essentially involving my brother's happiness, that for the present I merely thought it advisable to recommend a postponement of any decisive step, until the parties and their respective friends should have leisure to make acquaintance, and enquiry. I ventured so far as to hint at the propriety of his expressing in candour his sentiments of his eldest daughter's religious state. Mr Flemying hereupon instantly said 'Far be it from me to pass my daughter as a Child of God, I approve entirely of what you recommend.'

30 May 1814

After we returned from Mr Flemyng's on Saturday, my father and I met Joe in the market. Joe acknowledged that he believed my interference to proceed entirely from regard to him, and that he knew I was under the idea of his being insufficiently acquainted with Miss F.'s character, but that he was in her company a good deal during the last six weeks, that his mind had been made up on the subject of marrying her for a month, that he knew her thoroughly, and no power on Earth should keep them separate.

(Half past 12 o'clock.) I have just returned from a walk on the Dyke with Mr Flemyng ... He again declared in the clearest and most candid manner that he had no opinion of the spiritual state of either of his daughters; that he had used every means to convey to them a right knowledge of divine truth, and that he thinks they must understand it as a science ... that he had set his face as a flint against worldly maxims in the education and treatment of his children, that he could vouch for their moral deportment ... that he had been well pleased at the intimacy which he had observed between the females of his family and ours because its tendency was no less to lead his children into good company than to preserve them from bad. He assured me that all these feelings had passed in his mind without a thought of any union between our families; and from what I had said he resolved to continue quite neutral and passive in his future conduct respecting it.

22 June 1814

On Tuesday 14th June my brother Joseph K. Cummins married Charlotte, eldest daughter of Captain William Flemyng of the Royal Bengal Artillery – at the Glanmire Church. They proceeded to Youghal soon after, and remain in that town. James is with them.

My time has been employed latterly and is now employed in superintending alterations at our little country residence. Mr Brown the ship's carpenter is constructing a wooden parlour for us. I have given him many religious pamphlets and tracts to distribute and have hopes of good being done through his means.

7 November 1814

From seven o'clock yesterday morning till noon the Mass House bells kept tinkling almost perpetually, to my great annoyance. It is a novelty in this city [Cork], and may do much mischief. I console myself whilst I repeat the 79th and 80th Psalms, and hope the long dormant zeal of Protestants will at length be aroused.

The ringing of bells in Catholic churches had not been allowed since the Reformation.

20 December 1814

Our dear Marshall shews great thirst for knowledge, and I am glad to find him attracted chiefly by the Sacred Volume.

31 December 1814

Trees planted by Mr Thomas Harvey on N.M. Cummins ground at Dunkettle within the year ending 19th December 1814: 5000 oak, 200 ash, 5000 larch, 500 fir, 100 elm, 100 sycamore, 200 poplar, 100 chestnut – making a total of 11,200.

9 January 1815

The last has been a busy week with me. For by detention of the W. India fleet an opportunity was afforded us of continuing our shipments and we did so. This amounted to about Ten Thousand Pounds. Thos. Morton bade us adieu on Thursday or Friday, but they are in the Harbour still, I believe.

20 March 1815

On Friday and Saturday reports reached us of the landing of Bonaparte in the South of France. This evening an account is received of his having reached Paris and of the adherence of the people and the army to his cause. The common people here are in ecstasy. They always admired Bonaparte, but now the depression of Trade consequent on the peace, and England's triumph in accomplishing it, make them long for a renewal of War. I speak of the ignorant peasants of Ireland. May God for Christ's sake protect us, and if it be his divine will may he spare the effusion of blood, especially in the land of our Nativity.

23 May 1815

On the evening of the 22nd May we received intelligence of the insolvency, or at least embarrassment of Messrs French Son and Barton of London who are in our debt to the amount of about SIX THOUSAND POUNDS! Joe went off in the Packet for Bristol last evening on his way towards London. My father and those in our office acquit me of any blame in the affair, for I pleaded hard to prevent so large a sale to one House.

26 June 1815

A blow has at length been struck between the Allies and the French [at Waterloo]. The latter it seems are worsted.

15 September 1815

Our removal to Dunkettle on my father's return to Cork seems now determined on ... Whether Martha will feel comfortable in a long winter night, I can't tell, nor do I know how the boys will go on in learning at home. Whether we shall be annoyed by the visits of unwelcome neighbours I don't know, nor can I see whether the effect on our business may prove prejudicial. One thing gratifies me, and were I to mention it even to those who think most nearly as I do, they would laugh – it is my being placed beyond the sound of the Mass House Bells.

18 September 1815

When I returned to Monkstown on Saturday, I found Martha quite discomposed by the misconduct of Ellen the Cook, from whom she had received shameful abuse. The woman, it appeared, had pilfered some cambrick which was found in her possession. On her charging Ellen with the theft, the latter opened a volley of the lowest sort of ill language in which she mingled insinuations that the Protestants were in the habit of swearing away the lives of the Papists, and that many had in this manner been innocently hanged, but that the Protestants had better beware, for that these things might soon take a different turn etc ... I determined to put the woman out of doors on Saturday night, according to Martha's desire, and for that purpose went into the kitchen, and told Ellen that her wages should be fully paid at the office on Monday or Tuesday, so soon as every article had been counted. She contrived, however, to fidget about for near half and hour, looking, or pretending to look about, for her clothes etc. to take with her; but continuing to rail at Martha in a side way, and less violently than during my absence; flattering me all the while. I hated multiplication of words with such an impudent, vulgar, wicked creature, and for the purpose of getting her off, I tempered my language too much. This added to Martha's vexation, and as soon as Ellen parted she gave vent to it in many tears and bitter expostulations with me. She suffered in her side and head during the night. Hasty words fell on this occasion – such as 'I had rather be dead than have such torment with servants'; 'I will undertake their management no longer'; 'Those who should take my part, turn against me'; etc. etc.

19 September 1815
In our walk to visit the Quarrys at Monkstown last night, Martha accused me before her mother of reproving her in presence of servants, instancing the occasion on which I complained of unreasonableness because I happened to neglect one commission out of many given me to execute in town.

23 September 1815
Two or three mornings ago my dearest Martha ceased to feel the effect of the servant's misconduct, and again grew kind to me.

Marshall advances in history, but abhors dry study.

18 November 1815
Yesterday morning was a teasing one. The masons employed at the steam-kitchen required extraordinary recompense. A stone cutter, a third mason, two carpenters, and labourers all at work within doors, and making every part of the house uncomfortable. Above all, appearances of dry rot below stairs, and the north-west room absolutely rotten in the joists. Martha very ill. The children wandering about unemployed for want of our attention. Victuals greatly consumed. Linen and house articles exposed to plunder. And expense growing! James and his wife brightened us in the afternoon, but midnight brought back Martha's depressed

spirits, and my offences (I fear) in that unruly member, the tongue. Leaks near the cistern have been troubling us also.

3 January 1816

No part of the debt due by Messrs French, Son & Barton of London has since been recovered, nor is there any prospect of recovering anything out of it. The sum exceeds £6100, and many costs were fruitlessly incurred in endeavouring to recover it, and in hunting after a part of the goods which were shipwrecked.

2 May 1816

The progress in Marshall's education is so insignificant that I feel uneasy, and apprehensive that I may be guilty of negligence respecting him. Through mercy his health is excellent, and I am not without hope that his understanding expands. Advantages would unquestionably result from a regular course of instruction at some public school, particularly that great one of having fixed hours for study; yet I am swayed on the other hand by the fear of corruption from intercourse with boys already perverted in their principles. It is scarcely possible for me to avoid his questions on points which ought not yet to be made known to him. May that Wisdom which is from above be our guide, and may we ever act under its blessed influence through Christ Jesus, our Lord, Amen.

17 September 1816

A subject which has often proved the source of disquiet, arose in conversation with my dear Martha this evening; namely, Marshall's slow progress in learning, his idleness, refractory habits, and proneness to imitate the low and criminal language of the labourers. It produced a difference. I am blamed for neglecting to send him to school, or to provide a private tutor. The former I have a strong aversion to, from the remembrance of all the wicked company into which I myself was introduced at a public school, and its unhappy effect upon me. The latter I do not object to, whenever a suitable person can be procured.

18 September 1816

Last evening's consultation about Marshall led me to a measure of which Martha disapproves, viz. the engagement of Richard Harris to attend the two boys during the ensuing three months from 10 till 3 each day, to teach writing, arithmetic and English. The lad is but 17½ years old and of an appearance much more youthful; he is mild, very poor and perhaps boyish, yet of good *professed* principles.

19 October 1816

Our darling John began to be unwell since last Saturday, when he jumped out of the schoolroom window. Ever since he has been sickish, and has a sort of intermittent fever, but thanks to the Lord not violent. Chings Lozenges were given yesterday and today lest he should have worms.

Martha seems very confident that Richard Harris will never answer as an instructor to the boys. I must confess his abilities are inconsiderable, and there is a great difficulty in managing Marshall. But what better is to be done?

26 May 1820

A PANIC beyond example in our memory has been struck into the minds of the trading community of Cork and the South of Ireland by yesterday's events' namely, *the failure of Roche's Bank* at twelve o'clock, followed almost immediately by that of *Leslies' Bank*!

2 June 1820

Night after night my dear Martha and our family have been alarmed at every noise, lest robbers should attack us. May it please God to strengthen our faith in his Providential guardianship ...

8 June 1820

My dear Martha had a very painful time last night. So severe was her illness that we were awake for the greater part of the night and frequently spoke of sending for a physician. She doubts whether her lying-in may not be nearer at hand than was expected. I felt alarmed at the prospect of a *large* increase to my family; but why should I? – Am I not commanded to take no anxious thought for the morrow? Have I not always experienced the Lord's mercies to myself and my family?....

The diary stops in July 1821 and there are just two entries more, following a gap of thirteen years.

Sunday evening, 7 August 1834, near 7 o'clock

I think I have never, since my birth, suffered such deep afflictions as during the present year, hitherto. At the opening of it I found my most precious and ever beloved children Ellen and Joseph seriously ill ... My brother Joseph still affected by the removal of his Emily ... my brother Robert fearing the death (or illness as trying as death) of his elder daughter Eliza ... my brother James hardly venturing to rely on his wife's state of health after her dangerous illness in London ... sister Charlotte, sister Anne, sisters Eliza and Susan, *all* tried with illness and suffering in various ways; business not prosperous, James at a distance. ... In February and March my dear wife took my children to England – there trying all means, at Bath and Clifton etc., under the best physicians, deriving no benefit ... April carrying off Ellen and June following carrying off Joseph ... The totally unexpected illness and speedy death of precious little Lucy early in July, and before the end of that month the bursting forth of still greater sorrow than any experienced before, in the sad misconduct of another connected to us. Business neglected and heavy losses resulting from want of attention and system of affairs.

The almost sudden death of my brother Joseph's daughter Louisa and two of his infant sons.

6 July 1837

My dear wife and my darling daughter Martha went to England last Monday, both of them requiring something to be done for their health. The mother has symptoms of dropsy and the daughter great weakness after the measles.

Our John writes cheerfully to us from Lobs House, Delaware, Upper Canada, where he has been about half a year settled as agent to Lord MountCashell. Marshall is at Timoleague residing with his wife and child. We seldom hear from him or his aunts, Ann Coghlan and Eliza Cummins, who are situated in the Glebe of Timoleague.

Humphrey O'Sullivan
1780-1837

AMHLAOIBH Ó SÚILLEABHÁIN / HUMPHREY O'SULLIVAN lived in County Kilkenny. He had been born in Kerry, but when he was quite young his father, a hedge-school master, moved his family eastwards and set up a school in a small shed near Callan.

Humphrey O'Sullivan describes the shed as being only twenty foot by ten. The sod walls were put up in one day, the timber and lathes were added the next day and it was thatched on the third. Here O'Sullivan taught with his father before moving to Callan and starting his own school there. He married Mary Delahunty, with whom he had seven children, three of whom died as infants; his wife, whom he very seldom mentions, died in 1829.

The diary, which he kept from 1827 until 1835, is written in used school headline copybooks or account books. O'Sullivan wrote over the original writing, making it very difficult to decipher. He wrote in Irish for he loved the language and was fearful that it would soon be lost. He says, 'new schools are being built to teach the Saxon tongue, but alas! no attention is being paid to the fine smooth Irish language, except by wretched swaddlers, who are trying to see whether they can wheedle away the children of the Gael to their accursed new religion'. He was an ardent Gaelic scholar and his collection of manuscripts is now in the Royal Irish Academy.

Callan is a small market town on the road between Kilkenny and Clonmel. H.D. Inglis wrote in his book Ireland in 1834 *that he 'had not yet seen in Ireland any town in so wretched a condition as this,' and described people crawling in and out of their cabins – 'mere holes with nothing in them excepting a little straw and one or two broken stools.' Humphrey O'Sullivan calls the town 'Callan of the Ructions' because of the infamous faction fights in which several people were killed.*

The following extract is taken from the translation by Rev. Michael McGrath, SJ.

***

Monday 2 April 1827
At ten o'clock, I went from Callan to Kilmoganny in company with Margaret Barr, widow, and her daughter sweet-worded, sweet-voiced little Margaret. We had an old, half-blind, lean-bodied, heavy-hoofed, clumsy cart-horse; and we had as driver an unkept dark brown 'guide', to wit, Michael Cuddihy … Kilmoganny is a nice little country town. A considerable number of new houses are being built, at a yearly rent of five shillings for a site for a house and yard. Good brown stone

is to be had at the end of the town out of the side of the hill, with short haulage and plenty of slate at Aughnaslintacha hard by. We came home quietly and easily, after having had a little drop of whiskey at Power's public house … At the weir of O'Brien's Mill there is a waterfall and a fine pond, and an island of willow. The fair maid stood between me and the waterfall, singing, and the waterfall humming and the trees soughing. She stood like a banshee, amid the mist of the waterfall. My very heart was stirred …

Tuesday 17 April 1827

'… However long the drinking bout, its end is thirst.' 'It is sweet while being drunk; it is bitter when being paid for.' The street crowd were very uproarious at three o'clock, this morning. Some of them are still 'three sheets in the wind'. It is no harm to call them 'froth'; for they are the foam, the dirty pool-dwellers, bogtrotters, mountaineers without self-respect or manners. A stormy morning hiding from view and disguising the hills, the mountains and the dark woods around us: a brisk, rather harsh, east wind: sowing oats finished.

Wednesday 18 April 1827

A sunny cheerful morning free from fog: midday, with merry sweet-voiced Maggie Barr and another, I went to Desart, by the same roads which I took on Easter Sunday. We walked through dark evergreen pinewoods through fine laneways, now crooked, now straight, shaded from the face of the sun, listening to the fluting of the lark in the wayside meadows, to the delicate note of the blackbird, and of every other sweet-voiced bird, in unison with the soft sweet liquid-voiced Maggie Barr. We lost our way in a dark mysterious dell, so that we could no longer tell east or west, north or south. At long last we came through mossy hollows, through breaks of briar, glens of ash, groves of evergreen pine to a glade of puddles, pools and loughlets, of rivulets, waterfalls and chattering of birds and streams … 'I am tired,' said soft, sweet, liquid-voiced Maggie. 'So am I,' said I. 'Let us sit awhile on the moss of the rock.' What with the murmur of the waterfalls, soft-voiced Maggie slumbered … The wind blew gently through the weary wanderer's hair, laying bare a neck as white as swan on pool. Her tiny lips were red as rowan berries and sweet as honey, her white breasts like twin snowclad mountainets rising and falling like the waves of the King's River, her slim little waist, her tidy seat, her pretty little legs hidden by her satin gown even to her shapely feet. Suddenly two snipe darted, from a swamp close by, through the air as an arrow from a bow. The beauteous maiden started from her sound sleep … We wended our way faint and weary, her arm in mine, her head on my shoulder, her eyes bent on the ground. I do not recall a happier day.

Wednesday 25 April 1827

Morning, the north-west wind gentle: a grey frost on the high mountains … evening, I went with Patrick Shallow, merchant, to Graigueooly to see his farm.

We saw eight donkeys putting out manure for one person. Donkeys are now more numerous than horses in the neighbourhood of Callan and along the bog, though I remember the time when donkeys were so scarce that a horse would shy on see-ing one of them. A farmer, named Mullaly, from near Callan, paid sixty pounds two years ago for a Spanish jack ass, and he gets a pound for each service by him.

Thursday 23 August 1827
A fine sultry sunny day: sky fogless: a gentle north wind. The O'Sheas of Ratha-phooka are drawing their corn into the haggard. When the mill of Millstreet is working, its gentle whistling, soft and low, is in the distance like the sound of a weaver's loom.

Saturday 10 November 1827
... Thomas O'Looney, medical student, and myself went from the Fair Green ... to the delightful dell beside the mill of Kilbricken. From the eminence by the mill the aspect of the western sky was beautiful after sunset ... Some of the clouds red or crimson, others purple fringed with gold, some of the sky green. Slievnamon concealed by heavy black clouds ... the river the colour of blood from the reflec-tion of the sky ...

O'Looney is a pleasant little gentleman. The night before last I was along with him and other delightful company in O'Callaghan's hotel. We were merry and sweet-voiced, singing and saying 'Hip, hip Hurru,' when Dr Butler came upon us as a cat bent on war might come on nimble mice as they gnawed at cheese, and we all sat as though dumb. 'Go home,' said Dr Butler to O'Looney. 'I will,' said O'Looney bending his knees and bowing his head, his hand the while to the brim of his tattered hat. 'I don't know', said the Dr, 'what knowledge of medicine you'll have, when your term is complete, if you continue on these lines.' We broke up.

Sunday 25 November 1827
For the past fortnight I was not out any day, but at night I went for strolls like the owl. My reason for staying indoors during the day was a little black eye and another still blacker I got from Mr Butler, M.D., on Sunday night, the 11th or perhaps it was after midnight. It happened as follows: A merry company and I were drinking at Margaret Commerton's. Whiskey somewhat tepid, with water and sugar, was being drunk unstintedly by us. Thomas O'Kelly, a young man of business, caught John Forrestal, a medical student, to wrestle with him. Thomas O'Looney thinking that a real quarrel had risen between them, struck O'Kelly a 'bang' on the face and felled him to the ground. Up sprang O'Kelly and began to belabour everybody ... at long last mild Maggie and I succeeded in making peace. 'Alack my dear you have two nice black eyes,' said Maggie to Thomas O'Kelly. 'That makes me all the more like you,' said O'Kelly, 'for a ripe sloe is not black-

er than your two jet-lashed black-browed eyes, nor is the blackbird sweeter on a sunburnt day in May than your sweet red-lipped mouth, so let me sample your fine sweet kiss, my heart's treasure, as I am near you,' – and with this he gave her a kiss like the sound of a battered old wet boot on the bottom of a hot pot.

Hereupon we left O'Kelly courting mild Maggie and went to the public house of Sinclair, an ex-soldier from the devil's posterior in the north-east of Scotland ... O'Menton began to play his scrip scape fiddle. John Aheane and the rest of them began to dance wildly ... So we were enjoying ourselves till mad Butler burst in among us with a short brown blackthorn stick, the devil's own snarl on his face, and fire in his eyes for the flames of war ... 'When the cat's away, the mice are at play,' says he, and with that O'Looney and Forrestal ran off behind his back ... 'Pack up your violin. Don't awake the hatching geese.' But O'Menton kept on playing ... he ran to O'Menton who was huddled up in the ash-corner and dragged him out backwards on to the middle of the dirty floor. Here they both began buffetting and shaking and belabouring each other ... till they were bruised and battered before they could be separated.

Then Butler cast an eye on me as I was seated on my bench and he rushed upon me, as a wolf on a lamb, or a hawk on a lark; he struck me a blow of his fist straight in the eye and put the 'blue rag' on it in a trice. I fell backwards to the ground like a felled ox. This, however, did not satisfy mad Butler. Falling down on me, like a dead weight, he dealt me another blow in the other eye. 'Administer a vigorous blow to every inch of him,' said the alewife, – a yellow, malodorous, obese, yellow-loined, heavy-based, flat-footed, club-footed, dirty hag, with breasts like an old cow's udder, with wrinkled lubber-lips, snub-nosed and flat-nosed with teeth like a plug of tobacco and running red eyes ... 'Beat every inch of him, soft and hard on which his mother ever laid a finger,' said the devil in woman's shape. But, by the strength of friends I succeeded in slipping away from mad Butler ... That is how my little black eye occurred which kept me from seeing a leaf, green or dry, without hearing the murmur of the streams nor the voice of the waves, the lowing of the oxen, nor the sough of the winter wind through the trees.

Saturday 5 January 1828
... Some of the townspeople were putting in order a circulating library. It is a year established. Each member of the association pays five shillings a year. Alas! who will establish an Irish library? ...

Monday 7 January 1828
Pig market day ... My sister's son, James Costigan, was married this evening to Grant's daughter ... by Father James Hennebry the parish priest. We spent the night till three in the morning eating, drinking punch and tea, and singing Irish songs. We came home quietly and composedly, without hurt or injury to anyone.

There was a poor fellow lying at full length in a cart coming home from

Clonmel. He was nearly dead owing to the pouring of the heavy rain on his head and his whole body, and perhaps he had taken a considerable quantity of drink. We stretched him out at full length beside the fire, and we took off his boots and stockings; and thanks be to God, at the end of an hour or two he was cheerful, out of danger and sitting by the fire. He has a hurt on his knee owing to having fallen under a wheel of a cart at Nine-mile-House.

Friday 20 June 1828
... I had dinner with Father James Hennebry. We had two fine fat sweet substantial trout, one of them as big as a small salmon. We had hard boiled hen eggs and cooked asparagus soaked in melted butter with boiled new milk and salt. We had port wine, and punch as good as I ever drank, on the table; and needless to say it was not to throw stones at we put it in the jug.

Tuesday 8 July 1828
... Every window in town was filled with candles all a-light in honour of Daniel O'Connell who was elected in Clare County to be a member of the London parliament.

Sunday 3 May 1829
... Two May balls were taken up (that is a May bush covered with silk, ribbons, flowers, etc. with the ball in the middle of hanging down and covered likewise with adornments), the one from the Grants of Coolalong, and the other from the Walshes of the Fair Green. The young men played for one of them in a hurling match afterwards. Up to this day, no May ball has been taken for the past fifty years, since a man was killed on the cross roads of Callan taking a May ball from a newly married minister, Dr Lambart.

Finn's Leinster Journal *1782: '... A number of people in different parties, assembled at Callan in order to collect may-balls, they disagreeing, a quarrel ensued in which Nicholas Butler, of that town, cooper, unfortunately received a blow of a stone on the forehead and instantly expired.'*

Sunday 28 June 1829
... I sat up all night with my wife who is ill. The voice of the corncrake gives a feeling of lonesomeness.

Wednesday 1 July 1829
... Now, just now at eleven o'clock my wife died fortified, through God's will, after getting Oil and Repentance.

Friday 28 August 1829
... The cottage of James St John, the father of my servant maid, Peggy St John

at Cannafahy, caught fire at half past ten. In less than a quarter of an hour it was burned to the ground. The hen, the sucking pig, the pots, that is steeping vessels, an old straw-bottomed chair, a legless pot, a basin, piggin and a pot hook were saved. The pot-rack pin and the pot hook itself were burned ...

Sunday 27 December 1829

I left Callan after nine o'clock Mass. I got a dark chestnut trotting cob from James Lynch, at Goats' Bridge ... there was snow on every side of me, on plain and hill and mountain, but I did not feel it too cold till I came to Newmarket beside the mountain, where I drank a glass of spirits, half a noggin for three halfpence. On I went over streams dried up by the frost, beside icy lakelets whose names I forget, the needlelike snow swirling on myself and my graceful little horse, snow that was driven by a sharp stinging south-east wind over the breast of Tory Hill, the highest mountain within view. At length I reached Mullinavat, where I went to a good turf fire that blazed up on the hearth, and I got a glass of whiskey to keep me alive ... An excellent dinner was ready for me; a chine of beef new-salted and white cabbage, roast goose with bread stuffing in it; a leg of mutton and turnips, bacon and chickens and roast snipe. There was port wine and whiskey turned into punch; and there was something else, namely Mary Walsh, a fine tall ruddy-cheeked auburn-haired young lady, neat loined, high-chested with hard shapely snow-white breasts. She is about thirty-five years of age and her complexion is not too smooth, for it is lightly pockmarked; but she is well-bred, dignified, quiet, courteous, gentle. She would hardly look at me, or allow me to touch her fair hand with the tips of my fingers, for she knows that I came to see her, on invitation to woo her, or 'to get a hog's shoulder'.

Monday 28 December 1829

... I spent some of the day seeing the City of Waterford and the shipping, and some of it paying court to gentle Mary Walsh. I think I have found the way to soften her heart; for she gave me to understand that she will come home with me. It is many a soft sweet tale I told her tête-à-tête, for Father Simon, and the widow Murphy, and her two pretty young daughters kept out of the way on purpose. Nothing remains but to await the morrow of the 'Twelfth Day' to have us married. I am getting a good dowry with her and I think she will be a good step-mother to my four orphans, for she has an affectionate easygoing mien, as has her brother, Simon, the priest.

There is never another word about Mary Walsh and Humphrey O'Sullivan did not marry again.

Monday 28 June 1830

A fast day that is, the Eve of the Feast of Sts Peter and Paul ... Horse racing begins today near Danesfort south of Kilkenny City. I trust in God that the turf will be soft under the feet of the competing horses, though owners and jockeys do not wish it so; but I, naturally, am more interested in new potatoes than in the enjoyment of an hour on a race course.

Friday 9 July 1830
Pig fair day – few pigs. I sold my own little pig ...

Friday 16 July 1830
... This is my first day wearing new boots, and a black coat and vest ...

Sunday 18 July 1830
A fine thin clouded sunny day ... I went to Kilkenny on foot. I was wearing strong new boots. They hurt my feet severely. I spent the day drinking and in dissipation. This is a sorry trade. Bad was the bed I had. There were bugs in it. I did not sleep a wink.

Monday 19 July 1830
... I was home from Kilkenny at half past five in the morning. The sun was shining gloriously through an occasional cloud, the birds singing pleasingly and I walking barefoot, for the very strong boots are short for me yet, till I get accustomed to them.

Three persons were interred today who died of corrosive sublimate poisoning (I believe), which was, by mistake, in the soup which they drank. Many are ill for the same reason. It was in charity Dean Stephenson gave it to them ... The poor smith escaped the yearly distress, under which the poor of Ireland labour in food-scarce July ... It is well it happened that his wife and child departed along with him, that they did not stay behind him, sorrowful, heartbroken ... gazing vacantly at his forge tools, with no hand to set them to work, to earn for them their daily bread ... His hand will no more set a curved shoe on neighing stallion, on prancing mare, on unkempt gelding, or on kicking fierce colt ... The three coffins were side by side on a cart, under white sheets, and men, with bowed heads, drew the cart with ropes to their last resting place, where the smith was buried deep down on the exposed side, his loving wife by his side and their babe on her breast as was their wont in their marriage bed ...

Thursday 22 July 1830
I see oats being reaped near Goats Bridge. A fine sultry sunny day ...

My son, Denis O'Sullivan, a youth sixteen years of age, and I left Callan at five o'clock in the morning, in the cart of a sprightly little donkey, which trotted away, lightfootedly, with us to Thomastown.

A courthouse is a roasting place on a hot sultry day, when there are many people in it. One of my processes, namely, that against John Cormick of Cooliagh, went ahead: but that against Edmond Maher was adjourned by a trick. Indeed I shall have a long time to wait if Edmond Maher gets his way.

My son and I retired to rest in a fine feather bed, on which were a pair of white clean sheets and every other sleeping accommodation however soothing or fine, but a bagpipe player, Coltan to wit, kept playing, driving, pushing and wrangling with drunken people, so that they spoiled my sleep. My son and I arose and went over to Mangan's, where we slept soundly till six o'clock next morning.

Monday 26 July 1830
... A gentle southwest wind: sixpence for a little stone of potatoes, new or old. The poor are picking the potatoes out of the edges of the ridges or lazy beds. Stark famine is upon them. It is hard to say that God will avenge it on them; but, nevertheless, it is a bad habit; for, if the poor begin with petty pilfering, they will go on to robbery, plunder, rapine and brigandage ... July of the famine this month is called now. Yellowmonth is its name in Irish and it is an apt name; for if the cornfields are yellow, the faces of the poor are greenish yellow, because of the livid famine; for they are subsisting on green cabbage and other inferior odds and ends of a similar character.

Little Humphrey, little Jimmy, my two younger sons and myself went for a swim. The water of the river was quite warm. Many of the young people of the town were bathing.

Tuesday 27 July 1830
... There are labourers on the Owbeg road, at the end of the Common doing spade, shovel and pick work, at ninepence a day, and other men breaking stones, at three pence a day, that is, at three pence for breaking a heap of stones, containing three horse loads. This is a bad division among working men; namely, the gang of Maurice Reid of Kilmaganny to be in receipt of ninepence, and the working men from the Common of Callan receiving only three pence. But I will make serious complaint about this injustice to certain prominent persons, who will have justice done to the people of Callan Common ...

Wednesday 28 July 1830
... Two other gentlemen and I distributed much Indian meal to the poor of Callan, at half price, that is at two pence a pottle. This is a great help.

Friday 30 July 1830
A cloudy fine mild morning ... The diet of my family and myself is as follows: a hot breakfast, consisting of oat-meal stirabout made on milk; wheaten bread and milk at one o'clock, this is a cool midday meal; and potatoes and meat, or butter, towards late evening, as a meal in the cool of the evening ...

The heaps of stones are now made smaller for the people of the Common. They earn sixpence a day. It was no harm to expose the trickery of the vicious steward ...

My potatoes are growing wonderfully.

Monday 6 September 1830
I paid ten shillings to the mail-coach Company. A cloudy, boisterous morning after a windy night. I am going to Dublin to buy goods. I was in Dublin at nine o'clock at night, having left Callan at nine in the morning.

Thursday 9 September 1830 – Dublin
A grand thin clouded sunny day ... I spent a good part of the day looking at ships. The waves that arise from the wheels of the steamers are wonderful; great too is their smoke and harsh is the rough sound of the steam escaping after the steamer stops.

Friday 10 September 1830
... I came home by coach to Kilkenny, for six and sixpence. I walked home from Kilkenny to Callan. I was in my house at nine o'clock, having left Dublin at seven in the morning.

Saturday 11 September 1830
... Last Thursday, I heard an air being played by a band in Dublin Castle, which was like the music of demons. The bass instruments were like a sow grunting to her offspring; the music of the shrill-toned flageolet was like the screech of young suckling pigs ... the trombone like the rough cry of herons – it was not gentle like the lovenotes of the heron; and the clarinets were like the pewitting of the green plover and corncrakes; it was quite unlike tender, sweet, heart-moving Irish music.

Tuesday 26 June 1832
... I am superintending seven men with two carters with their horses which are drawing stones and yellow clay, to fill holes in Mill Lane, so that the cesspools may not bring the cholera to Callan ... The widening of this corner was badly needed, for it is many a time the mailcoach was capsized there.

There was a European epidemic of cholera at this time.

Monday 6 January 1834
Goodwives Monday. The last of the twelve days of Christmas. A heavyclouded, dry day ... Everything is now damp and moist. Bacon is growing mellow in the chimney and hung beef also. A dripping secretion down and an upward oozing in every hovel. Night as dark as Powl-a'Phooca. The rabble or the dregs or the cornerboys of the town beating one another.

Saturday 11 January 1834
A grand delighful, thinclouded, bright, sunny morning ... Fine, dry weather is
badly needed for the country is flooded and the yellow clay is oozing up through
the dirty streets of 'Wrangling Callan' and if it ever was 'Wrangling Callan' it is
so now; for there are two accursed factions, one either side of the River Rye,
throwing stones at one another every Sunday and Holiday night; namely
'Caravats' on the south side, especially round about Fair Green, Green Street,
Mill Street, and Rookery or West Street; and the 'Shanavests' on Guard Green,
Shepherd Lane or Flag Lane and Kilkenny Road. If these factions are not suppressed there will be murder between them ...

Thursday 28 May 1835
Ascension Thursday, a Holiday of obligation ... Hurling and cock-fighting and
a country dance and a cricket match on Fair Green. There are two games of driving: namely Irish, with a hurley and a ball which is struck on the pitch, through
the goal or the loop at the end of the playing pitch; and English cricket with a
bat and ball which is thrown by hand to knock down a little gate if possible, but
the gate is defended by the man with a bat.

Thursday 30 July 1835
A fine, sultry, blueskied day, bright and sunny.

Friday 31 July 1835
Much like yesterday.

This is the last entry in the diary.

Frances & Emily Ponsonby
1812–?; 1820–1856

THESE TWO SISTERS *accompanied their father, Bishop Richard Ponsonby, on a visit to his parishes in County Donegal. Frances (Fran) was his third daughter and Emily (Emmy) his fourth daughter. Emmy married Rev. Charlton Maxwell, Rector of Leckpatrick, in 1852, and died in 1856; Fan did not marry.*

Bishop Ponsonby, son of the 1st Baron Ponsonby of Imokilly, became the first Bishop of the combined dioceses of Raphoe and Derry after the Church Temporalities Act of 1834. Previous to this, the 852,064 members of the Church of Ireland had been governed by four archbishops and twenty-two bishops with a revenue of some £800,000, most of which came from the tithes gathered from the six million Roman Catholics in Ireland. With the reforms of 1834, the archbishoprics were cut down to two and the bishoprics to ten. The year 1837 marked the height of the tithe wars, and it must have been at this time that Bishop Ponsonby wrote to the Archbishop in Armagh an account of 'the destitute Rev. John Wilkinson, Rector of Mervagh, Co. Donegal, whose sons have been beaten up savagely, whose children are barefoot, and whose curate is literally starving, and the rectory without food. In a living worth £325 he received only £121 in tithes during the two years of 1835 and 1836. In 1837, he has received only £30.' It was fortunate that the Rev. Wilkinson did not have to entertain the Bishop and his entourage which consisted of his wife, his two daughters, their Uncle John and also a lady's maid and a man servant.

The Ponsonby sisters wrote the diary together, probably for the amusement of their siblings, and did not differentiate between themselves as diarists.

* * *

Tuesday 19 September 1837

We left Boom Hall on Tuesday for Letterkenny. The road was very rough and the rain very heavy all the way. However we got there safely without any adventure about six o'clock, and found a very good dinner prepared, consisting of every delicacy of the season. Very soon after dinner, we, being sleepy from the great shaking of the carriage, retired to look at our bedrooms. At first, they appeared very comfortable, and we saw a good large bed apiece for us. But, lo and behold! Mamma, in her usual search after spiders, discovered that the wall at the head of our beds was literally dripping wet. Luckily the walls destined for Papa and Uncle John were quite dry. And we, to escape colds, adjourned to the sitting room, for there was one beside the dining room and Mamma had a bed made for herself, partly on a couch, and partly on chairs. And we both reposed (or attempted to repose) in a very narrow *wardrobe* which when opened made a bed and answered very well to Goldsmith's description of 'a bed by night, a chest of drawers by day'.

Here we lay all night with a 'rushlight dimly burning' and surrounded by various prints and portraits, particularly one of the landlord, Mr Hegarty, in his state coat and waistcoat with basket buttons. In the morning we all agreed unanimously on one subject, viz., that though we had escaped the damp walls, we had slept in damp bedding and sheets, but fortunately no bad consequences ensued. There is nothing worthy of record at Letterkenny, being a very ugly country town.

Wednesday 20 September 1837
Soon after breakfast, just as we had made up our minds to stay there another day and spend another night in our wardrobe bed, Mr Irwin, the clergyman of the adjoining parish, came in and insisted on our dining and spending the night at his house, Barnhill, two miles from Letterkenny, which we all joyfully agreed to.

Accordingly we ordered the carriage, and in the first place drove there to deposit our baggage, and to take a view of the landlady's looks to see what we might expect for the evening. We must tell you that the landlady was *not* the landlady, being a married daughter of Mr Irwin's, who was there on a visit and did the honours in the absence of her mother who was in Dublin. Having examined her (who, by the way, was dressed in a figured plum silk gown with its compliment of Blonde, and a garnet Lyre on her forehead, in the *morning*), we drove to Ramelton and from thence to Ramullen, which is on a beautiful part of Lough Swilly. There is a very fine wood which we drove through, which belonged to Col. Knox of Prehen. We saw the Terror there, of which, of course, you have read all the accounts in the papers, of being shut up in the ice for a year. So we shall say no more about it.

In an expedition led by George Back in search of the Northwest Passage, the Terror *had been trapped in the ice for ten months and then nearly up-ended by an iceberg; the ship had limped back as far as Ireland where she had been grounded.*

After Papa had inspected the Church, and after we had seen all the beauties of the place we drove back to our promised dinner at Barnhill, where we did not arrive till near nine o'clock. When we got in we found the company assembled, viz., the man of the house, the married daughter (Mrs Miller, acting hostess) and her husband a Curate, Mrs Irwin's son (also a Curate and for all the world like Mick Buggles, voice etc., etc.). Miss Green, a Canadian niece, with ringlets a good deal below her waist and swivel eyes, and a *young* son of Mrs Irwin's (a regular riot in a jacket, and hair brushed straight over his eyes). Considering all, dinner, etc., was much better than we expected, with the exception of two sweating and blowing servants. A young Miss Irwin of eight years old appeared at dessert, hopping and looking very like an idiot.

After dinner, when we adjourned to the drawing room, the fire was out, and we had no candles. But with some difficulty they succeeded in making a blaze. And Mrs Miller's son and heir, nine months old, dressed in a red calico frock, with red feet and dirty toenails, without shoes or stockings, was brought down to be admired. After some time we got candles and tea, and we sat there till near twelve, when the gentlemen came out. By this time we were rather sleepy *after* the wind and *with* the conversation, which for the last two hours we had kept up by instinct, and we hoped that now bedtime was come. But, alas! on the stroke of one, Mr Miller called out to his wife: 'Margate[?], will you give us a song?' and all our hopes were destroyed! For he struck up a *thing* of which every refrain ended in 'my lassies' and lasted (we thought) for ever. Then we had to play waltzes, and at length towards two, we went upstairs, but not to bed. For when we *did* get to our rooms, we found that Charlotte and Tyrell were preparing to set out for Letterkenny, as they had no rooms for them. Luckily for Charlotte, Uncle John wanted to get rid of his feather bed, which we tossed up for her in a corner of our room, and then we went to bed and slept, you may be sure. Mama had some difficulties to contend with, for she had to skirmish with half a dozen spiders!

Charlotte was the lady's maid, and Tyrell the manservant.

Thursday 21 September 1837

At breakfast, *Micky's* fetch did the honours of the cold meat: 'Mr. I. (meaning his father) shall I help you to beef?' As soon as possible after breakfast we got away and we drove to Kilmacrenan to have luncheon at Mr Hastings, the Rector's House. On our arrival there we were ushered in to his wife, Lady Anne Hastings, who is a little, shrivelled, old woman and is a *great gossip*. Papa went out with Mr Hastings and left us for two hours with her. And by the time he came back, she had put us *au fait* of every report, etc., of the country. Her daughter, Miss McNeill (by her former husband), did not appear that day. After luncheon, having arranged to return there on Saturday, we set out on our way to Horn Head …

It was nine o'clock at night before we arrived at Horn Head House, which belongs to Mr Stewart (Dr Stewart's father). And as soon as were were ready for dinner we were ushered into the drawing room, where we found the company, all (we suppose) starving, and which were as follows: Mr and Mrs Stewart and seven grown-up daughters (virgins), a son and his wife, and a younger son, Mr Butler, the clergyman of the parish, and a Mr Denham (a police constable) who handed Fran in to dinner. Though the first appearance looked formidable, we liked the seven Miss Stewarts particularly and we made great acquaintance with them all during our visit. Nothing worthy of record passed in the evening and we went to bed as soon as we could, being very tired and sleepy after our long walk up the mountain. When we got into our room we flattered ourselves we should very soon be asleep, as our bed looked remarkably comfortable. But, alas! all is not gold that glitters. For after we had been in bed five minutes we felt ourselves *sticking to damp sheets*, so up we had to get, with our sheets on our backs, to air them at the fire which we luckily had in our room. So after doing that and making the bed again, we had not much time left for repose before breakfast the next morning.

It is remarkable how they all fitted into this house, which was a plain eighteenth-century house of five bays, for besides the host and hostess and their nine children plus a daughter-in-law there were the five of the Bishop's party, as well as the servants. Eventually Horn Head House was almost buried under storm-blown sands.

Saturday 23 September 1837
We went back, according to arrangement, to Mr Hastings, taking Ards on our way. It is built close on the sea coast and is a very fine house, beautifully furnished and the gardens and hot houses are very large. Mr Stewart was not at home to do the honours at his place. We believe he was in England. He keeps a large boat at Ards, mounted on wheels, which carries twenty people and in which he generally *drives* to regattas, a most appropriate conveyance.

We had a very good view of Doagh Castle which is nearly opposite Ards. It is a large square tower (looking rather like a ruin) which Captain Hart had fitted up for himself. He lives there quite alone and can exclude or admit visitors as he chooses, by means of a drawbridge and a portcullis. He generally receives his *expected* visitors with a salute of cannons, perhaps his *unexpected* visitors might be welcomed in a similar way, though not with an *amicable* salute, if they ventured to intrude. He is reckoned a very extraordinary man, not very far removed from madness. When we had inspected Ards we continued our journey to Mr Hastings. Instead of re-passing Lough Salt we went a different road and a very beautiful one, through the vale and the lake of Gartan, where we had the advantage of seeing moutain, lake, valley and trees combined. We got to Mr Hastings just before dressing time and we went down in due time to the drawing room anxiously expecting dinner. But, *there is a great deal between the cup and the lip*, as we had to wait a long time for it.

In the drawing room we found assembled Mr and Lady Anne Hastings and a Mr and Mrs Mansfield (neighbours). As yet we had not seen Miss McNeill; that remained in store for us. At length, a few minutes before dinner the door opened and from behind the screen appeared – Miss McNeill!!! Words can not describe her and the impression she made on us. She certainly is the most extraordinary person *we* have ever seen. We shall only *attempt* to describe her hair, which was dressed with a thing like a dumpling down her back and shoulders. Her voice must be left to your imagination. *All we can say is*, that it is *by no means pleasing*. With infinite difficulty we kept our countenances at this *apparition*.

And we had scarcely recovered from it, when the sound of a large *watchman's rattle* in the hall made us all with one accord scream and start from our seats. When we were sufficiently recovered to know what was saying around us, we were informed by our host that it was a summons to dinner used by him instead of a bell. And then – rather late, you'll allow – he apologised for not having warned us of it.

We then went in to dinner, and as there was no *beau* for Fran she was handed in by the formidable Miss McNeill. Nothing was heard at dinner but her voice going on like the dinner rattle – the only thing we can compare it to – and we were all staring at her in amazement. At one time we feared our fortitude must have forsaken us, and that we should have roared when she called out to the top of the table from the bottom: 'Tasty' (which she afterwards informed us was a nickname for Mr Hastings), 'send Franky' (meaning Mr Mansfield) 'some beef.' Surely everyone must have thought that we had great coughs as we choked ourselves with our napkins and were nearly suffocated with repressed laughter. As she ate scarcely any dinner herself, she kept ordering about the servants the whole time. Nothing particular happened in the evening and we all went up to bed. But as the house is very small and the rooms very near each other, and as she had told us she left the door of *her* room open all night, we had no opportunity of giving vent to our long-repressed mirth.

But it was not over for the night, as we had all occasion to go to a *certain apartment* which in most houses *serves but one purpose*. But in this house, we were surprised to see, was put to five or six different uses – being first, the *store room* for bread, groceries, pickles, fruits, and particularly dried lemon rinds hung round on strings. Secondly, it served as a harness room, as there were brackets with saddles, hooks for bridles, curbs, whips, net cars, etc. etc. which were in great profusion. Thirdly, it served as a lumber room containing quantities of old, coverless, deal boxes full of old glass, old brass, old iron, horse sheets, girths, carpets, torn check aprons, ragged night caps, glass cloths, unfellowed shoes, old armour, whalebone rosettes, broken cages, old hearth brushes, powder horns, shot belts, broken snuffers, candlesticks, baskets, 'mugs, jugs and porringers', 'rag, tag and bobtail' etc. etc. And fourthly, it served the purpose *most necessary in such rooms*, and in short, with the exception of *one* there was not *another hole* unoccupied. For filthily, it was the abode of spiders, rats and mice, which took up all the spare crevices. On one wall devoted to the purpose (on a nail put fast in the wall), there hung a most picturesque scarlet nightcap, *à la Turc*. Such is the rather incomplete inventory (for want of recollection) of this repository which *with all*, was so small that it required nice steering to arrive at the *right* seat, and good optics to distinguish it from the surrounding trunks, which you may guess were numerous, from our description. After we had in some degree recovered from our journey through the trunks, we went to bed. Ours was, we think, on three legs, so that we were obliged to barricade ourselves with chairs, boxes, etc. and then we slept, being more tired with laughing than with walking.

Sunday 24 September 1837

Mama was treated, *as the great lady*, to what was called a foot pail – which was, by the way, the only one in the house – but which was, in reality, a *handsome goosepie dish*, made so as to represent paste walls. Uncle John had to get up early to dress, as his bedroom also served as Papa's dressing room, and was so small that it would not admit more than one person at a time.

After breakfast we went to Church. There are the remains of an abbey, twelve hundred years old, close to the Church, the windows of which are made of a very curious stone, which is so soft that you can cut a piece off with a penknife. No one can find out where it was brought from. After Church and luncheon (which was principally supplied from the repository upstairs) we walked to see the Rock of Doon, where all the Kings of Donegal were crowned and where the famous Irish chief, Cahir O'Doherty, was shot. Near this rock there is a celebrated holy well which performed *wonderful cures*. It is especially good for lameness. The country people told us that a great number were cured in an hour, but that it never took more than three days. There are quantities of crutches and rags laid round it as offerings to the saint. At the foot of the rock a fairy is supposed to dwell. And they say that a boy who fell some years ago from the top of the rock to the bottom, and who was not hurt, was saved by the fairy's power.

That night at dinner we had no one but the apothecary of the village, who fell to Emmy's lot. Though we were this evening prepared for the rattle, we could not refrain from giving a slight start at the sound of it. This night we got on better in our voyage through the trunks, having engineered it so well the night before.

Monday 25 September 1837

We got up early and Fran was accommodated with the goosepie dish, which her feet did not get into comfortably. After breakfast we set out, accompanied by Lady Anne and Mr Hastings, to see Mulroy Bay – one of the most beautiful things we have ever seen. It is a very fine bay, full of small islands ... We went to the village of Fanad, where Papa went to see the Church and to visit the clergyman of the parish. But as his glebe was rather far off, we preferred staying about the village, looking at the pretty views ...

We got home in good time for dinner and in the drawing room we found assembled Miss McNeill, dressed rather like an actress and looking as extraordinary as before; Mr and Mrs Boyton and Miss Montgomery (Mrs Boyton's sister) – they are both reckoned great beauties, but we think they are ugly. There was also a Mr West there, who was busy *coorting* Miss Montgomery the whole evening. We had a long, stupid, and seemingly interminable sit after dinner, in which Mrs Boyton chatted incessantly on her passion for insects of every description, spiders included. This passion extends also to every sort of beast, fish etc. etc., and so far as to make her keep live crabs and crawfish in her dressing table drawer, a table covered with silk worms, spiders, etc. and a *ferret*, which she wears as a boa, when cold. Her sister, Miss Montgomery, sat all night without speaking. The only symptom of her living was a continual sniffling, which she certainly did keep up well. By the by, *en passant*, we hear that there either *is* or *was* a marriage on the tapis between Miss McNeill and some adventurous man – we do not know who – someone probably with *strong nerves* and a *good command* of countenance.

Thus passed the evening and we retired to bed, expecting to hear the ghost that haunts the house and gives ten heavy blows so loud that it often wakes the inmates. It has now been going on for years and no one can find out the cause. All the country people believe firmly it is the ghost of some person looking for a *limb*; as the house is built on the site of an old churchyard! However, we slept peacefully, notwithstanding the ghost.

Charlotte and Tyrell were highly amused by their visit at this place, as the cook, who did the honour of the meals to them, was the most extraordinary person. Whenever she offered them anything on the table, she used the language of which the following are specimens: 'I beg to be excused; may I offer you some mutton? pardon the poor cook; I beg to be excused; may I help you to a potato? Remember the poor cook.' And so on until they could keep their countenances no longer and were near asking her why she wanted to be excused!

Tuesday 26 September 1837
We left Mr Hastings to go to Drumboe Castle (Sir Edmund Hayes). The road to it is very wild and hilly. You do not see even a cabin for miles, till at last you come to the village of Convoy and two miles further on you come to Stranorlar, where old Harry Stewart has such a beautiful estate, so well planted. Drumboe Castle, which is close to Stranorlar, is a very comfortable house and a nice looking place ... Lady Hayes is a very nice person, and does the honours very well. Sir Edmund looks and, we believe, *is* stupid enough, but he was very good-natured to us and asked us to return there. We had a few of the neighbouring clergy at dinner and our bed here possesed four legs and was very comfortable ...

Wednesday 27 September 1837
... Immediately after breakfast we had to go to Inver ... We went to see a famous spa near the town [Donegal] which we tasted and it has a very disagreeable taste, but is reckoned very wholesome for people with delicate stomachs. There is a very nice establishment of hot and cold baths of every description, very well fitted up. We then proceeded to Inver ... This house and place and everything about it is the picture of comfort and Mr Montgomery is so hospitable and good-natured.

Friday 29 September 1837
We got into the carriage and drove to Killybegs which is quite on the sea coast ... We drove on to Mr Ewing (the rector)'s house and were ushered into a room con-

taining one white and three red haired girls. Mrs Ewing informed us she had not prepared any luncheon for us, as she had been invited to meet us at a *lunch* at Mr Hamilton's of Fintra, a mile further on.

Mr Hamilton is a great friend of Mr Johnston's, who had begged of him to show us *civility*. So the poor man thought he could do no less than have a *fine repast* ready for us, which he certainly had. We were ushered into the drawing room, where we were *astounded at the sight* that met our eyes, which was Mrs Hamilton in a butterfly cap made of tulle and blonde, and quantities of ribbon-wire, which seemed to say exultingly, '*I am* a butterfly!'

As Papa would not have luncheon, he set out immediately on a car to another parish, six miles distant, which a carriage cannot get to, and as there was no scenery worth seeing, we did not go. So we went into the parlour and the first thing we saw was a profusion of roses, hollyhocks, fuschias etc., in which a numberless quantity of dishes were embedded. One in particular attracted our notice, which was a bastion of rice, surrounded with a trench of custard and flag of fuschia, flying from the tower. In the middle of luncheon Mr Hamilton (who scarcely spoke from extreme shyness) rose and decanted two bottles, and approaching Mama with one, filled her out a capacious *beer glass* of a liquid, which she supposed to be cider and of which she was preparing to take a good drink, when she discovered it was champagne, and in consequence, took a more moderate share in it. After this magnificent repast, we walked to the seashore, where there is a beautiful strand. And having looked at everything worth seeing, and having taken leave of our hospitable entertainers, we drove back to Inver. At dinner Fan was very amused by one of the clergymen dining there saying to her, 'Miss Ponsonby, I was just going to *challenge* you,' meaning 'I was going to ask you to drink wine.'

Saturday 30 September 1837

We set out for Cliff. We again passed through Donegal and drove to Brownhall, a most beautiful place on our road, belonging to Mr Edward Hamilton. We had a great deal to see there, as there is a very curious subterranean river running through the place, which is well worth going a great way to see … We arrived at Cliff in good time to unpack before dinner. The house is built on a cliff overlooking the river Erne, which is a very beautiful river, having steep banks on each side covered with planting. The house itself is very ugly and badly planned inside. The ground floor is almost all given up to reception rooms and those are very cheerful and pretty; but the upper storey is very bad inside.

When we got there we found Mr and Mrs Fenwick who stayed there that night, and two or three clergymen, besides Mr and Mrs Hamilton. The Conollys are very pretty children. The two eldest girls were the only ones that appeared in the evening. After dinner the party broke up early and we went to bed with an injunction to be ready at nine o'clock in the morning for prayers and breakfast.

When we got upstairs we inspected our beds, which were small but apparently comfortable. Emmy had no pillow, but she did not mind that. But when she had been in bed about five minutes, she felt her head and cheek getting wonderfully sore, but still said nothing for a few minutes, when she felt her head aching more and more. And just when she was beginning to think she could bear it no longer, Fran began to complain of *her* head. As she had a pillow she was not so sensitive to pain at first. At last we resolved to get up and strike a light to find out what hard materials our bolsters were composed. We thought the best way of finding out would be to pierce a hole in one of them, which we did. And then indeed we had no difficult in accounting for our sore heads, as we ascertained that they were both stuffed with large-size quills, one of which we pulled out. And the next day we applied it to its *natural* purpose by making it into a pen and writing a letter with it.

Sunday 1 October 1837
We came down without broken heads, at nine o'clock to breakfast. We went to church at Ballyshannon, which was three miles from Cliff, and afterwards we walked to the village of Belleek, which is very near the house, to see one of the beautiful salmon leaps on the river. In the evening we had a large congregation at prayers, as a great many of the country people who lived too far from the church come there, and Edward Conolly reads a sermon and evening service. This night Emmy had asked for a pillow, which luckily they were able to procure, as Mrs Fenwick had gone away. But she had still some difficulties to contend with, as they were rather *too* generous and gave her Mrs Fenwick's pillowcover with the pillow (which she had not bargained for), and not liking the thoughts of her face having been on it, she had recourse to pocket handkerchiefs, which made a very good cover.

Monday 2 October 1837
… That evening at dinner we had two or three clergymen and the doctor of Ballyshannon and his wife, Mrs Crawford. The doctor never opens his mouth except to make a bad pun, which his wife seemed to think cannot be surpassed in excellence, and she kept continually saying 'that doctor must have his fun'.

The rest of the diary is torn away.

Sir John Benn-Walsh
1798-1881

SIR JOHN BENN-WALSH *owned 8900 acres in County Kerry and a further 2200 acres in County Cork. He never lived in Ireland, but ran his estates as a business enterprise with the aim of improving the profitability of his investments. He lived in Warfield Park near Bracknell in Berkshire and at Ormathwaite near Keswick in Cumberland, but his largest holding was in Radnorshire, where he possessed 12,400 acres. Between 1821 and 1864 he visited his Irish estates on twenty different occasions – usually in August or September for two weeks.*

The original family holding in Ireland was made in 1764 by his great uncle, John Walsh, out of the profits of a successful career in the East India Company. At first the lands were let on long leases of three lives to middlemen; of the eleven farms that comprised the Kerry property, seven were still in the control of middlemen in 1829. Benn-Walsh disliked the middleman system, which did almost nothing to improve the land and buildings, so whenever possible he took the properties into his own hands and from then on they were let only on an annual agreement to tenants who, if they were lazy, overworked the land or subdivided their holdings, were evicted. He did not allow fear of public abuse or unpopularity to deflect him from any action, though in one entry in his diary he describes himself as having 'a timid, anxious, apprehensive nature, always conjuring up possible misfortunes'. But his apprehensions and anxieties were only for himself and his fortune; he never attempted to visualize any future for his evicted tenants.

In the management of the land he was more exacting and more progressive than many of his fellow landlords, and during his ownership the productivity of his estates was greatly increased. Farms were enlarged to make them more efficient. Wet fields were drained, limed and fertilized with sea sand; rivers were banked against flooding; new roads cut and tile yards opened. He rebuilt farm houses and added barns and outhouses. As a result, his rents in Kerry rose from £3439 in 1829 to £5317 in 1847 to £7933 in 1866, though this last figure included an additional 700 acres.

A staunch Tory, he entered parliament in 1830 as one of the members for Sudbury in Suffolk and later for Radnorshire. His long and devoted service to the Conservative Party was finally rewarded with an elevation to the peerage as Baron Ormathwaite.

Though he visited his estates in 1821, the diary for that year is missing as are those for 1825 and 1829. In 1823 he paid his first recorded visit to Ireland. He was in the process of recovering from a middleman the possession of two of his farms, Derrimdaffe and Forehane in Kerry. He travelled from Dublin to Limerick by the 'new coach', which took sixteen hours. The next day he continued his journey to Listowel.

* * *

Friday 11 April 1823
I went over the farms of Derrimdaffe & Forehane again accompanied by Mr Gabbett [the agent] & Kane the land drainer. The latter assures me that Derimdaff in particular is an admirable subject for improvement. The peasantry of this part of the world are by his account totally idle eight months in the year; they will therefore cheerfully assume very high rents for their farms if they are allowed to work out a portion in labor, & thus a landlord may carry on very extensive improvements at little expense. On Derimdaff there is a superabundant population; however as there is so much work to be done, this is less to be regretted. I shall set to the tenants by the year, take a part of the rent in labor, & get rid of the poorest by degrees. We returned by Forehane where much may be done, though it is not so good a subject for improvement as Derrimdaffe.

Saturday 12 April 1823
We spent the whole morning arranging the setting of Derimdaff & Forehane, which we at last concluded very satisfactorily, at least so far as regards Forehane. The Derrimdaffe tenants are poorer & seem less regular characters.

Benn-Walsh went by coach from Tralee to Cork where he visited his Cork estates, which consisted of four large farms – Grange, Ballygromans, Classis and Fergus – all on the Ballincollig side of Cork city.

Wednesday 16 April 1823 – Cork
The subagent who has been acting for Mr Gabbett, a Mr Holland, called after breakfast & accompanied us to Fergus. This farm is let to the undertenants since it has come out of lease. Some of the poorest & worst have been refused & their lands let to others. They have kept possession, however, & it requires some firmness & address to get them out. We went all over the farm, followed by a rabble of tenants. We at length appointed them all to come to Cork tomorrow.

Thursday 17 April 1823
We were engaged all day in settling the claims for these tenants. I paid a short visit at the Bishop's & returned to my labors. We adjusted all these pretensions at last, except some people of the name of Danahy [Dennehy?] who must be proceeded against.

Benn-Walsh visited his estates again in 1824 and 1825; but though he writes in his diary that it is absolutely necessary that he 'must continue to visit and superintend, as the agent Mr Gabbett is a non-resident and has many partialities in the country, & would go over the business in a very slovenly, negligent manner if I were not to accompany him', he did not return until 1829 – for which year the diary is missing – and then not again until 1834. He came first to Cork and spent five days there before continuing on to Kerry.

Saturday 16 August 1834 – Listowel

I had a long day over at Derrimdaffe & Forhane. These were my pet farms on which I first tried improvement, & certainly I have much reason to be satisfied with the result. The whole appearance of them is changed. The tracts of coarse, wet, mountain, heathy pasture have disappeared, & good pasture meadows, fields of potatoes, oats, & wheat have taken their place. And all this has been done upon Derrimdaffe, although from some flaw or alleged incorrectness in the ejectment, the heir of Wall has been bringing suit after suit against me to recover possession, & now there is a trial pending in the courts in Dublin. These poor people have great merit in reclaiming all this land on so uncertain a tenure. They admitted to me that their farms would now bring in a great increase of rent. It is admitted on all hands that the Kerry farms, particularly those called mountain farms, by which is meant a wild, heathy pasture, have been vastly improved of late years. Whole tracts have been brought into wheat & other tillage, & sea sand & lime drawn to them in great quantities. The rents of all my farms used to be made by butter & stock; a great portion is now paid by corn. Forhane is quite as much improved as Derrimdaffe. As usual, I was beset by a levée of petitioners when I entered Listowel.

Monday 18 August 1834

I rode to see Crotto. This estate with a pretty moderate park, or demesne as they call it in Ireland, belonging to a Mr Ponsonby, & which is shortly to be sold under a decree of the court to pay off numerous charges upon it. Gabbett mentioned it to me, having just heard of the proposed sale, as a purchase which, were I inclined to invest here, would square my property, as it joins both Ballyrehan & Derivrin, and Mr Ponsonby, who is a young man, called upon me two or three days back to try & coax me into it … Accordingly I mounted on Mrs McElligot's pony & trotted over. It is six or seven miles from Listowel on the Tralee road. It is quite a Castle Rackrent as far as the building is concerned, an old ruinous house nearly two hundred years old, but the place altogether has capabilities of being converted into a very pretty gentlemanlike residence. There is a great deal of wood on the property covering some hilly ground.

Mr Ponsonby is, I find, a second son. The elder was disinherited by the father. This one was in the navy but left it & married on coming to this fortune, which is in fact a mere nominal thing, as it is eaten up with debts & charges. He seems a complete specimen of the embarrassed, broken down Irish squire – with rather pleasant, open manners & some plausibility, but with a thousand schemes & points & objects to carry, against whom one must be perpetually on one's guard. It was his plan, by getting me to buy the demesne & one or two farms at an extravagant rate, to raise money enough to pay off the charges & to clear the remainder, but I have no idea of purchasing at all, except it be the whole under the decree of the court. Then he had another design of getting himself appointed my agent & living at Crotto in that character. A pretty agent, a man overwhelmed with debts & encumbrances! Then, in case he could manage to retain his place, he wants to take Ballyrehan when it comes out of lease by Hilliard's death, & in truth it lies very handy to him, being close to his gate. I neither intend to make him my agent, not to let Ballyrehan to him, nor to give him more than the market value, nor to purchase only a portion of his property, but I endeavoured to parry all these attempts & to extract what information I could from him …

It certainly would make a pretty addition to my property in this part of the world &, by adding a place & residence, give it more importance. No property is more improving than Kerry, & this would pay a good interest now with ultimate increase. Yet on the other hand, there is the agitation here, the clouded political horizon. The chance of a combination against rents similar to that against tithe, and the trouble & risk of making & accepting title to an encumbered Irish estate. I took some luncheon with Mr and Mrs Ponsonby. She is a pretty young woman.

He did not buy the estate. His next visit was not until 1844, when again he landed first in Cork, having come over in his yacht The Arrow. *He visited again in 1848, when he came from Dublin to Limerick by train.*

Wednesday 4 October 1848
Mr Gabbett breakfasted with me & we started by 10. The Great Southern & Western is a slow railway. We arrived at Limerick at ½ past 5.

Thursday 5 October 1848
We left Limerick by the Tarbert steamboat at 10. The day was cloudy and windy, with occasional heavy showers. We had a pleasant sail nevertheless to Tarbert. Opposite Stafford O'Brien's place we picked up Sir William Clay & Mr Parker of Sheffield, the Lord of the Treasury, who were going to Killarney. Mr Gabbett & I found a car at Tarbert which took us to Gortshanavoe, where we stopped & went over the farm. I have not visited it since the middleman was ejected & it came into my hands about two years ago. Much has been done to improve it. I have got some good tenants & ridded the farm of some bad ones and some cottiers. Thorough draining has effected an improvement on several lots, & altogether it is now a very improving estate. But the failure of the potato crop seems universal. We rode into Listowel & took up our quarters at Mrs McElligot's.

Saturday 7 October 1848
We went all over Derrimdaffe. This farm & Forhane were the first upon which I began extensive improvements … after my first visit to my Irish estates in 1821 …

Derrimdaffe is wonderfully improved & in a few years more, if everything is not destroyed, will be extremely enhanced in value. Wall, the middleman I ejected, paid me £180. I raised it on getting possession to £260 & in 1838, after having made all the fences & roads, to £400. I am now underdraining it, & it will eventually, I dare say, be worth £600.

I have resolved to remove two of the younger tenants, Neligan & Hartnett, & to emigrate them. The farms will then be all large ones for the country ranging from 35 to 62 Irish acres & averaging near £40 rent.

Monday 9 October 1848

I did not feel very well. However, I went over Forhane. Captain Holmes called and asked us to dine with him tomorrow. Both on Derrimdaffe & Forhane we have got rid of some bad tenants & are throwing the farms into larger divisions. I have dispossessed young Corrigan from Forhane & given his division, which was £50 per annum, to one of the Curtins, who throws in his farm to his brother's & thus makes another £50 tenancy ...

He returned in his yacht to Cork in 1849 and after seeing his estates in Cork went on to Kerry.

Thursday 16 August 1849

The day showery ... At Gortshanavoe changes have taken place since last year. The fever & dysentery have made great work among my tenants in different places. Stack died of it. Michael Nowlan gives up his land & I emigrate him, & we have got a promising new tenant, Dillane, for these two lots.

I had this evening a conversation with Mr Flood, the Vice Guardian appointed by the poor law commissioners, which utterly dismayed & appalled me. The picture he draws of the union is frightful. Since last year the debts have increased eightfold & the union owes about £40,000. There are now 22,000 paupers on outdoor relief out of a population by the last census of 78,000, now probably 10,000 less. He estimates that there are not potatoes to feed the people three months even if the crop be good, & the blight has reappeared in many parts. The vice-guardians have already collected all the produce of the butter in rates, & they are prepared to strike another in September to secure the produce of the harvest. The fact is that the landed proprietors are now the mere nominal possessors of the soil. All the surplus produce levied by the poor law commissioners. If, after they have stripped the tenants of all their returns, the landlord presses for his rent, the stock is sold, the tenants abscond, the land is laid waste, rates accumulate, & finally the land is sold under the powers of the new act to pay these charges, which are enforced by powers so arbitrary & tyrannical.

These lamentations and the 'heavy stroke' in the next entry refer to the passing of the Encumbered Estates Act of July 1849, which forced the sale of bankrupt estates, but as

Sir John was perfectly solvent his anguish was unnecessary and indeed after 1854 the land values improved dramatically.

Friday 17 August 1849

I am deeply affected by this most heavy stroke, by which my Irish property is rendered as valueless as a Jamaica estate. I went today over Derrimdaffe ... Since last year I have emigrated the families of three insolvent tenants: young Hartnett & his wife, Cornelius Guerin, & Neligan. They are, I should think, nearly twenty persons. Patrick Guerin died of the fever and these vacancies have enabled me to consolidate the farms among the good tenants, which in better times was my great object. Derrimdaffe has been much improved and is still capable of great additional improvement. The tenants all appear in good heart & are trying all they can to manure & improve their lots. I was grieved to see upon Connor's land one great instance of the potato blight in a whole field. We are bored every night by a certain Mr Leslie Foster, a son of the late judge, a pragmatical coxcomb who besieges us with jabber.

Monday 20 August 1849

We went over Ballyhaurigan ... then passed by the road across the bog to Lissihane & Knockburrane & finished with Ballyrehan. We had quite an affecting scene with the pretty heiress of Knockburrane, Regan's daughter. It seems her mother has taken to drink, uses her ill, & is running through the property as fast as she can. The poor girl in despair thinks of going to America.

This day completed the survey of my estates, with the exception of Killarida which as being held by a middleman, I do not care to visit. At any other time I should have derived great satisfaction from the evidences of their improvement & the advantages perceptible from my having always kept the population in check & latterly reduced it so much by emigration. Now all is poisoned by the reflection that it is done in vain.

Tuesday 6 August 1850

... I left Dublin at 10, secured a place in the coupé, & enjoyed a most lovely day, though there were one or two thunderstorms. The carriages, line etc. are most admirable on this Great Southern & Western, but I observe very little traffic; they run but few trains & I could not but deplore my rashness in investing £5300 in 100 shares in this undertaking. I reached Limerick by 1/2 past 3 ... Cruise's is a comfortable hotel. I walked on the quay after dinner & saw an emigrant ship. They may talk of horrors of the middle passage, but I cannot think there is much difference between the accommodation for the whites & the blacks.

Friday 9 August 1850

We went today to Derrimdaffe & Forhane (my two first essays in the way of improvement). Since the potato famine I have emigrated several of the worst tenants & enlarged the farms. Everything is now promising & would be in the most rapid progress of improvement did not the famine, the poor rates, & the adverse spirit of legislation defeat all my endeavours. The tenants are still in good heart & exert themselves to improve.

We crossed the bog to Ballyduhig … where we are now making fresh divisions and reletting the farm. I have some promising tenants upon it, particularly Walsh & Kenagh. The latter is a most improving tenant and has a most notable, stirring wife. They gave us a little entertainment of tea, eggs, bread, & butter. It was pleasant to see so much activity & spirit. They seemed such good creatures. She exhibited her dairy, her calves, & her homespun linen & towels with great pride. How hard it is that the times should be so adverse to these industrious people.

For his visit in 1851, he again came by train to Limerick.

Friday 22 August 1851
It was a wet morning. We went over the workhouse & saw the paupers in a state of mutiny at the establishment of a capstan mill for them to work at. However, they succumbed at last …

Tuesday 26 August 1851
The weather is very stormy & wet. I went over Derrimdaffe, which is now in a very satisfactory state. No paupers, the farm let to good tenants, & the drainage & other improvements telling. The great criterion in these times is to watch whether the farmers are increasing their cow & dairy stock. If they are reducing their cattle & ploughing up their lands, depend upon it, they are going to the bad, but if they are adding a collop or two to their stock, the productiveness of their farm & the security for their rent are both increasing.

Saturday 9 October 1852
Mr Gabbett had a rent day & a very unsatisfactory one, only collecting £170. I went to see the workhouse. Phillips, the clerk, a very active, intelligent officer, gave me a good deal of information. There are now only about 1500 paupers in the workhouse, & the great majority of these are deserted children. All the auxiliary houses are now shut. Still, the rates this year have been heavy in consequence of our paying old debts & balances & building a large addition to the workhouse. Phillips is anxious to leave his situation & begged my interest to get him some employment. The active, resolute matron Miss Fitzall, whose manner of managing the unruly paupers struck me so much in former visits, is absent and alas, I heard from Captain Home that she is vehemently suspected of having left for the purpose of being confined. Phillips is supposed to be the father …

Saturday 16 October 1852
Rahilly came in & I promised him, after a long discussion, another year's trial.

Since my threats the tenants have come in. The first day we had only £170; now we have made up £630, which with the Cork levy, makes a sum of £1200. This is the best haul I have had since the famine ...

He came again in 1853 but not in 1854. In 1855 he was in Cork.

Saturday 16 September 1855
Gabbett came & we set out to visit Ballygromans & Grange at 12. Ballygromans may be taken as an example of the benefit which the emigration has effected for Ireland in spite of the clamour of the priests & anti-Malthusians. I come first to Henry Reid; he was in partnership with two brothers, both of whom have emigrated with their families; they were all struggling with beggary; he is now a thriving farmer; I have given him not only the three brothers' portion but a slice of Wiseman's & half of Pat Murphy's. He has 16 cows & intends soon to have 20. Pat Murphy I have ejected & divided his farm between Reid & priest Walsh. I have now but six tenants instead of eleven on the whole farm, besides having got rid of younger brothers & their families in every lot ...

Sunday 2 September 1855
I was a little indisposed yesterday in my walk through the farms with bilious diarrhea. I took two of Digby's mild blue pills & remained late in bed, amusing myself with The Newcomes, a very clever novel of Thackeray.

Wednesday 12 September 1855 – Listowel
This is the first wet day we have had and today was not a regular wet one, only showery & misty. We went to Derrimdaffe, a farm which I have always an interest in visiting because it was one of the first which I got into my own hands when I first visited the estates, & I can mark the improvement extending over 30 years. When I first saw it, it was a perfect illustration of the evils of middlemen's rule. It had been let by my great uncle Walsh about the year 1790 at a rent of £180 on a lease for three lives, the usual tenure then. Two of them were flourishing in 1822 & may be alive now. They were two tough, strong maiden ladies about 40. Wall (the middleman) had never resided on the farm a bit more than I had myself. He had sublet it to about twenty occupying tenants at a rent of, I think £250 ... The idea of improving the farm was never in his head for a moment or in those of the tenants. I do not recollect how many partnerships & subdivisions there were, but altogether the holdings scarcely averaged £10 each. The farm contained 763 English acres. A great portion was shallow bog & wet moor, what they call mountain land, not meaning by that hilly ground, but wild, heathery land which has never been cultivated and pasturable only for young dry stock. Stuck about in this wild, desolate tract were a number of poor cabins wherever the tenants could find ground dry enough for their potato gardens. There was some good land in the centre of the farm, some dry ground on the upper part, & a considerable

extent of wet, rushy fields sloping down to the river Smearlagh, on which cows yield a good deal of butter in summer, but which was useless in winter for tillage.

I remember that I owe recovering the possession of this farm to old John Sheahan, the driver or bailiff of those days. Old Mr Gabbett, who had a leaning to the middleman system, was always very averse to bringing ejectments. On my first visit to Kerry, I was talking over the farms with Sheahan, whose Irish accent, want of teeth, & a peculiar voice, or rather two voices, one high, squeaking treble, the other a deep, guttural bass, rendered him almost unintelligible to me. We were discussing which of my farms was nearest to me, by which he meant which would soonest revert to me by the determination of the middleman's interest. 'Be dad, please your honor, I think it is Derrimdaffe will be the nearest.' 'Derrimdaffe, Sheahan, why there are two good lives against me that may live these 50 years.' 'Bring an ejectment, please your honor.' 'Well, if I do, there is a valuable interest in the lease & they will be sure to redeem, for the arrear is not heavy.' I have old John Sheahan before me at this moment, his bent figure, his hard, crab apple face, his small twinkling, cunning eye, as he came closer to me, & striking his great, gnarled knotty fist upon the table he hissed out in a hoarse whisper, 'they canna redeem, they haven't the *manes*' ... Acting on this information, I brought the ejectment, which Gabbett rather reluctantly did, & the event justified Sheahan's prediction. I recovered possession.

... I began by dividing it into fields of about five acres & dividing the farms afresh by large bounds ditches & dikes. I think the farms were 17 in number, for we did not venture to eject many of the occupying tenants. This was the first great commencement of improvement. The land was partially drained by these deep ditches (underdraining was then unknown), & they managed to till a great portion. The bogs, which were shallow, were gradually cut out & reclaimed ... The time was now come when I thought I might reasonably derive some benefit from my expenditure & improvements, & I raised the rent to what it now is, a little above £400, about 12s an acre. I must mention that I built good, comfortable cabins for almost all the farms at a cost of about £20 a cabin, to which I added barns for £15. There was a great outcry at the time, but this farm has held its own better than most during the famine years.

The next start the farm made was the introduction of thorough underdraining by Bruce, the Scotchman I brought over after my visit in 1848 ... Another great means of improvement was the high road from Listowel towards Kanturk which was made through the farms & from which I made little farm roads to each of the holdings. The next event in the history of the farm was the great famine, which enabled me to reduce the number of farms to eleven, giving an average of about 70 English acres & a rent of £36, a fair size for Irish farms ... During the famine I also greatly extended thorough draining, & many of the lots are nearly completed. Such is the history of Derrimdaffe. It is now worth, I dare say, another £100 a year ...

Sir John Benn-Walsh

His last visit to Ireland was in 1864.

Wednesday 25 September 1864

… I leave Listowel tomorrow and thus complete my visit to my Irish estates. Shall I ever see them again? God knows. Forty-two years have passed since my first visit. I sometimes compare myself to a little king who has had a long reign. I have done much for these estates and never, I think, made any considerable mistake in their management. Things are going on pretty well now.

William Joseph O'Neill Daunt
1807-1894

*O'NEILL DAUNT inherited Kilcascan at Ballineen in County Cork when he was nine-
teen. His father had fought a duel with a cousin, Daniel Conner, over some very minor
dispute, and though both the protagonists escaped injury after the first exchange of shots,
they had been forced by Conner's second to fire again and Captain Daunt was killed.*

*When still quite young, O'Neill Daunt became a Catholic and began to interest
himself in politics. He was a passionate nationalist, regarding the Act of Union as 'a
wicked usurpation by England' and the tithes that were levied to support the
Established Church as a 'monstrous injustice'. He was elected MP for Mallow, but was
unseated on the petition of the Tory candidate. Daniel O'Connell, in spite of promises,
failed to come to his assistance and Daunt never again took public office.*

*Though his trust in the Liberator had been shattered, O'Neill Daunt remained a
friend and admirer of O'Connell who, by way of recompense, made him his secretary
when he was elected Lord Mayor of Dublin. O'Neill Daunt was one of the first members to join the Repeal Association (for the repeal of the Union) and was Repeal Director
for Leinster; he travelled, often by canal boat, to attend the 'monster meetings'.*

* * *

2 October 1842

On Thursday last we had a meeting at Castle Pollard, the Rev. Dr Burke D.D. in
the chair. At Mr Burke's house dined a Mr Campbell, a musical enthusiast, who
travels on a jaunting car with only two available seats, the rest of the vehicle being
fitted up with drawers and cases containing flutes, bugle, clarinets, a violin and a
bagpipe. The two seats were occupied by Mr Campbell and his piper, who usually travels with him. They duetted the whole evening, Campbell accompanying the
piper on his violin. Despite the nuisance of their noise I was amused at the manifest ecstasy of Campbell as he rasped away; the very curls of his oily brown wig
keeping time with their vibrations to the movement of his bow. My host is the
same Father Burke in whose parish, Castle Pollard, one of the sanguinary tithe
affrays occurred between the parsons and Catholic people. The soldiers on that
occasion were called on to fire on the populace, and some persons were killed.
Soon afterwards Father Burke received a Government circular inquiring the number of his flock, for the purpose of making up the census. He answered that as he
had not yet ascertained to what extent his people were thinned out on the last
shooting day, he could not furnish the required information with accuracy.

16 October 1842

We have had numerous and enthusiastic meetings at Clara and Banagher. The latter was indeed a noble display of patriotic zeal. The labourers engaged upon the Shannon works turned out in a body, to the number of several hundreds, to attend our gathering. Left Ferbane in the evening boat for Tullamore. Dark, cloudy sky; the moon peeped out at intervals as we slowly passed through the dreary expanse of flat bog. I could see no scenic beauty in that bog, yet I felt that I loved it better than richer scenes in any other land, because it is my own beloved Ireland.

14 December 1842

Left Macroom in the Killarney mail. From Killarney I proceeded to Darrynane by the Sneem road, and saw the faint outline of the glorious lakes and mountains by the light of a misty moon. Arrived at Darrynane at a late hour. Liberator in bed; Mrs Fitzsimon and her daughter in the drawing room.

17 January 1843

O'Connell hunted all yesterday and today. Yesterday we all dined with his cousin, Mr John O'Connell, who keeps the principal inn at Cahirciveen, and who gathered a numerous company to meet the Liberator. Our coterie last night were social and amusing, under the presidency of the Cahirciveen Boniface. There was, however, little to amuse in the way of conversation, the ideas of the most of the guests being limited to shooting, fishing, hunting and agriculture ...

26 January 1843

The week's Repeal rent yesterday was £209, and we had a very good meeting ... Last September, John O'Connell [O'Connell's son], [T.M.] Ray [Secretary of the Repeal Association] and I held a council to determine our immediate course. I said to my *confrères*, 'Our adventurous independence is amusing. Here is this colossal crime, the Union, that cost in cash three million pounds sterling ... and here are we, three hopeful adventurers, setting out to repeal that Union with a sum of £8 each (the amount of *viaticum* given us by the Association)' ...

28 February 1843

O'Connell brought on his motion for the Repeal petition in the Corporation today. He spoke for four hours and ten minutes, and made out his case conclusively as regards the argument. Butt replied in a two hours' speech ... He is a very fluent speaker, but his action is ungraceful. O'Connell is in buoyant spirits at his triumph in the debate. 'I don't think *you* could have done that quite so well,' he said to me with a most amusing air of self-complacency, when we were issuing from the Assembly Rooms.

5 March 1843
Good Repeal Meeting at Castletown-Devlin. I find that the march of dandyism has reached the stable. My friend Father Fitzgerald's groom uses eau-de-Cologne and plays the accordion …

O'Neill Daunt did not keep his diary for some time and the next entry is during the famine on his estate at Kilcascin in Cork.

15 August 1846 – Ladyday
… In the evening Tom [his brother] and I availed ourselves of the assembling of my tenants and their labourers to ascertain the number of persons living on this property. Notwithstanding large emigrations there are still 271 inhabitants. Of these there are exactly twenty Protestants, leaving a balance of 251 Catholics. The Reverend Doheny, P.P., receives about £12 per annum for performing the spiritual duties required by these 251 Catholics, whilst the law-established parson screws £50 a year out of me for performing spiritual duties for the twenty Protestants.

To provide employment, O'Neill Daunt borrowed money to open a new line of a road. The repayment burdened him for many years.

26 December 1846
Spent this day in inspecting our new road … There were 108 hungry men working weakly and lazily under a hard frost. When desired by the overseer to go to dinner, fully one-half the number sat down by the ditches, having no dinner to go to; the other half had nothing but coarse brown bread and water … Although large numbers in this country have died of starvation, I have not heard of any robberies.

28 March 1847
The news of Dan's death is confirmed. It is not easy to contemplate with indifference the exit of our old familiar leader, to remember how often I have been among the band who surrounded him on Repeal platforms; to have the tones of his noble voice still ringing in my ears, and then to think that I shall hear that voice no more!

O'Neill Daunt was much involved in agitation against the existence of an established state Church that culminated in the disestablishment of the Church of Ireland in 1869.

8 May 1869
… Gladstone's Bill has as good as passed the Commons. It falls so short of what a Disendowment Bill should be that I shall not be sorry if the Lords reject it …

26 July 1869
This morning's paper announces that the Bill has received Royal assent.

2 August 1869

The reception of the Bill by the Protestants in this quarter is comical. On Sunday last the Reverend Mr Myles announced from his pulpit at Dunmanway, that England had separated herself from God. 'We Irish Protestants', said he, 'have always been faithful to her, and now she requites our fidelity with desertion. Caesar has cast us off. I will not preach disloyalty, but I will say this – let Caesar take care of himself for the future without our assistance.'

Asenath Nicholson

c. 1796–1855

ASENATH NICHOLSON came to Ireland on a lone mission from New York to 'personally investigate the condition of the poor'. This was 1844, the year before the failure of the potato crop that caused the famine. She travelled the country, mostly on foot, so had every opportunity to see that the 'beautiful domains were sprinkled with walking rags' and to predict that there would be 'an explosion of some kind or other'.

In spite of the depth of the poverty she encountered, she was welcomed into the cabins and hovels much more warmly than into the larger houses. She stayed in the meanest cabins, frequently sharing the room and sometimes the bed with her hosts and their pigs, cattle and hens. Her sustenance was three or four potatoes a day and, if she was lucky, a bread roll for breakfast. Very often she was given her night's lodging free.

In 1844 Asenath Nicholson was almost fifty years old, and no beauty (a man with a cure had offered to remove the wart from her face). She wore a coat in polka-dot material, a huge velvet bonnet and shoes made of india rubber. She had spectacles that were of 'superior excellence, very expensive and had been specially selected in New York for travel', but she lost them while walking along the road to Lismore absorbed in the beauties of the scenery and tempted by the magnificent blackberries. She carried a parasol, a basket containing a change of linen, and a black bearskin muff which she found rather cumbersome; two bags slung from a strong cord round her waist held copies of the New Testament in English and Irish. As she walked along she sang hymns or read the scriptures to her fellow travellers.

A rabid teetotaller, she was never averse to telling imbibers of the Judgment that was to come, nor did she keep her vegetarian convictions to herself, writing: 'Oh what creatures however loathsome have not found a sepulchre in the stomach of man? The creeping snail, the forbidding lobster, the snaky eel and wallowing swine, have all made their way through the teeth and throat of Kings and Emperors.'

In New York she had run a temperance boarding house, and the servants that she had employed came from near Urlingford. She spent some of her happiest weeks staying with their families, who gave her a touching reception when they danced for a whole hour for her amusement and for her welcome.

Mrs Nicholson stayed eight years in Ireland – remaining throughout the famine, during which she was indefatigable in her efforts of assistance, using the money from her writing to buy food and clothing for the destitute.

She had arrived in Kingstown and after looking round Dublin, especially into the cabins of the poor, she went to Tullamore.

* * *

2 July 1844

I went at seven in the morning to the fly-boat, where I was packed as tight as live-stock could be in any but a slave ship. Here I found a company of Irish and English aristocrats, who, on 'both sides of the house', were professed enemies to the poor Irish, calling them a company of low, vulgar lazy wretches, who prefer beggary to work, and filth to cleanliness … In eight hours we reached Tullamore, a distance of fifty miles.

The appearance of the people here was not prepossessing.

I had always heard the Irish were celebrated for giving the pig an eminent berth in their cabins and in two cabins I found a pig in a corner snugly cribbed, with a lattice work around him, a bed of clean straw under him, and a pot of food standing near the door of his house, to which he might go out and in at option. And in both these huts, though the floors were nothing but the ground, yet these were well-swept; a peat fire was smouldering on clean hearths and the delf was tastefully arranged upon the rude shelves.

In the afternoon I visited the jail, which contained eighty-one prisoners; seventeen had been that morning sent to Dublin for transportation. They were all at work; some cracking stones, some making shoes and others tailoring or weaving. Their food is one pound of stirabout, and milk in the morning, and four pounds of potatoes for dinner.

The drop where criminals are executed is in front; four had suffered upon it within the last two years.

She returned to Dublin by coach and a few days later set off for Wicklow.

? July 1844

I found myself at the coach at half past five. For an hour were ominous fixings and re-fixings of trunks, chests hampers, sacks, and baskets. 'Where shall I sit? – my band-box will be all jammed up – and won't you please make a little room for my legs?' began long before the horses were brought, while I stood with basket in hand, waiting for a clearance of the ladder to ascend. Seeing an opening I improved it, and fixed myself in mid-air with one foot on terra firma, and the other seeking rest and finding none. And now the full tide of battle set in. I had been seated by the coachman in a few inches of space, just left by an old fat man in breeches, who had moved to have a trunk put up; and when he turned about for his seat, and found it filled, 'You have got my place, ma'am.' 'Sit still,' jogged another fat Irishman, 'make sure of what you've got; and here, sir, you can take it aisy on the top.' Behind us was a kind of scaffolding, of sufficient width to seat two. Here, after much grumbling, the old man with his bundle was adjusted, his footstool the necks of each of us, who in turn handed or whirled his heels to the next, while ever and anon he muttered to himself, 'That woman's got my sate.' 'Be aisy,' said my fat neighbour at the left, when I showed signs of pity, 'he's doin' quite well.' The storm rose to a tornado. A modest-looking young girl, who had waited patiently to be seated (for all this time we had not stirred an inch from the door), asked what she should do. 'What shall you do?' said the boor of a coachman. 'Sit on top of the luggage.' There was no alternative; what with hoisting from below, and the old man pulling from above, she was seated upon her perilous throne, while we had a second pair of heels to dispose of, to the no small annoyance of the poor man on my left, who did not like to make the same rude arrangement of them as he made of the old gentleman's.

We had proceeded a few miles, with nineteen upon the top, and one appended to the back, when a loud call from a car arrested us with, 'Can you take a few more passengers?'

'As many as you please,' answered the glad driver; the clamour, the entreaties, and threats of the passengers, were all unavailing; the car was emptied of four occupants, each with a box or two and baskets and lesser appendages, and all transferred to the coach. The terrified girl over our heads was now ordered to alight, and without ceremony was packed among us though we were already eight where five could only have a tolerable seat. A corner of a trunk rested on my shoulder, and twenty miles I rode without having the free liberty of my head or full turning of my neck. The beautiful Vale of Avoca we entered but my cramped position kept me from one solitary look at it; the ponderous coach was threatening at every jostle to plunge us headlong. The 'Please be so kind as to move an arm or a leg'; and 'Do be aisy, my good friends, you put my hat into all manner of shapes,' went on, and, taken as a whole, it was the most perilous, the most uncomfortable, laughable, provoking ride that could be imagined.

I was the first passenger called upon by the coachman when we reached Arklow. My carpet-bag was missing; and as the coachman would not look for it, I was left to make my way without it, a mile and a half to the house where my letter was directed. Endeavouring to take a shorter route, I was entangled in hedgerows and plunged in ditches. Everyone of whom I inquired gave me a different direction, but all of them agreed that I was 'goin' astray'.

At length I found myself at the gate. An open lane showed the placid sea, and far-famed mountains of Wicklow. About the door were roses, a shrubbery, and lilies. A daughter met me in the hall, and I gave her my letter, from a long-absent brother.

Her mother was called, and invited me in to a well-furnished table, very neat and orderly ... I felt as if I were seated at the dinner table of an intelligent New England family. After dinner the mother invited me to the garden, saying, 'We have made our arrangements for you to spend a week with us, and if we did not wish it we should not ask it.'

The carpet-bag was returned by the coachman the next day.

At the end of October, she was in Roscrea, and as she had only 4/6d, she resolved to go to Galway in hope of finding that money had been sent to the Post Office there for her from America.

4 November 1844

Early on foot towards Ballinasloe. The sun rose most beautifully; poor labourers were going to their work, smoking or singing, their tattered garments an apology for clothing. On the muddy path before me a little girl of eight years old, who was seated on a car, driving an ass, hummed a monotonous tune; and going to her, I said 'Will you let me put my basket on your car?' 'I will ma'am.' ...

In a neat little cottage I had a snug little room on the first floor, with a nicely curtained bed, a turf fire, two candles, and some crisped potatoes, and all for the bill of fourpence.

[date not given]

Early I prepared for a walk of eighteen miles to Galway. The road was muddy, and there was quite an appearance of rain. The kind people did all they could do for my comfort. Twopence a night for lodging was the stated price to all. I was soon joined by a man and his wife, with a car, riding alternately, which made the journey slow; they kindly relieved me of my basket, and I walked nine miles with tolerable ease. I was resting upon a stone when the post-car arrived, and offered to take me to Galway for a shilling. I paid it, light as was my purse, and reached the town at two o'clock, with half a crown.

I found a comfortable lodging-house in some respects, and in some uncomfortable; but knowing that slender purses must not put on airs, I went to the post-office for letters, but found none. Sixpence a night for lodging was the price, and find my own potatoes. I had five sixpences, and with these I must make my way back to Kilkenny. I had no fear for I knew all would be all right so I perambulated the town, and saw what I could see, enjoyed what I could enjoy, and then went home for the night.

She found the money waiting for her back in Roscrea and continued walking about Ireland handing out tracts and bibles.

18 March 1845

I concluded to go West, and visit Cahirciveen, a distance of thirty miles; to walk the first ten, and wait for the car till next morning at the town of Killorglin ... My feet were soon blistered, the road stony, and the rain threatening. Often I sat down upon a stone by the wayside, feeling quite unable to proceed. I could get nothing to eat. A carrier let me put my basket on his cart, and I trudged behind ... I endeavoured, as I followed the cart, to forget my pains by singing. This, to my wonder, drew upon the hillsides and path groups of all ages ...

Bye and by I saw a thatched house of considerable dimensions, and a pile of well-packed manure at the door, and looking in, saw a cow fastened at the entrance, standing upon straw and filth, and her young calf to the right, near the fire. The smoke was making its way as well as it could through the door, eight men were lolling upon a settee and benches, one stretched at full length upon a table, his head hanging off one end, and the mother, three daughters, two teamsters and myself with geese and hens at roost made up the group in the room and about the fireside of this 'stage-house'. I was quite indignant, and asked the consequential landlord why he lived with his cattle in the house, when I saw he had a barn nearby.

'The cow has a new calf, ma'am, and she is warmer in the house.'

My feet needing bathing, the pot which had been used for the boiling of the potatoes was presented, and in presence of ten male eye-witnesses gathered about, the girl washed my feet in spite of all remonstrance.

In half an hour my bedroom was in readiness with a splinter of bog-wood put into a crack to light me on the way thither. This bedroom contained three beds for father and mother, three daughters and myself. I was allowed to retire first, the same attendant standing by in real primitive fashion, to help me undress.

In May she was in Clifden and Roundstone, though why she was climbing Diamond Mountain with two policemen is not explained.

May ? 1845

Went with two policemen to Diamond Mountain, so called from having upon the top a transparent stone which resembles a diamond and is used in breast-pins and bracelets. We waded through bog till the ascent became difficult, in pouring rain. Here I lost a second pair of silver-mounted spectacles, used entirely for reading, which had served me years for that purpose ... I crept up an almost precipitous rock with my india-rubbers upon my feet, but so steep and so slippery was it that I could retain my position only by holding fast to the heath. Here was a cave like a room, with a stone in the middle for a seat, and the roof of square stones as if laid by the hand of man. In the descent my slippery rubbers exposed me at every step to a long slide which might be fatal. But by sitting down and sliding where walking was impossible, I succeeded in reaching the police barracks, leaving the diamonds to sparkle at a distance as all diamonds generally do.

I went supperless to bed, passed a sleepless night with cows, a horse, men and boys, and an old woman smoking in the cabin, and walked through mud and rain to Tully. Not a loaf of bread was in the town, and the Methodist lady where we stopped said there had been none for six weeks! Can you believe, that in 1845, when there had been no failure of crops, an assize town lived six weeks on nothing but potatoes?

Rev. William Sewell
1804-1874

SCHOOLS IN EARLY NINETEENTH-CENTURY Ireland had a poor reputation. A telling, if not necessarily representative, episode took place at the Royal School Armagh, where W.F. Trench, author of Realities of Irish Life (1868), received his education. The boys had rioted and locked out the authorities for three days, during which time they took pot shots at people passing on the road outside. In the end, boredom, lack of water and the pleas of the Mayor of Armagh made them negotiate terms of capitulation.

In 1839 an Irish collegiate school was proposed by Lord Adare, his brother-in-law William Monsell and the Earl of Dunraven, who were all very much attracted by Tractarianism. They approached William Sewell, an Englishman and a Fellow of Exeter College, Oxford, who was a member of the Oxford Movement with its aim to return to the Catholic ethos of the early Church. The idea was to found an Irish public school based on High Church principles with an emphasis on Celtic Irish history and the importance of the early Irish Church. Great significance was placed on learning the Irish language, partly in order to give the students a feeling of national identity and partly for the alumni to proselytize amongst the Roman Catholic peasantry. St Columba's College contributed towards a Chair in Irish at Trinity College and had for the first ten years at least one teacher of Irish on the staff. The Rev. Sewell wrote in his diary how they undertook to publish an Irish grammar: 'It is, I understand, an admirable philological work. Among other things, he has destroyed all the irregular verbs, a surprising feat, but one of great value.'

In 1843 Stackallen House on the river Boyne was rented by the Governors on a very short lease. It was not the most suitable place for a school: the chimneys smoked, and the great oak staircase took up much of the space in the hall, which was also used as a dining-room. When Sewell came for a protracted stay in order to see how the school was progressing in October 1844, there were twenty-five boys. The headmaster or warden was the Rev. R.C. Singleton, a graduate of Trinity College. In 1846 Sewell and Singleton withdrew from St Columba's owing to a controversy over the rules for fasting by members of the staff.

The school was looked on with the greatest suspicion in Ireland because of its High Church format, particularly after Lord Adare and Mr Monsell became Roman Catholics, but it did survive, moving to its present location at Rathfarnham, County Dublin, in 1849.

Back in England, Sewell founded St Peter's College, Radley, on much the same principles as St Columba's. He published the journal of his stay in County Meath shortly after he had resigned from being a Governor of the school.

12 October 1844

Arrived in Dublin this morning after a calm passage, and came immediately to Trinity College. Had a long conversation with ——. A very satisfactory account of the state of St Columba generally … Found that it was beginning to excite great interest in Ireland, and formed the subject of conversation at most parties; but the most absurd and scandalous stories respecting it gravely stated, and greedily swallowed … The arrival of our library was transformed into an importation of cart-loads of breviaries … The Fellows of course cannot marry, and the poor people in the neighbourhood were alarmed with the report that all the females within ten miles round were to be sent away; the boys were to be starved; and they were to sit at their meals with their hands behind them, and their backs to the table … The College said to be planned by ——, for the purpose of winning over the Irish to popery. I just put down these follies, to shew the feeling which prevails against us, and against which we have to struggle …

The Warden was in Dublin looking out for a cook. Irish servants proverbially bad; and they have found the greatest trouble with this part of the College … Rejoiced to find the Warden himself well, and in good spirits; and we made arrangements to go down together by the Drogheda Railway … It was late before we reached Stackallen; and the old house, with its high roof and ranges of windows, looked grand and solemn in the moonlight among the old trees, and surrounded by its park. … I found —— and —— in the library, busy in completing a sheet of our Irish Primer, which is now in the press. The room had been carpeted since I was there; and, with the books all round, and globes, and old chairs, and a good fire burning, it looked thoroughly comfortable. They use it as a common room …

The bell was rung for tea in a few minutes, and we adjourned into the hall. They had not yet taken away the great oak staircase and to bring the boys nearer the fire, and more into the light, and under their own observation, they had altered the arrangement of the tables – not an improvement. When all had taken their places, the Warden, in his gown, at the head of the table, with his great old oak chair, and the Fellows, in their gowns, at the table with him, and the boys at the other, one of the Fellows repeated a versicle from the Psalms, in Irish, as a grace, and the boys responded in another versicle also in Irish; for we hope to familiarize them with the language in every feasible way. I had heard a great deal of the gentlemanly appearance of the boys, but was greatly surprised to see them. A finer set of countenances in boys I never saw, full of health, cheerfulness, and spirit, and at the same time perfectly respectful and refined … There were twenty-five already, all in little Eton black gowns, with their clean white collars and open throats …

The Warden, and two of the Fellows, made tea for the boys and all, taking care, of course, not to make it too strong; but the object was that they might feel that all took their meals together. And boys brought up their cups and saucers for each other, I was delighted to see them come up to the Warden without the least fear, each with a smile upon his countenance. And there was the little question, or remark – the pat on the head, or the little admonition for each, which shewed that there was no reason to fear lest the strictness of the discipline interfered with his affection for them, or their regard for him. Another Irish grace and response from the boys followed after tea; and then the Fellows separated, some of them adjoining together to the library and common room, and others to their own room. And the boys went to the music-room, which is at the end of the same suite with the library, and there practised their music with the Warden taking part, till bed-time. I was tired and unwell and went to bed soon after.

13 October 1844

At six o'clock I was awakened by a bell ringing through the house, which I found was generally done by the Warden himself, on the principle that those who are at the head of an Institution must be the first to undertake the most disagreeable duties ... The first act is to call one of the Fellows, who goes to the boys' dormitory and rings a bell, and sees them all out of their beds, and that they say their prayers. I went into the school, a lofty plain room, about thirty feet long, well lighted, and very clean, which they had fitted up out of one of the outhouses.

The Warden and Sub-warden were both engaged in giving their catechetical instruction, to which they always devote the first part of the morning ... At eight o'clock we assemble in the chapel ... the whole congregation, boys and all, chanted the Te Deum and Benedictus. And when I remembered that fourteen months since the chapel had been a coach-house, and that none of these boys had a notion of singing, I certainly was amazed.

Immediately after chapel we met in the hall, where breakfast was served. No gentleman's table could be neater than that of the boys, the table-cloth spotless, the cups china, plain white with a little badge to mark it: 'Collegium St Columbæ'. Each boy had his little pat of butter in a little white plate, that none might be wasted ... Breakfast was begun and followed, like tea, by the Irish grace; and then the boys went to their school till about one, when a servant brought them each a great bit of bread for luncheon ... In the afternoon, the Warden and I walked about the grounds. They have completed an excellent dry walk round the lawn; and the flower-garden still retained signs of its having been in high perfection during the summer ... The garden and every part of the lawn is free to the boys, and I found that not a single act of mischief had occurred. On one occasion they had accidentally damaged one of the beds; but when the Warden spoke to them ... and told them that he was sure they would make it a point of honour to assist in keeping it nice, they voluntarily got their spades and set it right again. Few things indeed have struck me more than the neatness of the whole place ... Not a cut upon their desks or benches in the schoolroom, not a sign of scribbling on the wall in any part of the premises: and I found that they already made it a point of honour among themselves not to injure any thing, even to the extent of spilling ink upon the floor in the schoolroom.

At four o'clock the bell tolled again for chapel; and it was surprising to find what a venerable collegiate character was given to the whole scene by its deep mellow sound ... As it was Saturday evening, there was full choral service ... I do not think I ever heard it more beautifully performed. The organ is magnificent; and as the whole congregation join in the choral parts, down to the least boy, the effect of the full body of voice is very striking ... The whole body, boys and all, wore their surplices, white and neat; and the sight was delightful. I watched their manners narrowly, and did not see a single instance of irreverence, or talking, or lolling, or even of weariness; and the heartiness with which they repeated the Amen, proved that they were attending. We must make them use the Irish Prayer Book, in which English is one page, and the Irish on the other, to familiarize them to the language. And by and by we hope we shall be able to have the Lessons read in Irish.

Immediately after chapel we met in the hall for dinner ... The table was laid very neatly, with clean table-cloths; each with his neat cup for his beer, which, by the by, must not be poured out before they sit down, or it becomes vapid ... The boys' plate was given them by the Warden; and the table was well lighted with bronze candle lamps. The Fellows' table had much deteriorated since I was here last, partly owing to a bad cook, partly to the wish of the Fellows to help the boys from their own table; so that it was crowded with great joints of meat – and these were sadly hacked and hewed – and partly from the littery practice of serving up the potatoes in their skins, which is not uncommon in second-rate houses in Ireland, but much destroys the neatness of a table.

15 December 1844

Last night I had scarcely been asleep two hours when I was awoke by the ringing of the bell. I thought it was the usual signal of getting up. Presently I heard something like an explosion and a hurried voice, and jumped out of bed, slipped on my dressing-gown and shoes, and was hastening downstairs, when I was told the house was on fire. The fireworks for Monday, which had been brought down that afternoon from Dublin, had been deposited by the Warden, according to the directions of the maker, in a great oak wardrobe in his own room, with the greatest care, but they had ignited spontaneously, and exploded. There were rockets, blue lights, and the usual display of things to the value of £8 ... To our inexpressible relief we found the Warden safe; he had just got into bed, having closed the door of his bed room, from which, happily, there was another egress through his dressing-room. At the first explosion he thought it was a mob smashing the windows and breaking into the house; but when the rockets went off with their horrible hissing, he at once saw what was the matter, leaped out of bed, and escaped by the dressing-room to ring the bell, in which act, as so often occurs, a second frightful accident nearly occurred, for the bell broke, and if it had fallen on his head, would probably have killed him. We were all assembled in a minute or two; and our first effort was to open the door, so far as to discover, if possible, how much of the room was on fire. And one of the Fellows, with a noble spirit, insisted on creeping in on his hands and feet, but on opening the door there rushed out such a volume, not of ordinary smoke, but of dense sulphurous metallic pestilential vapour, that we could not allow him to penetrate, and dragged him back. He would probably have been poisoned. The room was on the ground floor, and we were enabled to get over the area to the window, and there perceived it wrapped in a tremendous blaze, which it would have been impossible to approach; we therefore ordered the doors to be kept thoroughly fastened, and stopped up with blankets the panes of glass which had been smashed in the windows; and then, with all hands, proceeded to deluge the room over the one on fire with water. Our first thought, of course, had been the boys, and they behaved admirably. No screaming or shrieking. They got out of their beds and came down stairs, though such a volume of pestilential smoke had rushed up the back stairs, on which the door of the Warden's rooms open, that candles would not burn, and we were nearly suffocated. We searched all the little cubicles or cells with miserable anxiety, in the dark, lest any one should be still there but on counting them in the hall, we were relieved beyond expression to find them all safe. And as the staircase became clear from smoke, the three senior boys went up with one of the Fellows, gutted the dormitory of bed-clothes etc. and they all came into the common room, which has a door opening on the lawn, and they lay down upon the floor, nestling close to each other, without a word, or apparent anxiety, knowing that of all our property, they were the most valuable; and putting entire confidence in our managing for them ... Having fixed a ladder at the bottom of the area against the window, we watched the flames raging, licking up to the ceiling, over both the fireplace, and where the oak wardrobe had stood ... Our fear was for the floor. I was on the ladder at the window, and after some hesitation, we resolved to collect as large a quantity as possible of wet blankets and buckets, and pans of water, at the door and then open it, and rush in at once to extinguish it. We had formed a line for the buckets from the scullery pump, and to our inexpressible joy and gratitude, the plan was successful, and the fire extinguished ... We ripped up the floor to satisfy ourselves that every spark was extinguished. And then all of us met in the music-room, as we usually do on Sunday for prayers, and, kneeling down, the Warden offered up our thanksgiving for our preservation, and I closed it with another for his own preservation. I never heard more fervent Amens than from the boys breaking out in the middle of the prayers; and not a few tears were shed by all. Mrs —— got the dormitory arranged again for them; and leaving two of the men up, we all went to bed, but I fancy, none of us to sleep.

There was an experiment to bring some Irish peasant boys from Castletownsend, County Cork, who, it was hoped, would familiarize the boys with the Irish language while they would be trained up to work as servants at the College in exchange for their keep and some education. If any were particularly bright, they could win scholarships to the College.

7 February 1845

... There arrived five little naked Irish boys from about eleven to thirteen, from the farthest extremity of Ireland, who are to form the beginning of our servants' department. We were all, Governors included, as curious as children to see them. But Mrs ——, with due regard to our dignity, persuaded us to postpone our interview; and, in the mean time, without any delay, she took them up stairs to their room, stripped off their rags, deluged them with soap and water, put on them the only apparel which had yet been made for them, in the shape of some stout clean shirts; and thus attired warming themselves by the fire, they were submitted to our inspection. The father of one of the boys came with them, an intelligent interesting old man. But the boys themselves were little rugheaded creatures, with many of the least graceful features of the Irish peasantry. They seemed entirely bewildered; as well they might, after a voyage from Cork, cold and frozen, and transferred suddenly from the side of a peat bog, and a smoky mud cabin, up in the mountains, into a large room, half filled with awful persons, in caps and gowns. But the Irish are not as dull as the English or so afraid of their superiors. And they soon began to answer our questions in a sort of half gibberish and to feel more at home. We soon left them to go to bed. Mrs —— had arranged their iron bedsteads very neatly, and provided combs, brushes, washing things, etc. etc. for them; and the drill sergeant has an inner room to himself where he is to take charge of them.

This not very altruistic experiment was a failure; the boys were so homesick and unhappy that they were returned home in a few months.

23 February 1845

An internal commotion in our little world. An offence against good manners and discipline, in itself trifling, considering what is common in Irish schools, committed by two or three boys, younger ones – names unknown. The College makes a principle that in all such cases the culprits are to give themselves up – and this is the only way of wiping the stigma from the whole school. Important to make them feel an esprit de corps. Usually they confess the moment the charge is made known ... In the present case there was a blunder of the Senior Prefect, as we found afterwards – and no boys came to confess; and upon this the Warden went into school, and laid the whole body under an interdict, till the stigma was wiped off. This was the first instance of the kind. He told them that during the interdict none of the boys should go to chapel – the chapel bell should not ring – of course there would be no music in the chapel. The Warden and Fellows would take their meals in a different room, and would hold no communication with them beyond what was absolutely necessary. No games would be allowed, and no talking at meal time; and any symptom of levity to be severely punished. This he did just before tea. And, for the first time the Fellows drank tea in the common room, leaving the boys in the hall, under the eye of two of the Fellows, to see that they were not infringing the rule. We wondered, and debated what could be the meaning of the culprits not giving themselves up. Meanwhile the Fellows in the hall reported that three of the bigger boys at one table had behaved ill, and shewn a great deal of levity, though, at the other table, they all seemed to feel as we wished. The Warden saw at once that this kind of punishment was, in itself, a mere farce, unless it were made serious by a proper moral tone and spirit, in which case it would have a most powerful effect; and that any infringement of the rules laid down was to be punished at once, and with great severity. Accordingly, after tea, to the great reluctance of all the Fellows, though all acquiesced in the wisdom of the step, they all went in a body into school; the offenders were called up; and the poor Sub-warden administered to them, before all the boys, a castigation, for St Columba, of no little severity. I was not present, but it evidently hurt them much. Poor ——, who is by no means hard-hearted, went up to his room in tears, and I had to go and console him. —— and —— were miserable. The Sub-warden came down the next morning with his eyes red. And the Warden himself came to me at six in the morning, declaring that he could not stand the estrangement from the boys any longer, and that some means must be found to put matters right. Happily I had received, just before, a note from the Senior Prefect, explaining that he had been the cause of the blunder, and that the delinquents were ready, and had been ready from the first, to give themselves up. This was done; and as it was found that the delay had not arisen from any fault of theirs, they were forgiven at once. The Warden made the school a little address, which he does very well, pointing out why little offences, in such a place, were dealt with gravely; how resolved the College was to enforce acknowledgement of offences charged on them even if the whole school was to be sent away … And then, he told them, that to shew the joy which he and the Fellows felt at their reconciliation, and the pain which the estrangement had given them, they should have a whole holiday, and go down to the river. This happened just before chapel; so that the most painful part of the interdict was avoided. At this announcement, the poor boys could not refrain from giving a good cheer, but we stopped it at once. Boys should never be allowed to applaud, any more than to hiss, their masters. Praise cannot come properly from an inferior.

It is difficult to reconcile the diary of William Sewell with the memoirs of E.W. O'Brien, the son of William Smith O'Brien, the Young Irelander. He went to St Columba's at the age of nine in 1846. In his memoirs he writes how astonished and shocked he was at being 'systematically instructed with every sort of wickedness and mischief that boys are capable of'. Bad language, bullying, and evil practices of every kind were rife. He recounts that during meal times in the hall, the boys would go on foraging parties to raid the butter from the other table. Another pastime was flicking lumps of butter from the points of their knives up to the ceiling.

The boys had built caves in a wood, where they cooked toffee, drank cherry brandy obtained surreptitiously in the village and smoked birdseye tobacco in clay pipes. He recounts how an unpopular master was 'hissed' when he was in sole charge of the schoolroom. The lights were put out and everyone jumped up and rushed to take part in the fray, yells and hisses filled the room and books flew through the air while the miserable master was knocked and hustled until rescued by some of the other masters. On another occasion, some leaving boys smashed all the windows in the chapel and schoolroom and threw most of the furniture into the moat. For this the whole school was docked two days from their vacation.

Possibly Mr Sewell was somewhat naïve, as he wrote happily in his diary how the boys had told him they had all stood and sung the Venite under the great dome of Newgrange!

Elizabeth Smith
1797-1885

Elizabeth Grant was born in Scotland and was proud of her old Highland blood. Her father, Sir Peter Grant, the laird of Rothiemurchus, was a lawyer and a member of Parliament, but ran up such huge debts that he had to take refuge in France from his creditors. In spite of this, he was appointed to a judgeship in Bombay and the whole family sailed for India with the newly made judge being smuggled aboard the ship from a small boat that put out from Jersey.

In Bombay, Elizabeth met and married Colonel Henry Smith, who was some fifteen years older than herself. In 1830 he inherited an estate in Wicklow and they came to back to Ireland.

Baltiboys, near Blessington, had 1200 acres that had been much neglected by the previous owner. He had pulled the house down in order to sell the materials and the tenants were so ragged and impoverished that Elizabeth thought a crowd of beggars had come to greet them at the gates. Over the next ten years the Smiths rebuilt the house and improved the farms, planting the first field of turnips ever to be seen in that part of the world; when they had the money they built chimneys and put windows into the cabins. Elizabeth set up a school.

The character that emerges from her diary is practical, intelligent, and a little priggish. It is clear that much of the management of the estate was in her capable hands. Occasionally she interferes too blatantly – the steward gave notice because she demonstrated to him how to weed turnips with a hoe in the Scotch way.

On 5 November 1845 her husband brought in two blighted potatoes, the first they had seen at Baltiboys. By the 11th the blight had spread through their fields. During the autumn of 1846, she and the Colonel with the help of the steward had worked out a plan to buy flour and coal in bulk 'for at the present prices it would require 21/= a week to support a labourer and his family, who earns 6/= to 8/= at the highest'.

In December 1847 she wrote: 'The people are starving and the poor house has 1100 where there never used to be 200.' At Baltiboys, they were giving milk and soup to their twelve workmen and soup to the sick and aged.

She was always railing against the improvidence of the Irish and wrote often of the indolence, ignorance and inanity of the other landlords. She had 'made up [her] mind that the distress of the poor demands a large sacrifice on the part of the richer', and to that end the family gave up many of the luxuries to which they had been accustomed, though she was rather sad when her husband would not let her daughters attend any of the festivities in Dublin for Queen Victoria's visit because of the expense. On 16

February 1847 she wrote, 'No news stirring – nothing going but misery, nothing thought of but the relief of it.' She organized a repository where things made in the school could be sold and where there was rice and corn at special prices. At night she wrote stories and articles for magazines, and with the money she earned she kept her school going with a meal for the children every day. It was not until Christmas 1849 that she could write, 'we had the pleasantest rent day we have had since the famine year, the tenants looked happy, no complaints, no demands and no shuffling. It will do little more than pay our debt to John Robinson [their agent] and the dues on the land, but to be even with the world again is comfort unspeakable.'

I have taken the first entry from the diary in October 1845, which was before the potato blight had spread.

* * *

26 October 1845

The month of October is running rapidly away, the weeks actually flying. The Colonel has been very much occupied with plans for the prevention of such extreme distress as the failure of the potato crop threatens the poor with. Just in Baltiboys there seems as yet to be no damage done but very near at hand this widespread disease has already attacked some large con-acre fields where the poor man's supply for the next nine months may without active measures speedily taken fail him entirely. The potato once attacked is quite unfit for food, it rots away, infecting all its companions, but the farina, the nourishing part of the root, is uninjured even in the worse cases so that by scraping down the potato at once and making it into what they call starch nothing fit for food is lost. This starch or flour mixed with a half of wheaten flour makes delicious bread, some of which we tasted to-day for Mr Shehan amongst others has been trying this experiment and he sent by young John Hornidge a sample …

Hal [her husband, referred to below as the Colonel] fears the want of energy of the lower orders, their idleness, and their ignorance, will prevent their setting to work to supply themselves with this change of food so he went to see Mr Owen on the subject of establishing a scraping manufactory and perhaps a bakery …

5 November 1845

… Hal has just brought in two damaged potatoes, the first we have seen of our own for on our hill few have been found as yet. It is a dull misty day, surely the rising barometer cannot have been for this cold wind instead of a continuance of bright weather.

13 November 1845

Still a heavy fog. Road sessions took the Colonel out early, while I was busy arranging a dinner party in honour of the grouse, for Saturday. The Doctor called and sat talking nonsense half the morning. *Half* the potatoes in this new field are tainted, some very badly.

30 November 1845
The last day of November, Sunday, fine ... Mr Robinson came down yesterday to collect the rents, the Tenants paid well, were in good spirits, made no complaints, not even of their potatoes, were well dressed, so that altogether it was a most comfortable gale day. The potato failure has been much exaggerated, the disease is by no means so far spread as was supposed and the crop so over abundant that the partial failure will be the less felt, particularly as the corn harvest was excellent.

4 January 1846
Our New Year's day dinner downstairs was a very satisfactory one to the company, inasmuch as they had a most bountiful display of joints and puddings, with tea afterwards at discretion. We only used to have the men, but this year the thought struck us that it would do a great deal of good to ask their wives with them and Mrs Fyfe tells me that cleaner, tidier, decenter behaved women could not be met with.

Margaret Fyfe was the housekeeper at Baltiboys, who had come from Elizabeth's old home at Rothiemurchus.

24 February 1846
Having finished my 'Lairds' I have actually written to offer them to the Messieurs Chambers. If they will encourage me ... I may make my £10 every now and then and shall, I hope, employ it ... to cheer the humble hearths and rouse the dormant energies of the miserably wretched around us. Clothe some of the naked children at any rate; and this spring will be one of deep distress, potatoes are now 6d a stone and that unhappy creature Jemmy Craig's wife told Mrs Fyfe today that she cannot do with less than ten stone in the week. Five pence a week for her lodgings, three pence half penny for the husband's tobacco – where is the firing, the clothing, and what they call the kitchen to come from for these five miserable creatures, even though he is in the Colonel's work, for he is so weakly he cannot earn as another man. The idea of such a pair of incapables marrying without a home, without employment; it is really a moral sin, though they none of them comprehend its enormity.

5 March 1846
Ploughing match very good yesterday. Upwards of sixty ploughs. An immense concourse of people, almost everyone in the country, high and low; the day though coarse kept up well.

There came a letter from the Messrs Chambers accepting the papers for consideration.

23 March 1846

The Doctor brought us yesterday a printed paper, published by Government to teach the people how to use the Indian corn flour. It will be very useful although the Dutch oven part might have been left out, even a griddle few of the poor possess, and to talk of yeast and butter and eggs and new milk to perfect paupers is a sort of mockery. Margaret and I can teach the porridge, the hasty pudding and the common cakes from seeing them made at Pau where the maize flour is much used. Unfortunately any trouble is so disagreeable to the habits of our indolent population, I doubt their taking it till actually dying from want, any food they are unaccustomed to they dislike equally, but the famine is coming, has begun in the plains and must reach the hills, and though those immediately belonging to our small knot of good landlords may feel little of it, all around are already in misery, the poor broom man among them who while walking up from the gate with me, his load on his back, told me has had no work, no food, and was reduced to one meal a day, himself, his wife & five children. Why will they marry on nothing?

24 March 1846

A milder morning. Could not sleep last night for thinking of the miseries of that wretched James Craig's wife and fifty others, who I daresay were sound on their straw under their scanty coverings and half open roofs.

1 April 1846

We heard that Lady Milltown had returned home, herself, her five children, her maid, her footman, all packed up in one hired carriage. I hope she may be so occupied with her home for a few days as to leave me in quiet; I am determined, however, not to let her worry me as she used to do. Whenever she tired of herself she drove over to bestow her ill-humour on me.

Lord and Lady Milltown lived at Russborough.

26 May 1846

My Lady, her two daughters, and her two younger sons came to tea, the children happy and agreeable, their mother such a mass of affectation as to be almost intolerable, beyond merely ridiculous. Half her words French – lolling on the sofa – dressed for a ball – grand to the sublime! and to crown all quite youthful – somewhere about five-and-thirty, and this to me who have often compared ages with her in our early days, and know it to an hour from old Mrs Wall who was present at her birth; fib after fib about Paris, as formerly about London. She must think me a fool, or else, poor thing, maybe she is only trying to cheat herself –

neglected as she must sorely feel she is by everyone: her own fault, for she has out-
raged everyone. The Children are really nice; the girls very awkward, very coarse,
and none of them one bit more than mere children.

27 May 1846
Went up Blackamore Hill, a large party, to eat our cold dinner on the top; yet
such was the force of much combined attraction that the day passed very pleasantly. The panorama was worth climbing up to view, the eye reaching far over the
hills at hand to the wide plains of Dublin, Meath and Kildare. All determining
to drink tea here and dance the polka afterwards, we passed a merry evening, not
breaking up till after ten.

One of the pleasantest sights of the day was our group of attendants over the
fragments – men who never taste meat twice in a year truly enjoying what we had
left of our luxuries; the saddest was one the Doctor and young John Hornridge
called me to look at – a little ragged frightened boy, the herd of some cattle graz-
ing on these uplands who had collected on a stone the *shakings out* of the table
cloth, and who was piling up crusts of bread with one hand and holding bare
bones to his mouth with the other – the impersonation of famine. Need I set out
that we added more substantial morsels to his store – enough too for the morrow,
and the Doctor slipt sixpence into the poor thin hand for milk hereafter.

*The Smiths had two daughters, Annie born in 1830, Janie in 1832, and a son, Jack, in
1838.*

4 July 1846
After dinner Annie and I drove to Russborough where I had long owed a visit; I
set out at four o'clock and did not get back till eight, so glad was Miladi to have
a visitor. Annie was sent off with the girls to gather mushrooms. I had to listen
to many complaints, a good deal of scandal, some fun, and a quantity of conjec-
tures, political and otherwise; all this in the Library; then was walked out to see
many real improvements in the grounds – a new flower garden, a hot house building, greenhouse preparing, iron gates projected. Brought to the Dressing-room
for a cup of tea and to review the whole of the Paris wardrobe. All the caps were
put on my head; all the flowers and bands and bows and streamers and fringed
ribbons and tissues and gauzes and a little hat and feathers on my lady's; the bonnets, a pale pink among them, were ferreted out of their boxes; a *pink* glacée silk
with two deep flounces, short sleeves, low neck; a light blue satin equally low, a
green and lilack, a rose and white, a red and green, a deep blue, were all paraded
before me. Also a Limerick lace with two skirts festooned up one side with bows
and flowers; and she must weigh twelve or fourteen stone and has become the size
of a house, and is one year younger than myself. Then there were shawls, scarves,
visites, dessus, furs, lace, embroidery beyond counting; more than two dozen

pocket handkerchiefs lay at one time on my knees, while a pile of habit shirts lay beside me.

It was quite a bridal array – and for what purpose? for the poor woman visits nowhere; none of these things will ever be on hardly as she herself acknowledges; it is a curious passion under the circumstances. She showed me some trinkets too, presents from him – sixty, seventy, eighty guineas. And in the last paper was his advertisement to raise ten thousand pounds upon her life annuity – the *third* insurance of the same kind, which with the interest paid to the Coates after the law suit with them went against him reduces her once handsome income by one half. Such infatuation! How will it end?

28 September 1846

Tom Darker [the steward] and I were the whole morning settling our affairs. He has dismissed the two old men who for the present have work elsewhere. James Doyle will most likely get enough during the winter to support his family, a brother in America having lately sent him £10, and written for the eldest son to go out to him. James Craig and his dirty idle wife must take their wretched children to the Poor House, old John Doyle may want a little help, and so may Pat Quin's delicate mother, but no one else. And instead of raising wages, a bad precedent, the Colonel with pleasure consents to give them meal at a low price instead of selling his oats in the market, and to ensure his supply lasting, the horses will get none unless the two working mares one feed each. Then we shall buy another cow, and so have milk all winter to divide amongst them.

29 November 1846

Sunday. The grounds covered with snow, a hard frost all yesterday, a storm at night of thunder and lightening, and regular winter to-day … Such a miserable creature as besought Janey and me yesterday to buy a straw basket that she might carry home a supper to four children and a husband who had fasted with herself since the night before. *He* has gone upon the roads but will not be paid till the pay day nor then in full …

I have made up my mind that the distress of the poor demands a large sacrifice on the part of the richer, and it must be our business to prepare for this and to give up luxuries to meet this. 'To feed the hungry' is a duty that cannot be shirked and Hal is not inclined to shirk it.

20 December 1846

Milder weather. I got out yesterday and again to-day. The Doctor has dined with us and says the famine has come, is in every house on Bishop hill, Pinmaker's hill, Holywood and the Radcliffes mountains … The Poor House is full, 1100 where there never was 200, and sheds erecting for hundreds more … After Christmas soup kitchens must be set up.

We have been trying rice and find it liked so have sent for a further supply ... We are paying 24/- and even at that price it is the cheapest food to be had. We will order a ton if necessary, and buy coarse beef which can make into soup to sell at cost price or below it where needful. We must all do our utmost, share our all. Mr and Mrs Moore called yesterday and my Lady and her girls in red clokes and black beaver gypsey hats and feathers cocked up behind like the cobwebs to catch flies. Lunaticks from Bedlam. She was not in a good humour. Wanted us all to go and dine and neither we nor Moores would go.

12 January 1847

... Hal has killed a beef for our poor and we make daily a large pot of good soup which is served gratis to 22 people at present. It is ready at one o'clock and I thought it quite a pretty sight yesterday in the kitchen, all the workmen coming in for their portion, a quart with a slice of the beef; half of them get this one day for a dinner with a bit of their own bread; the other half get milk and the cheap rice we have provided for them. Next day they reverse the order. The Colonel is giving them firing too; so they are really comfortable; there are twelve of them and ten pensioners, old feeble men and women, or those with large families of children; some of them no longer living on our ground yet having been once connected with us we can't desert them.

    ... I will describe my day. Wakened by a cup of tea at half after seven. Bathe in cold water, dress, without a fire; down by a quarter after eight, to keep tryst with Jack who meets me then with his lessons. We work together till nine, I knitting the while the little triangular pieces for a counterpane; whichever little girl is housekeeper for the week comes down at nine to make breakfast and while the tea is drawing they all go up to the schoolroom to prayers, then call in Papa and so we gather to our pleasant meal, after which Jack takes some warm milk to the cat, Annie the crumbs to the birds who actually know her; Miss Clerk [the governess] other little remains to Rover. At ten we all set to work again. Jack goes up to school. I have an interview with Mrs Fyfe, another with Mr Darker, and then I write for the post; then receive any applicant, tidy the drawing-rooms, by which time it is near one o'clock for a good deal of business is included under these few heads. On fine days I am out till four, walking, each walk having its object. Middling days I take the little covered carriage and pay visits – a job I hate. On wet days I have all these hours for my own private occupations the authorship time, but the weather is so fine just now that I am doing nothing in that line. At half after four all dine; afterwards if the Colonel has finished the newspapers in the morning I play backgammon or piquet with him. If the papers are still to read, I sew, mend or make or work for the Repository. At seven we go to tea, and then I read aloud till ten except on the two musick nights when I work. At ten we all retire, but as I sleep little, I sit after undressing for an hour or more by the fire reading, or knitting warm petticoats for the wretched ...

Elizabeth Smith described her survey of the tenants and people living at Baltiboys, whom she visited on five different walks that she made in January 1847, when the famine had become terribly severe.

20 January 1847

Walk 3rd. The distances being now greater I was able to take fewer houses on my round. I went up the hill again first calling on the Widow Quin who being left some years ago on her husband's death insolvent with a large and very young family and she an ailing woman, the Colonel relieved her of her land, forgave her seven years' rent, gave her the stock and crop to dispose of and left her the house and garden for her life ... All her sons are in good places, one them with us; her daughters married except one who lives with her and takes in washing. I put mother and daughter on the soup list, times being so hard. Two of the daughters are very well married; the third made a wretched one; she took a sickly labouring lad who is often laid up, and to whom she has brought seven children. They live in the mother's cowhouse where she had no right to put them and thus settle a whole family of beggars upon us ... It is the most wretched abode imaginable, without window or fireplace; mud for the floor, neither water nor weather-tight, nor scarce a door, all black with smoke, no furniture scarcely. Yet times are brightening for the nearly naked inmates. A brother in America sent them at Christmas ten pounds which paid their debts, and bought them some meal and fuel, and their eldest son is to go out to this kind uncle in March. I gave the poor woman a quarter's school fees for four of the children and put the family on the soup list, and when we come to the clothing which we must do for the very poor, she shall not be forgotten. Nothing could be cleaner or neater in the rude way only known here than the Widow Quin's comfortable three-roomed cabin.

The next visit was to a cousin Red Paddy Quin with a good farm which affords him every comfort from his good management; his wife latterly died in childbed and her baby; he has two fine boys, the eldest at school, a little tidy girl as maidservant; two men, and plenty of everything. Little Paddy, a copy of Jack: with his boots, frieze great coat, and cap! and quite familiar with me from our school intercourse, and only seven years old, insisted on escorting me to the next house on the hill, the abode of another old pensioner, the plague of my life though I am very fond of her.

The Widow Nary wants a few months of eighty, and there she is as brisk as a bee darning her stockings in the doorway without spectacles. As we provide her with everything in the world she wishes for I merely called in to see how she was ...

I came the back road home over the hill, down past the quarries and through the farm yards, looking in at the new room we have just contrived for the two men who sleep there to watch the cattle ... We have eight bachelor labourers who all know they leave us if they marry. As they are rich on their 6/- a week getting their soup or milk daily. Twelve out of door servants, four at 7/- ; eight at 6/-

makes a hole in small means, but this year we must keep them. Ten is our ordinary number ...

24 January 1848
Jim Doyle, the son of those miserable people upon the hill who went out last year to a kind uncle in America, writes home that this uncle met him on the quay and had two suits of clothes ready for him as people must be well dressed in that country and has put him into a factory where his wages are 20/- a week ... Will the poverty-stricken parents let this well doing lad alone or let him really help them by sending by and bye for a brother or sister? I fear that neighbour-like they will try to draw all he can spare from him to help them exist in their wretchedness, and they are so wretched, so very nearly destitute all of them, we can hardly wonder at the pauper family clinging to and draining a prosperous member.

8 December 1848
We have got our third drainage loan without the Surveyor thinking it necessary to look after us; they deduct eight pounds odd however for expenses. Mrs Doyle came here on Saturday last with her tale of destitution which I can well believe is entire seeing that she has five children at home and a cripple for a husband, an incurable; she is blind herself and her only grown up daughter hopelessly lazy. I told her we could not help her nor the farmers either; she must go to the Poor House towards which this little estate pays ninety-six pounds a year and sends hitherto no paupers to it ... She told me they would take no more into the Poor House, it was full. The Colonel rode into Blesinton, got her an order, hired a cart to convey them and they set on the carter to beat him and would not hear of the Poor House ... have forbidden her applying again here. At the same time I hate the Poor House. A sink of vice: idleness finishing to corrupt the miserable inmates; but when people have brought themselves down to it, they must put up with it. I begin to think a pestilence in this darkened land would be a mercy to it.

21 January 1849
I was shocked at our own school, no rosy cheeks, no merry laugh, little skeletons in rags with white faces and large staring eyes crouching against one another half dead. How can we remedy it? No way; how feed sixty children? If we were to coin ourselves into halfpence we could not give a meal a day to one hundredth part of our teeming neighbourhood. The poor little Doyles so clean, so thin, so sad, so naked softened my heart to the foolish parents. They are on our own hill, although not our own people, they must not die of hunger. If I could manage to give a bit of bread daily to each pauper child, but we have no money, much more than we can afford is spent on labour, the best kind of charity, leaving little for ought else ...

21 February 1849

… The party for Monday appeared to swim gallantly on in spite of one or two apologies – but – 'twas a lull before a storm. Mrs Wills came beautifully dressed, Mr Wills really grown presentable, the Doctor very gay. The dinner was very good. Coffee was all right, tea laid, but the urn was not to be had. Ring, ring, ring, and call, call, call, nothing of any use. At last Jack descended to the kitchen and after some delay up it came. The next event was the real actual fainting of Mrs Wills from having eat *crab* at dinner, and she never recovered this crab all the evening, spent most of it up in my room with brandy and water etc. etc. Mr Wills walking up and down wringing his hands in despair.

Next event was George quite drunk, could not lay the supper, could not understand what was said to him, would not go out of the way either. I tried to get him in his room, not a bit of him. Sent the Colonel to him and the Doctor and between them they took him off and got him a little quieter. The maids laid the table, the company waited on themselves and all did pretty well. At last all were gone but the Doctor and Mr Owen, whom we had asked to stay for fear of another outbreak, and there was a fearful one. I found my girls as white as two corpses, comforting Jack in tears. George had got a pistol, had pointed it at Jack in the passage on his way to the kitchen to shoot Mrs Fyfe, which he most assuredly would have done had the pistol not been locked most providentially. 'Life for life', said he as he held it to her ear. He looked, they say, like a demon. Not being able to cock either barrel she had time to fly into her storeroom where she cowered down behind a sack and was found after a search more dead than alive, quite cold and weak, and shrunk to half her size … it took an hour to revive her during which time George had been seized and turned out of the house first and yard last, he going off pretty coolly, giving up the pistol to Pat. The Colonel had some time ago, quite unknown to me given him this pistol to protect the house with, being unaware of the dangerous temper of the man. What an escape we have had from great misery …

7 April 1850

Our Schoolmaster, poor young man, came out of the hospital and has had to return to it. He is totally unfit to resume the school which I shall therefore give up as a bad job and save my pocket thereby. There are very few boys left on our side of the country; there will be few men soon for they are pouring on in shoals to America. Crowds upon crowds swarm along the roads, the bye roads, following carts with their trunks and other property. We have forty children as yet in the girls' school; but really I don't think there will be half that number by autumn.

In December, as part of the marriage festivities for her daughter Annie, Mrs Smith held a party for the school 'with bread and butter and the Piper'; and she was going to reopen the boys' school with twenty-seven pupils.

21 July 1850

Sunday again. Our chief business within has been preserving fruit, a small proportion of the immense crop of small fruit actually over-running the garden. The farm looks as well as the garden. Such corn and hay and potatoes as we have not seen for many a day and difficult to get people for field labour. Eight turnip weeders after searching the country and we have to take them off to make hay. Two mowers only; so here is the rain before that heavy crop is safe ... The markets have fallen again, the cattle markets and very much too – 20/- to 50/- a head. We sold our last lot of lambs wonderfully well considering – 17/6 ...

Our actual income now is nine hundred pounds, five hundred of which is spent outside this house. On the remaining four hundred pounds we live: butcher, baker, grocer, wine merchant, chandler, carrier, wear and tear, house servants' wages, Jack's dress and education, the girls' pinmoney, the Colonel's pocket money, mine, our little journeys, charities, Doctors' fees, extras. Four hundred pounds a year pays it all with the addition of the garden and dairy; but then I pay nobody for doing my work. I do it myself or the girls do it; and I buy no luxuries till we are plentifully supplied with necessaries ...

Elizabeth Smith continued to live at Baltiboys, which was inherited by her son Jack and was where her great granddaughter, the ballerina Ninette de Valois, spent her childhood.

William Clements, 3rd Earl of Leitrim
1805-1878

ON 3 APRIL 1878, *Lord Leitrim left Manor Vaughan, his house in north County Donegal, on an outside car accompanied by his young clerk of the estate to be driven by his coachman to the railway station at Letterkenny. At the place where Cratlagh Wood goes down to the shore, he was ambushed by three men hidden behind the wall. As the outside car passed they fired, killing the coachman. The young clerk jumped from the car, but collapsed with a heart attack and died. Lord Leitrim had had his elbow shattered by the shot and was unable to get his loaded revolver from his attaché case. He fell on to the road, but getting to his feet, blood streaming from his face, caught one of the attackers (McElwee) by his red beard and the two men struggled together. The other assailant, Sheils, seeing McElwee was getting the worst of the encounter brought the butt of a gun down on Lord Leitrim's head. With the old man on the ground, they picked up a rock and broke his skull to make sure that he was dead before rolling the body into a flax dam and rowing back to Fanad. It is said that that night every man in Fanad shaved off his beard.*

William Sidney Clements, 3rd Earl of Leitrim, owned nearly 100,000 acres in Leitrim, Galway and Donegal, and a house and demesne in Kildare. In folklore he is known as the 'wicked' Lord Leitrim with a reputation as the most tyrannical and lecherous of landlords. His diaries bear out his autocratic, inflexible, and sometimes paranoid attitude towards his tenants, though undoubtedly he saw his actions as improvments to the estate and increasing the general prosperity. Ten days after his death, Frank Hugh O'Donnell MP alleged in the House of Commons that the real cause of the murder was Lord Leitrim's sexual immorality on the Donegal estate. The House was cleared of strangers, so we do not know what evidence was produced.

Though he never married, in his diaries there are entries about a girl called Mathilda whom he educated and took on two trips to the Continent. It is presumed that she was his illegitimate daughter, but she displeased him in some way when she was about sixteen and she is not referred to again.

He quarrelled with his tenants, his neighbours, his relations and with the administration in Dublin, and there were incessant law suits. He made passionate speeches in the House of Lords on the Disestablishment of the Irish Church and on Gladstone's early Land Acts. Before he succeeded to the title, he had sat in the House of Commons for County Leitrim as a radical Whig. By the 1850s, however, he had become an extreme conservative.

He was adamant that landlords should reside on their estates and he himself con-

stantly travelled around his properties attending to the minutest details of their management – buying cattle at fairs, collecting the rents in person and recording the dismissal or engagement of his domestic servants. His houses were Killadoon in County Kildare, Lough Rynn in County Leitrim, Manor Vaughan (today Mulroy) in County Donegal and Ross Hill in Galway. He also owned the town of Manorhamilton and had a house at Milford and a lodge at Fanad.

As he grew older he became ever more domineering, arrogant and repressive; evicting his tenants for any infringement of his exacting regulations, antagonizing his fellow landlords and squabbling with his relations.

In his will he left all his property to a cousin, and nothing to his surviving brother and sisters or to his nephew, the heir to the title.

Marcus Clements, a descendant of this cousin and who at one time owned Lough Rynn, transcribed Lord Leitrim's diaries; the explanatory notes below are his.

* * *

18 April 1857 – Kildare
Went to Dublin and to Killadoon.

I was shot at passing through Tooman. Two copper caps snapped. The gun or pistol missed fire. I went into the house of the widow Burbage and her son Mch'l Burbage appeared to be the person who had done the act.

12 October 1857 (to 19 October) – Leitrim
Mohill rents – £1918-12-0d.

6 November 1857 – Leitrim
Newtowngore rents – £505-5-11d.

10 November 1857 (to 13 November) – Leitrim
Manorhamilton rents – £2872-18-1¹/₂d.

21 January 1858 – Donegal
[Tenant rights meeting in Milford] Engaged all the Public Houses. Police came in – about sixty. People came in two mobs of about two hundred strong each. The meeting held on the hill above the town – not on the estate.

17 July 1858 – Leitrim
Evicted Widow McRann of Eskerkilen and obtained possession from the sheriff.

The Rent Book of c. 1852 shows a holding of under seven acres with the comment 'good farm badly laboured, dirty house, cows tied in the kitchen (7 children)'. The 1878 Rent Book shows Eliza McRann occupying 2¹/₂ acres.

13 September 1860 – Leitrim

Received a challenge from James Murphy by post. Sent to Mr Wm Jones [Murphy's landlord?] who called on me. I gave him the letter I had received from James Murphy and called on him to protect me.

15 September 1860 – Leitrim

Went to Mohill Poor House. Was shot at in the Main Street of Mohill by James Murphy from the door of his house in that town about half past one in the afternoon. The ball struck the house near me, the splinters fell on me. James Murphy was arrested and committed.

8 October 1860 – Leitrim

Received an address from the town and neighbourhood of Mohill to congratulate me on my escape from assassination.

16 October 1860 – Leitrim

Ditto from Newtowngore.

18 October 1860 – Leitrim

Received a deputation from the tenants of the Mohill estate congratulating me on my escape from assassination.

20 October 1860 - Leitrim

Answered the address from my tenants …

27 October 1860 – Leitrim

Received a deputation from the Persons in my Employment who presented an address, signed by 121 in daily employment, expressing their attachment to me.

28 October 1860 – Leitrim

Sunday – at home writing a codicil to my will.

4 December 1860 – Leitrim

Leave Lough Rynn at 7.30 a.m. Arrived Manorhamilton at 1 p.m. Received rents. At night a tar barrel was burned and a band played through the town to greet my arrival.

5 March 1861 – Leitrim

Leitrim Assizes – Trial of James Murphy for firing at me in Mohill on 15th Sept 1860. Verdict acquittal on the grounds of insanity.

Lord Leitrim was not at all satisfied by this verdict and continued to pursue the matter – going as far as writing to all the jurymen on the case.

6 March 1861 – Leitrim
Inquired into the cutting off of the tail of Thompson's cow in Farnaught. Found that there was every reason to believe that the tail was cut by young Malachy Fanning and his brother Charles. Thos Cunnion of Farnaught and Edward Corr of Farnaught were with Malachy Fanning in his father's house. The father Fanning was absent. Ordered that Fanning pay Thompson £1.

7 March 1861 – Leitrim
Inquired into the stealing of my potatoes at Clooncoo. There was not sufficient evidence to show who took them. The Irwins were accused by James Carroll, but there is much reason to suspect that the Carrolls took them.

I gave £25 to each of the Constables who arrested James Murphy.

3 August 1861 – Donegal
Ballyhooriskey – saw a schoolhouse partly built. Stopped the building and called on Mr Boyle the priest and told him that the school must be my property.

This was the start of bad relations with Father Boyle which went on until Lord Leitrim's death.

15 January 1863 – Donegal
Sat in Petty Sessions. Seaweed cases of M. Fausset [?] came before me, which I postponed as they were for the collecting of seaweed below the high water mark – which I consider my property.

17 January 1863 – Donegal
I assembled 12 tenants of Fanad and conferred with them as to the seaweed on the shore, they appeared all determined to respect my rights.

12 May 1863 – Fanad, Donegal
Went to Doaghbeg with Wilson [his bailiff], gave notice to Michael Martin No 10, Pollet and Pat'k Kelly No 8 that I would evict them; also to Wm McAteer, Doagh Beg, I would evict him and to Dennis Boyce of Ballinacrick that I would remove him for harbouring McGinley who was evicted.

13 May 1863 – Fanad, Donegal
Saw John Martin who was evicted from Pollet & told him that I would not give him land, but would evict all of his name if he gave me trouble.

13 October 1864 - Leitrim
Received intelligence by Telegraph that Rob't Wilson my steward at Ballyhiernan had been shot on Wednesday the 12th.

15 October 1864 – Fanad, Donegal
Arrived at Ballyhiernan, found Wilson alive and doing well.

16th October, 1864 – Fanad, Donegal
I met twelve of the tenants and heard their opinions as to the late outrage.

17 October 1864 – Fanad, Donegal
Mr Butt & Captain Latham came to Ballyhiernan but they did nothing and seemed to think that the matter was in other hands, and that they should not interfere. I told them that I attributed the outrage to the conduct of the Gov't in giving up my letters for the purpose of the trial in Dec '63 by Studdart against me.

19 October 1864 – Fanad, Donegal
There was an investigation at Tullyconnell schoolhouse respecting the shooting of Mr Wilson. Present: Capt. Hart, Capt. Latham, Mr McLeod, stipendiary magistrate. Nothing achieved.

15 November 1865 – Donegal
The first night at Manor Vaughan.

16 November 1865 – Donegal
The House Warming at Manor Vaughan. Forty-three tenants etc. at dinner in the hall – twenty Bailiffs in the kitchen – twenty-seven servants and others.

21 March 1867 – Leitrim
Gave directions that Thos O'Neill should be dismissed in consequence of his having allowed a Priest, O'Bierne, to hold a station in my house occupied by him as my servant, and making use of it to obtain an opposition to Noble's election [to the Poor Law Guardians?].

23 March 1867 – Leitrim
Thom O'Neill came to me and asked to be allowed to remain in my service. Told him it was impossible.

27 March 1867 – Killadoon, Kildare
Saw Makim ... instructions that Thom O'Neill should leave immediately (Then to Killadoon) Went to the river, found the water within $6^{1}/_{4}$ of the top of the weir wall with the edge plank removed and found the water $3^{3}/_{4}$ inches deep in the house sewer.

10 January 1870 – Dublin
Went to Dublin – Called on C. Fortescue at the Park – had a long conversation.

He appeared at first inclined to give me trouble and talked about the *harsh* way in which I treated my tenants. I told him that it was *false*. I asked him to remove Hill, County Inspector of Donegal.

This is Chichester Fortescue, later Lord Carlingford, Chief Secretary – 'the Park' is his house in the Phoenix Park in Dublin.

17 January 1870 – Killadoon, Kildare
A robbery took place this night – two shirts, two pocket handkerchiefs taken out of the Bleach Green at Killadoon – some lemons taken from the Green House & some of the Gardener's tools.

20 January 1870 – Killadoon, Kildare
Went to the garden and examined the footmarks of the man who had been there on Monday night. I took a model of them and compared with Rutherford's and remarked his mode of walking which left no doubt of his being the man.

26 March 1871 – Donegal
Leave Derry by the 6.20 train – changed carriage at Omagh and was unable to find a privy fit to be used. At another station, I think Ballybay, they were going to remove me from the carriage but the Station Master civilly allowed the carriage to proceed. Dundalk – the carriage was again changed. The privy at Enniskillen was also unfit for use.

15 December 1871 – Dublin
Met Robert (at the Bilton Hotel). He talked to me about his marriage to Miss Norah Westenra, to whom he stated that he is not engaged …

Robert was his nephew and heir and Norah Westenra was the daughter of a neighbour, Lord Rossmore.

30 September 1872 – Leitrim
I received a letter from Robert stating that he was engaged to marry Norah Westenra.

5 October 1872 – Leitrim
I received a letter to say that Lady Rossmore and her daughter would come here [Lough Rynn] on Monday.

8 October 1872 – Leitrim
I drove out in the drag with Lady Rossmore, Norah & Robert. Left Robert in Clooncarne to shoot. Home and took the ladies thro' Clooncahir, Mohill and returned by the bog road. We afterwards went walking to Errew and Gortletteragh, returning by Doyle's gate.

9 October 1872 – Leitrim
Robert refused to go out shooting … In the afternoon I walked with Lady Rossmore and told her my intentions towards Robert – viz. that he should live at Manor Vaughan and that I would pay him for his services. I afterwards talked to Norah on the same subject, and told her that she should be comfortable at Manor Vaughan. She asked me if she might change the servants, and I said yes if necessary. Robert told me he would not accept my offer.

The note at the end of the year reads:
… I told Lady R. that I saw no objection to Robert marrying Norah Westenra … I afterwards told Norah to the same effect and that she should have the use of the garden and that he should have the use of the Carrick farm. She asked me if I would require them always to be there, that she would like to go and see her brothers at times. I told her that I would be willing to give them leave of absence, but that I should like to be asked.

I afterwards told Robert the same and that I would give him at the rate of £500 a year. He was not satisfied, and he afterwards told me that he would not accept my offer. He was exceedingly rough in his manner and said that he would not marry.

10 October 1872 – Leitrim
Lady Rossmore, her daughter & Robert left Lough Rynn for the early train at Dromod to return to Rossmore Park.

22 October 1872
I received a letter from Norah Westenra saying that her engagement with Robert was at an end. She returned to me a cheque for £50 which I had sent to her as a wedding present to buy whatever she wished for. She stated that she had herself broken off the engagement.

23 October 1872 – Leitrim
I wrote to Norah and asked her to consider carefully the step she was taking.

1 January 1873 – Kildare
Received a letter from Canny stating that his life had been threatened.

Presumably Canny was a Bailiff in Galway.

2 January 1873 – Kildare
I wrote to Canny and told him I would protect him and I would provide for the family if he should be shot. Wrote to Mr Robinson on the same subject.

John Sarsfield Casey
1846-1896

THE IRISH REPUBLICAN BROTHERHOOD – *familiarly known as the Fenians – was founded in New York and in Dublin in 1858 with the aim of winning independence for Ireland. It was envisaged that the American Fenians would supply the army in the field with arms, officers and funds. In Ireland the Fenians attracted the working man: agricultural labourers, building workers and first-generation rural migrants, shop assistants, clerks and a high proportion of soldiers in the British regiments.*

It was arranged on the lines of a secret society, with local 'circles' and the members bound by oaths, but the organization was riddled with informers. An uprising planned for 1865 had to be postponed after the police, on the night of 14 September, raided many of the Fenian centres An insurrection was planned for 5 March 1867, but the government, aware of the conspiracy, was well prepared and the attempted insurrection was a complete failure. In spite of this, Fenianism remained a political force in the country into the twentieth century.

John Sarsfield Casey was born in Mitchelstown, County Cork. As a young man he worked in Cork as a clerk for J.J. Geary, who had a public house that was a 'head centre' for the IRB. Under the nom de plume *of 'The Galtee Boy', John Casey wrote letters to the newspaper, 'The Irish People'. This brought him to the notice of the police and he was arrested in September 1865 on a charge of treason-felony and sentenced to five years. The notes on his charge sheet read: 'Very young man, but a very determined Fenian. Used to write very violent letters and "poetry".' He went from Mountjoy to Pentonville and from there to Portland where he was breaking stones before being transported to Western Australia.*

He was granted a free pardon in 1869 and arrived back in Dublin in 1870. He spent the rest of his life in Ireland, eventually becoming coroner for County Limerick. The extracts are from the journal he kept on his way to Australia.

* * *

7 October 1867 – Portland
Monday went to work as usual till dinner – at 1 o'c inspected in company with some 120 prisoners by Surgeon Superintendent – Confined to cell during remainder of the day – supplied with clothes etc. Received no information as to time of leaving.

8 October 1867
At work again till 9 a.m. at which time summoned 'inside' by Officer – Went

through form of leave taking with comrades – prevented by Russel & ordered 'within' immediately …

12 o'c Prepare to depart – our kit consists of 2 shirts, 2 flannels, 2 drawers, 2 pocket & neck handkerchiefs, 2 stockings & 1 suit of clothes.

Chained and drawn up in hall – Governor and naval officer entered – Beg permission to bid adieu to our comrades – Governor refuses – upon second thought he consents – All men very much affected.

Drawn up in yard – Governor addresses *other prisoners* on conduct during Voyage. Depart.

Meet for the first time Men convicted '66 and '67. Converse with them during walk to pier. Officers repeatedly reprimand us for talking and at length separate us, yet other prisoners are laughing & chatting at pleasure. Escorted by several companies of soldiers – Crowds collected on shore – Tender at hand – As we cross pier P. Dunn's sister rushes to embrace him, she is violently pushed back by Coastguards who take her in charge – Enter tender the 'Earnest' – quarter of an hour brings us along side the 'Hougoumont' – Enter vessel – showed down between decks to our apartment. Total number of prisoners on board 280 of which 62 are Fenians, majority of other prisoners Irish victims of the 'Special Dispensation'. Receive plenty of tobacco etc. from men – During remainder of day conversing with our companions in misfortune, hearing news of the world outside – astonished & indignant at facts we hear especially of perfidy and treachery of Stephens.

Supper; Bread & tea for first time these two years. Glad to see that our apartment is separated from other prisoners. After supper our friends entertain us with some well-known songs of our dear native land and once more we roam in spirit over green fields and through the romantic ruins of Old Erin.

8 o'c to bed – no sleep for us talking all night. A new life to that of Portland.

James Stephens, veteran of 1848 and founder of the Fenians, had been arrested but had made a dramatic escape from the Bridewell prison. In New York, at the end of 1866, he had been accused of cowardice and incompetence and was deposed from the leadership; a rumour was put about that he had been foiled of misappropriating funds to spend on fast horses and faster women in Paris.

9 October 1867

On deck at 6 o'c & wash – Beautiful morning, smart keen breeze, promenaded deck till 12 o'c. Several boats with visitors sail round vessel.

Scale of dietary: 10 oz biscuit; 1 pint of tea & chocolate on alternate mornings. Dinner in part fresh meat an' tea, beef & pork ½lb with bone on alternate days with oz of flour & raisins with beef and oz of preserved potatoes and pint insipid pea soup with pork. Supper 1 pint thin gruel – 2 o'c 1 glass of wine; 11 o'c ½ pint Lime juice very palatable. Spent day in recounting stories of my prison life.

12 October 1867

Sails set – Blue Peter hoisted – 2 p.m. set sail, fair wind. Take a farewell glance at Portland as we sail within one mile of its rock bound coast. Emotions of the pleasant kind. Towed out by the gun-boat 'Earnest', Pass the evening in playing Chess etc.

13 October 1867

Ship rolling very much. On deck nothing visible but sky and water save a few solitary sea-birds that kept eternally skimming over the crested waves. Had several interviews with Mr Deleany RCC. Begs of me to serve Mass for him I consent – I serve with difficulty in consequence of being seasick – Majority of hands, troops etc. on board Catholics – Mass in main hatchway.

Still towed out by 'Earnest'. Eat very little today – None sick but myself 'spued' off everything I eat – Water distilled & measured out ³/₄ pint per man per diem – find I cannot read. Ordered below for night at 4.30. Amuse ourselves every night with a concert of which the following is the programme:

Mr Michael Cody		Chairman
Mr Con O'Mahony		Vice Chairman
Song	Paddies Evermore	Mr M. Moore
Song	Lamh Dearg Aboo	Mr P. Doran
Song	Ned of the Hills	Mr D. Bradley
Recitation	The Spanish Champion	Mr Duggan
Song	Freedom's War	Mr C. Keane
Song	The Penal Days	Mr I. Kearney etc. etc.

At 8 o'c the whistle sounded & all retired to rest, save the sentry in the hatchways who cried out every half hour 'No 2, Alls Well'.

15 October 1867

Morning very gloomy – ship rolling – Feel terribly sick can neither eat nor keep anything on my stomach – remain below all day. Bradley says that plum duff is a cure for sea sickness – intolerable thirst – with Dr – says he can't cure seas sickness – got 2 pills – Prisoner hooked a dog fish 4 feet long about 14 lbs weight.

17 October 1867

Blowing exceedingly hard – still sick.

2 o'c Sail ho – A Fenian cruiser? All hands rush on deck and in an instant bulwarks & forecastle are crowded with anxious faces chatting and pointing in direction of supposed cruiser who is bearing down on us – she hoists no colours – when within ¹/₂ mile of us dreadful excitement prevails on deck – Captain and Surgeon examining her with a glass – She is still 'incog', a faint cheer is heard from her and scarcely has it died away ere a deafening cheer bursts from all hands who expect that the hour of deliverance has at length arrived, but alas another minute

and the Union Jack is proudly waving to the breeze and the 'Fenian cruiser' turns out to be an English merchantman bound for Liverpool with a cargo of rice.

26 October 1867
... A prisoner received 48 lashes from boatswain today without wincing for beating another prisoner most inhumanly – At conclusion cheered by his comrades – got cross irons on his feet ...

24 December 1867
Glorious morning – Mate has caught 2 albatross very large.

6.30 All below – Endeavour to celebrate Christmas in this den as well as circumstances will permit, having neither 'mountain dew' nor sparkling Rhenish to make us merry, we form a circle & pass the night in singing some songs of our dear native land. Such a celebration of Christmas by exiles for the cause of liberty in the Indian Ocean & the mention of names of many others who were keeping their solitary vigils in the cold & cheerless cells of Portland and Millbank made our hearts almost burst with grief to think to what a condition Ireland has been reduced not only by the —— but more so by the perfidy & treachery of her sons, especially during the past two years.

29 December 1867
One of the most eventful days of my life. Two years to day since I stood in the dock in Cork & heard my doom pronounced by Mr Justice Fitzgerald. Two years! Oh God to look back through that vista what memories, what painful associations rush upon my mind. December 29, 1866 I spent 'knobling' stones in Portland: the same day in '67 finds me ploughing the trackless ocean on board the Convict ship Hougoumont, 14000 miles from the green hills of old Ireland ...

9 January 1868
Blowing hard all night – sailing under scarcely fifty yards of canvas.

7.45 Land ahead – on our lee bow a long low range visible surmounted by a lighthouse.

The pilot boat now appears in the distance, 7 men in her. Fremantle now visible after dinner, a few merchant vessels in the roads. Prospect cheerless in the extreme – A sober sadness now assails me at idea of being separated from many of my comrades. Look in vain for the emerald green hills dotted with sheep, the waving meadows, the yellow corn fields bowing beneath the golden ear, the broad transparent river meandering through the deep garment of the fairest green and the darkly shadowed mountains in the background which gladdened the sight on nearing the shores of Holy Ireland – There all is grand. Here all is dreary desolate & cheerless. How many of the stout hearts now beating are destined to lay their bones in this land. How many will again tread the fair hills of Holy Ireland. Oh! for a dip into the gloomy dark future.

Thomas Johnson Westropp
1860-1922

THOMAS WESTROPP *was the fifth son of John Westropp of Attyflin, County Limerick, and had seven older half brothers and sisters. The Westropps had been in Limerick since the seventeenth century and were related to most of the other Protestant landlords of the area. Until he went to college, Thomas Westropp was educated entirely at home. At Trinity he read engineering, but he abandoned that field in favour of archaeology, for even as a boy he was a keen antiquarian.*

In the nineteenth century amateur archaeology flourished in Ireland. In 1849 James Graves, a Protestant clergyman, and John Prim, who became editor of the Kilkenny Moderator, *founded the Kilkenny Archaeological Society. Twenty years later it became the Royal Historical and Archaeological Association of Ireland and in 1890 took the name the Royal Society of Antiquaries of Ireland and soon after moved to Dublin. (The Kilkenny Archaeological Society was revived in 1945.) Thomas Westropp was a distinguished President of the RSAI. His chief interest was in prehistoric forts, on which he was the leading authority.*

He never married: in one of the entries in the diary, he writes: 'I am very practical & don't think paupers have any right to marry so never trouble myself about ladies society, dress or an amentia —'

The diary is entitled 'Chronicum Westropporium'. It was originally written when he was a boy, but he added and revised it later as part memoir part commonplace book.

* * *

7 July 1875
Ralph, Bessy, Mother & I drove to Doonass. Now Ralph had some shopping to do in Limerick & I during the delay purchased 13 odious delicacies viz. fig cakes for a shilling, of which as no one else would eat them, I demolished 7 on route, leaving 6 to give to my cousin Anne Westropp at Doonass, but she did not care for any so I kept them. Now Aunt had two parrots, one the old grey one, the other a parrot which had once broken two of its toes and cracked its bill through sticking it through the wires of its cage (& ever since the gardener had to prune its beak once a month because it grew crooked, during which surgical operation Aunt used to retire to her bedroom having shut all the intervening doors and would hide her face in a pillow for fear of hearing the dear bird scream). To each of these two I gave half a fig cake.

Next Ralph asked me for a fig cake and when he broke it we discovered, much to my horror, that it was full of small white worms. Now allow 30 for each cake which equals 330 worms consumed by me this day, and to add to my discomfort I was informed that Aunt had found them crumbled in the parrots' cages and had wondered who gave it as almonds were deadly poison to parrots. You may fancy my horror at what I had done & I expect to hear by every post that the parrots are dead. Horreseo Referens.

Ralph and Bessy are his stepbrother and stepsister.

28 March 1877

There was an auction at Faha where we got a quantity of furniture. For Mr Robert Massy was leaving, rumour said, because his house was haunted. The ghost of the deceased Mrs Russell walking into the dining room in the dusk of the evening and sitting at the head of the table and the ghost of an old gentleman appeared in the passage one night as Mrs. M was going to bed and bowed to her. Nay more. The ghost of a man holding its head under its arm & emitting blue light was seen stalking through a shady walk at the foot of the pleasure ground.

In short there was a choice variety of ghosts round Patrickswell and I cannot do better than append a list of the most prominent.

Attyflin:
1. Ghost in back room rattles fire irons and drags about furniture.
2. Cannon ball ghost (now extinct)
3. Slipper ghost (ditto)
4. Haunted Danish fort
5. Banshee
6. Coachabower or headless coach attending on the Westropps.

Ballyhandrahan: In the Kyle or Roses private burial place are two vaults where reside several chained ghosts & skeletons which rattle heavy chains at night.

Faha: Ghost of lady; ghost of gentleman; & headless ghost as given above.

Greenmount: Ghost of Lady Peacock who committed suicide; ghost of man in shrubbery.

Turret Hill is haunted by many & venomous ghosts; coachabower attendant on the Green family etc.

Others: Ghost of man haunts road near Attyflin gate; coachabower drives near Annagh; haunted fort in Lissard; *Total* nine ghosts besides colonies in Kyle & Turret Hill, three coachabowers, a banshee, two haunted forts & several skeletons etc.

31 July 1877

We, having been invited by the Revd Mr Humphries, drove to the Rectory at Tulla. Our intentions being to explore the hill, churchyard and see the family tombs. We went through the rectory garden, a quaint pretty spot with its sunny old fashioned flowers & beds & going through Tulla we entered the churchyard in which was an old man with a flock of geese & a woman looking for a hen. The new part of the burial ground lies farthest from the gate; when it was taken in, some of the more bigoted guardians wanted to insist on its being kept for the Protestants alone & walled off. But one Mr Dan O'Connell [not the Liberator] standing up said, 'Gentlemen you had better leave things as they are, for the Catholic & Protestant ghosts can whack each other as well over the wall as if there was none at all.' This new aspect of the question silenced all the malcontents.

On entering the church you first see the mural tomb of the Hartes fallen across the little doorway, on your right are three shattered arched windows; before you is the railed-in vaulted chancel on the north of which is the O'Callaghan tomb embellished with the figure of a 'horned wolf looking out of a bundle of sticks'. A travesty of the family arms.

8 January 1878
The long looked for Histrionic Ball came off ... I had a pleasant enough evening and a fair share of dancing seeing that I was a novice and not the heir to large estates. But the humblest has friends and is often happier than the most fortunate. The Ball was at the Atheneum and it was rather crowded and kept up till seven o'clock on Saturday morning. And on this day the news of the death of Pope Pius the Ninth reached us, as also a false report that England had declared war with Russia to protect Turkey ...

22 March 1878
Johnny Westropp 'the Mayor' having come to us from Limerick the day before. He, I, Ralph & Bessy drove to Rockhill, they to hunt, I to see the meet at which Prince Arthur, Duke of Connaught, or as we called him Prince Paddy, was to be present. Sir David Roche master of the Foxhounds & as usual in a profane passion met him at the station and nobody saw the Duke well till in a narrow road near Coolruss the riders passed in single file between the carriages. No one bowed, no one took off – nor touched their hats even – to the prince. We all stuck out our heads and stared him in the face with grim determination of making the most of what little royalty filtered into our remote country. Pat Scott (who drove me and James Horrigan who had ridden Bessy's horse Ruby for her down to the meet) was very much disappointed at seeing a slight unremarkable looking young man, not a patch on some of the Limerick Anakim in appearance, instead of a grand person in fancy dress wearing a crown and wolloping his horse with a golden sceptre (à la travelling play) which he doubtless expected to see. We then went on by Ballyheany to Liskennet hill passing a wretched hamlet of mud lean-to huts against a churchyard wall, the most miserable human habitations I ever had seen.

Johnny, the Mayor, met with an accident for he was riding Ralph's

Connemara cob 'Bob' and he put him at a ditch before the prince and the whole field. Bob flew at it, John felt his hat going – could not get his poor still whilom broken arm up to it, so he let go the reins and put up the good arm. At that instant the horse took the ditch like a bird & Johnny was landed sitting in some tough yellow clay which – all the more as he wore black breeches – branded him for the rest of the day. He was perfectly frantic with rage and cursed the horse as the cause of what he had brought on himself. The hunt however was very cold so we had no means of proving our speculations of the early part of the day as to whether Sir David would get in a passion if the prince got before him and would call him a bloody tinker (which the gallant Bart had applied even to ladies within the year).

30 April 1878

News reached us of the death of unfortunate George Westropp of Fortanne. Spending his sober moments at the feminine employment of sewing and knitting and worn out by living in a chronic state of delerium tremens he after a long struggle realized the family prophecy and died ... E'er his death Jont came up one evening to Maryfort in great alarm shouting as he saw my sister 'Arrah Mayery, I've seen the white owl. It flew three times round me near the corner of the house & some Fortanne Westropp will die ... it never told false and I think it is George it has come for.'

George died and two of the neighbours and all the servants during the long night with difficulty kept the rats which infested the decaying house from mangling his body.

Thomas Westropp and Vere Valentine Hunt from Curraghbridge were working together for their entrance to Trinity College, Dublin. Valentine Hunt was a relation of the diarist Sir Vere Hunt (q.v.).

17 September 1878

Vere insisted on my taking him to Greenmount to see his cousins the Greens (for Mr. 'Mon' Hunt had recently paid out tin to Sir Bernard Burke to make out a swell pedigree & had thereby discovered hundreds of relationships). Vere actually brought a clothes brush with him and got me to brush his coat at Greenmount gate to appear fascinating. He was not over lucky however in his fascinations, for the three Miss Greens, two Miss Russells of Lemonfield & Mary Massywestropp of Attyflin all snubbed him severely – poor fellow –

31 October 1878

Vere David Hunt [cousin of V. Valentine] was married to the daughter of Arthur Russell of Lemonstown.

We were all in the Attyflin pew at Kilpeacon church and outside on the window sill behind us stood various gossoons looking in and as Mr Gubbins said most impressively, 'Vere David Urquhart Hunt will thou have this woman to be thy wedded wife?' one of them slipped off hitting his chin on the sill and turning a somersault with a loud yell, we looked up and saw his legs vanish in the bushes. Ralph and John looked at me and we all laughed despite our efforts to choke it down & Madge looked scissors at us.

George Hunt of Limerick got very tight and tried to sing 'The Hardy Norseman' to the time of 'There's a Land of Pure Delight', but as he forgot the words and always sang two octaves at least above or below the accompaniment he gave up his intention. As the happy couple left, I put a handful of rice with fatally correct aim down the bride's back and it must have made her very uncomfortable.

25 December 1878
We had the Massywestropps to dinner and passed a very pleasant evening. The male guests went masquerading into the kitchen and hunted Anne Nestor the housemaid downstairs and upstairs. Now there was mistletoe in the hall and Jane O'Dea the foxfaced kitchen maid was washing plates under it thereupon much to the delight of us boys, John despite her very unattractive appearance kissed her on the spot.

20 March 1879
Hugh Westropp of Clorane & his son little Johnny were invited to come to Attyflin with their terriers to kill rats and mice. When the corn stacks were taken down the mice appeared ... When Madge, Mary and Mrs Hess came out, a mouse got under the latter's petticoat making her execute a frantic misery dance. Madge and Mary squodged several but afterwards when the latter took off her waterproof she found one mouse up her back and several in her petticoats, nearly all were killed.

Hattie Cowper
1863–?

HATTIE COWPER *of Trudder, Newtownmountkennedy, County Wicklow, began her diary in June 1877 after she been taken away from a Dublin boarding school. It is not explained why she had left school other than she had been ill 'and other reasons only known to Mama'. She and her sisters Ada and Ethel and her two younger brothers had lessons with their governess, Miss Bernard.*

Hattie's father owned a wine-importing business in Dublin and spent most of the week in town. During the winters the family left Trudder and lived in their house in Fitzwilliam Place.

Hattie married Robert Rynd of Black Hall near Naas.

The diary is in a very small book, written mostly in pencil. An indignant adult has written on one page: 'Such fearful writing for a girl of fourteen, to say nothing of the spelling!'

* * *

4 June 1877
I made a radish bed and did up my garden. It rained all day. We have been here for four days. I have just come home from school having been there for one month. I got a gastric attack and Doctor Blythe said it would be better for me to stay at home, but there are other reasons only known to Mama.

5 June 1877
Miss Bernard came today, and she and Ada went into the village and telagraphed to Mama that she had come, they counter ordered Bell. Mama came however in the evening; she was very angry with Miss Bernard for interfering with her arrangments. Very fine here in the morning, but poured for the rest of the day. Planted Calcies in my garden, they were the colored ones. Dreadful rows with Ellen and Eliza, Ellen refused to obey Eliza. She would not wash or sweep the oilcloth. I found a birds nest full of young birds in the shrubery near the tennise ground. I am very lucky. The trees are only just out and they are a lovely green. Papa is coming down on Thursday and the carrige tomorrow.

Eliza looked after the children and Ellen was the housemaid.

6 June 1877

Miss Bernard refused to come into breakfast, alleging that Mama *had* been rude to her. She has behaved most extronenly. Mama says she is like a sulky child, she wont come into meals but eats them afterwards when everybody is gone.

15 June 1877

Started for Greystones this morning at ten. The five of us and Eliza. I took the pocket handkerchif case that I am making for Ethel to work on on the car – it is getting on nicely. We got a box [bathing box] almost directly and we had a most delightful dip. Ethel made a rush out into deep water. Eliza had to call her in. Eliza would not let the boys take off their shoes and stockings. We told Mama and she was very angry. Alick cried a good deal and called Eliza a filthy beast. When we were going to eat our lunch Eliza said we should have it on the road and when we would not she walked off to the car and we had to get a woman to open one of the lemonade bottles, however she came back and drank a glass of it soon enough. I had no nuts for my mouse so I gave it some picnic biscuits which it ate. Lovely day.

22 June 1877

This morning when I went up to see Mrs Smythe, she attacked Ada and me and gave us a most *awful* jaw I ever had, at last it became so bad that I rushed out of the room down stairs, after cursing her very badly finished a story out of The Quiver and then seized with a sudden desire to practise, went to the piano, but first I opened the window as wide as I could and then attacked the piano and practised my scales and exercises for a whole hour – didn't I give her a dose of music. I hope very much she has a headache, I pounded so.

The Collins came to dinner. I ate prunes and a fig behind the blind. Mr Collins thought I was sentimental. Stayed up till twelve o'clock.

Mrs Smythe is always talking about her ailments. She is wrapped up in herself. Ada and I call her 'old number one'.

Mrs Smythe was a friend of the family, who was staying for a few days at Trudder.

23 June 1877

Went to Mrs Irwin [wife of the Protestant rector] and got a kitten for myself. Tried to paint but did not manage very well. Mrs Smythe still very unwell and does not come down to breakfast. Watered my garden with manure water. Miss Burns promised me a hedgehog on Monday. Had a hot bath, mended my clothes. Went to bed.

25 June 1877

The Smythes went away today. Mrs Smythe has been very ill here. She got up for dinner yesterday but had to go to bed after it. Kitten quite well. Fine day.

5 July 1877

Ethel's birthday. She got a parosol, a knife, a shoehorn and I gave her a handker-chief case. She did not have a holiday as Miss Bernard left today. I don't like her atall. She was so impertonent to Mama. Mama says no governess was so rude to her in her life. Mrs La Touche thinks my dormouse might have young ones, so we must not handel it atall. Alec ate all the strawberries out of my garden. I will pay him out. I am so glad Miss Bernard is gone, Hurrah Hurrah. Ada cut her fin-ger with Ethel's knife. Ada and I fought dreadfully this morning.

7 July 1877

Mama went to an At Home at the Thiges [Tighes]. Adolpe came in the after-noon. I cleaned out and settled all my goods and chattels this morning. Mended my clothes. All our potatoes are run out. Newman never said a word about it and then he thought to dig the kidneys for the servants. Mrs Mannering brought me a hedgehog today, I am so glad I have wanted one for so long. Played lawn ten-nice this afternoon with Adolpe, he does not play very well for a man. I don't like him very much and I know he does not like me.

Newman was the gardener. Hattie is obviously repeating her mother's views. Newman gave in his notice a few weeks later.

10 July 1877

Went to see the Drill at Wicklow and to dinner at Mrs Welches, we met Mr Wynne in the town and he talked to Mama a great deal about gardening. We then went to Mrs Welches to dinner. The room was very small, two militia men came in. We had chickens and lamb, gooseberrie pie and a white mold, champane and sherry and very sour strawberries and cherries. Mrs Welche smirked and smiled as usual. She is a booby. We went out and stood for an hour watching the drill. C. Cunningham came up to us and made the men march past with the band. Then we went in to tea and strawberries at the Wynnes. Papa did not like it at all. He was very cross all the way home. Papa says he will not go to Poulafoca tomorrow he is disgusting so he is. I am going, I think, instead.

11 July 1877

Started at eleven. The boys screamed and shrieked when Mama told them that she was going to Blesington – they said they must go with her and Freddy took all the things out of the valise in order to prevent her going. When she said good-bye, Freddy clung to her neck and yelled. Eliza had to tear him away. Came to Roundwood where we changed horses. Bought some ginger bread biscuits. Went in to the little hotel and sat in the garden as the parlor smelt so of sour meals. Came to Luggelaw and passed up quite a difficult road, very hilly. We walked a great deal of it – lovely scenery about here. Stopped at a little rock for dinner. I had a whole bottle of ginger beer. It was great fun. We passed the Murdering Pass

– Lost our way, we were a very long way until we came to Blessington. Very dusty hotel and we waited an hour and a quarter for tea.

12 July 1877
Did not sleep well, thought the bed was dirty and I spilt some water. Had nice fresh eggs for breakfast, stale butter and good tea. We had dinner at the Smiths of Baltiboys. It is a very large house and there are a hundred acres attached to it. There was a very pretty little girl called baby Graydon, she will have all this place. There was a large retriever dog named Freke, he was very nice.

We drove to Poulafouca, just as we came into the courtyard we saw some hawthorn trees cut into some curious shapes. One was a pig or a fish, two were peacocks. We had to go down to the river – suddenly we came upon the fall which is under a beautiful bridge. It was most lovely. I sketched it. There was an old bagpipe man, who said he had played there for 46 years, indeed he did not play at all badly. Drove back to Baltiboys, where we were made to have tea in the nursery so we did all sorts of things like throwing cake out of the window to the dog. Strolled about the house and read some books. There are a great many books in this house. Mrs [Elizabeth] Smith [q.v.] is a funny old lady. Drove back to the hotel.

24 July 1877
I have got the most delightful rabbit – Papa got him in town, he is quite tame and will eat out of my hand. His name is Saint Sebastion – I think he is a buck, I am going to get a doe.

19 August 1877
My black rabbit that I got in Blackrock had young ones this morning. I have had the rabbit exactly three weeks – lots of things have happened since I wrote last.

26 August 1877
Rabbits eyes are not open yet.

14 September 1877
This is my birthday. In the morning while I was in bed, Mama came in and gave me a belt – Ada gave me a gum bottle & Ethel two reels of cotten, the boys needles. I was not happy – I felt discontented. It was very wrong I know, but the tears would come. After breakfast, I looked at my rabbits and tied a blue ribban on the neck of Hildegarde, the pet.

We started for Greystones at half past ten and we took up Ellie Hassard on our way, but her cousins would not let her bathe – old pigs. Ada and I bathed, it was rather cold – I went out up to my neck. After we bathed, it began to rain.

Dear Grandmother sent me a book named 'Clare Avery' and Aunt Ann sent me a white tie embroidered with poppies – both sent such nice letters. Dear me, I am fourteen, I always wanted to be 14, but I am not at all happy – I had a nice soda current cake for tea.

16 September 1877

Went to Sunday School. Mr Irwin came out strong on the proper place of women. I think the old brute wants taking down.

8 October 1877

Did my lessons badly as usual, Oh dear me – Was naughty at work, would not do any – forgot to say my prayers and other things. Little hedgehog seems sick, drank porter I am afraid.

6 December 1877

I am going to school in the last week in January to Blackheath. I don't mind it, indeed I am glad. I can't learn at home. I have been very wicked. Mrs Mannering finished my dress yesterday, it is of corduroy and has a very evil smell. I have lost my gold thimble. I have five shillings, the fruits of my rabbits. I have caught four mice in a hole behind the shutter in the room where I am now sleeping. Ward [the gardener] has cut down nearly all the shrubs round the house, the place looks so bare. Goodbye dear Trudder, I will not see you for a long time.

Joseph Holloway
1861-1944

JOSEPH HOLLOWAY *was born in Dublin, the son of a baker in Camden Street who died when Joseph was a boy, leaving him with enough money to be independent. When he was quite young, he and his mother and sister moved to 21 Northumberland Avenue, where he lived for the rest of his life. After attending the School of Art in Kildare Street and being apprenticed to an architect, he set up in his own office. In 1904 Annie Horniman employed him as the architect to renovate the old Mechanics Theatre on Abbey Street for the National Theatre Society, but he was never diligent in his profession and said that the First World War 'killed his business of domestic architecture altogether'.*

Joseph Holloway made himself into a Dublin character by devoting his life to the pursuit of culture; his small, rotund figure, with a bowler hat set squarely over his rather heavy face with its straggling moustache, was to be seen going to every concert, every art exhibition and every 'first night' in the city. The many literary and artistic societies and clubs that flourished in Dublin found in him an enthusiastic audience and viewer, though he had no desire to create anything himself. He had a passionate love for the theatre and was an early supporter of the Irish dramatic movement. For over sixty years he attended thousands of performances, all of which he described in his journal. He made a huge collection of theatre memorabilia, and commissioned portraits and drawings of actors and writers so that his house was crammed to overflowing; pictures had to be stacked because there was no room for them on the walls; there were narrow pathways between piles of programmes, prompt copies, scripts, playbills etc. When his study table collapsed under the weight of books and journals, it was left to lie undisturbed. But his monument – a very substantial monument – is his diary, which runs to about twenty-five million words and is entitled 'Impressions of a Dublin Playgoer'. Frank O'Connor described the journal as 'that donkey's detritus', for it records every detail of trivia including the most uninteresting conversations that he exchanged with the great and the good over a period of fifty years.

* * *

Monday 8 May 1899
At last the Irish Literary Theatre is become an actuality, and the red letter occurrence in the annals of the Irish Literary movement took place in the Antient Concert Rooms where a large and most fashionable audience filled the hall. There a pretty little miniature stage, perfectly appointed, had been erected. W.B.

Yeats' miracle play in four acts, 'The Countess Cathleen', was the work selected to inaugurate the Theatre, and from one cause or another the event was looked forward to with considerable excitement and interest, owing to the hostility exhibited in certain quarters to the author.

Expectation was satisfied, as an organised claque of about twenty brainless, beardless, idiotic-looking youths did all they knew to interfere with the progress of the play by their meaningless automatic hissing and senseless comments ... Thomas Davis seemed to be the particular 'bee in their bonnets,' as they frequently made reference to the poet ... Their 'poor spite' was completely frustrated by enthusiastic applause which drowned their empty-headed expressions of dissension.

... By the way, taking his call, Mr Yeats seemed most embarrassed and did not know what to do until, prompted by the 'devil' in the person of Mr Trevor Lowe, he took Miss Whitty's hand and shook it heartily, and afterwards that of Miss Farr which he treated similarly. My, Yeats must have felt very proud at the complete triumphing over his enemies.

Monday 21 October 1901
The Irish Literary Theatre is with us again for the third season. The Gaiety Theatre is again the scene of operation ... Everybody who is anybody in Dublin seemed to be there, and the attention paid to the plays was remarkable in its intensity. A few years ago no one could conceive it would be possible to produce a play in Irish on the Dublin stage and interest all beholders, yet such was the case to-night when Dr Douglas Hyde's little Gaelic piece 'The Twisting of the Rope' was produced for the first time by Gaelic-speaking amateurs ... Dr Douglas Hyde, the author, as 'Hanrahan', though villainously made up, made love very persuasively, and rated those who would deprive him of the young maiden with delightful glibness and sincerely expressed abuse. I have always been told that Irish is a splendid language to make love in or abuse, and having heard Dr Hyde I can well believe it. His 'soft-talk' and 'hard words' flowed with equal freedom and apparent ease from his slippery tongue ...

Saturday 27 August 1904
In connection with the Irish Revival Industries Show being held this week in the Antient Concert Rooms, a Concert was given to night at which I was present. The attendance was good, but the management could not have been worse ... The substitute appointed as accompanist ... was so incompetent that one of the vocalists, Mr James A. Joyce, had to sit down at the piano and accompany himself in the song, 'In Her Simplicity' from Mignon – after she had made several unsuccessful attempts to strum out the programmed item, 'The Croppy Boy', over the singer's name ... I do not yet give up hopes that some day I may be present at a 'grand concert' ... where things may go smoothly in their proper order,

the advertised time adhered to, the doors closed during each item, and the audience conducting themselves with some semblance of good manners and not demanding encores for every item or leaving noisily during the items that do not please them.

Irish-Ireland audiences have little discrimination and seldom display any artistic taste. A good shout is dearer to them than all the artistic vocalism in the world, as witness the enthusiastic reception of Mr J.F. McCormack's vigorous rendering of 'The Irish Emigrant' (a most crude bit of abominable, inartistic vocalism to my mind). This young vocalist is gifted by nature with a remarkably strong, pleasing tenor voice, but as he has no idea how to use it, nor a scrap of emotionalism in his rendering of any ballad, the effect to me of his singing is very painful ... greatly fear his voice has been ruined past all redemption by the blind folly of unthinking, popular audience; and what might have been a remarkable voice, if trained properly, will fizzle out into a cracked robust tenor of the pothouse order of merit ... Mr James A. Joyce possesses a light tenor voice which he is inclined to force on the high notes, and he sings with artistic emotionalism. 'Down by the Sally Gardens' suited his method best of his selected items, and as an encore he gave 'My Love Was Born in the North Country' – a short and sweet item – tenderly. 'In Her Simplicity' struck me as too high for him.

Saturday 26 January 1907
The Abbey was thronged in the evening to witness the first performance to Synge's three-act comedy *The Playboy of the Western World*, which ended in fiasco owing to the coarseness of the dialogue. The audience bore with it for two and a half acts and even laughed with the dramatist at times, but an unusually brutally coarse remark put into the mouth of 'Christopher Mahon', the playboy of the title, set the house off into hooting and hissing amid counter applause, and the din was kept up till the curtain closed in.

On coming out, Lady Gregory asked me, 'What was the cause of the disturbance?'

And my monosyllabic answer was, 'Blackguardism!'

To which she queried, 'On which side?'

'The stage!' came from me pat, and then I passed on and the incident was closed ...

'This is not Irish Life!' said one of the voices from the pit, and despite the fact that Synge in a note on the programme says, 'I have used one or two words only that I have not heard among the country people of Ireland, or spoken in my own nursery before I could read the newspapers,' I maintain that his play of *The Playboy* is not a truthful or just picture of the Irish peasants, but simply the outpouring of a morbid, unhealthy mind ever seeking on the dunghill of life for the nastiness that lies concealed there ... Synge is the evil genius of the Abbey and Yeats his able lieutenant. Both dabble in the unhealthy. Lady Gregory, though she backs them up when they transgress good taste and cast decency to the winds, keeps clean in her plays, and William Boyle is ever and always wholesome ...

Monday 28 January 1907
... Henderson and I went down to the Abbey ... and on our way spoke of Synge's nasty mind – to store those crude, coarse sayings from childhood and now present them in a play. The influence of Gorki must be upon him ... By this time we arrived at the Abbey. Two stalwart police at the vestibule suggested trouble, and we found plenty and to spare when we went in. The performance was just concluding amid a terrific uproar (the piece had not been listened to, we were told). The curtains were drawn aside, and W.G. Fay stood forward amid the din. After some minutes, in a lull, he said, 'You who have hissed to-night will go away saying you have heard the play, but you haven't.'

'We heard it on Saturday!' came from the back of the pit, and the hissing and hooting were renewed.

The scene which followed was indescribable. Those in the pit howled for the author, and he with Lady Gregory and others held animated conversation in the stalls ... after about a quarter of an hour's clamour, the audience dispersed hoarse ...

Tuesday 29 January 1907
Arrived at the Abbey when *Riders to the Sea* was half through ... We waited in the side passages near the radiator until it was over ... I noticed that the youths in the stalls were mostly under the influence of drink (and learned that the management had allowed them in for nothing to back up the play that the crowded pit had come there to howl down). This precious gang of noisy boys hailed from Trinity, and soon after *The Playboy* commenced one of their number (Mr Moorhead) made himself objectionable and was forcibly removed by Synge and others, after a free fight amongst the instruments of the orchestra.

... This set the noise in motion, and W.B. Yeats again came on the scene and with raised hand secured silence. He referred to the removal of one drunken man and hoped all that were sober would listen to the play. The noise continued and shortly after a body of police led on by W.B. marched out of the side door from the scene dock and ranged along the walls of the pit ... A gent addressed the audience from the stalls, and the students with Hugh Lane in their midst behaved themselves like the drunken cads they were. At the end chaos seemed to have entered the Abbey, and the college youths clambered onto the seats and began the English national anthem, while those in the body of the hall sang something else of home growth. I felt very sad while the scene continued. The college boys had ultimately to be forcibly ejected by the police, and they marched off in a body singing, police-protected, to the college. One of them was arrested for beating the police and fined £5 ... Despite all, *The Playboy* was not heard.

Thursday 31 January 1907

The police-protected drama by the dramatist of the dungheap ... got a fair hearing tonight, and was voted by those around me very poor, dull, dramatic stuff indeed. After the first act all interest of any kind ceases, and were it not for the claque imported into the stalls very little applause would be forthcoming. A Free Theatre is a droll cry where police line the walls and block the passages ... ready to pounce on anyone who dares say 'boo' to the filth and libels of the Irish peasant girl on the stage. 'Free' indeed! The theatre is forever damned in the eyes of all right-thinking Irishmen. One sack, one sample. Yeats, Synge, and Gregory are all degenerates of the worst type; the former pair indulge in sensuality in their later work, and the latter condones with them ...

Saturday 26 October 1907

... Synge personally is such a nice, unassuming, silent fellow in private life. One has to draw him out to get talk from him at all. Frank Fay ... took a walk one day up the mountains with Synge and hardly a word passed their lips for hours. To meet Synge and not know the nature of his work beforehand, you would never suspect him of such a strange output. He is mildness itself, and never a coarse or suggestive word passes his lips. He was a dark, silent boy, I've been told. He is the same as a man.

Saturday 11 December 1909

As I was looking over the papers in Eason's this afternoon, I saw James Stephens doing the same. He is a strange-looking little fellow with a head much too large for his burly, bandy frame, and set almost neckless on his body. Major MacBride, meek of look and fair of hair, came in to have a look round at the papers also ... I saw George Russell looking into Naylor's old curiosity shop in Nassau Street. His overcoat hung carelessly unbuttoned about him, and a big pipe struggled through his ample straggling beard and moustaches from his well-concealed mouth. He wore a soft felt hat perched on his long unkempt hair – a strange mixture of the dreamer and businessman.

James Stephens, the author of The Crock of Gold *(1912), published his first book of poems in 1909. I have included extracts from his diary in 1916. John MacBride fought against the English in the Boer War and in 1903 married Maude Gonne; he became one of the leaders of the 1916 rebellion and was later imprisoned and executed.*

Tuesday 10 November 1910

The limit was reached surely in Lady Gregory's new comedy *The Full Moon* at the Abbey tonight before a good house. One would imagine that Lady Gregory considered her audience a pack of lunatics to put before them such a hopeless inane production. Oh, the pity of it all, to see fine actors and actresses having to make such fools of themselves just to please the whims of a conceited old lady who happens to be the boss of the show and who must be obeyed. Such undramatic rot it has never been my misfortune to see before. It led nowhere. All the characters talked and talked, and every now and again behaved like people in a pantomime rally.

Monday 25 November 1912

As I passed by Essex Street, I saw an extremely long queue of wretched, hungry-looking men ranged against the wall in twos awaiting to get relief from the Dublin Distress Office in the corner house. Numbers of others, as hungry-looking as themselves, stood looking in from the other side. It was a picture of Dublin I had not seen before, and it distressed me very much when I thought of the hundreds of poor wretches that stood shivering and hungry lined up in the street awaiting help.

Wednesday 23 August 1922

News reached Dublin that General Michael Collins, Commander-in-Chief of the King's own Irish army, was shot dead in an ambush near Bandon, Co. Cork, R.I.P. He served his English masters only too well. Nightmarish Civil War stalks the land. Oh, that the dawn of peace were at hand!

Friday 17 April 1925

Heard one workman say to another in D'Olier Street, 'You're a bloody fool to work for anyone if you can help it.' And when I told Sean O'Casey what I overheard, he replied, 'Work was made for mugs.' He hasn't been working at the new play of late. He is lazy. 'I like to read adverse criticisms of my plays,' was what he said when I told him of Carey's comments in *Honesty*.

Sunday 7 February 1926

I attended the dress rehearsal of O'Casey's *The Plough and the Stars* at the Abbey, which didn't commence till after six o'clock and concluded some minutes after ten. The last act will save the play; the second I am of the opinion is quite unnecessary. On the whole, I imagine, as far as I can judge from such a performance, it is not nearly as interesting and gripping a piece as *Juno and the Paycock*. There are some moments of real drama in Act III. Act II is very badly managed, the bar being placed to one side, cut off from half the house. Ria Mooney's part, a prostitute, in Act II is quite unnecessary; and the incident in Act I about the naked female on the calendar is lugged in for nastiness' sake alone …

Monday 8 February 1926

There was electricity in the air before and behind the curtain at the Abbey tonight … The theatre was thronged with distinguished people, and before the doors opened the queue to the pit entrance past old Abbey Street – not a quarter of them got in. The play was followed with feverish interest, and the players being called and recalled at the end of the piece. Loud calls for 'Author!' brought O'Casey on the stage, and he received an ovation.

... The street outside the theatre was packed on either side with motor cars. In Abbey Street a policeman was stalking after four 'Rosie Redmonds' [prostitutes] who flew before him, and I am sure the dispersing audience found no interest in their flight, although they had applauded 'Rosie' plying her trade in Act II of *The Plough and the Stars*. The fight between the two women in the pub scene was longly applauded, yet who is not disgusted with such an exhibition when one chances on it in real life?

Tuesday 9 February 1926
The Abbey was again thronged ... Some four or five in the pit objected to the Volunteers bringing the flag into a pub in Act II. Kevin Barry's sister was one of the objectors. The pit door had to be shut to avoid a rush being made on it, and two policemen were on the scene. The audience relished the fight of the women in Act II and didn't object to the nasty incidents and phrases scattered here and there through the play ... Lord Chief Justice Kennedy frankly declared he thought it abominable. Kevin O'Higgins was silent until Monty thanked God he was off duty, and added, 'This is a lovely Irish export.' Then O'Higgins owned up he didn't like it. Meeting Dr Oliver Gogarty, Monty said, 'I hope you are not going to say you liked it?' 'I do,' owned up Gogarty (whose reputation for filthy limericks is very widespread), 'It will give the smug-minded something to think about.'

'Monty' was James Montgomery, the Irish Film Censor.

Thursday 11 February 1926
The protest of Tuesday night having no effect on the management, a great protest was made to-night, and ended in the second act being played in dumb show ... After Act I, was the first I heard that a storm was brewing from Dan Breen, who was speaking to Kavanagh and said, 'Mrs Pearse, Mrs Tom Clarke, Mrs Sheehy-Skeffington, and others were in the theatre to vindicate the manhood of 1916' ...

Few really like the play as it stands, and most who saw it are in sympathy with those who protested. Some of the players behaved with uncommon roughness to some ladies who got on the stage, and threw two of them into the stalls. One young man thrown from the stage got his side hurt by the piano. The chairs of the orchestra were thrown on the stage, and the music on the piano fluttered, and some four or five tried to pull down half of the drop curtain, and another caught hold of one side of the railing in the scene in Act III ...

Mrs Sheehy-Skeffington from the back of the balcony during the din kept holding forth, and at the same time others were speaking in the pit; all were connected with Easter Week ...

Monday 1 March 1926

... I had tea with Eileen before going on to the Mills Hall to hear the discussion on O'Casey's play *The Plough and the Stars*. The hall was thronged ... T.C. Murray, Mrs Despard, Maude Gonne MacBride, John Burke, Shelagh Richards, Gabriel Fallon, F.J. McCormick, Arthur Shields, Ria Mooney, Joseph O'Reilly, Mrs Tom Kettle ... and many others I knew were present.

Arthur Clery was in the chair and opened the proceedings by merely introducing Mrs Sheehy-Skeffington to the meeting. Sean O'Casey was received with applause as he walked up the aisle ...

Mrs Skeffington spoke mostly about the right to disapprove as well as approve in theatres, and was totally opposed to the police being brought in, and spoke most interestingly in soft, low, carrying tones. She is an easy, agreeable speaker and says what she wants to say clearly and well.

... O'Casey came forward again, and in a speech put his point of view as a dramatist before the meeting, and then drifted into a sort of Salvationist address at a street corner ...

O'Casey said he had no use for heroes in his plays, and Maud Gonne said she didn't see the play, but from what O'Casey said he had no right to introduce a real hero – Padraic Pearse – into his play, and from O'Casey's own words could clearly see why the protest was made. Donaghy spoke again, and Mrs Skeffington responded in a very subtle speech, full of sly thoughts and humour, and then the discussion concluded. It had been conducted in the most peaceful way and in the best of humour, each taking or receiving hard hits in their turn.

James Stephens
1882-1950

A NOVELIST AND POET, James Stephens is best remembered for his novel The Crock
of Gold *(1912). He was born in the Dublin slums and educated at a Protestant industrial school in Meath. When he was working as a solicitor's clerk, he contributed some
poems to* Sinn Féin, *the paper that was edited by Arthur Griffith, and became friendly
with Yeats and George Russell, who encouraged him with his writing, though they did
not always admire it. James Joyce is quoted as having said that the only writer (besides
himself) with the imagination to complete* Finnegans Wake *would be Stephens.*

*At the time of the Easter Rising in 1916, described in the diary entries below,
Stephens was the Registrar of the National Gallery.*

* * *

Monday 24 April 1916
This has taken everyone by surprise. It is possible that, with the exception of their
Staff, it has taken the Volunteers themselves by surprise; but, today, our peaceful
city is no longer peaceful; guns are sounding, or rolling and crackling from different directions, and, although rarely, the rattle of machine guns can be heard
also ... I awoke into full insurrection and bloody war, but I did not know anything about it. It was a Bank Holiday, but for employments such as mine there
are not any holidays, so I went to my office at the usual hour ... At one o'clock I
went to lunch. Passing the corner of Merrion Row I saw two small groups of people. These people were regarding steadfastly in the direction of St Stephen's
Green ... I also, without approaching them, stared in the direction of the Green,
I saw nothing but the narrow street which widened to the Park ... My return
[after lunch] to business was by the way I had already come. At the corner of
Merrion Row I found the same silent groups who were still looking in the direction of the Green, and addressing each other occasionally with the detached confidence of strangers. Suddenly, and on the spur of the moment, I addressed one
of these silent gazers. 'Has there been an accident?' said I indicating the people
standing about. 'What's all this for?'

He was a sleepy, rough-looking man about 40 years of age, with a blunt red
moustache, and the distant eyes which one sees in sailors. He looked at me, stared
at me as at a person from a different country. He grew wakeful and vivid.

'Don't you know,' said he. And then he saw that I did not know. 'The Sinn

Féiners have seized the City this morning.'

'Oh!' said I.

He continued with the savage earnestness of one who has amazement in his mouth: 'They seized the City at eleven o'clock this morning. The Green there is full of them. They have captured the Castle. They have taken the Post Office.'

'My God!' said I, staring at him, and instantly I turned and went running towards the Green.

As I drew near the Green rifle fire began like sharply-cracking whips. It was from the further side. I saw that the Gates were closed and men standing inside with guns on their shoulders. I passed a house, the windows of which were smashed in … In the centre of this side of the Park a rough barricade of carts and motor cars had been sketched. It was still full of gaps. Behind it was a halted tram, and along the vistas of the Green one saw other trams derelict, untenanted.

I came to the barricade. As I reached it and stood by the Shelbourne Hotel, which it faced, a loud cry came from the Park. The gates opened and three men ran out. Two of them held rifles with fixed bayonets. The third gripped a heavy revolver in his fist. They ran towards the motor car which had just turned the corner, and halted it. The men with bayonets took position instantly on either side of the car. The man with the revolver saluted, and I heard him begging the occupants to pardon him, and directing them to dismount. A man and woman got down. They were again saluted and requested to go to the sidewalk. They did so.

The man crossed and stood by me. He was very tall and thin, middle-aged, with a shaven, wasted face. 'I wanted to get down to Armagh today,' he said to no one in particular. The loose bluish skin under his eyes was twitching. The Volunteers directed the chauffeur to drive to the barricade and lodge his car in a particular position there. He did it awkwardly, and after three attempts he succeeded in pleasing them. He was a big, brown-faced man, whose knees were rather high for the seat he was in, and they jerked with the speed and persistence of something moved with a powerful spring. His face was composed and fully under command, although his legs were not. He locked the car into the barricade, and then, being a man accustomed to be commanded, he awaited an order to descend. When the order came he walked directly to his master, still preserving all the solemnity of his features. These two men did not address a word to each other, but their drilled and expressionless eyes were loud with surprise and fear and rage. They went into the hotel.

I spoke to the man with the revolver. He was no more than a boy, not more certainly than twenty years of age, short in stature, with close curling red hair and blue eyes – kindly-looking lad. The strap on his sombrero had torn loose on one side, and except while he held it in his teeth it flapped about his chin. His face was sunburnt and grimy with dust and sweat … 'This morning,' he said, 'the police rushed us. One ran at me to take my revolver. I fired but I missed him, and I hit a —'

'You have far too much talk,' said a voice to the young man.

I turned a few steps away and glancing back saw that he was staring after me, but I know that he did not see me ...

The Irish Citizen Army under the command of Michael Mallin and the Countess Markievicz held St Stephen's Green and the College of Surgeons.

Tuesday 25 April 1916
A sultry, lowering day, and dusk skies fat with rain.

I left for my office, believing that the insurrection was at an end. At a corner I asked a man was it all finished. He said it was not, and that, if anything, it was worse.

On this day the rumours began, and I think it will be many a year before the rumours cease ... An attack reported on the Post Office by a troop of lancers who were received with fire and repulsed. It is foolish to send cavalry into street war.

In connection with this lancer charge at the Post Office it is said that the people, and especially the women, sided with the soldiers, and that the Volunteers were assailed by these women with bricks, bottles, sticks, to cries of: 'Would you be hurting the poor men?' There were other angry ladies who threatened Volunteers, addressing to them this petrifying query: 'Would you be hurting the poor horses?'

The lancers retreated to the bottom of Sackville Street, where they remained for some time in the centre of a crowd who were caressing their horses. It may have seemed to them a rather curious kind of insurrection ...

I went to the Green. At the corner of Merrion Row a horse was lying on the footpath surrounded by blood. He bore two bullet wounds, but the blood came from his throat which had been cut.

Inside the Green railings four bodies could be seen lying on the ground. They were dead Volunteers ...

Wednesday 26 April 1916
... Shooting, indeed, proceeding everywhere. During daylight, at least, the sound is not sinister nor depressing, and the thought that perhaps a life had exploded with that crack is not depressing either.

In the last two years of world-war our ideas on death have undergone a change. It is not now the furtive thing that crawled into your bed and which you fought with pill boxes and medicine bottles. It has become again a rider of the wind whom you may go coursing with through the fields and open places. All morbidity is gone, and the sickness, and what remains to Death is now health and excitement ... I crossed Dame Street some distance up, struck down the Quays, and went along these until I reached the Ballast Office. Further than this it was not possible to go, for a step beyond the Ballast Office would have brought one into the unending stream of lead that was pouring from Trinity and other places.

I was looking on O'Connell Bridge and Sackville Street, and the house facing me was Kelly's – a red-brick fishing tackle shop. This house was being bombarded ... About five o'clock the guns eased off Kelly's. To inexperienced eyes they did not seem to have done very much damage, but afterwards one found that although the walls were standing and apparently solid there was no inside to the house. From roof to basement the building was bare as a dog kennel. There were no floors inside, there was nothing there but blank space; and on the ground within was the tumble and rubbish that had been roof and floors and furniture ...

Thursday 27 April 1916

... At 11.30 there came the sound of heavy guns firing in the direction of Sackville Street. I went on the roof, and remained there for some time ...

This night also was calm and beautiful, but this night was the most sinister and woeful of those that have passed. The sound of artillery, of rifles, machine guns, grenades, did not cease even for a moment. From my window I saw a red flare that crept to the sky, and stole over it and remained there glaring; the smoke reached from the ground to the clouds, and I could see great red sparks go soaring to enormous heights; while always, in the calm air, hour after hour there was the buzzing and rattling and thudding of guns, and, but for the guns, silence ...

Friday 28 April 1916

... Rifle volleys are continuous about Merrion Square, and prolonged machine gun firing can be heard also.

During the night the firing was heavy from almost every direction; and in the direction of Sackville Street a red glare told again of fire.

It is hard to get to bed these nights. It is hard even to sit down, for the moment one does sit down one stands immediately up again resuming that ridiculous ship's march from window to the wall and back. I am foot weary as I have never been before in my life, but I cannot say that I am excited ...

Saturday 29 April 1916

This morning also there has been no bread, no milk, no meat, no newspapers, but the sun is shining. It is astonishing that, thus early in the Spring, the weather should be so beautiful ... The approaches to Merrion Square are held by the military, and I was not permitted to go to my office. As I came to this point shots were fired at a motor car which had not stopped on being challenged. Bystanders said it was Sir Horace Plunkett's car, and that he had been shot. Later we found that Sir Horace was not hurt, but that his nephew who drove the car had been severely wounded.

At this hour the rumour of the fall of Verdun was persistent. Later on it was denied, as was denied the companion rumour of the relief of Kut ...

The rumour grows that the Post Office has been evacuated and that the

James Stephens

Volunteers are at large ... The rumour grows also that terms of surrender are being discussed, and that Sackville Street has been levelled to the ground.

Sunday 30 April 1916
The insurrection has not ceased.

There is much rifle fire, but no sound from the machine guns or the eighteen pounders and trench mortars.

From the window of my kitchen the flag of the Republic can be seen flying afar. This is the flag that flies over Jacob's Biscuit Factory, and I will know that the Insurrection has ended as soon as I see this flag pulled down ...

It is half past three o'clock, and from my window the Republican flag can still be seen flying over Jacob's factory. There is occasional shooting, but the city as a whole is quiet.

At a quarter to five o'clock a heavy gun boomed once. Ten minutes later there was heavy machine gun firing and much rifle shooting. In another ten minutes the flag at Jacob's was hauled down ...

Joseph Campbell
1879-1944

Comes any hope from the hard heart of stone?
From gates with double locks, thickets of wire?
From guards, gun-ready, pacing floor and roof?
A shot cracks in the circle.– No! no hope!

So wrote Joseph Campbell when he was in Mountjoy prison in 1922. As an anti-Treaty member of the IRA during the Civil War, he had been arrested while bicycling into Bray to attend a meeting to organize accommodation for wounded republicans and he was held for seventeen months in the very severe conditions of Mountjoy and later on the Curragh.

Joseph Campbell was born in Belfast into a family with strong nationalist and artistic leanings. His father was a prosperous road contractor, but Joseph had little inclination for the business and after a short time had given it up in favour of writing in the Gaelic tradition. He published several books of verse and songs among which are The Garden of the Bees, The Rushlight *and* Songs of Uladh; *this last includes his most popular song, 'My Lagan Love'.*

After some years in London, he settled in County Wicklow in 1912, teaching Irish history in Padraic Pearse's school in Rathfarnham, County Dublin. He was an enthusiastic member of the Gaelic League. He had one play, Judgement, *put on by the Abbey.*

After 1916 Campbell became more politically involved and was an active member of Sinn Féin. He was wholly opposed to the Treaty and worked for the republican movement until his arrest.

In prison, he was older than most of the other inmates and he was often deeply depressed by the ugliness, fear and lack of stimulation. Fellow prisoner and later novelist Francis Stuart described him as 'a bit of cultural yeast among the prisoners giving the cause ... an intellectual prestige'.

Some time after his release, he went to the United States where he founded the School of Irish Studies under the auspices of Fordham University. He returned to Ireland in 1939, disappointed and embittered by his failure to find recognition for his work. In Ireland he had some success with his radio talks. He died of a heart attack in 1944.

In Campbell's shorthand, F.S. stands for Free State; R. stands for Republican.

* * *

Joseph Campbell

[Letter on a scrap of paper]

6 June 1922

I am a prisoner in the Royal Hotel, Main Street, Bray. Arrested by the Free State Army on information of an ex-soldier in the street. Rotten accommodation and no food so far. The O.C. is a grocer's assistant in Clerys shop in Main St. Treats me like a dog. No charge formulated yet. I am one of six other prisoners ...

Up the Republic, Joseph.

[Prison Diary]

22 September 1922 – Mountjoy

A wonderful picture made by the band at the dancing class in the prison compound. Tommy Dukes, perennially interesting figure as the fiddler, his bow arm crooked, his head leaning pathetically across his fiddle – all in black. The young drummer astride the stool beating a roll/ruffle on his drum. Tom McG. with the English concertina, his black red face aglow with pleasure. The gentle melancholy of a banjo player. The flute players trilling the quick passages of 'Miss McLeod's Reel'. The dull gas flores partly illuminating the heads of the dancers and the loungers against the wall. Such a scene as Jack Yeats might have delighted in painting.

'I hear you are about to get married', said old R.D. (aetat 61) to T.B. 'Let me give you a bit of advice. Never marry a girl who is as old as yourself. I married a girl my own age. Today she's not able to oblige me, but old D. is (game ball still – not bet yet).'

10 October 1922

About 8.30 a heavy burst of revolver fire, then the Q.M.'s voice: 'Orderlies! Get back from the gates. Back to your cells.' More firing, then the running of feet along the compound floor. Several orderlies ran past cell door (No 9) on A2 landing. The wings began to echo with the concentrated revolver and rifle fire, the detonation making a head-aching racket. Silence which you can positively hear – about 9.15 a.m. – 'the beating of the wings of death', as I said to Dr R. Firing back again. Voices from the cell doors: 'Waste it away, Churchill will give you more.' Intense rifle fire until 11 a.m. Banging of prisoners on cell doors. 'Give us our breakfast. We are hungry.' Like primitive animals. In the intervals of the rifle fire could be heard the tap, tap, tap of an industrious ring maker in a cell down the wing. About 11 a.m. I ventured forth and got a can of water to make tea. Broken glass littered the floor below and plaster and limewash everywhere. Rumours afloat. Dead sentry's cap in hall of A2 landing and pool of blood. Two F.S. dead. One R. dead – nine or ten wounded about 9.30 a.m. In an interval between the shots, the bell of Berkeley St church began to ring for mass. How paradoxical it seemed! Dr R. talking to me from his mattress at the time: 'Reaction after crisis'

'Psychic vibrations' 'Second sight' etc. etc. 'What a joy to be a Republican Prisoner.'

There has been an ominous calm all day after the battle in the morning. Rumours that 3 are dead, 2 F.S. and one R. First report that nine were wounded, but it is now down to one R. The F.S. wounded not known. The sentry's cap lay in the pool of blood on A2 landing for quite a long time, the poor devil himself was not removed for quite 15 minutes after he was hit owing to intense fire. The guard are white-faced, tense and generally 'windy'. No breakfast this morning except for a cup of tea which we made over the gas ring in No 9 cell. Not allowed out into the exercise ring all day. As darkness fell it was quite jumpy to be out on the landing at all. About 7.30, I went down to the gas jet at A2 lavatory to boil some milk. R.B. & Dr R. were in No 9 cell playing chess. A shot suddenly rang out – rifle – which gave me a shiver down my backbone. It was fired at young Perry who was crossing the bridge near the sentry's post (against orders). I wondered if I would be able to get back to my cell. Dodged along from door to door. When I got to 13 was quite relieved to think that I was so near 'home'! As I got in R.B. and R. were on their feet. A mug of milk was spilled all over the cell floor. A prisoner passing along landing from tap, dashed in for cover as shot went off and capsized his supper. R.B. immediately left for his own cell.

There were disturbances among the prisoners, which the inexperienced Free State guards found difficult to contain.

Dr R. is Dr James Ryan, with whom Campbell shared a cell, and R.B. is Robert Barton.

11 October 1922

(C wing kept out in Ring all day without food.) Andy Cooney arrested and taken to basement. C wing cells raided and property broken or stolen.

All normal again, more or less. Exercise yard open. Watched J. Begley, Scully, R.B. and Dr R. play auction bridge in 16 cell. S.D. came in about 5 p.m. with 'Buckshee' tobacco from an unclaimed parcel. He distributes it around. Very grateful for smokes, for parcels have stopped as punishment for the attack yesterday morning. Still unsafe to be on landing after dark.

12 October 1922

This morning between 1 a.m. and 3 a.m. heard lorries arriving and shouting of men outside in yard. Then shuffles outside the guard room in central hall; shouting and one shot from revolver fired. 'Double to it!' from the guard and then scuffling feet running and suppressed screams. Prisoners maltreated as they arrive. Kicked more than likely on the backside and threatened with revolver butts.

Just before dinner 11.30 to 12 noon we were sitting, R.B., Dr R. and myself in the cell chatting when in walks a tall F.S. policemen – 'P.A.' – in uniform with a drawn revolver in his right hand. He pushed open the cell door without warning. Outside a rifleman at the ready stood guard. 'P.A.' looked closely round the cell – at pictures on the walls and behind the door – and without saying a word went out again. Sinister and menacing. Prisoners, white-faced and expectant at cell doors (how they hug the door posts since the shooting) discussing the situation.

31 October 1922
7.45. Just as the Fianna were getting ready to produce Pearse's play *Íosagán* and *Buttingli* (2nd time) two F.S. policemen with revolvers came up to the stage and said: 'Take these blankets down and —— quick about it!' Protests were made, but to no avail. The O.C. Wing asked the G. [Governor] by note: 'Was the stopping of the play done with his sanction?' He received back his note with the G.'s ukase – 'No play' written across it. All prisoners moving about in the cold (how cold!) A1 landing with gloomy faces. There is not much heart among us since the parcels were stopped. We are permitted to exist, to breathe and no more.

11 p.m. A quarter of hour after 'lights out' a concert organized by way of protest against the stopping of the plays began ... Sharply at 11 p.m. the number 100 was called out, and A. O'C. began from his cell to sing 'Dark Rosaleen'. Great chorusing and applause at end. He called 101 and D. O'D. began 'The Battle Hymn' (very well sung), then 102 Joe B. followed with 'Fireship'; Paddy M. 'Dawning of the Day' D. O'D. 'Avenging and Bright'; L. QM Wing 'Rose of Tralee' (A3) M. The Workers' Song (Maryland). Wrap G.C. around him. Revolvers shots began to ring out after A. O'C.'s song. The guard in circle fired 5 times. Then after Paddy M.'s, 2 rifle shots were fired up the wing. I could hear the locks of the wing gates being opened and the guard crept up in canvas shoes into the wing A1. 'If you don't stop I'll, I'll give you 303!' cried the guard. The singing stopt, deathly stillness. Then a song and recitation could be heard far off in the other wing and cheering. The 'jerry' was thrown down from A3 (against orders) followed by a bottle which smashed itself to pieces on A1 floor. The guard was changed and no further molestation took place.

At the Soldier's Song sung about 12.30 am, the guards below (I was told) stood to attention. All ended quietly when O.C. shouted —- 'To sleep now lads. Parade at 7.30 in the morning and two minutes "stand to" in silence for the 2nd anniversary of Kevin Barry's hanging.'

1 November 1922
Parade 8 a.m. and 2 minute silence 'at attention' for K.B. Parted with Dr R. as cell mate. Could not stand eternal hammering and crowds in cell. Sean M. to come to me as cell mate.

3 November 1922
A tin of rice, half a pint of milk, piece of dry bread (without butter) for dinner

today. A fine clear, cold sunshiney day inducing appetite. Everybody very cross and hungry. The primitive need food.

4 November 1922

Clear, sunshiney, 'hardy' morning, still, biting air after night's frost. Ice on pools in yard. After parade I was touched on the shoulder by O'S. the machine gunner from Bantry who said: 'A nice morning for a couple of grouse on the hill.'

As I was going round as food orderly with tea about 4.30 p.m., I was asked by Dan D. 'Had I heard the bad news?' 'What?' The news had been so good from the Republican side for the past few days that I suppose we must be prepared for reverses. 'Dev' captured in a house in A. road; E. O'M. killed in the scrap; Mary MacSwiney T.D. arrested.

5 November 1922

Meeting outside Gaol gate. Cool gloomy November day. Whirring of double-turreted armoured car in yard, stuck in a collapsed 'shore'. Shouts of soldiers; cheers from Republican crowd outside walls, now faint now loud but enthusiastic. The emotion behind the cheering 'Is that cheering I hear?' (Kathleen ni Houlihan) Procession with banners seen from A3. Armoured car running up and down to disperse procession.

7 November 1922

It is four weeks now since the fatal shooting up of the 10th of October, 1922. No parcels allowed in since. Yesterday and today the prisoners have been irritable and dissatisfied owing to the shortage of food rations. I have been hungry myself – never knew what hunger was until now. Indigestion etc.

Campbell went on hunger strike in protest at the lack of food.

9 November 1922

4 p.m. Nothing to eat or drink since 8 p.m. last night. A bit weak and tottery, a dull headache, taste in mouth. The first day of a hunger strike is largely experience of nerves. Will settle down I imagine. Several 'Job's comforters' in to see me. Washed two shirts and handkerchiefs. Slept better than I thought (back at 11 p.m.), but woke several times during the night.

Infernal din from guards in 'Circle' all night.

10 November 1922

Kept in bed until about 2 p.m. Prison M.O. (C.C.) in to see me. Told him would cease hunger strike if G[overnor] gave me an account of official ration and promise that each man would get his quantum. Very weak on legs. About 7.30 p.m. three Fianna boys came and told me they were thinking of going on hunger strike. Short rations and very hungry. Decided weakness about heart. 8 p.m. Sent for prison M.O. Forty-eight hours now without taking food.

11 November 1922
This morning at breakfast in No 9 cell we were talking about the good things of this world, comfort, culture, women, travel, wine, fame etc. and how few of them we had in our lives. 'When I get out,' said M., 'I'll get my own back again, I'll get it anywhere and by any means.' He spoke with the percipiency of youth. 'Ah,' said I, 'when you get out, you will have your whole life before you, but I'll be a grey-haired old man.'

12 November 1922
Fine foggy morning. The bell of St Joseph's Berkeley Street is ringing for mass. Outside our cell window one hears the sharp words of command given to the guard on inspection parade. 'Port arms' bolt and clicks. Inside in the gaol there is nothing but petty tyranny, spleen, shortage of food, no parcels, no letters, no papers, no books, no tobacco – we are just allowed to breathe the fetid air and no more. How mean and weak the tyrant ever is.

15 November 1922
Word brought in today that B's cat was lying dead in the yard with four revolver bullets in it. Killed by the F.S. Guard. Alas for so bad an end to J.B.'s cat 'Nigger/Skipper' – how it used to lie on his bed in the cell – on its back with its legs spread out; and how it used to scrounge milk – 'There is a cat here!' And fat meat for its dinner and breakfast. Cat fed first thing in the morning before B. got up. How he shielded it from the white-footed lady cat – 'catnagospa'. Its nights out in spite of all precautions – alas alas.

16 November 1922
Cat not dead. Sleek, black shiny stretched on Joe B's bed. The white-footed female mate shot.

18 November 1922
News brought in by Sean M. who had it from D. O'D. that Erskine Childers and David Robinson are to be executed on Monday. Everybody very serious – drawn anxious faces. Can the wretched P.G. [Provisional Government] survive the executions? Tom Johnson supposed to be for the executions, yet he could not understand why no notice was given of the executions of the four men in Kilmainham. Twelve hours elapsed after executions and before public informed. Kilmainham of unhappy memories for Ireland. Erskine Childers was a man they *hated* – he seemed to attract this *hate*. F.S. guards said this would do for the P.G. It is good to see the rank and file dissatisfied.

Erskine Childers was a member of Sinn Féin and a supporter of de Valera; he had been arrested for carrying a pistol given to him by Michael Collins. Before taking up Irish politics he had been Clerk in the House of Commons and had written the popular thriller The Riddle of the Sands *(1910).*

19 November 1922

A lovely mild misty sunshiney morning. Bells ringing for mass. A feeling of sick horror all the same grips me because of these executions. Will Erskine Childers die tomorrow, poor melancholy strange-mannered Childers – the most hated man in Ireland, a damned Englishman ...

Today at noon all the men in A wing were paraded. The orderly officer read out, standing on the iron stairs, the names, addresses and history of the four executed men. Before the rosary was said, I asked D. O'D. did he think they would execute Childers? He had his doubts if they would – Spoke cryptically – something might happen. About 11.30 a.m. the sentry outside exercise yard fired two shots at prisoners – nobody hit.

22 November 1922

Horror follows on horrors! News came in by word of mouth today about 5 p.m. that Erskine Childers, David Robinson and seven other prisoners have been executed ...

Lady Gregory
1852-1932

AUGUSTA PERSSE was born at Roxborough in County Galway, the youngest daughter in a family of sixteen. In 1880 she married Sir William Gregory of Coole Park, County Galway, who had been a Conservative MP and later Governor of Ceylon. After he died in 1892 she became more and more absorbed in Irish affairs, learning the language, collecting folklore and joining Horace Plunkett's co-operative farm movement and the Gaelic League.

With W.B. Yeats she started a national theatre in Dublin which was established as a permanent company in the Abbey Theatre in 1904. She involved herself in every aspect of this theatre, from management to writing, directing and even acting in plays.

The Abbey is her great memorial, for Coole Park, which she loved and worked tenaciously to keep going for her grandson, was sold to the Land Commission and pulled down. Her son Robert had been tragically killed in the First World War, an airman shot down by mistake by an Italian ally. His widow Margaret owned Coole and she and her three children, whom Lady Gregory adored, spent many holidays there.

The journals were begun in 1916 to record her negotiations for the return of the Lane pictures. Her nephew, Sir Hugh Lane, a successful art dealer, was drowned with the Lusitania. In his will, his collection of French Impressionist paintings was left to the National Gallery in London, but in an unwitnessed codicil he bequeathed them to the City of Dublin with Lady Gregory as sole trustee. For the rest of her life, Lady Gregory made every effort to get the British Government to return the pictures. She pleaded and petitioned every one of influence but to no avail. Until 1959 there was a room left empty in the Municipal Gallery for the Lane pictures. In that year a compromise was reached and they are now divided in two groups that alternate between London and Dublin.

The journals were written in forty-four penny notebooks. At the end of her life she edited and transcribed them, then sent them to her publishers, Putnam & Co.

* * *

8 September 1918

... I went to Dublin on Abbey business. I was tired next morning, Sunday, but in the afternoon I went to the National Gallery to see Hugh's bequest ... I stayed there a long time looking sadly at the Goya, and at the Rembrandt I used to look at so often when I came in late and tired to Lindsey House [Lane's house in Chelsea], there was such sunshine in the face ... Hugh's portrait by Sargent was hanging in one of the rooms, lent by the Municipal Gallery. Sargent had told me how Hugh had gone to him for a drawing, but he had painted him instead, he was so interested in 'the nobility of his face'. It looked very sad and tragic. The eyes seemed to follow me, seemed to reproach me for not having carried out what he had trusted me to do, the bringing back of the French pictures to Dublin.

I had worked so hard in London, and after I left all seemed to be abandoned; and the papers, even the *The Times*, all but the *Nation*, having rejected my protests made me very hopeless. I stayed there a long time and prayed …

16 March 1919

I went to the almost empty matinée at the Abbey. The bills were there for Monday with *Kathleen ni Houlihan* and *Minerals* [*Boyle's Mineral Worker*], but [Charles] Millington [business manager] said casually that Miss Walker has to go to Manchester after all and so can't play Kathleen till Wednesday, and *Rising* is to be played in its stead. A bad moment to make a change, when we are already weak with the loss of players. I left a card for [Lennox] Robinson asking him to come round, and told him I would rather myself play Kathleen than let it drop (after all what is wanted but a hag and a voice?). He said it was 'splendid' of me, and we arranged a rehearsal for today but my heart sinks low; remembering the words will be the chief difficulty, and I could joyfully welcome Maire Walker should she return, yet if all goes well I shall be glad to have done it.

In the evening I set out again for the Abbey, but when the tram reached O'Connell Bridge, at about eight o'clock, there were immense crowds blocking the street and I went on to the pillar. I asked a newspaper seller what was going on and he said excitedly: 'The Countess is coming back!' I got into another tram seeing it would be difficult to get to the Abbey and perhaps impossible to get anywhere, and we set out but very soon came to a stop.

Then a band was heard and then came a waggonette and a pair and I saw Madame Markievicz standing and waving a bouquet, yellow, white and with long green sprays (I had noticed a man carrying it through the streets earlier and had thought regretfully that we have no actress now to whom it could possibly be on its way as a tribute) …

'The Countess' was Constance Markievicz, who had been born into a distinguished Anglo-Irish family, the Gore-Booths of Lissadell in County Sligo. She had adopted the republican cause enthusiastically, and in 1916 had commanded the rebels in St Stephen's Green. While in prison, she had been elected as Sinn Féin member to the House of Commons, the first woman MP, though she never took her seat.

18 March 1919

To the Abbey, and ran through *Kathleen* with Shields, my heart sinking more and more at the thought of the stage …

Tea with Lady Ardilaun. She looks very handsome, handsomer I think as an old woman than in her youth even, though she had then her flashing eyes …

On to the Abbey, and my face was painted with grease paint – white with black under the eyes and red inside the lids – dreadful! Luckily my own hair is grey enough without a wig. And I had got a slight cold so I was a little hoarse and felt miserable. When I went on to the stage it was a shock to find the auditorium in black darkness, I thought for a moment the curtain was still down and hesitated. But I got through all right, only once Shields had to prompt me. He was kneeling beside me so it didn't matter. Seaghan was behind the fireplace, book in hand, but didn't have to use it. There were few stalls, but as I guessed from the applause and saw afterwards, the pit and gallery were full. Of course the patriotic bits were applauded, especially 'They are gathering to meet me now', and I had two curtains all to myself. I wish tonight were over for all that. The actors seemed pleased, and Mrs Martin [charwoman] came and hugged me with enthusiasm. Home very tired and hungry, and the fire out, and had stale bread and butter and a glass of milk.

4 June 1921 – Coole
… Coming back from Galway and near Athenry, the train was stopped – 'A military search'. Soldiers who had got in at Galway, I thought as passengers, produced rifles and ordered everyone out, and all luggage out, and with some demur people scrambled down the six or seven feet drop on to the line. I looked and saw I could not attempt it, or if I did get down with help, could never get up again, so I sat down and stayed there, the only one who did. Soldiers passed and repassed and pulled out suitcases and parcels and threw them out for search, but they passed as if I and my little fish bags (fresh mackerel for the workmen) were invisible. I looked from the window and could see the luggage opened and the men searched, pockets and inside coats and waistcoat 'hands up'! Once they took out a pocket book and read its contents hopefully. But they found nothing. 'They never do,' said one of the young men. The passengers scrambled back and we went on, and I got home, and found the children well and happy at the sheep shearing, and M. looking sometimes as if the terror was with her, but tranquil and told me all the story of the ambush.

She had had that morning a letter signed 'I.R.A.', apparently a threat, wanting her to give money to T. Diveney. She very properly sent it to Nolan in Gort. He answers that it has nothing to do with the I.R.A. but is probably written by a young chap at Coole who is giving trouble and they will investigate the matter …

M. was Margaret, her daughter-in-law and owner of Coole Park. Three weeks before, on 15 May, she had been to a tennis party at Ballyturn House and the car in which she was leaving was ambushed and the four other people in it killed.

4 January 1922
On St Stephen's day Guy walking in the woods saw two young men with guns, who seeing him 'ran like hares'; and these had also been seen by Mick and by S.,

a Quarter master in I.R.A., and they had followed them in vain. There had been many boys and young men coming in with dogs, killing rabbits or taking timber, and I felt as if the woods were slipping away from our hands. But yesterday evening the children Richard and Anne were out at dusk in the nutwood with their bows and arrows and say they met a man who told them they need not be afraid of him (as indeed they were not) as he was one of the I.R.A., 'one of its police', and was taking care of the woods 'for her ladyship'. And I find that there are four of them told off to do this, C., S., M. and another but not wishing their names to be given. This brings fresh courage to me and gives me hope.

Guy Gough from Lough Cutra later married Margaret.

13 May 1922

Yesterday a nice motor drive with Guy to Ballylee and to Burren, sea and mountains beautiful. I went to bed tired, and at 11 o'c Mike knocked at the door – 'There's men downstairs knocking at the hall-door. I think they are raiders.' I told him I would follow him down, put on a dressing-gown and a veil over my hair. He said they had called out to him to open the door. He said he had not the key. 'Where is is it?' 'Upstairs in Lady Gregory's room' (it being in the door all the time). When I came to the door they were knocking again. I went to it and said 'Who is there?' 'Open or it will be the worse for you,' a young, unpleasant, bullying voice. I knew one would not gain anything by speaking to such men, so stood at the foot of the stairs. They kicked the door then and I expected every moment they would break in the unshuttered window and come in. I prayed for help though without much hope, and stood still. After a while the knocking ceased. I thought they had gone to look for another door and whispered to Mike to come up to the playroom by the backstairs as we could see from there. But the door on the backstairs was locked and the moonlight was so bright on front staircase I didn't like to show myself upon it. We could see nothing and hear nothing. Once I saw a red light as though they were coming back with helpers. But no one came and I could see no one from any window and at 1 o'c went back to bed and Mike to his. It did shake the nerves. Yet at the worst moments I felt it was right, somehow, I should know what others had suffered in like cases, and that I might be glad later to have known it.

The Civil War began in June 1922.

28 July 1922

This morning a letter from M. saying she has taken a house at St Ives to take the children to for the summer. I did not know I should feel it so much. I had been hoping against hope they could come. My strength gave way, I had to lie down for a while, trying to realize it and not to break down. Then I wrote to M. making the best of it and saying that though I believed they would be safe here, there would be the danger of news of things happening that one would rather keep them from the knowledge of. Then I went out, heavy hearted enough, all had been prepared and ready, the tennis ground rolled and mown, the gooseberries wired in to keep for them ... And then John told me it is true about Mr Edmunds, he has been shot, he and his chauffeur, and not they say through accident but because of some division of land. A terrible thing, indeed it is better the children should be away.

1 October 1922
The summer over and the children have not seen the flowers or gathered the fruit. An anxious month, it may bring peace, or failing that a more bitter war. I think if the idealists among the Republicans could realise that against the high light of the desire for freedom are to be measured these dark shadows of covetousness and crime, they would themselves call for peace ...

This has been a good Sunday, the sun came out after church, the people looked in good humour, I felt so much at peace that it seems as if peace must be in the air! Two Killeen children came for apples, I gave them damsons as well. And a rather deaf young H., son of the harness maker in Gort, passed having been in the woods picking nuts, and I took him to the garden for apples, and I liked his brightening and excitement when I said he might have damsons – his sister is an invalid 'and will be so glad of them' ...

23 January 1923
... I took the children to the Convent to learn step-dancing. Sister Enda and Sister Columba teach it, 'they didn't learn it here but before they came to us,' the Rev. Mother said. All the infant-school learn only in Irish, speak Irish; the elder ones all learn it. Such a difference from that old day when the Rev. Mother wrote to thank the Turkish Ambassador for a donation she thought came from the Sultan because the letter was written in such a strange-looking language she thought it must be Turkish (and they always remember the Sultan's charity in the '47 famine time). But he denied it and she took the letter to Monsignor Fahey and he burst out laughing and said that the strange language was Irish! One of the older nuns there today said, 'It was you, Lady Gregory, were the first to bring Irish to this neighbourhood,' and spoke of Miss Borthwick, who had given classes at our gate lodge ...

15 April 1923
At the Abbey I found an armed guard; there has been one ever since the theatres were threatened if they kept open. And in the green room I found one of them giving finishing touches to the costume of Tony Quinn, who is a Black-and-Tan in the play, and showing him how to hold his revolver. *The Shadow of a Gunman* [Sean O'Casey's first play to be performed by the Abbey] was an immense success, beautifully acted, all the political points taken up with delight by a big audience. Sean O'Casey, the author, only saw it from the side wings the first night but

had to appear to make his bow. I brought him into the stalls the other two nights and have had some talk with him ...

Casey told me he is a labourer, and, as we talked of masons, said he had 'carried the hod'. He said, 'I was among books as a child, but I was sixteen before I learned to read or write. My father loved books, he had a big library. I remember the look of the books high up on the shelves.'

I asked why his father had not taught him and he said, 'He died when I was three years old through those same books. There was a little ladder in the room to get to the shelves, and one day when he was standing on it, it broke and he fell and was killed.' ...

1 November 1924

... When I said last evening, 'I must write to Robinson about the list of plays,' Yeats said, '*The Image* [a play written by Lady Gregory] will cause a drop, but as you and Lennox want it, you may put it on.' I told him I was getting work finally into order and must see it to know if it is really for the rubbish heap or if I could amend it before I die. I read him an excited letter from Sally [Sara] Allgood, crying out at being given the old woman's (a far better) part instead of Mrs Coppinger, 'this last insult!' But Yeats waked up then, said he might like it better with that change; I think he is preparing to come round. But of course I am anxious and I can't go to look after next week's rehearsals because of having him here.

25 November 1924

The Image last night, a small Monday audience but appreciative. It was beautifully acted. Sara Allgood held the audience even when the kitten Seaghan had brought escaped from her in the last act and walked down to the footlights ...

14 February 1926 – Russell Hotel, Dublin

On Friday, I left for Dublin to see *Plough and Stars* ... I got the post and papers in Gort and when the train had started opened *The Independent* and saw a heading right across the page. 'Riotous Scenes at the Abbey. Attempt to stop O'Casey's play'; and an account of wild women especially having raised a disturbance, blown whistles etc., prevented second act from being heard and had then clambered onto the stage – a young man had struck Miss Delany on the face etc. etc. ... The train was very crowded, groups of men getting in at each station. I thought at first there must be a fair going on, but they were going up for the football, England v. Ireland next day.

Yeats met me at the station and gave his account of the row, thought of inviting the disturbers to a debate as we had done in *Playboy* riots. But I was against that. In *Playboy* time our opponents were men. They had a definite objective, they thought the country people were being injured by Synge's representation of them. These disturbers were almost all women who have made demonstrations on

Poppy Day and at elections and meetings; have made a habit of it, of the excitement. Mrs Skeffington who leads them lost her husband in 1916, but he was not a fighter but a pacifist, killed by order of an insane British officer.

We found the Abbey crowded, many being turned away … I thought the play very fine indeed. And the next day at the matinée, when though the House was full and overflowing there was no danger of riot and I could listen without distraction, it seemed to me a very wonderful play – 'forgiveness of sins' as real literature is supposed to be. These quarrelling drinking women have tenderness and courage showing all through, as have men. At intervals in the public house scene one hears from the meeting being held outside fragments of a speech of Pearse's (spoken in Stephenson's fine voice) with extraordinary effect. One feels those who heard it were forced to obey its call, not to be afraid to fight even in the face of defeat. One honours and understands their emotion. Lionel Johnson's lines to Ireland came into my mind:

> For thy dead is grief on thee?
> Can it be thou dost repent
> That they went, thy chivalry
> Those sad ways magnificent?

And then comes what all nations have seen, the suffering that falls through war and especially civil war on the women, the poor, the wretched homes and families of the slums …

The morning's excitement had been an attempt to kidnap Barry Fitzgerald, 'Fluter', the chief actor in the play. A motor with armed men had come to his house and demanded to see him. But he was not there; someone said he now lived elsewhere, but when I spoke of it he told me he had not gone home that night, had some little suspicion in his mind. I said if taken he would now be wandering in the Wicklow mountains like some man who has latterly been carried off.

It was thought safer for the Players to stay in the theatre between matinée and evening performance. So there was a meal made ready for them. And G[eorgie] Yeats brought Rummel who had been giving a concert and he played for the actors in the auditorium, Chopin – several pieces. During Beethoven's Moonlight Sonata, Yeats fell asleep and awakening said he had dreamed there was a storm going on; and when he awoke and saw Rummel playing his last chords he thought 'they can't have noticed it'! The players were delighted. Rummel had arrived on Saturday morning for his concert. There was a great crush in the boat and he could not get a cabin until he happened to say he was coming over to play, and then he was given a cabin at once – he thought from respect for music – but found they thought he was one of the English football team! …

Frank McEvoy
1925–

For a small inland city, Kilkenny has been the home of a remarkable number of influential societies for the promotion of knowledge and the arts. At the beginning of the nineteenth century, immediately after the Act of Union, Richard Power of Kilfane put on plays acted by the local gentry for an annual three-week season. The leading parts were played by professionals such as Charles Kean, and it was in Kilkenny that Tom Moore met his Bessy, an actress in the company. The theatre season became very popular; it was said 'the streets of Dublin were deserted for Kilkenny'. The Rev. Peter Roe, an evangelical divine, wrote that even clergymen 'crowded to Kilkenny to waste their time, and squander their substance, and drink the maddening draught from the cup of fashionable riot and ungodliness'.

In the 1840s the Rev. Graves and John Prim founded the first Archaeological Society in Ireland, which I have referred to in my introduction to Thomas Westropp.

The Kilkenny Art Gallery Society, which owns an outstanding collection of contemporary paintings and has put on a very credible programme of exhibitions, was founded in the 1940s in the belief that culture need not be metropolitan.

In the 1950s there was also an Arts Society - Frank McEvoy's diary entry for 4 March 1958 describes a lecture given to the members by Patrick Kavanagh. But societies are no sooner formed than they divide. In January 1960 James Delehanty founded the Kilkenny Literary and Bibliography Society. By May of that year, it boasted of over a hundred members and had already had lectures by such distinguished literati as Kate O'Brien, Denis Donoghue and Monk Gibbon, and published the first number of The Kilkenny Magazine.

The magazine was edited by James Delehanty with McEvoy as assistant editor. It continued for ten years and eighteen numbers, publishing works by Seamus Heaney, Brian Friel, John McGahern and Roger McHugh among others. It was one of the few literary magazines in Ireland at the time.

Born in Kilkenny, Frank McEvoy has spent most of his life there, first as a law clerk in a solicitor's office in High Street and then, after recovering from TB, as a civil servant. He has had short stories published and has also written for the radio. For some years, after he retired from the Civil Service, he ran an antiquarian bookshop in High Street.

***

4 March 1958

Well Kavanagh has come and gone: like the monsoon, the mistral, Hurricane Annie: things will never be quite the same again, even if it only meant that somebody told Lady Bellew to shut up, and went on to declare later that he hates Prods. I was supposed to put Kavanagh up for the night, but thank Heavens he insisted on a hotel; wanted the Club House but we diverted him to the Metropole. He travelled down by train, first class, with a bottle of whiskey before him and immediately did a tour of the town, unaccompanied since he preferred to remain incognito. In the afternoon I saw him going into a bookie's office and when I introduced myself in the Metropole bar, he announced he had already backed two winners, though he finished up with a loser. He was sprawled over a stool, in a worn gabardine coat and a hat turned down all round. His face had a rather angry expression, no way mollified by the heavy glasses which were like a winkers. His hands were workman's until you felt the soft palm, though the nails were dirt grimed. He had a heavy flannel shirt of harness lining, and the effects of the pneumonectomy were evident to my trained eye.

For company he had a barrel-shaped man with fair hair, suety complexion and drops of porter on his fawn jersey.

Kavanagh announced that he was going to take a rest, so I arranged to call back at half past seven and walk him up to the Tec.

By then he was in nice condition, sitting at a bottle-strewn table, with broken biscuits underfoot. To make conversation I mentioned other poets, other lecturers. Each one was dismissed with the same categoric phrase, 'No fuckin' good'. I foresaw a disastrous night, and enquired diplomatically if he had notes or if he spoke *ex tempore*, so he said he couldn't say a sentence unless it was written before him. He did keep an eye on the clock and more than once asked how long it would take us to walk up.

Along the street, he kept talking at the top of his voice: 'I must find a pisserie. Where is there a pisserie?' and various people were described as fuckin' cunts. From the corner of my eye, I could see knots of people looking after us in wild surmise. The yarn about Dylan Thomas at a University of California dinner when he regretted that the whole company were not hermaphrodites was bellowed aloud by Kavanagh, passing the town hall.

In the Tec he was introduced to Dr Walsh who brought him into his room. At this point he seemed to be keyed up to a certain pitch of nervous excitement. How many more minutes would he give them? How many were in the audience? Were there fifty people there? Eventually he could not be held back another minute and strode into the lecture room. He gave a vague gesture with his hand to the sharp burst of applause that greeted him. J.D. introduced him and when veering to the too-eulogistic was brought back to earth with Kavanagh's snorting and shifting. 'I won't stand any longer between you and the speaker,' J. said, thumping off the rostrum.

Kavanagh produced his notes and laid them gently on the table and heaved back a step. He took a leather case from an inside pocket and substituted his glasses for another pair held together with elastoplast. He opened with an eloquent phrase: 'Parnassus is not a place; it is a point of view', and then went on to decry the provincial scene, the awfulness of the community we lived in – he knew, he had been brought up in a similar one – and Kilkenny is a terrible place. He said this with a kind of groan, as though it physically pained him. Looking vaguely over the small audience, or perhaps at the blank wall, he would repeat 'This is a terrible place. It is terrible that people would go to those places of worship instead of coming here.' (Earlier when he asked me if there would be many young people at his lecture, I said jocosely that they would be going to a novena in the Friary.) He spoke of the drama festival in Dublin, denouncing O'Casey as a charlatan or at any rate a non-poet because he upheld the Protestant view. Joyce he admired, and even praised Yeats. Then, like a recurring theme in a rondo, he would groan, 'This is a terrible place. This is terrible.'

It was at this point that Lady Bellew interjected, 'I don't know who showed you the town that you got such an impression.' 'Don't interrupt me,' he said. 'It's bad manners to interrupt the lecturer.'

He had a recent illness, he said, had cancer of the lung and everyone said poor Paddy is finished, but he got better, underwent a re-birth, more than spiritual and like a Russian prophet talked of his new Christianity. Then the theme returned on the double-bass. 'This is terrible. Really I never thought it would be so terrible.'

When he was a chap, his mother and himself went to the fair in Carrickmacross and had to take shelter from the rain under an archway. A lounger stood beside them. The mother engaged him in talk and asked him what he did. He was with a circus. 'Ah musha, anything is better than work,' she sighed.

This was greeted with laughter and Kavanagh looked down with a smile, but on seeing again the row of old women, widows, and spinsters, grey heads right under his nose, his face assumed a pained rueful look. 'This is terrible,' he said once more and at last let us understand why it was so terrible. He had expected crowds of young people, 'I mean between fourteen and twenty', in the audience, and 'to think instead of being here they are in those places of worship, it is terrible, just terrible'.

Then ironing the creases out of his foolscap sheets, he said he would give us the privilege of hearing four poems written last autumn, after his recreation. In utter stillness we listened to the four poems and the intensity of the speaker was transmitted to us, his unfathomable emotions and beliefs, his grasping for truth. We were given a glimpse of a vision, beyond our power to describe or understand, but illuminated with the light of heaven striking on Parnassus.

Back in the Metropole he immediately demanded a drink, and when a small Jameson was set before him said that wasn't even a drink. He was quickly brought another, which was down with a brisk gulp. He had visited Ezra Pound in Washington last October, in the biggest madhouse in the world, fifteen thousand, buck niggers going along the corridors showing their penises. But Pound's poetry was too obscure. Eliot's? He was all right, he contributed £25 to Kavanagh's law appeal. The only poet worth talking about was George Barker.

He looked across at the stately looking woman sitting on the opposite side of the fireplace. 'What's your name?', he demanded. 'Bellew.' 'Mrs Bellew?' 'Yes.' Somebody whispered 'Lady Bellew'. 'Are you a Prod?' 'I am.' 'I hate Prods,' he let his head fall sideways in a stupor and put out his tongue.

The company who had come to be entertained drifted away one by one. The question of his expenses came up and Kavanagh, downing another glass, said 'Ten pounds and I'll pay my hotel bill.' We demurred. It was to be three guineas and reasonable expenses, S.L. pointed out. 'Keep your bloody money. I don't want any. I have plenty of my own.' He produced some notes from his pocket and thrust them back again. We fell to squabbling among ourselves about what to give him and J.D. took Leo outside – the beer-barrelled fellow who was with Kavanagh in the afternoon and never moved from his shoulder since – to confer about the cheque. 'Where's Leo gone?' Kavanagh demanded. I looked at the two women on the sofa and said 'Gone to the gentlemen's'. 'He's gone for a piss. Why don't you say he is gone for a piss?'

We said S. had recently become a widow – she indicated her black garments – and was looking for another husband. He held back his head and surveyed her. 'She is too fuckin' auld for me,' he croaked. Though later on he announced he was going to bed and looking at the two portly dames said in an off-hand tone, 'Stay around because I might ride one of yous afterwards.' The women exchanged a look of scandalised happiness.

The others came back and the haggling continued more bitter than ever. 'Give me six guineas and pay my bill,' Kavanagh said, by now half-asleep. Next morning I learned that he got the six guineas and paid the hotel bill himself. I did not wait for the end but left with the two fat women. They professed themselves disgusted with his coarseness.

'At any rate, you didn't learn any new words. You heard them all before,' I said. 'That's true anyway. There was nothing new in it.'

? May 1958

Last night I started talking to a woman lighting sprigs outside a caravan. They are there for the last week collecting rags, doing the whole town.

Woollen and serge are the only things worth gathering. You get nothing at all for silk. She tossed a nylon stocking on the rising flame. Nothing for nylons either? No, they uses them for stitching up the sacks. Monday they sent six sacks to Dublin and the cheque would come tomorrow to the post office. No, they don't drink when they get the money; they are too cute for that. Plenty of money they're making. They goes to the pictures. Not every night, I wouldn't let them. They'll come home now looking for tay. They'll be drinking tay till three in the morning. They had six piebald ponies and a stallion which she herself owned. The man in the other caravan, he was a Protestant. His name was Gentle. His wife was buried there above. They wouldn't let him marry again. Who wouldn't? His sons and daughters. And why should they anyway; let him bring in another woman and they grown up men and women. His son in Galway has a van for collecting rags. They gets six shillings a stone for woollens, but they gives you nothing for silk. It's no good.

She opened the caravan to show me the inside, the toy stove, the seat beside it with a copper band, the wireless, a wet and dry battery. She turned the knob and Luxembourg music flooded out, drowning her commentary. It seemed so incongruous somehow that the wireless in this caravan should be playing Luxembourg. She turned it off and resumed the circuit of the caravan, the mirror with a transfer stencilled on it, the bed stretching transversely at the end of the caravan under the window. Beneath was a double door like a cupboard. Her daughter slept in there; it was another bed. On either door was painted a red scrolled motif, her son's handiwork. Where did she come from, herself? Athy in the county of Kildare. The short grass. She came from a farmer's place herself. There were fifteen of them but when she married a travelling man they had no more to do with her. Only a short time ago they camped just beside her brother's gate, but little he knew who was in it. She saw him all right, an old man now, and he never noticed her. Another brother of hers died lately, died sudden too, and left a thousand pounds and they all got some of it except her. But when you marry a travelling man … In the country when they see them coming, the children run inside and say 'Mammy, here's the tinkers coming.'

They only get four pence a pound for lead. It's the worst it weights so heavy. Copper and brass are all right.

She hung the tarry kettle on the crook and fed the fire with long dry sticks.

16 February 1960

Kate O'Brien. This day week I met her, though some days earlier I observed a squat foursquare woman with green tweed coat, walking stick and mannish hair crop sauntering in front of me.

J.D. has founded a literary society [the Kilkenny Literary and Bibliography Society] and invited Kate O'Brien to give the inaugural lecture. It was widely publicised under her picture in last week's local newspapers. On Saturday, just about this time, I went into J.D.'s shop and found him in a winded state. Only a few minutes earlier he had learned that the Arts Society was up in arms against his new venture and that two members had individually approached Kate O'Brien and told her she had been 'got at' under false pretences by a schismatic group. Word even went abroad that the lecture would be boycotted on Monday night.

There was no way of knowing the strength or vehemence of the opposition, so he asked me if I would accompany him to the hotel and explain the situation to Kate. On phoning we learned that she was having tea but would allow us ten minutes. After that she had to go up to her room and do some writing. Admirable Kate to take her job seriously! If it were my metier the least excuse would put me off writing.

J. arrived out of breath and told his tale. Kate laughed in describing how young S. came the previous evening and told her she was being misled into giving this lecture. That morning when she was buying apples at the country markets, Lady B. drew her aside and gave her the same warning. 'I am sorry I shan't be there. It is not that I am boycotting your lecture but I have to attend a Corporation meeting,' she explained grandly.

Anyway that was Kate, planted in an easy chair, a woven shawl draped about her knees, a strong jaw thrust upwards as her head rested against the back of the chair. Her eyes were lost in the bland plump flesh, no eyebrows, pale fat hands like Oscar Wilde's with a small square emerald on her middle finger. Her voice was deep and brisk, amused at the imbroglio over her lecture.

For the lecture she was dressed as the quintessential lady writer, in black with a kind of stole affixed to the back of her garment, ornamenting her shoulders like a professor's toga. V-necked white blouse, a gold bangle on her left wrist and a monocle strung on a gold chain. All the while she read she polished the monocle between thumb and forefinger and not once called it into play. It was a delight to hear her give the full Spanish lisp to words like Andalusian and the sonorous title of St Teresa's grandee papa.

After the lecture a number of us went into K's for tea and drinks. I veered into Kate's orbit and mentioned how difficult it was to read Don Quixote. It is not a book to be ploughed through conscientiously from start to finish, she explained. One need only read the first hundred pages to get acquainted with the characters and then the book can be picked up anywhere.

After a few stiff whiskeys, Kate sat back and demanded if someone could give a song in a nice fluting tenor. T.L. did his party piece about the Spanish hacienda. J.D. sang one which he hoped would be sentimental enough for her taste, 'In the Shade of the Old Apple Tree'. Such a singularly unmusical bunch must have been hard to come by, for after T.L.'s encore, 'The Auld Orange Flute', we lapsed into what gradually became an embarrassed silence.

'Can nobody sing a nice sentimental ballad?' Kate persisted in sleepy tones. '"I saw from the Beach". Can nobody sing "I saw from the Beach?" Can you not sing?' she fixed her gaze on me for a moment. 'I am afraid not; you have already heard the best the company can offer.' 'That was nothing.' She dismissed their efforts with a fluttering white hand. 'Can nobody even recite a poem he wrote himself? This is proving a hopeless evening. When we disperse we won't have one thing to remember this evening by. Something is needed to ... to ... What is it?

No, no, don't interrupt me. You don't understand what I am trying to say. Something is required to give this evening an accent, and there has been nothing.'

'Maybe before the evening is out, someone will draw a pistol and shoot someone else dead. Wouldn't that give it an accent?' I said. 'Anyway what you must do, Miss O'Brien, is to view the evening in reverse. Picture all this not as an anti-climax but as something leading up to your lecture, which was the highlight of the evening. Look at it through the other end of the telescope and then it is a perfectly rounded evening.'

She shook her head sadly, 'No, no, no,' and the maudlin disappointed expression on her face almost made me burst into tears. It was too late now, just on midnight, to rout out any ballad singer. Even the street singers, if such existed, would have long gone to sleep.

Kate lit another cigarette and immediately pitched it into the fire. Dispiritedly and in almost complete silence we got to our feet. The host took Kate firmly by the arm. She bade us a very tired Good night, and her sandalled feet found their way unsteadily downstairs and up the steps of the Club House to bed. We put on our overcoats and huddled in the hallway a moment, resembling nothing so much as a group attending a wake.

Seán Ó Ríordáin
1916–1977

Seán Ó Ríordáin was born in Ballyvourney in West Cork and moved to Inniscara when he was sixteen, after the death of his father. He started work in the Motor Taxation Office in Cork city, but a short time later was diagnosed with pulmonary tuberculosis. It was not thought that Ó Ríordáin would survive, but as he wrote; 'I hung on to life when I should have died. I am paying for it.' His physical health was permanently damaged and though he continued to work for Cork Corporation until 1965, there were long bouts of sickness. He once said he had graduated with TB rather than a BA.

Seán Ó Ríordáin published his first poem when he was in the sanatorium in Doneraile, and his first collection, Eireaball Spideoige, *came out in 1952. He wrote in Irish, believing that only through that language could a national consciousness be transmitted. The rich vocabulary and texture he introduced into modern Irish verse writing has been an influence to subsequent writers. From 1967 he was appointed a part-time lecturer in University College Cork and he also wrote a column in* The Irish Times.

In his diary he recorded his reflections in the form of essays and appraisals that shows him to have been a man of intense feeling and a subtle and original thinker.

The passages from Seán Ó Ríordáin's diary have been translated by his biographer Seán Ó Coileáin, Professor of Irish at University College Cork.

* * *

11 August 1964

I have just returned from a funeral. A Protestant who died yesterday was being taken to the church at seven this evening. I went into this church for the first time and felt a strong sense of eeriness. I stood at the door and looked in. A small chapel was visible. The congregation was standing, its back to me, facing the altar. It was divided in two, a path in the middle. The altar and the minister could be seen at the end of the path. 'Holy - Holy - Holy' was written on the altar cloth. The place had the appearance of poverty, although the building seems ostentatious from the outside. The coffin was at the foot of the altar. I must confess that I was deeply moved, that is to say that every part of my mind was moved and renewed, and every moment of my life back to the days of my youth, and I might even say that I felt the hundreds of years between me and the Reformation slipping away when I looked into that holy place this evening. It was as though I had opened a door in my own soul that I had not had the courage to open until now. That was the strangest thing of all: that it seemed to me that I was looking at something which concerned me closely but that I had neglected, and I felt guilty. It was though I had visited relatives with whom my own family had long been at odds, people whom we had denied and avoided, and suddenly a hidden part of my own heritage was revealed to me. I found it difficult to satisfy my eyes. If allowed, I would have remained till midnight, peering about. There before me was Protestantism within which I hitherto had seen only from without. These are the people whose faith and way of life and destiny I had thought was to remain outside. This evening I saw them inside – inside though still outside. I felt that here was spiritual shelter. Although they had separated from the larger flock at the time of the Reformation, observe the heed they paid to the altar, to the altar cloth, to the priest's vestments, to the rail, to the chapel itself, and observe how they had preserved these and other things. Who would claim that they did not preserve something of faith and sanctity and efficacy? Who would claim that their prayers are not heard?

I have long known a man of this congregation, but I never saw him pray to God until today. I looked on his back and on his grey hair and felt guilty. Why guilty? Because, I suppose, this thing has been happening among us for ages and we closed our eyes firmly to it. I felt also that I had been here before, although I had not. There is a part of Ireland and a part of the Church and a part of me here that exists nowhere else. Simple and not so simple people have been worshipping God, in this way, in this kind of church, for hundreds of years. Behind this worship is one great historical deed: the rejection of the Pope's authority. It took great courage to risk damnation, but it required even greater faith to believe in the teaching of this severed Church. What a thing a great deed is, be it right or wrong! To do is to live! Think of the suffering, the love, the hate, the bloodshed, the philosophy, the history that followed this deed. All this activity must have contributed greatly to the light of truth.

3 March 1962

The sun of spring on the window casts a framed light on the wall where hangs a picture of my grandmother as a young girl. I knew her when she was old. She has been dead for thirty years. My own mother has been dead for seventeen years, may the Lord have mercy on them all. There is nobody but me in the room now, and yet many people, living and dead, crowd my memory. I can call them and they will come to mind. There is no difference between living and dead in their coming. Neither category is physically present. Is there any difference between the living and the dead when they come disembodied to mind? I hardly think so. We simply recreate in our mind the personality and appearance of the one who is absent, be he living or dead. Sometimes it's easier to recall the dead. For that reason, in so far as concerns personal recollection of this kind, it makes no difference if our acquaintances are living or dead. When I looked at the picture of my grandmother a short while ago, it occurred to me that each has his dead – that they are part of one's mental furniture. My grandmother had pictures of her own dead on the wall, which must have set her thinking. Now the dead have a certain standing as distinct from the living, much like priests as distinct from laity. The dead have attained a rank that we have yet to reach. There is a mysteriousness about the *una nox perpetua* of which Catullus spoke. Their mental presence is a draught of wind from our own death. They are unreal only to the extent that they tend to be shrouded in a wonder that was never really theirs. But do not make light of their importance for you will shortly be among them.

1 August 1963
I feel that I know my own death, and have known it for a long time. I feel that I died long ago, the same death I shall die later on. When I think of my own death, I do not think of something that has yet to happen, but of something that happened long ago but was forgotten. When I am of this mind, it seems to me that my death is what is most me. I think it is much more me than all the rest of my life.

Like everyone else, I am a rich man for I have death in the bank. I cannot be drawn upon, however; death cannot be spent until it has matured. Death is land that cannot be sold or tied up in money, and we must live our life without it. We are often impoverished, without as much as a penny to spend, despite all this wealth we have stored up.

2 June 1964
I saw a fat, ugly, middle-aged woman the other night. She is long married. Where is the snow that was so bright last year? I remember when she was a vision, when I thought I was in love with her. There was no beauty or contentment in the world then but what could be found in her. Now I wouldn't care if she didn't exist. She is a fat, ugly, old woman. Other, younger women, now hold the sway that she once held. This is an old story - the departure of youth and beauty. But it is even worse when they don't depart but still remain, and we continue to crave them. People matter not a whit. They come and they go. But youth and beauty are eternal, and however old we may be they remain our constant goal. It was always people between twenty and twenty-five that Marcus Aurelius saw on the Appian Way. That is enough to break one's heart.

21 March 1974
I have been grasping for breath today and yesterday. Perhaps death is near. It doesn't bother me in the least. I remember a fine, sunny day long ago in Clondrohid. I lived in Ballyvourney at the time, and cannot have been yet fifteen. I think my aunt Kathleen (now dead) was there. I don't remember who else, but there were many. I got a spin in a large motor car that had no roof. The world was very airy. It is only a memory. Everyone is dead.

Gemma Hussey
1938–

A Fine Gael/Labour coalition took power following the general election of December 1982 with Garret FitzGerald as Taoiseach. Gemma Hussey, who held a Dáil seat for Wicklow for Fine Gael, was appointed as Minister of Education, the only woman in the Cabinet. Towards the end of the four years of that government, in the Cabinet reshuffle of 1986, she was made Minister of Social Welfare.

During her days in office, the government had a serious economic crisis, there was a referendum on abortion and divorce, and, in an attempt to bring about peace in the North, the Anglo-Irish Agreement was signed.

Mrs Hussey is a native of Bray, County Wicklow. She was elected to the Seanad Éireann in 1977 as representative for the National University of Ireland and became leader of the Upper House. In February 1982 she had taken a Dáil seat in Wicklow and was opposition spokesperson on Broadcasting, Arts and Culture. She retired from politics in 1989.

* * *

15 December 1982

Today the papers are full of the whole doings of yesterday, a bit of a sensation about me getting Education which is forecast as being a big job, but I suppose as the only woman there'd be bound to be a bit of attention.

At about 10 a.m. (having dealt for ages with family phone calls, friends ringing, telegrams, and flowers, constituency delighted) the rather rickety black Mercedes arrived – I hate that car, it is ostentatious and noticeable – and we drove to Marlborough Street to the dour stone building which is the Department of Education. Peter Baldwin is my private secretary. He was hovering at the door and brought me up to the rather morgue-like office which I'm to have. (The sooner I get pictures on the walls and a few lamps the better.) The first person I met was the 'Runai' [Secretary of the Department], Liam Lane, a most erect, correct and impressive man, and then the Assistant Secretaries. They seemed to me to be a group of rather elderly men, all with impenetrable Irish names. I wondered who was the more shocked, they or I.

After an exchange of pleasantries I left and went to Government Buildings where we had a more structured meeting about getting down to brass tacks, and Garret and Alan Dukes outlined the awful situation and how we had to take decisions to put flesh on the Fianna Fáil estimates of last month, and do even more cutting because of the massive debt servicing which Charlie Haughey and Jack Lynch had piled up for us.

Nobody directed us where to sit when we arrived into the Cabinet room via the double doors, so it was sort of accidental. I sat down between Austin Deasy (who's at the end of the table) and Michael Noonan; Liam Kavanagh is on the other side of Michael. Austin pulls lugubrious faces and whispers to me that the reams of figures which Alan and Garret pour out are all Greek to him – most of us are a bit glazed when they go on about EBR, PSP, GDP, at great and detailed length, but we certainly know enough to realize that the huge accumulation of debt since '77, particularly in the last eighteen months, has left us in a desperate crisis. When looking around at them all I feel that we're an unlikely bunch to inspire a country the way Ireland is going to need inspiring ...

We get messages into the room by rather a cloak-and-dagger sort of method, but I suppose it's necessary: there's a red light over the door, which goes on with a click; usually Dermot Nally gets up to answer it, or if he's immersed in something with Garret, one of us will do it, and the civil servant who sits ensconced in the Communications Room across the corridor is waiting outside with whatever note or document he has. Austin said to me that he can see how one's prestige could be determined by how many messages one receives. John Bruton and Barry Desmond already seem to have an endless stream of them.

5 January 1983
The storm about the next series of cutbacks in Education is now breaking over my head. Big headlines in *The Irish Times* this morning. To my intense anger and amazement an *Irish Independent* reporter rang me at 2 o'clock in the morning about it – unbelievable! I was, however, as polite as I could bring myself to be.

Up very early this morning with the usual massive schedule: opening the Department of Education Inspectors' Conference at 9.30 a.m. (wonder what they think of me?), funeral in Bray, back to Cabinet meeting, long encounter with the Irish National Teachers' Organization in the Department etc ... Deaf ears are turned when I tell them that even more cuts are going to be needed – 'yes, but not us' is everyone's response ...

1 February 1983
Exhaustedly sitting here. We had another marathon Cabinet session which ended at 2 a.m. It was punctuated by a good lunch but no supper until they sent out a driver for chips and sausages about 11.30 p.m. when a sub-committee started to work on the final figures. God, the tiredness! So we ate them out of bags, the only time in my life I ate chips and sausages washed down with gin ...

13 July 1983
... Spoke to the Confederation of Irish Industry lunch at 1 p.m., which seemed

to go alright. I wish I had more time to write these speeches myself. I sometimes have to rely on body language to convey goodwill …

Went to the ear doctor because I thought I was going deaf – I couldn't hear what they were saying at Cabinet; and the doctor, in quite an amused fashion, told me that I had absolutely no problem at all and should tell my colleagues to stop mumbling. So I did, and told them as well that it had cost me £45 to find that out.

7 August 1983
I attended the Aga Khan Cup at the RDS on Friday in the President's box. Everybody was very elegant and well dressed but it went on far too long. I was fidgety and worrying about wasting time, I couldn't believe the hours and hours it took.

23 October 1983
The Fine Gael Ard Fheis has just ended – the big, brash, annual 'love-in' one has come to expect.

When the time came for my speech, Peter Barry described me as 'our charming and pretty Minister for Education', which raised a number of hackles and caused some annoyance. So I thanked him when I spoke and described him as 'the silver-haired and handsome Peter Barry'. He didn't seem amused …

3 June 1984
Home from the State Banquet for Ronald Reagan in Dublin Castle, which I suppose must be described as an historic occasion. Elegance and some excitement, tinged with a slight reserve and ruefulness on account of the mixed feelings in Ireland about it all. It was done extremely well and I think I looked okay, if only I didn't feel so plump! Garret made a very good speech, suitably light but touching the right note. Ronald Reagan and Nancy looked exactly as they do on television. He is erect, wrinkled, but ruddy, lively-faced. She is very small and thin, pretty and elegant, but with that fixed vacant expression which is so peculiar. When I was introduced to them in the VIP reception line the President launched into quite a discussion: 'So pleased to meet you, Mrs Hussey. I've heard a lot about your Education reforms and understand you are particularly working on the Curriculum; of course you know at home we are quite worried about our Education system' etc. The fact that he was sufficiently well briefed and remembered to say all that took me somewhat by surprise. Nancy just shook my hand glacially. All in all, despite the bloody security everywhere – which was obtrusive and annoying – it was good …

16 December 1984
The Achill trip, would you believe, happened after all. The Air Corps decided to 'have a go', so I dashed to the Phoenix Park and up we went. Across Ireland,

through the driving rain, in a six-seater military helicopter with a cool pilot called Gus, the rolling fields of the midlands looking peaceful and empty and the majestic hills and water of Clew Bay. It wasn't frightening really and the only complaint was the cold. Then we swooped down in sudden sunshine to meet the waiting crowds in the beautifully placed new Vocational School, where it all went merrily and I seem to have been a big hit. Even my chunk 'as Gaeilge' went down well, and as I descended from the skies I felt like a combination of the Virgin Mary and Margaret Thatcher, with a dash of the Queen thrown in for good measure. Immediately after my speech, because of bad weather looming, we zoomed off skywards again, bearing flowers and a Christmas cake and lots of goodwill. The swooping up and up was a lovely feeling and then the weather became appalling, sleet and rain and cold, and we battled our way through desperate visibility across Ireland because I had to be into the Dáil for the final Adjournment Debate vote at 4 o'clock, which was the reason I had to take the helicopter trip in the first place. We made it to Leinster House just in time to see Charlie Haughey walking out of the Dáil with all his cohorts, in disgust at some remark of Garret's, so in the end there was no vote.

14 March 1985
Arrived in Miami for the St Patrick's week celebrations and seemed to be immediately surrounded by large American cops in plainclothes with bulges in their jackets.

16 March 1985
We went to an amazing Mass in St Patrick's Church on the beach: the 'colleens' in strapless dresses bringing up the Offertory gifts, everybody in bright green and shamrocks, St Patrick himself greeting us (a Hispanic called Manuel), the church nearly empty except for the people involved in the ceremony, mostly very old people there, me festooned with the biggest, ugliest confection of orchids, plastic clay pipes and green polka-dotted ribbons – Unbelievable.

We have now acquired a security woman called Maria and a blond man with a briefcase full of automatic weapons which he clutches, but which we are supposed to describe as a telephone to the White House!

The big parade: Derry and myself in a bright green open convertible, riding along Flagler Street, the main thoroughfare, being greeted and escorted to the reviewing stand. Lots of presentations to me at the most unexpected moments. Everyone in green – blacks, whites, Hispanics – lots of bands and colour, hot sun. I made some of my speech in Spanish which went down very well ...

Then we went to the elaborate Coral Gulf Chamber of Commerce Annual International Ball at the Hilton. I sat beside the Lieutenant Governor of Florida who was a nice, old, conservative gentleman, who knew absolutely nothing about where Ireland even was. But he knows now.

There was a long prayer at the beginning of dinner, when we all held hands with heads bowed and prayed not to be too materialistic …

16 November 1985

The day after the Anglo-Irish Agreement. The launching at Hillsborough went extremely well, except that Haughey has categorically and immediately rejected it in the strongest language. He, Blaney and the Provos are on the same side and the Unionists are rejecting it equally strongly from the other side. It has been, however, a marvellous success for Garret. Thatcher behaved herself perfectly, well almost perfectly − the whole international scene is good, but the Unionists are going bananas altogether. Thank God there has been no bloodshed or sign of it yet. That is our greatest worry …

21 January 1986

I'm still in bed at 10 a.m. because Cabinet met until 4 a.m. this morning. How can I describe the cold light beating down in the large Council Chamber, the thin stale air, the coughs and snorts, the occasional nervous hilarity or high spirits when things seem to be falling into place and the silent despondency when it turns out to be worse than expected, the chicken and chips eaten out of brown paper bags at night, wine out of a tea cup (we only have drinks very late to keep going)?

John Boland produced a scheme last night which looked for a while like our salvation, occasioning hours of examination by his experts and Department of Finance experts, but eventually producing a fraction of what we hoped for. Garret manages to keep going through it all, how I don't know. Meetings seem to have been going on non-stop for days and it seems like forever.

8 November 1986

Last night we went to the Wicklow Cheviot Sheep Owners dinner dance in Blessington. What a night: a semi-edible meal which was more or less thrown at us, not a drop of wine during the interminable dinner and even more interminable raffles for fertilizer and sheep dip. Then I was totally ignored while Liam Kavanagh was invited to speak. So all in all it was a messy and unsatisfactory night and I wish I didn't have to go, not to mention poor Derry …

2 December 1986

… I had a sort of sick feeling about what might greet me in Bray [following the announcement of social welfare cuts] and there was a nasty violent scene and demonstration as I was leaving my clinic in the Royal Hotel. The crowd was very small when I went in, but all during the clinic I could hear it building up on the street outside, chanting and shouting. A crowd of Sinn Féin activists from Little Bray, not the ordinary people of Bray at all, were pushing, fighting and shouting and I had to be escorted through a protective cordon of Garda to the car, being squashed and buffeted and cursed at, keeping a totally calm and expressionless face ... The manager of the hotel wanted me to leave by the back door, but I said 'no way' – I was going to go out the way I came in – How could they imagine I would slink out?

15 December 1986
A sort of gloom has settled over us all ... The impossibility of getting a Budget together stares us in the face.

We have had about 14 hours of Cabinet this week, the rumbles are that John Bruton wants still more Social Welfare cuts, but the ones that are there already are quite horrific – have they lost their reason?

Long Dáil session, Cabinet meetings that get nowhere ... I'm beginning to think it would be a miracle to keep my seat. Do I want it? Yes I do. After all these years of crucifying work and ill-treatment, I certainly do ...

On 20 January 1987 the Labour Party led by Dick Spring withdrew from the Coalition Government.

22 January 1987
Well, the Election is on. Our final Cabinet on Tuesday was slightly strained and obviously very hard for Dick. We took a formal vote at 12 noon and then Dick handed over his prepared letter of resignation. There was a session of slightly sad, slightly emotional handshakes (warm embrace for me from Barry and Ruairi). We were a very subdued bunch. Some of us then went off to Aras an Uachtaráin (Garret nearly forgetting to notify me formally of my appointment as Minister for Labour) where we accepted our new seals from Dr Hillery, who was inclined to delay us by chit-chat. None of us felt in the humour for chit-chat. Wish I'd been given Labour last February instead of now ...

A general election was called for 18 February 1987. Gemma Hussey retained her seat, but Fianna Fáil led the new minority government with Charles Haughey as Taoiseach.

Sources

ANON. [SIEGE OF LIMERICK CASTLE]. Edited by M.J. M'Enery, *Journal of the Royal Society of Antiquaries*, 5th series, vol. XIV, 1904.

BELLINGHAM, THOMAS. *Diary of an Officer under William III*, ed. Anthony Hewitson (Preston, 1908).

BENN-WALSH, SIR JOHN. Edited by James S. Donnelly, Jr, *Journal of the Cork Historical and Archaeological Society*, vol. LXXXI, 1975.

BOYLE, RICHARD, 1ST EARL OF CORK. 'Autobiographical Notes, Remembrances & Diaries of Sir Richard Boyle, First and "Great Earl of Cork"', ed. Rev. Alexander B. Grosart, *The Lismore Papers*, vols 1-5 (First series), 1886.

CAMPBELL, JOSEPH. By courtesy of the Library of Trinity College, Dublin (MS 10173-6).

CASEY, JOHN. From a transcription by Martin Kevin Cusack.

CLEMENTS, WILLIAM, 3RD EARL OF LEITRIM. From a transcription by Marcus Clements, owned by Charles Clements.

COWPER, HATTIE. Diary owned by Maura Toler-Aylward.

CUMMINS, NICOLAS MARSHALL. Diary owned by The Very Rev. Dean Nicolas Cummins.

FARRELL, RICHARD. Edited by George Little, *Capuchin Annual*, 1944.

FITZGERALD, JOHN. Edited by T.A. Lunham, *Journal of the Cork Historical and Archaeological Society*, vols 24-26, 1918-20.

FORTESCUE, MARIANNE. Diary owned by Imogen Hamilton.

FREKE, ELIZABETH. Edited by Mary Carbery, *Journal of the Cork Historical and Archaeological Society*, vol. XVI, 1913.

GREGORY, LADY. *Lady Gregory's Journals*, ed. Daniel J. Murphy (Colin Smythe, Gerrards Cross, 1987).

GODDARD, LUCY. *The Hamwood Papers*, ed. Mrs G.H. Bell (Macmillan and Co., London, 1930).

HOLLOWAY, JOSEPH. *Joseph Holloway's Abbey Theatre*, ed. Robert Hogan and Michael O'Neill (Southern Illinois University Press, Carbondale and Edwardsville, 1967).

HUNT, SIR VERE. Edited by R. Herbert, *Dublin Magazine*, April, June & August 1943.

HUSSEY, GEMMA. *At the Cutting Edge* (Gill & Macmillan, Dublin, 1990).

LEADBEATER, MARY. By courtesy of the National Library of Ireland, Dublin (MS 9292-9346).

MCEVOY, FRANK. Diary owned by Frank McEvoy.

MÜNCHHAUSEN, LUDOLF VON. Translated by Andreas von Breitenbuch.

NICHOLSON, ASENATH. *The Bible in Ireland*, ed. Alfred Tresidder Sheppard (Hodder and Stoughton, London, 1926).

O'NEILL DAUNT, WILLIAM. *A Life Spent in Ireland*, edited by his (unnamed) daughter (T. Fisher Unwin, London, 1896).

Ó RÍORDÁIN, SEÁN. Translated by Seán Ó Coileáin. Published in Irish as 'Sleachta Fáin as Dialann' ('Stray Passages from a Diary'), *Comhar*, Bealtaine 1967.

O'SULLIVAN, HUMPHREY. *The Diary of Humphrey O'Sullivan*, ed. Rev. Michael McGrath (Irish Texts Society, Dublin, 1929 [1936]).

PONSONBY, FRANCES & EMILY. *Donegal Annual*, 1973.

RICHARDS, ELISABETH. From transcription by a granddaughter of Elisabeth Richards, Enniscorthy Library, Enniscorthy, Co. Wexford.

RODEN, ANNE, DOWAGER COUNTESS OF. *Diary of Anne, Countess of Roden* (Dublin, 1870).

SCOTT, JOHN. From John Stevenson, *Two Centuries of Life in Down 1600–1800* (White Row Press, Belfast, 1990).

SCOTT, JOHN, 1ST EARL OF CLONMELL. From William J. Fitzpatrick, *Ireland before the Famine* (W.B. Kelly, Dublin, 1867).

SEWELL, WILLIAM. *Journal of a Residence at the College of St Columba in Ireland*, 2nd edition (Oxford, 1848).

SMITH, ELIZABETH. *The Highland Lady in Ireland*, ed. Patricia Pelly & Andrew Tod (Canongate Classics, Edinburgh, 1991).

STEPHENS, JAMES. *The Insurrection in Dublin* (Colin Smythe, Gerrards Cross, 1992).

STEVENS, JOHN. *The Journal of John Stevens*, ed. Robert H. Murray (Oxford, 1912).

TENNENT, JOHN. From a transcription owned by Dan MacLaughlin, Public Records Office of Northern Ireland (D.1748/E/14), Belfast.

TONE, THEOBALD WOLFE. *Life of Theobald Wolfe Tone*, ed. Thomas Bartlett (Lilliput Press, Dublin, 1998).

WESLEY, JOHN. *The Journal of John Wesley* (Charles Kelly, London, 1903).

WESTROPP, THOMAS. From a transcription owned by George Stacpoole.